Reflective Network Therapy in the Preschool Classroom

Gilbert Kliman

Contributing editor Elissa Burian

UNIVERSITY PRESS OF AMERICA,® INC.

Lanham · Boulder · New York · Toronto · Plymouth, UK

Dedication

This book is written with love, to each of my own five children—Becky, Amy, David, Steven and Jodie—who, during their childhoods, shared thousands of reflective hours of often delicious and variously difficult conversations in the small social network of our family. My wife, Harriet Wolfe MD and youngest daughter Becky have valiantly supported my labors on this task for a decade. During that time, Dr. Wolfe took time from her psychoanalytic practice and administrative duties, giving her energies not only to the Presidency of the San Francisco Psychoanalytic Institute, but also generously contributing many hours of fruitful discussion about the reflective network phenomena. She brought her considerable insight to her review of my writings and treatment videos. She helped found and served on the Board of Directors of The Children's Psychological Health Center, a nonprofit agency which has supported Reflective Network Therapy activities. Jodie Kliman, PhD, my oldest child, grew up with the Cornerstone preschool and its reflective network as if it were a sibling. Then, as an accomplished network and family therapist herself, she helped edit this book.

Reflective Network Therapy has two forms. One is school based, and this book harvests knowledge gained from RNT treatment of over 1500 preschoolers. The second form uses psychoanalytically informed guided activity workbooks, including the manualized Personal Life History Book. In the guided activity workbook form, the reflective network is community and family based for children of all ages.

The present book only touches on knowledge gained while using the simple derivative method which over the years has served more than 60,000 stressed or traumatized children of all ages, especially during natural disasters. This book is about RNT's daily school based work, in which children are treated in the classroom by networks of parents, peers, therapists and teachers. It is an introduction and guide for caring parents, educators and mental health professionals, hoping they will take this knowledge and use it in real life spaces. In-classroom use of Reflective Network Therapy can enhance their own best efforts to heal and educate children.

Contents

Tables and Figures

Preface

This book describes a remarkably effective school based treatment method which harnesses small social networks for the good of seriously emotionally disturbed (SED) preschool children and those with pervasive developmental disorders (PDD or ASD). It explains the method to parents as well as teachers and mental health workers who struggle to help disturbed or developmentally disordered very young children, many of whom seem to have stopped loving and learning. The contents come from testing the method's feasibility with hundreds of patients treated with Reflective Network Therapy in therapeutic services and projects. The clinical value and testing results of the projects took many years for me to fully appreciate. This book is not only a legacy of my own forty five years of treatment work using this method. It is also the legacy of dozens of colleagues who practiced the method and many hundreds of parents who experienced its benefits for children treated in sites on two continents. It is written at a time when few, if any, other methods for treating young children have shown as much versatility, safety and scientific evidence of good outcome as has Reflective Network Therapy. If you, as a professional educator, mental health clinician, or a well-read parent, are an informed skeptic, you will notice differences between Reflective Network Therapy and most forms of child psychotherapy. Unlike many interpersonal psychotherapy methods, the RNT method described throughout this book has a reasonably substantial evidence base. The method relies on about the same number of subjects and a larger number of comparison and control cases as the published IQ results of the most widely used comparable school based method. It has been well tested for feasibility, replicability, IQ effects, as well as children's global mental health results (CGAS), and has been used in many real life environments, classrooms and other therapeutic settings. It has been replicated by many people other than its originators. The Reflective Network

Therapy method is peer inclusive; it does not separate the child from peers by pairing him with an aide. It is carried out in the natural environment of a classroom. It gives the mental life of the child a cognitive and emotional scaffold on which to stand and build as well as the encouragement of a structured context in which formal learning and socialization can occur. The method is ready for more widespread use.

When first used with preschoolers, Reflective Network Therapy was officially known as The Cornerstone Therapeutic Preschool Method and was often called "The Cornerstone Method." It was originally developed for stressed children between the ages of 2 and 7. The treatment surprised us by being very helpful for children with autism spectrum disorders as well as for traumatized children. Readily individualized, RNT has been used by many teams, adapted for and helped over 1500 preschoolers, including those with attention deficit disorders, oppositional defiant disorders, posttraumatic stress disorders, anxiety disorders, reactive attachment disorders, and conduct disorders, as well as for many with autism spectrum disorders. We offer practical hope to families and schools struggling to meet the special needs of children who have lost or damaged capacity to care about and learn from others. A dynamic psychological and psychosocial network method, Reflective Network Therapy (RNT) enables many emotionally disturbed or cognitively impaired children to become healthier and receptive to learning. It helps developmentally challenged young children on the autism spectrum develop empathy, relate to family and peers, and grow intellectually. Almost all initially IQ testable and then later re-tested preschool patients regularly show highly significant clinical and IQ gains.

Public school special education administrators struggling with an epidemic of special needs children will appreciate the inclusive structure of the method. It can be carried out using a fraction of the financial and personnel resources usually required for other in-school methods.

Reflective Network Therapy is an evidence-based advance among efforts to provide for the emotional and cognitive needs of very young children who qualify for special education. The book includes a replication manual for the benefit of preschool directors, therapists, teachers, parents, administrators and researchers. I try to strike a balance between making complex material accessible to the general reader and keeping to the rigors of scientific presentation. Real life classroom narratives and discussion of more formal case studies enhance the reader's understanding and are a basis for theoretical explanations.

RNT's evidence is time-tested by clinical, comparative, and controlled clinical and psychometric studies. Children are described who have been treated by over 20 teams in two hemispheres using the (Cornerstone) method of Reflective Network Therapy since 1965. Parents will be encouraged by the emphasis on valuing their input and feedback and by how the method provides regular guidance and support to families.

Reflective network experience in huge disasters and other stressful situations is published online (www.childrenspsychological.org) and will be the subject of later articles and books. The Massachusetts School of Professional Psychology, Tulane Department of Psychiatry, Mercy Corps, Amurthaiti and Ekol Akasya (Acacia School) in Petion-Ville (Haiti) have all collaborated with The Children's Psychological Health Center, Inc. on the use and study of RNT as a resource for responding to children's psychological well being following the trauma of disasters.

Acknowledgments

I thank more than 1500 treated preschool children whose lives have touched mine in classroom contexts, and their parents. Parents' generosity of heart and mind permitted us to use videotapes of their children to help teach more Reflective Network Therapy teams how to apply the method to heal many more children. I thank 60,000 disaster-stricken and foster families who have used Reflective Network Therapy derivatives in their real life spaces throughout the world. They were helped using small social networks assembled around guided activity workbooks. Doris Ronald Gorin gave the last twelve years of her life to helping me found the first Reflective Network Therapy site, The Cornerstone Therapeutic Preschool. She was a loving, highly creative teacher with empathic and communicative abilities which made my work in the classroom far easier than I had expected. Many other teachers (listed in an appendix) have been influential in developing the interdisciplinary aspects of the method. The Center for Preventive Psychiatry provided a womb for the birth of the project which developed the method. I doubt the method would have survived and evolved without Myron Stein, MD and later, the help of Arthur Zelman, MD and M. Harris Schaeffer, PhD during a time when I was physically disabled. Zelman, beginning in 1978, took over Medical Directorship of the Center, and nurtured its vigorous growth, as did M. Harris Schaeffer as Executive Director. In 1994, the Center's team of Zelman, Abrams, and Samuels rediscovered the IQ rise phenomenon which is so vital a product of RNT. Their published archival studies (1985, 1986) are extensively drawn upon in this book, as is the prospective work in a California public special education system carried out by Miquela Diaz Hope, PhD (then a determined Wright Institute student). A well-funded National Institute of Mental Health project (RO1 MH 27944) serving foster children was an important predecessor. Only after its conclusion did I see clearly how much more powerful Reflective Network Therapy can be than other psychotherapy, and how little IQ is influenced by supportive-expressive psychotherapy. I was assisted in that project by co-principal investigator M. Harris Schaeffer, PhD and colleagues Murray Friedman, PhD, Bernard Pasquariella, Saim Akin, MD, Rose Bianco MSW, Judith Goldston, PhD and Helen Graham, MSW. My first wife, Ann Kliman, MA, poured her energies into developing the Center's situational crisis intervention service, which became the nation's largest preventive resource for mentally healthy but situationally stressed persons. Her work with orphans and other traumatized persons constantly informed that of my own work using Reflective Network Therapy.

The deepening of psychiatric and psychoanalytic thought about this in-classroom method was profoundly helped by my child analysis supervisor, Marianne Kris, MD, who dedicated hundreds of hours voluntarily. Methodologically vital were my first Associate Medical Director, Myron Stein, MD, and Thomas Lopez, PhD., the latter having trained with Anna Freud. The techniques benefited from the insightful work of Arthur Zelman, MD, Daniel Feinberg, MD, Norma Balter, MSW, Susan Howard, MSW, Ruth Rosenfeld, Harriet Lubin, MSW and Marianne Lester, EdD. All contributed perspectives they gleaned from psychoanalytic training either in England or the United States. David Trimble, PhD's intellectual contributions to the neurophysiology of reflective discourse enhanced my thinking in the Theory chapter. Catherine Henderson, PhD of Seattle Psychoanalytic Institute's Child Analysis Program has been a great partner in my Seattle work and training of others in this method, as have Alicia Mallo, MD in Buenos Aires and Linda Hirshfeld, PhD at the Ann Martin Center in Piedmont, California and Keith Myers, LICSW Vice President of Wellspring Family Services. Jessie Rios provided indispensable administrative help including organization and replication of treatment videos for training. Editing by Elissa Burian, MA, Jodie Kliman, PhD, Thomas Lopez, PhD and Teresa Reitinger was especially helpful in completing this manuscript. We would be nowhere without the initial support for my work given by The Foundation for Research in Preventive Psychiatry. Trustees of that Foundation included three great psychoanalytic pioneers: Marianne Kris, MD, Peter Neubauer, MD, and Mary O'Neill Hawkins, MD—each of whom encouraged me with what was then an experimental application of psychoanalysis.

Vital support came from The National Institute of Mental Health, The County of Westchester Community Mental Health Board, The New York State Department of Mental Health, John and Mildred Beatty, The International Psychoanalytic Association, the Esther and Joseph Klingenstein Fund, W. T. Grant Foundation, Cleveland Foundation, Foundation for Research in

Psychoanalysis, The New York State and Westchester County Community Mental Health Boards, the Estate of Flora E. Haas, Harrison Foundation, the Aaron E. Norman Fund, Pettis-Crowe Foundation, Steven H. and Alida Brill Scheuer Foundation, Van Ameringen Foundation, Yasseen Family Foundation, Lavenburg Corner House Foundation, Kelly and Farren Law Firm, Irving Harris Foundation, Lillian Foreman, David Kosh Family Fund, Daniel and Florence Guggenheim Foundation, San Francisco Chapter of Odd Fellows, Morris Stulsaft Foundation, Preventive Psychiatry Associates Medical Group, Windholz Foundation, Sobrato Family Fund, Cadence Corporation, Sophie Mirvis Fund, Laird Norton Family Foundation (thanks to Chalan Colby), Tim Treadway, Geoffrey Fletcher, Harriet Wolfe, and the Board of Directors of The Children's Psychological Health Center, and many generous Friends of CPHC, notably Rita Schreiber. Recently the Casey Foundation, Downtown Rotary Club of Seattle, Bill and Melinda Gates Foundation, the Maritz Foundation and Lisa Menett supported Reflective Network Therapy classrooms and training for therapists and teachers serving homeless and traumatized children at Wellspring Family Services of Seattle.

Introduction

Alexandra Harrison, MD

As a child mental health clinician with more than forty years of experience, I welcome this book on Reflective Network Therapy as an inspiring opportunity to bring cost-effective, theoretically sound, and scientifically tested treatment to a population of children in great need. It makes important contributions to vital fields for parents, teachers, child therapists and finally taxpayers: current new knowledge about brain development and the need for early interventions for children at risk. Kliman vividly and compellingly describes a type of therapy—Reflective Network Therapy—carried out in the classroom by a collaboration of individual therapist, preschool teacher, peers and parents, with seriously disturbed children. The facts that the therapy occurs in multiple short (15–20 minute) sessions a week, and that these sessions are optimally designed to help the children make sense of their otherwise chaotic and frightening worlds "on the spot," makes it an essentially practical therapeutic modality. Finally, Kliman has done something very unusual in the field of child mental health: he has conducted scientific studies to test the efficacy of the method. In addition to the anecdotal evidence that child mental health practitioners usually put forth to support their methodologies, Kliman has real data to demonstrate its effectiveness, including striking improvement in IQ scores. Thus the method is shown to be a remarkably "cost-effective" treatment for young children with severe mental health disorders—autistic spectrum disorders, pervasive developmental disorders, trauma, behavior disorders and serious emotional disorders. Kliman does not mention this specifically, but I would add disorganized attachment disorders to the list, in keeping with his in-classroom work with a series of thirty foster children and his series of studies of guided activity workbooks for foster children.

Kliman provides a very practical and helpful introduction to the reader interested in learning more about therapeutic interventions in early childhood—mental health clinician, teacher, or parent. It is comprehensive, including a manual as a guide to practitioners, numerous case examples, and scientific data, in one place. It is also helpful that the book compares the method to other current methods in use today in terms of theoretical foundation, technique, and available scientific data, in a thoughtful and respectful manner.

I have already started using an adaptation of reflective network therapy in treatments of preschool children; two of these children are autistic and one has a disruptive behavior disorder. The method has proved extremely effective. The first child I treated lost her autism diagnosis after less than two years of four times a week therapy. The second two, now in therapy for about nine months, are much improved. All the children were treated by a team including parents, O.T., speech therapist, and teachers. The RNT approach was central to their improvement.

In my treatments, I begin with a videotaped parent consultation evaluation and a recommendation for Reflective Network Therapy. I discuss the method and the conceptual background with both the parents and the teachers. In the classroom, I start each session with a "briefing" by the teacher to me about the child's day, in the child's presence. Then I spend approximately 20 minutes playing with my child patient in the classroom or on the playground. We finish with another briefing, this time with me briefing the teacher about the session. I add frequent—sometimes daily—communications with the parents.

My RNT treatments aim to help the child make sense of his or her world through a particular use of play and language. The play is based on psychoanalytic play therapy and attempts to develop the capacity for pretend play and the capacity to make meaning through elaborating potential symbolic themes. The language makes links between inner motivations—cognitive and affective—and behavior, and uses repetition to keep the elements of meaning in awareness long enough to allow the child to attend to them and begin to reflect on them. In this aspect of the method, the presence of others in the child's environment is critical. The collaboration of peers, teachers, and parents, is a crucial piece of the work.

In my work with these children, I as the therapist make use of the group of peers and the teachers to elaborate a simple narrative linking behavior to inner affective experience. The chance for multiple iterations of the communication, displaced slightly to other listeners than the target child, allows the child the safety to consider the message without having to shut down his emerging reflective capacity. Often, the peers contribute variations of meaning in their own words as part of the growing meaning. Through these experiences in the classroom, OT and speech studies, and play with parents, the child patient is given an enriched developmental opportunity, with the potential for great therapeutic benefit.

Although Kliman (1970), Lopez and Kliman (1975), and Lopez et al. (1996) report some profound child analytic work during the eight month span of a school year in Reflective Network Therapy, it is not a substitute for years of a full scale child analysis. The short duration of the sessions does not easily allow long evolution and elaboration of symbolic themes. Instead, the analyst prepares a child to think symbolically and teachers can report back on much response to interpretation after the analyst has left the classroom (Kliman 1970 and the Manual chapter of this book). More traditional methods of play therapy or analysis may become appropriate for the same children at later times in their development. Child psychoanalysis (unlike Reflective Network Therapy) though enormously effective and gratifying to provide, can be available to only a few children because of the high cost of four times a week sessions in the analyst's office plus the additional need of parent meetings. As with varying doses of RNT, the most intensive psychoanalytic treatment has been demonstrated to be more effective than less intensive treatments of severely mentally ill children (Fonagy et al. 1999).

Reflective Network Therapy offers the great advantage of high frequency of sessions in combination with an intense involvement in the fabric of the child's relational and educational life, at a fraction of the cost, and without extracting the child from his or her daily routine. I have succeeded in using it in a normal nursery school, where I bring my patients. Especially in terms of the lesser cost and avoiding the requirement that parents bring the child to and from the therapeutic sessions, RNT takes some of the burden off the shoulders of the parents of these children. The design of the treatment is ideal, in my opinion, for scaffolding a young child's development of competencies such as "mentalization," requirements for healthy functioning. In all these ways and for these reasons, Reflective Network Therapy is a significant contribution to the future practice of child psychotherapy and psychoanalysis.

—ALEXANDRA HARRISON, MD, Assistant Clinical Professor
of Psychiatry, Harvard Medical School, Training and
Supervising Analyst, Certified Psychoanalyst for Children,
Adolescents and Adults, Supervisor, Child Analysis Program,
Boston Psychoanalytic Society and Institute.
Dr. Harrison has a private practice in Cambridge, Massachusetts.

Part I

REFLECTIVE NETWORK THERAPY: THE CHILDREN IT HELPS AND HOW IT HELPS THEM

Chapter One

New Hope for Children with Psychiatric and Developmental Disorders

INTRODUCTION

For children with serious emotional, developmental and cognitive disturbances, effective treatment early in life is essential to fully support two precious human functions: loving and learning. We report here on a surprising method of therapy in which a therapist harnesses small social networks of children, teachers and parents in a therapeutic setting (usually a preschool or kindergarten classroom) for the benefit of each child. It has often produced unexpectedly rapid gains for seriously disturbed or traumatized children, and for preschoolers with autism. All had ceased being fully able to love and learn.

Measurable gains produced by Reflective Network Therapy (RNT), especially when used in a therapeutic or special education preschool class, include positive behavioral changes, improved relational skills, regularly and substantially expanded learning capacity, and increases in IQ. All of these outcomes are measurable by children's Global Assessment Scores (CGAS) and IQ testing (WPPSI-R). Rises in IQ occur regularly. This treatment method yields very significant IQ gains in a school year for most testable children, especially those who are numb from trauma or withdrawn due to autism. With a high number of sessions, IQ rises are even more significant. It works without medication. Those who begin treatment who are already using psychotropic medications are routinely able to do without these medications within a month. The treatment is much less expensive than early intervention methods such as child psychoanalysis for anxious children or the Applied Behavioral Analysis method for children on the autism spectrum.

Just before Christmas, 2007, RNT met another milestone for replication in a community based mental health center in a state (Washington) which never had an RNT service before. Having seen videos of children being helped by the method in San Francisco, San Mateo and Argentina, Wellspring Family Services' staff and shelter caregivers in Seattle wanted to offer Reflective Network Therapy to their child clients and some parents wanted to sign up their children for this therapeutic option. I was supported by the Casey Family Foundation to spend three days providing initial intensive training in Reflective Network Therapy to fourteen potential RNT therapists and teachers at Seattle's Wellspring Family Services. On the third day, I demonstrated the method for the Wellspring staff, working with children already in their program for services.

I invested my energies with Wellspring Family Services partly because of their desire to learn about RNT, but also because of the agency's particular ability to serve substantial numbers of disturbed preschool children. Wellspring serves about 90 homeless traumatized preschoolers and infants each year as well as middle and upper class preschoolers with anxiety disorders, and children of all economic classes in the community, including some children who suffer from autism.

It was my job on the third day of training to demonstrate the method with traumatized children already known to their preschool teachers. I did so right in the agency's shelter preschool classroom serving recently homeless families in transitional housing.

Working with the Seattle children in their old and new classrooms moved me greatly. I saw my best professional legacy—this method—once more at work, flexibly adapted for treating children in their shelter classrooms, in a new city and state, and with eager therapists and teachers learning from me how to replicate the method. We videotaped the work, providing more living proof that the Reflective Network Therapy method is especially valuable for young children who have been made numb or frantic by life's hardships. Working with the children with whom I initiated our Seattle project were excellent teachers from the children's own community. The teachers quickly learned to brief me about what each child had done that day. "Briefings" and "debriefings" are important techniques, which promote mentalizing and exercise reflective network effects in any RNT classroom. The children participated, playfully telling me their personal stories and showing their emotions without much prompting.

Videotapes of treatment sessions conducted at the end of this intensive long weekend training in Seattle are available for study by qualified professionals. But ingrained in my memory, without the need for taping, is Kevin (not his real name) a homeless boy I worked with whose father had been shot dead. At first, terrified of working with a stranger, Kevin hid under a sink while another traumatized but feisty child tried to climb and claw his way out the classroom door. But within only a few minutes, Kevin played with me at a doll house where he had a man doll shouting: "Let me in. I'm back. I'm home. Let me in the door." The "man who couldn't come back" was his focus, appropriate to a father-bereaved boy. He persisted in having the man piteously struggling to get in the home, to take his place in the family car, to get up the elevator from the garage, and into the child's house. Within fifteen minutes the usually agitated, seemingly thoughtless and attentionally distracted little boy showed increasing calm and thoughtful focus. His sentences grew longer, his expressed vocabulary more advanced. He began speaking in paragraphs rather than short phrases. He declared what was on his mind: a missing man whom he desperately wanted to come home.

Teachers who witnessed this process later told me that their jaws dropped as they saw the immediacy of the usually distraught and anxious child's progress. They easily understood the cognitive advantages of the method which were so manifest in Kevin's spoken thoughts. After Kevin's short therapy session, we had a debriefing. Kevin and I reflected together to his teachers and the other children in the class: "Kevin is thinking a lot about a man who isn't home but wants to get home. Kevin feels it is very important for us to know about this man. The man somehow isn't able to get back into the home. It makes Kevin feel a lot better to tell us these thoughts. Kevin talks with bigger words and longer sentences now that he is telling us. He has lots of ideas about why the man can't get back to his family."

In 2010 the Seattle agency moved into a wonderful, much larger new building with multiple classrooms, made possible by support from the Seattle Downtown Rotary. Bill and Melinda Gates grant, Marritz Family fund and Lisa Minnet, and many other major donors. The expansion and new training funds enabled them to plan to later add more classes delivering Reflective Network Therapy services. The possibility of creating a model program for all economic classes of children and those suffering from varied problems gripped me. In addition the project had inherent potential for high quality video-conferencing collaboration among several agencies. These include The Children's Psychological Health Center (for which I am the Medical Director), the Ann Martin Center, Cornerstone Argentina, the Cambridge Cornerstone project.

We hope that text and videos of my own experience and that of other RNT therapy teams will stimulate new studies for further independent verification of our findings. To that end, we offer the support of a replication manual (see chapter 3) and a video library of in-classroom treatments. Published papers and records of scientific presentations about Reflective Network Therapy also support training in the method. We are now engaged in an effort to have transcriptions made of videotaped treatment sessions (created at various service sites) augmented with clinicians' and teachers' notes. Transcribed and thus readily indexed and searchable video archives add a deeper level of objective data for study by independent researchers. (See Appendix A regarding required confidentiality agreements for viewing treatment videos which are made available for training, study and research at no charge).

WHAT IS REFLECTIVE NETWORK THERAPY?

Reflective Network Therapy is a deliberately synergistic combination of in-classroom psychological treatment for emotionally and/or developmentally disordered young children. It is the best studied of the two forms of RNT. Its techniques include individualized in-classroom psychodynamic psychotherapy for each child, briefings, debriefings, and parent guidance—all of which take place within the context of an early childhood educational process.

The network is comprised of a classroom team. The team has usually up to eight preschooler child patients (with a maximum of twelve for one group), their parents, classroom teachers and a classroom therapist. This network is dynamically engaged with each child, one at a time in the classroom, every day the class meets. A psychodynamically trained therapist intensely focuses on and attunes to each child in turn, for about a quarter an hour at a time. The session can go longer if time permits. During that attunement, the therapist tactfully and regularly verbalizes his or her reflections about the child's feelings, and behavior, especially the therapist's thoughts about what the child is doing and thinking in the here and now of the classroom. Children's resistances to education, refusal of affection, and inhibited or inappropriate enjoyment of socialization are spoken about and often interpreted on the spot.

Each child hears directly from the network of helping adults who, with leadership from the in-classroom therapist, verbalize what they think and understand about what is happening in his or her behavior and play. The child is encouraged to participate in these thoughtful conversations, structured around the natural events of his own real actions in the classroom. The network reflects about the child in predictable and specific ways, including joint adult-child briefings and debriefings before and after each therapy session and at other times throughout the classroom day. Intersubjective reflections organize and semantically encode each participant's theory of the child's own mind and to some extent reflect on the minds of all the others in the classroom. The child's classroom peers are a vibrant part of this network. Everything happens in the real life space of the classroom, and takes advantage of what comes up between and among the children both as educational and therapeutic opportunities for growth.

The Reflective Network Therapy method differs from other interpersonal psychotherapies and educational approaches in marked ways. In other methods, children are treated psychodynamically and individually but in no other method does the child's treatment take place exclusively within the learning and play activities of their special or regular education classroom groups. No pull-out therapy is involved. The child is simply not removed from the five day a week classroom. The children served are two to seven years old, in classrooms with small populations. Six to twelve children work best, usually with two teachers and a therapist for a group of up to eight children. The adults include one head teacher and one teacher's aide as well as one therapist. Parents are often in the classroom and are welcome for however long the parent's presence promotes the child's use of the process. One on one behavioral aides are not used. However, a child's existing aide is welcome, and urged to come at the beginning of a child's treatment. Behavioral aides are rarely required after a few days. Medication is hardly ever recommended and children often have medications previously prescribed eliminated entirely as they improve.

Each child is a pupil as well as a diagnosed patient, treated and educated with parental permission and with the cooperation of his public or private school or day care center. In RNT's most intensive form, a child has a psychotherapy session every day of school. Less intensive forms have been effective, two or three times a week, always right in the classroom, giving 15–20 minute long individual psychotherapy sessions per child plus briefings and debriefings with the reflective network of adult helpers and peers. The psychotherapy sessions go on within the classroom in the midst of classroom educational activities of all kinds. Sessions are witnessed, shared and inwardly or outwardly reflected on by everyone in the classroom, right in the real life space of the classroom using the themes, symbolic expressions and behaviors which arise naturally in this setting.

Before a child has an RNT session in which he is the therapist's focus ("index patient") the teacher and child brief the therapist about what the child and family have been doing. The child is encouraged to be an active participant and his or her parents participate when they are present. They might speak about any new events in the child's life and any current behaviors or immediate expressions that the child may have just made in the classroom. The events could be as simple as playing with a piece of string or avoiding another child's friendliness. The adults might comment on interactions they have just observed between the child and other children in the class. After the 15–20 minutes of individual therapy, the child and therapist close the session by a debriefing, telling the teacher together about the contents of the session. If other children show interest, they can participate in all aspects of an index child's session, provided they allow that child to "be the boss of his own session," which means leading the play and talk.

Parents are encouraged to be in the classroom, especially but not only during the early weeks of a child's treatment. Parents regularly receive a 45 minute guidance session in private with the head or assistant teacher each week except that once a month their parent conference is with their child's RNT therapist. This guidance conference includes the opportunity to give and get feedback about the child's current behaviors, preoccupations and progress.

The teachers and therapists meet as a team for 90 minutes each week, often viewing a recent videotape of their work, and always sharing the teachers' many hours of classroom behavioral observation. The teachers are expected to greatly amplify the knowledge the therapist gains in the daily therapy sessions. Similarly, the constant daily briefings before in-classroom individual therapy sessions immediately augment the therapist's access to important themes and behaviors based on the teachers' observations. The content of the therapy sessions varies as greatly as the individual children vary. Content may include a full range of psychoanalytically useful material such as talk, play, fantasies, dreams, interpersonal dramas, art work, responses and interpretations (the therapist's verbalized explanation of the meaning of a patient's remarks, dreams, memories, experiences, and behavior). The content may be quite simple and seem barren at first, among children who are autistic or otherwise delayed or primitive in their development at the time therapy starts.

For decades, the method now more precisely called Reflective Network Therapy (RNT) was known as The Cornerstone Therapeutic Preschool Method. More simply, it has been called "The Cornerstone Method." Over the years, as we gathered scientific data, documented case studies and developed the method for manualized replication, I have analyzed the data and written about the method in an effort to isolate and explain unique features of the method which make it an effective response to multiple diagnoses. A few years ago I introduced the term "Reflective Network Therapy" which is shorthand for some central and critical aspects of the method's structure and procedures. In addition to being more specific, the term has the merit of avoiding any possible confusion with endeavors (some of them Lutheran "Cornerstone" churches and schools) which also use the word "Cornerstone" to identify themselves.

After the method's forty five years of evolution, and its increasing emphasis on how a network of others cares about, reflects on and responds to each child's thoughts and emotions, with that child and with each other in the child's presence, I found that the more descriptive name "Reflective Network Therapy" is more useful. We are transitioning over to the more precise term as of this writing while several recent endeavors still have associations with the older term. Throughout this book, therefore, you may notice some instances of the terms "The Cornerstone Therapeutic Preschool Method," "Cornerstone Method" or "Cornerstone RNT" used interchangeably with Reflective Network Therapy. As a matter of historical record since 1965, and for ease of referencing previously published articles, studies and presentation, I have retained the term Cornerstone frequently in this book, particularly in presentations of some case studies. Nothing of the method is "lost in translation". The name "Cornerstone" was originally used when the first therapeutic preschool service using this method opened in 1965 at The Center for Preventive Psychiatry in White Plains, New York. The founders chose the name to convey "building" the foundations of personality, as the stone at the corner of a foundation is the stone upon which all else depends and by which all else is measured and built.

The method's hallmark network always includes a small social group. It uses in-classroom briefings and debriefings about each child, and the exclusive location of the child's treatment sessions in the real life space of the classroom. Emphasis is given to how we reflect on one child at a time, with multiple participants thinking, feeling and speaking about the child's inner and outer world. Within a flexible and child-tailored (individualized) framework, we have settled on criteria which appear crucial and which distinguish Reflective Network Therapy techniques from other methods. We have included a statistical meta-analysis (an overview, gathering data from comparable projects into one statistical analysis) providing a comprehensive view of the data. A primary goal of presenting this book and its "how-to-do-it" manual is to help future therapeutic teams replicate the method and help researchers scientifically study our method further. The method usually initiates treatment early enough in life to make a big difference. We start during preschool and kindergarten, before the children enter first grade, hopefully before a child has become irreversibly stuck in his or her development disorder or psychiatric illness. Appropriate settings for Reflective Network Therapy are any regular preschool, therapeutic preschool or public special education classroom, day care or Head Start which includes disturbed or developmentally disordered young children. The process can be continued for as long as it helps, but a typical useful time is one or two school years. Groups of parents and children treated by RNT who started in preschool have continued to find the method positive and productive in after-school groups well beyond pre-school, (Zelman, 1996).

Twenty years after the method's invention and following initial publications about "Cornerstone treatment" (Kliman, 1968, 1970, 1975), Stanley Greenspan's excellent DIR /Floortime method of bringing resistant children into affectionate emotional contact came along (Greenspan, 1992). It was initially not considering rises of IQ as one of the outcomes. In fact, that is not surprising. Reflective Network Therapy's effect on growth of intelligence (which my psychological colleagues measure by Stanford Binet and Wechsler Preschool Scale of Intelligence IQ tests) occurred in our first therapeutic nursery school without our initially noticing the regularity of this result. It happened right under our eyes, almost immediately after we founded the first school in White Plains, New York. In the first class, a mute three year old boy with autism began to speak. Others just seemed smarter, but we didn't start measuring them with IQ tests for another year or two. The regularity of IQ growth (as formally measured by psychologists using Stanford Binet and Wechsler Preschool Scale of Intelligence tests) was clear enough by 1970 that I assigned psychology interns the task of giving IQ tests regularly to our child patients. In 1974 I began presenting preliminary reports on the IQs of the first 11 twice-tested children. They all showed significant IQ growth. In 1976 I designed, and in 1978 I implemented, a generously funded NIMH study at the same Center, including IQ testing and retesting of the majority of 104 consecutive foster children in the design and actual project. They showed no IQ growth when treated by two forms of non-RNT therapy. The children's results in this study are now included as a comparison group in statistical consideration of outcomes with the twice tested children treated by Reflective Network Therapy.

Curiously, the data from testing by interns and my presentations themselves, as well as the IQ testing of most of the 104 foster children in the NIMH grant project on foster care were all largely forgotten by the White Plains staff during a traumatic time. This happened when I became disabled for several years by a severe physical illness and finally moved to another state. About the same time our educational director (Doris Gorin) developed a fatal carcinoma and our executive director, M. Harris Schaeffer, PhD had to retire. The agency's staff was psychologically overburdened. But, my associates, Arthur Zelman, Shirley Samuels and David Abrams continued working on aspects of the project. Although my earlier data on 11 consecutive RNT children with IQ rises was not included, they reported on 42 more twice-tested children at the same Center (Zelman, 1996). Without consciously recognizing their forgetting of the preceding foundational data, they renewed and brilliantly extended my cognitive research with original and deep considerations of variables related to IQ rise, such as the number of parent sessions and clinical characteristics of the families.

Fortunately, the remarkable intellectual growth of RNT treated children seen in New York has continued to occur in services over the years and continues to be seen regularly among our child patients in comparable current projects. All but two of the 69 children in Cornerstone's twice-tested follow up series have shown the IQ rise effect. The shortest testing follow ups are eight months and the longest has been nine years. Clinical follow-ups of our earlier work span as long as 40 years. In IQ follow up studies, 63 children who were treated at the same sites, often by the same staffs, and six children in an untreated public special education control group showed no IQ rise. Unlike the RNT treated children, some children in the comparison group had declines of IQ, as did Zelman's medicated children.

When we originally created the first therapeutic preschool using this method as a way to help children who had experienced the death of a parent, the idea was to create an educational and therapeutic service to give emotional support and preventive guidance to bereaved families with very young children. We also began working with another kind of psychological orphan—foster children. Soon many other children with differing neurotic and behavioral problems, stressful or traumatizing life experiences and family troubles came to us for treatment as well.

In the early years of applying the method, we were often impressed with how rapidly and measurably some of the children grew, both emotionally and intellectually. Responding to an early publication of mine (Kliman, 1970), Anna Freud made an editorial comment that the child described in my paper had an unusually adult way of expressing himself (Newman, personal communication 1970). Freud was so skeptical about the accuracy with which we quoted the child's vocabulary that we were particularly pleased with an event which occurred shortly thereafter. The child's grateful grandfather donated a video recorder so that we could begin highly objective documentation. In retrospect, I think Anna Freud was noticing in my account (Kliman, 1970) the unlikely but nonetheless actual growth of a particular child's intelligence and development. After a few more years, similarly striking growth became regularly and objectively noted in series of 11 and then an additional 42 twice-tested children (Zelman, Samuels and Abrams, 1985; Zelman and Samuels, 1996, Hope, 1999; Kliman, 1979, 2006), as described in later chapters.

Ultimately, a deliberately prospective (forward-looking) controlled and comparison condition study was designed by Hope (1999), who did so in a California public school special education setting. She found very strong IQ rises among ten consecutive Cornerstone treated children, but not among six control and three comparison children. Similar effects now continue to be observed in San Francisco and Piedmont, California, Cornerstone Argentina in Buenos Aires and Seattle.

Development of the Method and First Hypotheses

I began developing Reflective Network Therapy when I was young, eager, and devoted to bringing a scientific approach to the field of child psychiatry.

That field was then intellectually dominated by the subspecialty called child psychoanalysis. Freshly emerging from a combined science and psychiatry program at the Albert Einstein School of Medicine Department of Child Psychiatry in New York, I was also enrolled as a student of child psychoanalysis at the New York Psychoanalytic Institute. Imbued with scientific measurement oriented approaches since medical school at Harvard, where I studied the blood chemistry of stress hormones (Kliman, 1955), I was frustrated by the fact that child psychoanalysis at the time seemed so aloof from and even hostile to ordinary scientific methods, particularly concerning objective measurements. My year as an Interdisciplinary Fellow in Science and Child Psychiatry had allowed me to do some rigorous experiments, using objective measures, on adult psychological defenses against reading and visual recognition (Kliman, 1965; Goldberg, Kliman & Reiser, 1966). Working with children, however, appealed to me most as a doctor, because the opportunity to prevent or intervene early in psychiatric disorders was so clear and my personal heroes were preventive medicine heroes: Lister, Koch and Pasteur. Developing preventive or early treatment methods which could be tested scientifically, however, was much harder than doing the treatment work.

I acted on the advice of Morton Reiser, MD (then a senior scientist at The Albert Einstein College of Medicine) and set up my own scientific "shop" establishing The Center for Preventive Psychiatry and within it The Cornerstone Therapeutic Nursery School (Kliman, 1968, 1970, 1980). That preschool service, especially with the emotional and supervisory support of Marianne Kris, MD, rather unexpectedly led me to be able to test therapeutic actions with several scientific hypotheses, the proofs of which turned out to have social value. Four of these hypotheses (another term for testable predictions) provide part of the hopeful message of this book:

1. In-classroom therapy and education combined with parent guidance (Reflective Network Therapy) can regularly raise objectively measured intelligence of testable treated children. Data which comes from studying this hypothesis shows that IQ rise with RNT is very substantial (Zelman, 1996; Hope, 1999; Kliman, 2006). It does not occur among controls and comparison children. The rise is greatest among those children who would ordinarily be the hardest to treat: those with multiple psychiatric disorders, such as combinations of pervasive developmental disorder with a major depressive or posttraumatic disorder (Zelman, 1996). Traumatized children, also ordinarily hard to treat, also respond very well. Number of child in-classroom sessions and number of parent guidance sessions are both correlated with the amount of IQ gain.

2. In-classroom RNT therapy and education combined is clinically effective compared to control and comparison groups when measured by standardized global mental health scores such as The Children's Global Assessment Score. A chapter will describe the testing of this prediction in a public school special education class, showing Reflective Network Therapy as clinically effective, an important dimension of improvement which is missing in reports of a widely used and costly educational method called Applied Behavioral Analysis.

3. Among RNT treated foster children, one can objectively test for reduction of a symptom called "behavioral enactment" or "the repetition compulsion". There is a tendency for children to actively repeat traumas, and among foster children that produces new disruptions. We demonstrated that RNT in-classroom therapy reduces the repetition compulsion as measured by a practical and highly measurable index: transfer rates among homes. After millions of dollars were invested in our teams' studies of foster children, including National Institute of Mental Health and Daniel and Florence Guggenheim grants in which I was the principal investigator (Kliman, 1982, 1987, 2006; Kliman & Schaeffer, 1990), the best scientific measurement turned out to be that simple one—rate of transfers among foster homes. We literally counted rates of this highly damaging process: unplanned transfers (bouncing) of populations of children among foster homes. This highly quantifiable index was considered to be largely a measure of children's behavioral enactments, which often provoke expulsions from a foster home struggling beyond its abilities to care for a traumatized child. It was used to report how many times for whatever reasons—children's behavior or foster parent response—caused children to "bounce" around in the sense of an unplanned removal and transfer. According to our hypothesis, if RNT treatment, rather than no treatment (control status), reduces the numbers of bounces a foster child experiences in his social service system, that confirms the treatment is reducing the foster child's compulsion to repeat trauma. RNT treatment was applied to a population of 30 consecutive foster care preschoolers, sharply reducing the transfer measure of repetition compulsion to zero for the study year and also raising IQs. The untreated rate was 25% per year. We also designed a simpler RNT derivative, a small interpersonal network method employing a Personal Life History Book developed by our team. That simpler method was manualized, replicable, could be used in groups of up to 16 children, and also reduced bouncing very powerfully (Kliman, 1982, 1987, 2006, Bondy 1990).

4. After some good early results, we hypothesized that therapeutic optimism is justified for use of Reflective Network Therapy with preschoolers on

the autism spectrum. Among preschool children with Pervasive Developmental Disorders, including autism, we believe there is often much capacity for developmental plasticity of their young brains. In other words, we thought many children with these brain-based disorders can be markedly responsive to interpersonal therapies, showing global mental health gains as well as IQ rise. This interpersonally based hypothesis and our interpersonally based treatment data contrasts with hypotheses and data from interventions which are symptom-targeted behavioral modifications or chemical treatments. RNT's combination of education and treatment has demonstrated that autistic children can benefit greatly and quantifiably from this interpersonal method, showing a combination of significant IQ rises (demonstrated by changes in WPPSI-R scores) and global mental health gains (demonstrated by improvements in CGAS scores) scores as well as improvements in Childhood Autism Rating Scales (CARS). Chapter 9 of this book discusses such surprising and socially important results in more detail.

Concepts and Processes

We conceptualize Reflective Network Therapy as an interpersonal method, one which enhances brain functions without adding medicines in the form of psychotropic drugs. Especially hard to treat by ordinary medical methods are those preschool children who have stopped loving and learning. RNT's combination of psychotherapy and education helps many such children. Almost every child treated with RNT has improved without using the medication they formerly received. Recently, we treated and prospectively studied a series of 15 testable and later re-tested California and Argentina Cornerstone RNT children who were not medicated. All but two of the 15 had Pervasive Developmental Disorder. All children but one achieved IQ rises. All but one had Childhood Autism Rating Scale (CARS) improvements and/or global mental health gains. In Zelman's 1996 archival study of 52 children treated in New York, none of the 42 Cornerstone RNT children were medicated. All had IQ gains and most had mental health improvements. Four of 10 control-comparison children in Zelman's study were medicated and received educational psychotherapy on an individual basis. In contrast to Zelman's in-classroom treated Cornerstone RNT patients, those medicated individually treated children had IQ declines averaging 4 points.

The "network" concept has at least three levels or components:

1. Interpersonal: defined as relationships between the child, peers, parents and professional people in the child's treatment situation.

2. Intrapsychic: defined as the mental representations of other persons and the emotional life of the child who is being treated.
3. Brain and nervous system: defined as the effects on the child of having his brain neurons, synapses, and brain connective pathway development enriched. These effects result from neuronal growth and plasticity responding to stimulation by education, treatment and peer and family activities conducted for the child's benefit.

In practice, Reflective Network Therapy employs tuning into a child, thinking about and expressing the caring and thoughtful mirroring of a child's inner life. The therapeutic team of adult and peer helpers (therapist, teachers, parents/primary caregivers, and classmates) externally express their thinking or internal reflections—tactfully sharing their perceptions about the child. They talk and express feelings about what the child is thinking and doing, as well as reflections about his or her behaviors, relationships, events and interactions within the classroom. The child's, therapist's, teacher's and peers' internal reflections of the participants, when expressed and externalized in language, emotion and complex behavior, produce thoughtful and complicated "mirroring" for the child.

Tuning in, engagement and reflection by a therapist is done in a manner which stimulates emotional as well as unemotional data-processing exercise in the child. That processing includes exercise of the limbic system and associated mirror neurons, as well as the brain's entire cognitive apparatus. The cognitive apparatus is a widely distributed highly communicative neural system. The two brain hemispheres have parts which actively communicate with each other, so information travels multiple pathways back and forth to many brain centers and to the lower brain structures and entire physiologically involved endocrine system and whole body.

The in-classroom use of Reflective Network Therapy also gives emotionally charged, rewarding, pleasurably and positively toned support for the child in the midst of social and cognitive experiences. These charged internal reflections of others about and for the child, externalized in verbalizations and emotional expressions, reflect back to the child how he is perceived as experiencing, thinking and feeling. It teaches him how others think and feel about his mental life while enlivening his interpersonal world. Many theories of his mind and those of others are available for the child to assimilate, adopt and use.

Moreover, everyone in the network shares reflections. The child becomes a member of the reflective team on his own behalf and for the sake of others, being both constructively selfish and constructively altruistic. The team's reflections are produced on the spot during Reflective Network Therapy's structured and unstructured educational activities, during individual therapy sessions, and most reliably during hundreds of briefings and debriefings about what has been going on with the child to which the child is not only privy but in which the child also participates. A complex network of therapeutic interactions follows throughout the classroom day. These interactions exercise the child's emotional and underlying brain processes, leading to mental health improvements and cognitive development. Rather than focusing on whether the child's behavior is socially acceptable or on task, this method quickly generates internal rewards, motivation for social and cognitive tasks and develops skills which are emotionally positively charged by interpersonal transactions. Learning becomes based largely on intensive practice in exercising self-perceptions through in-classroom and team-guided family relationships.

The term "network" also underscores the value of an interdisciplinary and multigenerational team. A child's treatment situation in RNT is deliberately designed as a multigenerational network of children, parents, teachers and therapists—with mental and emotional mirroring and reflections among all of them—right in the children's school or real life classroom space.

The fact that therapy is conducted within the real life space of the classroom provides immediate access to a network of meaningful connections, a wealth of associative material which contributes to the interpretations a therapist can usefully make, often material shared with a child on the spot. Of course the word network has many other meanings. It captures and indicates the author's interest in the brain's and the rest of the body's neural networks, and major new neurological findings being made all over the world concerning the effects of interpersonal networks and mirrored connections on the actions and development of primate brains.

Many interconnected clusters, centers and pathways of neurons are involved in the child's brain and in his learning processes. The neurons in a child's brain are activated by external and internal events. Recent neurological studies indicate a child's brain neurons can be switched on and off, even kindled into high activity and growth, through seeing, hearing, touching, tasting, smelling, moving, and through processing the many layered networks which connect data and the meaning of perceptions and memories. Scientists have literally observed very special functional brain changes that are caused in primates by interpersonal events and transactions.

During Functional Magnetic Resonance Imaging (f-MRI) studies, when one primate is watching another primate perform an action, the certain brain neurons called "mirror neurons" light up or activate in the viewer as if performing the act it is witnessing (Di Pellegrino et al., 1992). That is, one animal watching another animal performing activates not only neurons in the perceptual areas of the brain, but also the neurons in the motor areas the viewer would use if it, rather than its companion, were performing the act. Similarly, if a chimpanzee watches a keeper reach for food, its own motor neurons light up as if it, rather than the keeper, were reaching for food, neuronally mirroring the keeper's actions and behavior. The existence of mirror neurons is probably a brain basis for empathy. Their use leads to social rather than purely solitary (or dyadic, one on one) individual learning. Using the brain's mirror neuron system, primates, including human beings, learn from each other by viewing actions of others (Iacoboni 2005). Emotional comprehension is enhanced by perceiving the facial expressions and body language of others.

Mirror neurons probably activate when people notice other people's facial and bodily movements which help convey feeling content. However, as reviewed later in this book, autistic children and many children who have been psychologically numbed by trauma seem to lack the capacity to understand and respond to others' feelings. They are often highly deficient or numbed in comprehending and predicting, having a theory of or caring about what is on someone else's mind.

A review of neuroscience literature indicates the readiness of that branch of science to study and theorize about the brain functions of autistic as well as traumatized children in ways that may at least begin to explain the cognitive growth (IQ rise) which occurs in applications of Reflective Network Therapy. Functional MRI studies clearly show that the brain's internal networks of connections (especially the white matter and inter-hemispheric connections) are deficient in autistic individuals. Autistic patients are literally deficient in their connective neural systems for using brain centers, centers that otherwise are functioning well (Just, M. 2004, 2007). In addition, among autistic children, amygdala volume in their brains is reduced. It is probably no coincidence that the amygdala is crucial to enable the processing of emotion. The autistic children with the smallest amygdalas had most difficulty distinguishing emotional from neutral expressions and had the least fixation of eye regions. They were the most socially impaired in childhood, so that social deficits literally correlated with amygdala under-development. (Nacewicz et al. 2006). We think it likely that Reflective Network Therapy exercises the emotional processing system, necessarily including the amygdala, the limbic system generally, and mirror neurons.

An analogy can be drawn to cerebral palsy which may help parents understand some of the tasks involved in helping children with autism or severe posttraumatic disorders. The therapeutic task with cerebral palsy is to help develop the child's brain to muscle connections. With CP, many such connections are atrophied from before birth, but some are still present. Exercise helps strengthen the cerebral palsy victims' residual brain connections to re-sidual motor muscle systems. Similarly, the task with autism or severely trau-matically numbed children includes helping develop the child's atrophied, but still present, residual brain networks among the brain's social, emotional and cognitive systems. Therefore, I often talk to parents of autistic children about a "kind of cerebral palsy of the brain's emotional and interpersonal sys-tems", and the need for treatment to provide constructive emotional exercise for such children. Neural imaging studies in PTSD, showing atrophied areas of the emotion processing centers, suggest a similar analogy about therapeu-tic action is appropriate for the effects of RNT in promoting brain growth in such traumatically numbed children.

The autobiographical account of a remarkable and severely autistic child who recovered is included in this book (chapter 4) giving me pause about settling for pessimism even in severe cases with mental retardation secondary to the autism—if vigorous treatment is given sufficiently early. Cornerstone Argentina (Buenos Aires), a San Francisco Cornerstone, and the Ann Martin Cornerstone Service (in Piedmont, CA) have been working successfully us-ing RNT with some children who presented with mental retardation second-ary to autism. All but one of ten autistic children with pervasive developmen-tal disorder treated so far in Cornerstone Argentina have improved in their Childhood Autism Rating Scores (CARS). Two Buenos Aires children have become IQ testable and have already been showing marked IQ and clinical gains. The Ann Martin Cornerstone (Piedmont, California) has begun to show similar CARS findings. All of the RNT-treated children in Hope's series of 10 public school pupils had mild to moderate pervasive developmental dis-order, some combined with other disorders. All ten improved markedly in IQ and clinical status. They all went on to inclusive public education, spending most of their time in regular (not special education) classes.

THE PROFESSIONAL NEED FOR
REFLECTIVE NETWORK THERAPY

There are not nearly enough child psychotherapists to provide an often-needed intensive therapy for even a fraction of the troubled children in the world who could benefit. Psychodynamic and psychoanalytically informed therapists are simply in very limited supply. They do come from many profes-sions, but some of those have small memberships. As a member of various associations, I know there are fewer than 8,000 medical doctors who are child psychiatrists in the U.S. The Psychiatric Times of September 2010 reports that recruiting for child psychiatric jobs is the most difficult of all medical recruiting tasks. Many of this small number of my medical colleagues do not even practice psychotherapy with children of any age, because insurance will not pay for psychotherapy at medical rates, or they are needed as consultants or they prefer to specialize in the use of parent guidance, or child psychiatric medications. To provide intensive therapeutic sessions is rarely possible for child psychiatrists. There are very few child psychoanalysts among the psychiatrists, and only a few hundred non-medical child analysts are certified in child psychoanalysis by other certifying bodies such as the American Psychoanalytic Association, the International Psychoanalytic Association, or The Association for Child and Adolescent Psychoanalysis. I belong to each of these associations and know my colleagues are hard pressed to do intensive work with young children. Among psychologists, social workers, marriage and family counselors and other non-medical psychotherapists, there are probably fewer than 3,000 child analysts in the entire world trained sufficiently to receive certifications from the major associations I have listed. In the face of this small and hard-working supply, it is valuable that Reflective Network Therapy multiplies the effectiveness with which that short-handed profession can use its time to meet the demand for child therapy. In less than 20 hours a week, a single RNT therapist can intensively and powerfully treat eight or more children daily and include their teachers and parents in the process. A child therapist working daily and intensively by ordinary means would be able to treat only four children daily in that same 20 hours, and then would need more time to meet with their parents and teachers.

Early age of onset of a disorder requires involvement of the child's caregivers for optimum treatment. We doubt that individual psychotherapy without benefit of vigorous involvement of the child's family and school is an answer for the problems of most children in need of mental health services between ages two to seven years. They are still highly dependent on family, school and peer emotional influences. By creating and harnessing reflective networks within early childhood groups or classes, we are attempting to meet an unfilled need for a method that can be used as part of an existing school or agency setting, either public or private, or in a community clinic setting. Instead of being taken elsewhere, children can be treated in their real life settings, with minimum artificiality and no transportation time.

Reflective Network Therapy makes it possible for a short-handed profession to help more children, and more effectively use fewer human resources than are used in other programs. This is terribly important because we are seeing a world-wide increase in detection and perhaps of real prevalence of early childhood emotional disturbances (Achenbach and Howell, 1993; Lavigne et al., 1998, 2001, 2009). In the United States, where considerable resources are spent to support early childhood treatment, countless children still go untreated or receive more limited treatment and less of it than can be provided in classes using Reflective Network Therapy.

After decades of documented success and proven feasibility, we are sharing this therapeutic method with as wide an audience as possible. Our nonprofit agency is ready to supplement the information in this book with a variety of additional training materials and expertise to support new Reflective Network Therapy service sites. We do so preferentially, focusing our resources on groups promising to document at least some outcome data, such as initial and follow up test results for clinical and cognitive condition measured by standardized means.

EARLY LIFE TREATMENT OF
PSYCHOLOGICALLY TRAUMATIZED CHILDREN

Often the cause of a child's emotional disorder is a clear psychological catastrophe rather than a genetic or developmental problem. Even the youngest of children can have posttraumatic stress disorders, and they are often traumatized easily. They are victimized by molestation, domestic violence, hurricanes, earthquakes and tsunamis, as well as by the destruction of family and community supports by the bombs, bullets, fears, fires and sieges of wars and terrorism.

More than half the children confronted by hurricanes Katrina and Rita have shown signs of posttraumatic stress disorder (Lawrence et al., 2006, 2007; Mishkin et al., 2007). At this writing, children are being psychologically as well as physically traumatized in large numbers in Haiti, Iraq, Lebanon, Israel, Palestine, Somalia, eastern Congo, Afghanistan, Pakistan, India, and Sudan (to name a few places). Hundreds of thousands of war-torn child refugees are dying in Darfur, and more are being traumatized by observing the mutilations and deaths around them as an uncaring or impotent world fails to protect them.

In a way very different from what happens in autism, yet in a subtly related way, surviving psychological trauma can also close children's minds to learning. Many thousands of very young children live in large communities with severe psychological adversities and traumas in their families and throughout their regions. A portion of those traumatized children become psychologically numb (Eth and Pynoos, 1985) or so anxious that they become hypervigilant against the adults who care for and teach them. Their minds can become so closed to new experiences that they almost completely squander what should be the most precious years of early childhood learning.

FOSTER CHILDREN / SOCIAL SERVICE
NEEDS FOR CHILD THERAPY

Emotionally disturbed and traumatized foster children constitute another large population of troubled and increasingly difficult to educate young children. The foster children among our patients have done remarkably well. One of the unexpected effects among RNT treated foster children has been a reduction of bouncing among foster homes (Kliman, 1996, 2006).

A half a million U.S. children are in foster care during any one time. Most are placed before age seven (U.S. Department of Health and Human Services, 2010). Many are resentful and perplexed, closed off by the effects of adversity, and have turned away from loving adults and peers by the time they are in grade school. Many have been traumatized, abused, neglected or abandoned. They become wastefully angry, inattentive, defiant, hopelessly withdrawn, or even hateful. Cycles of family dysfunction add tremendously to these childhood burdens, often leading to family collapse and children being given up to social service systems followed by further disruptions of bouncing from foster home to foster home and from school to school (Kliman, 2006). Finally, a common pathway or result is that many repeatedly rejected foster children firmly refuse love and learning.

GREATER IMPACT ON COMMUNITY RESPONSE

All of the frequent and increasing assaults on childhood mental health make this book about Reflective Network Therapy timely. All these recognized mental health diminishing factors create more recognized needs for bringing effective, community-based treatment to very young children. Responding to such increasing needs, we have shown that RNT projects can work in a shelter for homeless children (The Golden Gate Shelter of the Salvation Army, San Francisco and Morningsong in Seattle), in a day care center (The Union Day Care Center, Greenburgh, NY) in a public Special Education Department's preschool (San Mateo, CA), a public special education kindergarten (D'Avila School, San Francisco Unified School District) as well as in community mental health agencies (The Ann Martin Center, Piedmont, CA, The Center for Preventive Psychiatry, White Plains, NY, Wellspring in Seattle, WA), in our own non-profit mental health agency, The Children's Psychological Health Center (CPHC) in San Francisco and over a dozen Community Mental Health Centers in Oklahoma (Fran Morris, Report, 2002; personal communication to Kliman).

We have concluded that Reflective Network Therapy is a versatile and practical child treatment method which many communities agencies can learn, adopt, adapt and highly individualize for the very varied special mental health needs of young children. In this book, we will show communities, agencies, schools, practitioners of mental health and mental health agencies how children can be helped before they enter first grade, before they have a career of potentially life-long mental and emotional handicaps which inevitably add to the social and financial burden on the community.

At a governmental level, young children's needs for special education and early mental health services are so great that they are officially recognized in many parts of the world. The U.S. federal government recognizes that handicapping emotional and mental conditions can arise early in childhood, and often seriously impede education. The Individuals for Disability Education Act (IDEA) makes special funding available in U.S. public schools for children who need in-school treatment services in order to be educated or to protect children in regular classrooms from undue interference with their education. In light of great need, this book is an effort to show how excellent results can be achieved with diagnostically varied young children who can be helped economically using the Reflective Network Therapy. It combines treatment with early childhood education in varied and highly versatile ways which can be easily tailored to the individual needs of each very different child.

SYNERGY OF LOVE, EDUCATION AND THERAPY

In RNT classes, preschool education includes benevolent loving, attuning with, coaxing, introducing and cautiously intriguing the child into the world of words, verbalized thoughts and abstractions. In the Reflective Network Therapy classroom, through the psychotherapist's thousands of moments of shared patter over the course of a child's preschool year, changes are induced during a developmentally valuable process. Because the therapist is always hovering, observing, and translating a child's actions and play into his or her own thoughts and skilled words (a constant process in RNT) the treatment encourages each child's developmental shift from behavior into thought expressed as semantic abstractions. This is called "mentalizing" (Fonagy, 1995, Fonagy and Target, 1996, 1998; Fonagy et al., 2002). Evolutionarily, mentalizing is developmentally and adaptively light years more advanced and efficient than action, providing a child's mind with speedier thought and data processing abilities. Rather than only behaving about a topic (such as missing an absent Mommy, expressed as angrily breaking loved toys in the classroom) a child can now think, verbalize and contain emotions about that painful topic. A dialogue can evolve with a therapist over several minutes and over many cumulative hours of regular 15-20 minute sessions of mentalizing during which the therapist describes the child's anger, jealousy, greed, longings or other affectively charged processes almost immediately to the child, as close as possible to the moment an event happens, and especially before the child has repeatedly acted on or forgotten the emotions involved. Here is a brief and deliberately over-simple example of the effectiveness of mentalizing during a boy's separation-induced tantrum:

Therapist: (to teacher and child together) "Jack is showing us that he misses his Mommy. He is angry and wants to hurt her."

Child: (angrily) "I hate these toys."

Therapist: (thoughtfully, slowly, caringly, deliberately using the third person) "Some children get angry at toys when their Mommy is not here. Jack, I noticed you were angry at the toys when Mommy left."

Child: (less angrily) "Mommy went home"

Therapist: (conveying her sense of discovery) "Yes, that's why you hit the lady doll and broke the toy sink."

Child: (mournfully, agreeably) "I want Mommy here."

Like a baby's or toddler's parents, the RNT therapist and teacher team are regularly attuning to the child's facial expressions, body language, rhythm of movement, tone of voice and spontaneous play choices. They are constantly recruiting the child into a dialogue or multi-person conversation. When a therapist repeatedly shows mildly affectionate interest in a child, that child develops an emotionally charged attachment to the therapist. That is part of appropriate therapeutic loving. The interpersonal process is not only in the child, it is also in the therapist and between the two of them. The process has a force and structure, rooted in the therapist's past, and is the opposite of transference. Transference is defined as a process in which emotions associated with one person, such as a parent, unconsciously shift to another, in this case to the therapist. For the treating adult, the internal experience almost always has some features from her past, and thus is called a "countertransference." While we are aware of the current professional debate about the concepts and value of "transference" and "countertransference" in psychoanalytic therapy, we consistently find positive use and positive effects of understanding these phenomena in RNT. The attuned therapist has feelings which empathically engage with the child. Her reactions are built around responses to the child's mental products, play and utterances. Tender interpersonal emotional investment in each other through such transferences and countertransferences are vital to our method. Without this form of attunement which includes the psychologically intimate feeling of caring for a growing child, useful social and cognitive learning by the child is limited. The tender transferences and counter transferences are a forerunner and necessary part of some disturbed children's attachment to ideas and concepts. The therapist's and child's attunement to each other—their mutuality of interest in the child's mind—is a precursor to the child's thoughtful and abstract form of attachment to his or her own inner world.

The child's and the therapist's mutual or separate hostilities are valuable for them to discuss. The child's prior relationships with adults have often led him or her to rage and hypervigilance. Unless these are confronted and worked upon, they may remain as permanent obstacles to development and learning. When the RNT therapist enlivens the child's inner world with attunements and stimulates mental activity through benevolent interactions, the child regularly grows cognitively. If the child did not mentalize well before, now, in an environment charged with benevolent loving, he or she accesses the interest and energy, and gets some tools to begin mentalizing better than ever.

The teachers in the RNT classroom are very busy with lovingly socializing, disciplining and teaching what, for each child, is an advanced mode of thinking. We constantly aim for physically and developmentally appropriate educational and therapeutic forms of love with our child patients. These are both nurturant and mental forms. We do not allow inappropriate forms of love,

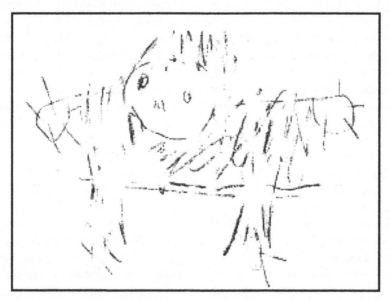

Figure 1.1. A child's drawing shows a fragile self-concept.

such as erotic, angry or cruel actions by adults. An in-classroom therapeutic method utilizing a participatory network provides additional safeguards against any form of child abuse. The entire classroom network witnesses individual therapy sessions, parent-child interactions and everything else that happens in that real life space.

Fortunately, inappropriate behavior initiated by the child (including any kind of socially inappropriate touching, curiosity or sexual physical contact) is usually not difficult to deal with at these ages. Once a child is to some extent in tune with and attached to a therapist and teacher, we can almost always channel the child's interpersonal activities and impulses into developmentally useful dialogue, interpersonal play, story telling and ultimately, into verbal discussion and sublimation. We turn children's raw urges into more socially acceptable, often verbal, playful and artistic forms.

DISCIPLINE IN A REFLECTIVE
NETWORK THERAPY CLASSROOM

Teachers are supported by a clear division of labor. They maintain primary responsibility for impulse control affecting safety in the classroom. RNT teachers use such disciplinary methods as group discussion of a child's unacceptable behavior, firm limit setting, and consequences, such as "time outs" or withholding privileges. The latter, for instance, involves having to wait to use equipment if a child is selfishly or destructively misusing the equipment. We constantly redirect children, offering them choices or suggesting alternative activities. If a child tries to make inappropriate physical contacts, we deflect and reflect on the behavior, encourage and allow the child to express and understand their urges and curiosity safely, through play with dolls and other toys, for example. Frustration of the child's interpersonal sexual or aggressive urges actually promotes learning, as the child is less excited and less anxious when well-contained in behavior. Cognitive activities seem to derive strength from the child's redirected desires for love, affection, admiration, praise and triumphs.

HISTORY OF THE METHOD

When I devised Reflective Network Therapy (as the Cornerstone Method) and first began using it with teachers Doris Gorin Ronald and Florence Herzog in a suburb of New York in 1965, my intent was to combine physiological and interpersonal psychiatry for the benefit of children. I already had an interest in neurophysiology, had published on stress hormones (Kliman, 1955), and made some presentations about an autistic child to Margaret Mahler, while a trainee in child psychiatry. Marianne Kris was then my supervisor in child analysis, as I was a student myself, at The New York Psychoanalytic Institute. She was very encouraging, and voluntarily contributed two hundred supervisory hours to the project between 1965 and 1967, particularly helping me tell her about and receive her feedback about my first discovery (Kliman, 1970)—that a real psychodynamic and psycho-analytic process was occurring, in a very unusual setting—the children's real life school. She, together with Peter Neubauer, Mary O'Neal Hawkins, and Al Solnit, formed a Foundation for Research in Preventive Psychiatry, for which they were trustees. They helped me start a flow of funding, resulting in over 50 grants which have supported the projects. Soon a nonprofit agency was formed, which was supported in part by contracts with The Westchester County Community Mental Health Board and the Dept. of Mental Hygiene of New York State.

Over the ensuing forty-five years, more than 1,500 children of diverse ethnic and socioeconomic communities have been treated and educated using Reflective Network Therapy. Research colleagues and I have begun to follow up the results and now various teams have twice-tested 69 of those children for IQ. IQ follow ups exist now on a larger number of control (completely un-treated) and comparison (otherwise treated) children; (Zelman, 1996; Hope, 1999; Kliman, 2006). The research data provide a strong confirmation of the favorable experiences of therapists, educators, and parents in multiple RNT projects and sites. Many emotionally disturbed children and a large propor-tion of children with developmental disorders—especially mild to moderate autism spectrum disorders—are included in our outcome data.

In my own career of practicing psychotherapy and psychoanalysis with individual children and their families over more than five decades, Reflective Network Therapy has proven to be an outstandingly successful method. My best outcomes in several diagnostic categories have been among young RNT treated patients. My colleagues and I have also had failures, especially among children who were so totally emotionally unrelated and nonverbal that they could not play at all. But for those children who are interpersonally related enough to ultimately take IQ tests, we have documented lasting and remark-able successes. These successes include preschoolers with the very difficult problems of severe anxiety due to trauma and interpersonally avoidant chil-dren who suffer from autism spectrum disorders.

RNT outcome studies should give some cheer and encouragement to the hundreds of thousands of families, teachers, and therapists trying to help very young children in need of mental health services. In keeping with favorable data, these pages offer hope for overcoming some of the serious developmental delays and early childhood emotional disturbances that keep children from loving others and from learning in school. Our work has been far from a cure-all. But, despite some failures, parents, therapists, and teachers have seen the method work well with most of the 1500 children treated in all projects carried out since 1965. These projects have been carried out by many different teams, in White Plains, Mt. Vernon, Peekskill, Greenburgh and Yonkers, New York; San Mateo, Piedmont and San Francisco, California; Norman, Oklahoma, and Buenos Aires, Argentina.. As we write, a new Reflective Network Therapy pilot project is going forward in Cambridge, Massachusetts under the direction of Dr. Alexandra Harrison and the Wellspring Family Services project in Seattle is solidly launched and has already been able to expand services since moving into a larger facility.

SCIENTIFIC THRESHOLDS WE HAVE CROSSED

Reflective Network Therapy has passed some important scientific study thresholds. These include service feasibility, prospective, consecutive, controlled and comparison treatment studies, and replication. Collaborating with Keith Myers, Director of Wellspring Family Services in Seattle and Dr. Alexandra Harrison, Director of the Cornerstone project in Cambridge, Massachusetts, we hope to augment our outcome data by using two other factors: random assignments and cost benefit comparisons. We plan to randomly assign child patients and support independent study of RNT outcomes versus other methods such as ABA, DIR, TEACCH, psychopharmacologic, and regular special education.

1. Feasibility: RNT is possible to carry out in locations as varied as daycare centers, private therapeutic nurseries, mental health clinics, Head Start projects and shelters for homeless families, as well as public school special education classes.
2. Prospective study: RNT has been studied by forward-looking research on outcomes, as well as and in contrast to backward-looking research on archives.
3. Consecutive study: Study of outcomes included several series of children with no omissions.
4. Controlled study: A study included reasonably well matched untreated same age, race and gender children with the same diagnoses in the same school system.

5. Comparison-treatment study: Results with RNT treated children were compared with results with children given other treatments, such as supportive-expressive group therapy, and individual psychotherapy.

6. Replication readiness–including by manual and by video instruction: These are factors necessary in scientifically based therapies. The manual within this book is a vital tool for further replication. Also essential for replication are the use of training videos and observation. Several sites are helpfully creating training archives of Cornerstone techniques: one at the Ann Martin Center, near Oakland, California, one in Buenos Aires, Argentina, and one at the Seattle project at Wellspring Family Services. They supplement the archives of training and research videos from our older California projects. Five sites are ready to provide training to other sites.

Although treating some very young children is often difficult, very few have been completely unimproved using this method. I have found failures to rise to ability to live in the community in one of four long-followed autism cases, two with very early arising autism with minimal language development. Another child developed what seems to be an early arising paranoid schizophrenia. It is likely that other treatment failures have occurred about which I have not yet learned. But treatment failures have been offset by many more encouraging experiences like those described above. We now have hundreds of videotaped longitudinal studies (studies that follow the same child, over time) of emotionally and cognitively improved children treated by Reflective Network Therapy. These videos are an archive which scholars, teachers, and therapists have parental permission to study when our agency receives evidence of professional purpose and a signed confidentiality agreement.

RESULTS—MORE ABOUT UNANTICIPATED IQ GAINS

Psychologists will readily recognize the importance of significant gains among RNT treated children's IQ scores, as these measures usually change very little over time. After decades of studying the method at work and its feasibility in various settings, I am confident in predicting that Full Scale IQ gains will continue to be produced and this measure will remain robust in other settings as RNT is more widely used. The easily and objectively measured increase in the standardized intelligence quotients of so many children is compelling in its statistical proof of one of the good effects of Reflective Network Therapy. Usually an individual's IQ test varies by only a few points when it is repeated after a patient is treated by other methods (Siegel, 1987). Thus, our results showing IQ growth with RNT treatment are generally surprising outcomes But they are even more surprising sources for therapeutic optimism about children with pervasive developmental disorders on the autism spectrum. One study reported in this book (Hope, 1999) deals with 10 out of 10 such children (an uninterrupted series) all of whom benefited. Our overall twice-tested group of 69 children, including those ten could simply not be predicted to grow this much in their intelligence.

When I began therapeutic preschool work, I did not expect the large IQ gains our child patients experienced. I was surprised that Zelman and Samuels (1996) found the children's IQ gains are so orderly in correlation to the amount of RNT treatment. The Zelman and Samuels findings are statistically powerful evidence that the number of sessions matters. The quantity of RNT treatment over the months of a school year is a crucial factor in the children's intellectual improvements. In a prospective study, Hope (1999) also exquisitely confirmed that the amount of treatment was crucial. Her IQ outcome data distinguished between children who received RNT twice a week versus four times a week. The more sessions children received using this method, the greater were their IQ gains. Researchers (Zelman, 1985, 1996; Hope, 1999; Zelman and Samuels, 1996) have compared our method's intellectual outcomes with those of classical child psychoanalysis, parent guidance, individual educational therapy, regular special education in a public school, and other psychological treatments for very young child patients at the same treatment sites, as well as with children who have not been treated. These experimental studies (some described in more detail later in this book) confirm the advantages of Reflective Network Therapy over the other forms of preschoolers' treatment.

Objective raters (defined as professionals who were not involved in any of the children's treatment) found an average IQ increase of one to two standard deviations. That translates to an increase of 14 to 28 points on full-scale IQ scores. This rise occurred only among children treated by RNT. No IQ rise occurred at all among the children with similar disorders treated with other methods and none among the untreated control children. All of the IQ testable RNT treated children with Pervasive Developmental Disorder showed an IQ rise upon retesting, at this writing, only two of the entire group of 69 twice-tested RNT-treated children treated for any diagnosis has failed to show a full scale IQ rise upon retesting. Again, the amount of IQ rise positively correlates with the number of classroom sessions with RNT treatment and also with parent guidance sessions as procedurally described in the replication manual. Such orderly correlations cannot be reasonably considered due to chance. Only with autistic children does another method (Lovaas, 1987) reliably give similar IQ findings (Sallows, 2002, 2005) and in most of that method's research, highly flawed incomparable measures (such as "Developmental Quotient" erroneously compared with IQ) were involved at baseline with follow-up.

Prospective Study of Reflective Network Therapy in Public School Special Education

Reflective Network Therapy worked well in a six year project where RNT was provided to children in a public school special education program in San Mateo, California. Table 1.1 shows the clinical outcomes for ten Cornerstone children treated by RNT and six Control children who had pervasive developmental disorders. Three Comparison treated children had post traumatic disorders and developmental delays combined.

RESULTS: IMPORTANT MENTAL HEALTH GAINS

General improvement in mental, behavioral and social behavior is rated by a scale called "The Children's Global Assessment Scale" (CGAS). It is not nearly as precise as an IQ test, but is perhaps the most widely used measure of childhood general mental health. It has been a principal measure used in the study of other methods, such as child psychoanalysis, (Fonagy et al., 2002). CGAS Mental health gains are strong among children treated in Reflective Network Therapy service sites that have kept track of their young patients' outcomes. These very encouraging results demonstrate the method's portability, a capacity for improving the general mental health of the patients in many different communities.

Colleagues are currently studying treatment videotapes of Reflective Network Therapy and other methods to see if we can further refine our understanding of the reasons for the mental health and intellectual gains achieved with children by using RNT. Meanwhile, the IQ research results are so striking that we have heard argument (Hope, 1999) that in the future it would be unethical to require controlled studies if these would require the investigators to randomly withhold Reflective Network Therapy from agencies and school systems capable of providing it.

ACTUAL TREATMENT DESCRIPTIONS OF CHILDREN WITH SED AND PDD

The children RNT helps (and their problems) fall roughly into two categories: those with serious emotional disorders (SED) and those with pervasive developmental disorders (PDD). Often there is overlap, because a child has both an emotional and a developmental disturbance. Surprisingly, we can help these two very different kinds of children in the same classrooms. We don't have to segregate the children by diagnosis, and can easily tailor-make each treatment

PROSPECTIVE STUDY OF REFLECTIVE NETWORK THERAPY IN A PUBLIC SCHOOL SPECIAL EDUCATION CLASS: CORNERSTONE RNT-TREATED, CONTROL AND COMPARISON CHILDREN

C**	= RNT/Cornerstone - Seen four or five times a week by therapist.
C*	= RNT/Cornerstone - Seen once or twice a week by therapist
C-SA	= RNT/Cornerstone Salvation Army Shelter - Non interpretive Therapy 3 to 4 times/week
SEC	= Special Education Control - Untreated

Site	#	Initial CGAS	2nd CGAS	Initial CGAS score	2nd CGAS score	IQ test (1)	IQ test (2)	Initial IQ	2nd IQ	CGAS Gain	IQ Gain
C**	160	Sep-95	Jun-96	33	58	Aug-95	Apr-99	72	106	25	34
C**	160	Oct-95	Jun-96	34	67	Nov-96	Aug-98	108	131	33	23
C**	100	Sep-95	May-96	54	58	Oct-95	Jul-99	78	117	4	39
C**	150	Sep-95	Jun-96	52	55	Nov-96	Apr-99	65	84	3	19
C*	80	Oct-97	Jun-98	48	71	Oct-97	Jul-98	98	108	23	10
C*	80	Apr-97	Jun-98	54	60	Oct-97	Jul-98	70	87	6	17
C*	80	Mar-97	Jun-98	60	70	Oct-97	Jul-98	69	91	10	22
C*	80	Feb-98	Jun-98	43	79	Aug-98	Feb-99	52	63	36	11
C*	80	Sep-97	Jun-98	50	74	Oct-97	Jul-98	66	79	24	13
C*	80	Jan-98	Jun-98	59	59	Aug-98	Mar-99	87	102	0	15
C-SA	50	Sep-97	Jun-98	81	81	Aug-98	Apr-99	117	102	0	-15
C-SA	50	Sep-97	Jun-98	69	70	Nov-97	Aug-98	115	123	1	8
C-SA	70	Sep-97	Aug-98	61	69	Jan-98	Aug-98	94	95	8	1
SEC	0	Feb-98	Jun-99	48	40	Oct-98	Apr-99	46	45	-8	-1
SEC	0	Oct-98	Jun-99	18	41	Oct-98	Apr-99	80	72	23	-8
SEC	0	May-98	Jun-99	48	46	Oct-98	Apr-99	61	63	-2	2
SEC	0	Oct-98	Jun-99	55	50	Oct-98	Apr-99	128	115	-5	-13
SEC	0	Mar-98	Jun-99	50	49	Oct-98	Apr-99	57	59	-1	2
SEC	0	Nov-98	Jun-99	44	40	Nov-98	Apr-99	54	64	-4	10

= No. of Sessions   IQ = Full Scale IQ Score   CGAS = Standard measure of children's mental health

Table 1.1.   Prospective study of Reflective Network Therapy in Public Special Education Class

to fit each individual patient. Here are some of the other children you will read about in this book, indicating the range of their disorders.

Among children with primarily Serious Emotional Disorders (SED) you will meet in this book are:

- Charles, a physically very ill and initially very frightened child who rose to the challenge of having leukemia with the help of Reflective Network Therapy. With the help of in-classroom therapy, he took the lead in his family. Actively understanding his own impending death, he took charge of communications about his illness. His mental health improved, he achieved a rich mental life, and he behaved heroically.
- Jay, an overanxious boy who came to us struggling with his own aggressive cruelty, from which he recovered very well. He also became able to cope with unexpected and severe new adversities in his life, including the deaths of his father and brother and has since become a successful artist.

Among children with Pervasive Developmental Disorders (PDD) you will meet are:

- Lonny, a child with Asperger's syndrome. Lonny was assaultive, hated to have his clothes changed and had been expelled from several preschools because of violence. He has become friendly, empathic, and a leader in sports. A ten year follow up shows that he has a very successful life, with a sustained 23 point IQ rise.
- Oscar, a traumatized witness to domestic violence, had become psychologically numb and avoidant of intimacy. He had oppositional and defiant behavior, and a pronounced receptive and expressive language disorder. He has become strong, healthy, smart and capable, with a 31 point IQ rise.
- Daniel, a highly anxious, sound-sensitive, change aversive, separation avoidant boy had probably been traumatized by repeated orthopedic surgeries, and also had an autism spectrum disorder. He too has grown much healthier and brighter.
- Monroe, a boy from a severely intellectually and economically impoverished environment, was greatly enriched emotionally as well as cognitively by Reflective Network Therapy. His IQ rose from mental retardation to normal.
- Dorian entered Reflective Network Therapy with a full blown autistic disorder, at age almost three years. When referred she was considered retarded as well as autistic; she was initially untestable. We have followed her remarkable social and cognitive progress for most of four decades. Ultimately, at a three year follow up, she had an IQ of 80. Her Full Scale IQ

was 149 upon retesting at age 12. Today, in her forties, clinical interviewing confirms her emotional health has continued to be rich and strong, and her cognitive growth and delightful sense of humor has been sustained and intricately adaptive throughout adult life. She is no longer autistic at all, though retaining remarkable gifts of memory and a pattern of thinking in pictures and cartoons.

Chapter Two

Welcome to a Reflective
Network Therapy Classroom

The interpersonal network process in the classroom is multifaceted, with some of the qualities of a hall of mirrors. Each person is an interactive participant, communicating and reflecting back perceptions and responses to all the others. Communications initiated by the adult helpers are warm and caring, delivered with consistently calm, positive regard for the children.

We present these experiences in the way they are lived, using points of view of the teachers, parent(s), the individual children and their peers and the therapist. In this particular classroom, I am the therapist. The identities of everyone else are disguised to further preserve confidentiality.

Let's enter a Reflective Network Therapy project in a public special education preschool class in a large city. As we enter, the day has already started. Two public school teachers are running the classroom: Miriam (fully credentialed with training in special education) and her teaching assistant, Carmen (uncredentialed). As the classroom's child therapist, I am working with each of the eight children in this classroom group, one after another, one at a time. The preschoolers, whose parents and school have determined that they need a therapeutic program, attend this class for several hours, five days a week. The parents have authorized videotaping for (scientific and educational purposes). Sam (the father of a boy in this class) is our volunteer videographer and he has already arrived. Historically, half the volunteers who have videotaped RNT treatment sessions have been parents. Other volunteer videographers have been psychology or social work student interns working toward a degree or doing a practicum for licensure.

Both schooling and treatment for these emotionally troubled or developmentally disordered three to seven year olds is provided in the Reflective Network Therapy classroom. Parent(s) or primary caregiver(s) are in the classroom process a good deal, and are part of the child's reflective network.

Teachers or the therapist who works with their children support and guide the parents with weekly parent conferences held before or after class hours.

Several parents are present and engaged with staff now. They are dropping children off, talking to teachers and to me informally about recent child behaviors and family events, and receiving some feedback. Most of the children stand close by listening and sometimes chiming in during these brief conversations (as they are invited to do).

Lonny has just arrived at school with his mother. Lonny is a "new boy". This is only his tenth day in Reflective Network Therapy. Lonny's mother, Rhonda, had entered the classroom on this day with guarded hope. An Asian American woman of great energy, she had a busy professional life, a tight schedule, and another child to care for. She carried in her mind the history of Lonny's failures in other schools. She scarcely knew me (Lonny's therapist) and teachers as persons she could really trust. She wanted to comfort Lonny during his transitions, but he barely glanced at her, and often turned his back on her, apparently hostile and avoidant in response to her persistent gentle efforts to engage him. Miriam and I shared some brief remarks with Lonny and his mother about Lonny's turning his back on his mother, as if he didn't care that she was leaving. Miriam moved toward Rhonda, and put a hand on her shoulder comfortingly, expressing some empathy for the rejection the mother was receiving, appropriate to Miriam's role as the major provider of support to parents. Lonny watched this exchange fleetingly. Then he joined the teachers and seven other children who were having a calendar lesson.

On Lonny's very first day in the RNT classroom, he was greeted by the school director, to whom he took an instant and anxious dislike. When the director leaned over to greet him, he was distraught and punched her hard in the face, actually bruising her and almost knocking her over. We knew that such sudden violent behaviors at times of transition were not at all unusual for Lonny. He had already been dismissed from several preschools for his uncontainable and frightening actions. Going to a new place was a torment for Lonny, whether a school, an unfamiliar home, or a restaurant. Even simple transitions such as changing clothes frightened him. He had succeeded in getting his family to wash and dry his clothes each night so he could wear the same pants and shirt the next morning.

Lonny's history of enormous reactivity to change had been on my mind so it was not surprising to find him in a rage today. He was storming mad, both howling and weeping. I had entered the classroom just in time to participate in the reflective briefing the head teacher was having with Rhonda. It was during this reflective briefing that I learned that Lonny had just kicked Daniel, apparently in retaliation for Daniel having touched some dishes with which Lonny was arranging a "tea party."

Earlier in Lonny's treatment I had realized that Lonny, who had an almost average IQ, suffered from Asperger's syndrome, a disorder which was then becoming increasingly commonly diagnosed. It is a mild form of autism, usually associated with normal intelligence but characterized by limited understanding of the mind and feelings of others. Occasionally, Lonny seemed intellectually bright. He loved to talk about mechanical things, regardless of how others responded to his monologues. I thought we might be able to harness his particular set of interests to his benefit and I looked for opportunities to do this. Lonny seemed sweet, despite his history of violent outbursts. On this occasion, although it might sound odd, I was not sorry to see him angry at another child's actions. I considered this an opening to be seized, because his response was at least in part to a living human being, rather than to a piece of new clothing or a change of physical situation. Further, his extremely aggressive behavior had immediacy; it was right in front of his and my eyes and was being discussed in his presence. He might not be able to avoid realizing somewhat that his injured peer, his teachers, and I were all perceiving and thinking of his behavior as unreasonable, unacceptable and self-defeating.

Lonny's classroom head teacher (Miriam) felt responsible for protecting other children and staff from Lonny. She found him a fascinating and complex child, but also puzzling and remote. Later that day, when Miriam talked with me about Lonny's violence, she expressed that knew she had not been as empathic with him as she would have liked, because she was predominantly concerned with the welfare of the other pupils. She also was sad–not only for Lonny, but also for his mother, whose loneliness she could feel. She knew that being Lonny's mother this morning–relating to an unresponsive and wildly overly reactive child–was painful. Because Miriam was able to observe Lonny's psychotherapy session with me in the classroom today, she reflected that she felt she knew Lonny better and experienced renewed hope.

As his therapist, Lonny presented me not only with many professional challenges, but also induced important personal emotions that shaped my responses. He seemed extremely remote as a person, not quite able to have a relationship. He did have considerable receptive and expressive language, which was encouraging. Could I really reach him emotionally, could I help him? Was his Asperger's Syndrome so hard-wired in his brain, so genetic and chemically based that no mental process would affect it? Would trying to give any "talking cure" be ridiculous? Would he hurt me physically—as he had the school director—if I came close to him? Would I have to protect the teachers and other children from him and lose my cool? Could I find a way to relate to him with words and feelings?

WHAT LONNY'S PSYCHOTHERAPY SESSION
IN THE CLASSROOM WAS LIKE THAT DAY

That day, Lonny had the first session among the eight children, each of whom had daily fifteen to twenty minute in-classroom sessions with me. As his session began, Lonny was in disciplinary trouble. We began, as usual with a short briefing. Miriam briefed me about the trouble, while Lonny listened and howled, with some attention to the rhythm of the dialogue Miriam and I were having. It seemed he was part of the communication, with his howls punctuating our conversation like a chorus which did not interrupt the main singers. Lonny, Miriam told me, was being given a time-out for having kicked Daniel. Lonny had chosen to take his time out by taking shelter under a small, round classroom table. Miriam wasn't sure why Lonny was so upset with Daniel, but she thought it had something to do with Lonny not wanting the things he was working with touched. I listened, thought and observed Lonny while sitting near him on a tiny chair designed for small children, but quickly moved onto the floor beside the table under which he crouched, gauging and adjusting my proximity to his changing receptivity.

I also had some associations of my own. Miriam somehow reminded me (by the stern and unmusical tone she had uncharacteristically just used momentarily) that Lonny's mother had pointed out during a parent guidance session how Lonny liked a soothing musical voice. He liked to be sung to! Miriam was not singing. She was rightly occupied with maintaining order in the classroom, teaching lessons, protecting Daniel, all the while promoting circumstances in which Lonny would have a turn to work with me. I decided to talk to Lonny by singing to him (although my own children have told me they would gladly pay me not to sing). From my position on the floor near Lonny's refuge, I began reflecting verbally on the immediate events preceding his time out and his self-imposed physical isolation under the table. I "talked" to Daniel by singing in a simple repetitive "sing-song" rhythm, using the nickname Jack in my song, as Lonny often referred to himself as Jack:

"Jack was having tea. Jack was serving tea...Somebody named Daniel—"

At the mention of the name of the boy who had offended Jack, his howling and screeching momentarily increased with a vengeance! But I continued singing:

Daniel took Jack's tea and he shouldn't have taken Jack's tea...
And Daniel took the tea from Jack without Jack's permission—

Hearing this, Jack's howling very suddenly diminished to silence and he became very attentive. His sudden shift into receptive attention was marked by his deliberate sideways shift in position in my direction, which moved him a little closer to me. Encouraged by this, I strove for even greater creative heights, incorporating obvious or approximate rhyme when I could. Continuing in "sing-song," I let him know how I thought about his distress and I interpreted some of his feelings:

Jack was having a big tea party.
For everybody.
And Daniel spoiled it.

At this point, Jack is seen (in the videotape of this session) briefly wiping tears from his eyes and, a moment later he inches even closer to me, wrapping one arm around the table leg closest to my position and leaning towards me. Lonny seemed enchanted. I sang on:

Daniel didn't listen to Jack.
Daniel turned his back.
Daniel didn't take the tea very nicely.
And Jack felt sad. And Jack felt bad.

I never witnessed Lonny suddenly get so quiet and become so calm in the ten days he had been with us, until now. I silently indulged in the thought, "What a great compliment to me". My own associations were active. Little did he know I had a great uncle who actually sang in the New York Metropolitan Opera in the early 1900's and would be ashamed of my unmelodic voice! What was going on in Lonny's emotions and thoughts? He actually looked a bit friendlier and certainly more tranquil. I thought he might be receptive to more:

And Jack gave Daniel a kick.
Jack said names and Jack said words. And Jack was very angry.
Poor Jack, he's so sad. Poor Jack, he's so mad.
He doesn't know what to do. He says boo hoo.
He wanted to serve a tea party. He wanted to serve a tea.
He wanted to be so friendly. And all that happened was:
People were mean and people were seen.
And people were in between all of Jack's ideas.

After these reflections and interpretations by me, Lonny began to arrange a bucket of tea party cups and toy pots which he had dragged under the table with him earlier. He energetically laid out his things and suddenly said to me quite clearly and with feeling: I'm going to share it with you.

I was astounded. Lonny's verbal communications were usually rare and not marked by relational intent. He was considered to be a minimally spontaneous though verbal child. When he did speak, his tone and affect was usually remote, his voice hoarse, ratchety and his melody robotic. In addition, much of his scant speech consisted of invented nonsense words lacking in any obvious order or thoughtful intent and even those utterances were usually not directed to another person. Now he said one whole sensible sentence, relating to me directly, coherently and with clear intent to do something nice for me: to share his tea party. That wonderful sentence—*"I'm going to share it with you"*—was followed by yet another with increasingly clear statements of emotion:

Jack: *I'm not going to let my teachers or the kids.*

Therapist: *No. You're not going to let the teachers or the kids have any of this.*

Jack: *Uh-uh! Cause me don't like what they done. I'm very mad at them!*

I repeated his coherent words back to self-named "Jack" (Lonny) without confronting him about how they contrasted with his earlier expressions that day, when he used private, incomprehensible gibberish and violence. Jack became thoroughly absorbed in making us a tea party. We exchanged further short sentences. Soon this conversation and meaningful activity attracted the attention of other children. Daniel (whom Jack had kicked earlier) came over to the table and sat down and wanted to play with the tea things and made a move to that purpose. Jack verbalized: *"Uh-Uh! He done some mean things."* He then said with emphasis and directly to Daniel: *"Stop it! I don't like that!"*

When I supported Lonny's choice not to share, he talked some more about details of his plan which included covering up the toy tea things so they could not even be seen by others. Daniel grew content to sit close to me as an observer. Daniel was perhaps also soothed by knowing that he too would soon be the focus of my full attention and support in his own therapy session later in the morning.

This was a very long stride in a very short span of time for Lonny. Not half an hour earlier, he had viciously kicked Daniel when he didn't want Daniel touching the bucket of tea dishes he was working with. Now he was satisfied—and effective—with merely stating his feeling and wish in coherent verbal communication. Though a small step towards socialization, it was a giant step towards Lonny's realization of his capacity to relate his internal states to others. Watching a series of videos of his treatment sessions, I began to think that the therapeutic events around the tea party incident marked a veritable revolution as significant to Lonny's life. This first major turning point in Lonny's treatment did not spontaneously occur out of the blue. It was precipitated by classroom events: the reflections of teacher, parent, therapist and peers followed by an on-the-spot therapeutic psychoanalytic session.

It was a good day. Lonny was never violent in the classroom or at home again. It is important to realize that for nine prior treatment days, many events, behavior and expressions that involved Lonny had been verbalized for Lonny scores of times in similar ways. We had exercised Lonny in mentalizing by using many expressions of a theory of his mind and emotional states, reflecting to him how he was perceived in the minds of others, modeling relationships and talking about behavior, feelings and events during his sessions and also during daily briefings and debriefings among teacher, therapist, parent (when present). I think this network of reflections about shared experience is an emotional resonance system, an interpersonal way to stimulate children's brains. It eventually improves their empathic capacity. As children practice and become able to mentalize their own inner world and communicate it, they become more able to generate their own theories about how others think and feel. Thus empathy and relational skills are growing.

On this day as usual, after Lonny's individual session with me ended, Lonny had a debriefing. He listened while I explained to Miriam that Lonny did not want to share with Daniel. Daniel came over again and tried to be friendly during this debriefing discussion, but Lonny persisted in rebuffing Daniel's overtures. Lonny still refused to let Daniel even see the tiny dishes he treasured. Lonny and I had already discussed how he was not even going to share the sight of the dishes. After this debriefing, the teacher helped Lonny to have his juice with the group, and I saw both tenderness and firmness in her demeanor. I worked with Daniel shortly after this. In Daniel's session we discussed his feelings about this rejection by Lonny, and the tea party events. Daniel and I then agreed that we were both trying to help Lonny be friendly to Daniel.

Thus began Lonny's highly successful treatment in a real life space. Not all of our treatments have such particularly dramatic moments or well-defined favorable turning points. In Lonny's case, however, the reflective network team soon became secure in feeling they could contain this child, and educate him to enjoy an age-appropriate social life. Lonny's treatment went on for the remainder of an eight month school year. It was a few years later that I realized that this treatment session, and perhaps the turning point moment I just described, was a powerful force in changing Lonny's life for the better. Rhonda, his mother reported to me that Lonny ultimately went on to become sociable, well liked and even admired by peers. He became comfortable going to restaurants and other public places. He gradually took his place in regular public school educational classes, and he was never violent again. Public athletic events and participation in a little league team became quite feasible for this boy, who had previously had no social life or successful schooling, and previously been confined in private, psychotic language. We will hear more detail about Lonny's treatment in this chapter and visit the treatments of two other children.

In this account of Lonny's tenth day in the RNT classroom, we have seen a team that includes the child, teacher, mother and therapist as well as other children at work. Even though teacher Miriam could naturally not immediately fully understand this child, she protected him, protected other children from him, and respected Lonny's need for psychological space. She knew Lonny couldn't stand to have his personal play territory invaded. She also set the stage for me as Lonny's therapist to tune in to Lonny's mental and emotional life without my having to worry about the safety of others. On this day we have just visited, during the psychotherapy session, the teacher observed some of the work and this created a warm feeling in her because she felt that she understood Lonny better–well enough to be a help to him.

The use of "marking" defined as communicating with marked emphasis and specific tone for naming what goes on in the child's mind, was present in the work described above. Marking is used to help transform behavior and feelings into words, a process called mentalizing. Marking is especially present in the above therapeutic sequence when the therapist sing-talked what he had to say to the child. The reflective network team of adult helpers in the classroom often "mark" or punctuate events and emphasize them in a manner similar to the exaggerated way that mothers or primary caregivers might speak to infants (akin to a "language" psychologists used to call "Motherese"). Marking employs voice modulation characterized by use of a higher than usual tonal range and calm tone but with strong emphasis on important words. This manner of speaking comes naturally to most people when speaking to infants and very young children. After some weeks of practice, this emotional marking is effortlessly employed by other adult helpers in the RNT classroom. Emotional and developmental problems often partially result from the differing ways children process (or do not process) auditory, visual, motor and spatial information. Marking for emphasis can be deliberately employed to help mitigate consequences of early deficits of brain function. I think marking exercises some pathways and creates new opportunities to open brain pathways by replicating some aspects of a type of language exercising most adults naturally use with infants. It is a kind of auditory code for opening a secret brain door with a sound-responsive lock that allows entry into mental processes. The neuroscience behind this practice is discussed by Patricia Kuhl (2004). Linda Hirshfeld. PhD, Jodie Kliman, Ph.D., David Trimble, Ph.D. and I produced a video in which we discuss the case of another mildly autistic child who emerged dramatically in an RNT classroom, with the help of marking and mentalizing, (Children's Psychological Health Center (Producer, 2009).

Next, we will look more deeply into the method at work to see how some of the richer techniques and procedures of Reflective Network Therapy play out in the real life classroom, returning to Lonny's case and the treatments of two of his peers.

CASE SAMPLES: LONNY, OSCAR AND DANIEL

This section is a disguised and composite example of a group of children in a Reflective Network Therapy service. The real children's names and grouping have been altered to protect their identities. We first describe the problems for which each child was accepted for treatment and indicate developmental history. We then follow these children through their day at a particular point in time based on videotape of their experience in the classroom and sometimes incorporate additional interactions from other sessions which shed light on the classroom experience for each child. The children described were a part of a reasonably representative group of seven children, including five boys and two girls. By "reasonably representative" I mean that pervasive developmental delays and a variety of other disorders were present among the children. [Professional therapists and educators who wish to study the actual work must sign strict confidentiality agreements to obtain underlying treatment videos available for research and training from the Children's Psychological Health Center. See Appendix A for information about viewing clinical tapes.]

Here are some disguised (and some deliberately altered) personal details about these children. Each of the three children discussed in this section were twice-tested and experienced significant IQ increases between starting treatment and graduation (indicated in a summary of each child's treatment outcome):

1. Lonny, the 4.5 year old boy with Asperger's disorder introduced above.
2. Oscar, a 4.0 year old with pervasive developmental delays and posttraumatic stress disorder secondary to domestic violence.
3. Daniel, a 4.5 year old with a physical disability aggravated by mild autism manifesting as hypersensitivity to sound, touch and personal interactions, and excessive anxiety.

Other children in this classroom group who are not discussed in this section but who were included in the classroom attended by Lonny, Oscar and Daniel were: Chris, a 4.0 year old with pervasive developmental delays and oppositional defiant disorder whose IQ rose from 78 to 102, and three more children for whom IQ testing had not yet been done: Sheldon, a boy with pervasive developmental disorder and exposure to extreme domestic violence; Tracey, a 2.5 year old who had been neglected and sexually abused before adoption at age 18 months, had pervasive developmental delays; and Katy, a 3.0 year old girl with multiple bereavements who was deeply depressed.

LONNY—A HIGH LEVEL AUTISTIC CHILD WITH ASPERGER'S SYNDROME

Presenting Problems: When first seen, Lonny was four years, three months old; a boy from an intact family of hard-working Asian-American professional parents, with a one year old younger brother. Three prior preschool programs had expelled him for violent behavior around transitions such as arrival or moving about within parts of the preschool. His behavior had included tantrums, screaming and violent assaults. He insisted on sameness in many aspects of life. Though seeming of average intelligence, his interests were narrow and encompassed mainly Thomas the Train, other train related facts, and airplane types. He would speak extensively to adult and child strangers on these subjects without apparent awareness that the topics were of brief and limited conversational scope and interest value to most other persons. Toilet training was poor for bowels. He sometimes smeared feces deliberately. He had several speech problems; his tone was hoarse, rhythm and intonation were odd and clumsy sounding. Coordination was a bit clumsy for gross motor, but not for fine motor movements. Eye contact was limited but not absent with familiar persons. Vocabulary was within normal limits, but incomprehensibly odd and bizarre invented words were frequent. He had little understanding of other people's states of minds, interests, and their dyadic (two-person relationship) or group conversational rhythms.

Lonny's Developmental History

The mother's pregnancy and Lonny's delivery were unremarkable. His condition at birth was excellent, onset of smiling, crawling, walking, short sentences, and motor skills such as riding a tricycle and building with blocks and Leggo pieces had all been on time. Lonny was attached to and mildly affectionate with both parents and a customary baby sitter. He had little social life otherwise. He had lost an important baby sitter a few months before the family took him for evaluation. An evaluation for an IEP (Individual Educational Plan as required by federal law for special education services in public schools) was precipitated by his unacceptable behaviors in preschools. Both parents were professionally successful, emotionally low keyed and socially skilled. One close relative was said to be professionally effective but a loner, socially remarkably unskilled, with a very limited theory of other people's minds. The younger brother seemed quite well emotionally and cognitively. Lonny was often markedly avoidant of eye contact and interactive play for prolonged periods. He used brief sentences and occasional paragraphs correctly. Neologisms, such as *"kinus," "germus"* and *"beautis"* were abundant and undecipherable. Lonny appeared taller than his stated age and markedly aversive to other children. He played rather mechanically and with an apparently high degree of focus, mostly with toy cars and trains, usually with no people or animal participants represented in the play.

Lonny's Further Development with Reflective Network Therapy

One day we captured Lonny on video—earlier in his treatment than the session discussed above—in an interaction with his mother which was revealing of her probable suffering due to Lonny's disorder. Though his mother tried to be friendly to others and affectionate to Lonny, in class, Lonny was as usual cool and aloof to her when she accompanied him into the classroom. Despite her persistent interest in engaging him during this transition, he kept looking away from her. When she tried harder, he looked down and sideways, assiduously ignoring her gaze. As usual, he kept his back to her when she approached him from behind, and turned his face away from her when she left. He did not return her "goodbye." Later that day, Lonny masturbated while looking at an airplane book. He spoke of an airplane going up and the space shuttle "going down" on the runway. I gently remarked to Lonny: *"This airplane stuff makes you scared and then you hold yourself between your legs."*

Lonny interrupted and began a half-joking, half-serious attack on me with a mop. Self-protectively deterring the mop (and then a broom) from hitting me, I felt some worry about my own safety. But I also was confident that teachers were right there to restrain Lonny if needed. Looking at the video later, I wondered if I would have been so calm and confident dealing with Lonny's assaults in a private therapy room with no one but me assigned to control and contain Lonny's violence. Video shows a surprisingly reflective moment in the midst of Lonny's distressing aggression. He explains to me why he is mopping, sweeping and cleaning me:

Lonny: *Pigs got you dirty. They threw mud all over you.*

Ultimately, I interpreted:

Therapist: *I know what that piggy thing was. That piggy, dirty thing that needs cleaning is that I talked about holding yourself between your legs. That's what the piggy thing was.*

Lonny listens intently and continues to clean me very gently with his mop, pretending that I am covered with mud all over my body. Magic private language talk appears during this session for almost the last time:

Lonny: *Your highness is a kighness [sic]. Your beuutis [sic]. You are not the only one. Don't push it! [Pause] This is your last chance!*

Some of the language is affectively appropriate enough for me to feel an understanding of Lonny's mind and emotions, allowing another interpretation, this time of his resistance:

Therapist: *This is my last chance if I talk to you anymore about private things.*

Lonny's response is to become calm and interested in me. This interest marked a trend in his development of ever more complex and affectionate play over the next days and weeks. Later in the same session, nurturant themes became evident, particularly concerning food and feeding others. Lonny created an imaginary restaurant—the kind of place his parents had dreaded taking him to because of his screaming and inappropriate personal actions. He appears to have accepted the class as a benevolent, nurturant place.

All of Lonny's psychotherapy treatment occurred in the midst of other children. They all had behavioral difficulties, including a spectrum of autistic and pervasive developmental problems. Two other children combined pervasive developmental delays with severe traumatization by domestic violence. Daniel, for example, was a highly anxious, hyper vigilant, sound-sensitive child who had mild autism and an IQ of around 70. Some had much more severe cognitive limits than others. In this class, Lonny eventually became a constructive leader. His therapy sessions revolved around his intolerance of interference by other children. His reactive and hypersensitive rages about his toys being touched were sometimes the subject of immediate therapy sessions. As if he were just being born into the interpersonal world, Lonny was seen rapidly changing and emerging into full human interactions. Lonny soon abandoned his idiosyncratic and self-absorbed isolation and became strongly interested in other children.

Weekly parent sessions, including feedback in both directions, to and from his parents were vital. His mother helped the work by telling how Lonny could sometimes be soothed only when someone sings to him. Thereafter, occasionally therapy sessions were conducted using rhymes and song, a medium which Lonny appreciated. (An example of this is cited above.) Such sessions allowed him to process unpleasant emotions such as his own otherwise unmodulated, sensitive and reactive rage. At times I could comment on his inappropriately public masturbation with a dynamic interpretation about the connection to his excitement and fear about the topic of the moment. Initially, such interpretations made him react with assaults and heaping of angry-toned, psychotic neologisms on the therapist. But Lonny took the comments to heart, and to the great relief of his family, he stopped public masturbation permanently soon after these interpretations were made.

Further, to my amazement and that of his teachers, Lonny slowly came out of his idiosyncratic use of language in proportion to the way he became quite attached to me, as his therapist. When pressed hard interpretively, (such as when the therapist discussed Lonny's own anxiety about separation from treatment during vacation, a fear which Lonny attributed to the therapist) Lonny would sometimes try to end the session. Other times he resisted by identification, even a re-enactment of benevolent therapy, saying: *"I've got to talk to the other kids. It's my 'sponsibility."*

The Role of Love in Lonny's Treatment

Despite his evident resistance, initial aversion to and even grim avoidance of intimate relationships, Lonny's identification with and growing fondness for me and for the teachers was also evident. Further, this feeling was reciprocated. As in other particularly successful cases, I (as the therapist) felt fondness and tenderness toward Lonny, a condition which I believe greatly facilitates my work with very difficult children. I became convinced that love, in the form of tenderness, affectionate acceptance, optimism, and benevolent attitudes, was an essential ingredient in the treatment. I tried to cultivate the whole team's capacity to hold each child in positive regard and to love them in appropriate ways. It was a special achievement to love Lonny, who was initially so noisy, aggressive, injurious, quarrelsome, and resistant to following classroom routine. It was hard for teachers to manage him when he screamed, hit, and refused to make changes, such as to go to outdoor play, or replace his dirty clothes. At times I felt that I had to give the teachers "permission" to be affectionate.

Knowing a great deal about and thinking a lot about children who can be very difficult to work with is essential to loving them. Through this sublimated and focused form of love, the whole network of participants (including therapeutic and educational professionals) matures and develops emotionally and introspectively. In the practice of Reflective Network Therapy, most of us think a great deal about our work, but more importantly, we have strong affective investments in the children. These mental and affective processes are acceptable to us as a tender kind of love, easily combined with much intellectual thought about the inner and behavioral worlds of each child.

The triumph of love in this method becomes clear when, after giving attention, thought, team discussion, and contemplation with parents over the family dilemmas, the team sees evident progress among several children. The self-esteem of teachers and parents grows in proportion to the increasing tenderness the children themselves show toward the adults. We find a reciprocal growth in adult expressiveness of caring when it is rewarded by children's responses, but the adults always give more to the children, as is to be expected.

Receiving and giving love and related nurture became an important treatment and educational theme for Lonny. He became increasingly affectionate to parents and peers. When he invented a restaurant, he thoughtfully fed others, inquiring about their tastes. He joined in the treatment sessions of two other children, focusing on what they did with food. He verbalized a great deal as he helped one child cook—although what they cooked was "*a scary, disgusting spider*".

Lonny's increasing identification with and mirroring of me continued for months, so that at times, in videos of the sessions, one can see Lonny fleetingly peeking at me and then precisely paralleling and mirroring my postures, gestures, intonations, and direction of gaze. Even more important, Lonny ultimately expressed empathic understanding, appropriately verbalizing about the states of mind of other children in the classroom whom he knew and increasingly cared about. At times, videos of Lonny's treatment show Lonny and me (his therapist) gazing in precise parallel, very close to each other, discussing Lonny's theories of how other children are feeling at the moment in the classroom. At one point he and I gaze at another child (Daniel) while Lonny speaks. He correctly comments, empathically, "*Daniel doesn't like to share, but he is sharing more and more. I am sharing my things, more, too.*"

Briefings and debriefings about intersubjective experiences were increasingly important for Lonny, in proportion to which he became affectionate with the teachers and interested in whatever they had to say to me. Teachers' praise was a major reward, and teachers' ability to stop his aggression when his toys were touched seemed to relieve all parties in the classroom. Some videos show teachers praising Lonny for socializing outside of class, a change reported by his parents.

Cognitive and Clinical Outcome of Lonny's Treatment

Lonny's growing empathy was accompanied by a reduction of private language, increased eye contact, and most remarkably, an impressive leap in IQ. Lonny's WPPSI-R Full Scale IQ rose from 98 early in his treatment to a Full Scale IQ of 119 points when he was tested only eight months later. From a scientific point of view, this was a very significant increase from low-average to high-average, only one point short of the superior range of intelligence. His initial Children's Global Assessment Score (CGAS) also rose markedly. Therapists interested in this well standardized rating should refer for definition and scoring method to the Diagnostic and Statistical Manual of Mental Disorders, DSM-IV-TR (American Psychiatric Association, 2000). Lonny's initial dismal score of 35 rose to 60 (out of 100 points). [See also, regarding CGAS: Shaffer et al. (1983).] This measure of mental health improvements was also taken after only eight months of Reflective Network Therapy. At the end of the school year, he clearly felt emotionally exuberant and connected to the other children affectionately. Acting like an orchestra conductor, Lonny vigorously led the other children in a marching parade around the classroom, during which he spontaneously and creatively expressed an original song of "Goodbye" to his therapeutic classroom mates and helped the other children to do the same. My singing to him months earlier was re-enacted by Lonnie with originality.

Lonny went on to regular, full-time mainstream public school classes, without supplemental tutoring or psychotherapy. He did well academically, and his parents report that most people cannot tell that he ever had a form of autism. Ten years later, he is well respected by other children, liked by many, and plays a team sport effectively in front of hundreds of people, participating in national travel and major competitions. He goes calmly to and from restaurants and school events, without his previously evident anxiety about transitions. His conversational ability is described as age-appropriate and the topics of his discourse are suitable to the interests of others. He is proud of himself and his parents are happy with him, though worried that his adolescence may be difficult as they fear he might then once more become socially inflexible.

DANIEL: AN OVERANXIOUS BOY WITH AUTISM SPECTRUM FEATURES (PDD)

Presenting Problems and Development: Daniel entered treatment at four and a half years of age, a Caucasian boy of medium height and weight, freckle-faced and pale, looking somewhat angry and disdainful. He was referred because of pervasive developmental problems including a speech disorder, with indistinct, hyper-rapid, high-pitched speech, a cognitive deficit, including a vocabulary markedly below age level, hypersensitivity to sounds, excessive anxiety about transitions and social anxieties, especially fearfulness of other children. He also suffered an empathic deficiency with a seeming lack of a theory of mind of others. He had a marked tendency to treat children and adults without seeming to care whether he hurt them physically or emotionally. He exhibited oppositional tendencies and occasional moderate tantrums. He also presented with hyperactivity, short attention span, low frustration tolerance, and poor coordination in all extremities, which resulted frequent falls.

Daniel did not have some other symptoms of autism. For instance, he had no echolalia, rituals, perseveration, or stereotypic movements, such as flapping or twirling. Also, he made eye contact frequently with familiar adult persons. On taking a history, we suspected a traumatic medical history contributed to his high anxiety level. He had multiple surgeries earlier in his life for a congenital anomaly of finger-webbing and an extra finger. His middle-class Hungarian American family, which was intact, well-functioning, and close to the child, was deeply concerned about Daniel's social isolation and his seemingly cruel treatment of others. Although he acted cruelly to most others, he treated his two year younger brother with indifference, as if he were not there.

Daniel impressed us as highly hypersensitive to noise and stimuli, easily made overanxious. His developmental delays were pervasive; his intellectual areas of vocabulary, speech articulation skills were immature and his rhythms and phonations were oddly intoned. His interpersonal skills and theory of the minds of others did seem very limited. We hedged our diagnosis and called his troubles a Pervasive Developmental Disorder (PDD) with marked overanxious features. The origins of his difficulties appeared to be obscure, since his congenital anomalies and resulting surgery may have reflected an underlying, constitutional pervasive developmental disorder, in which with other genetically induced physical features coexisted with the brain problems.

Daniel's Treatment

Daniel's treatment was also entirely in the classroom (as all RNT takes place in that real life space). Briefing and debriefing occurred in Daniel's treatment with unusually high verbal participation by the child (as compared with other children's level of active participation). Within a few weeks of therapy, he got into a distinct rhythm of relaxation while listening to his teachers' daily briefing of the therapist (me) about how he was feeling and what he had been doing. His usual frenetic and rapidly roaming pace within the classroom would suddenly slow, as he stood in tranquil proximity to me. The tendency for hyperactive children to slow down during briefings and debriefings varies. But with remarkable consistency, children generally slow down within minutes after starting a treatment session. This was certainly the case with Daniel; he seemed to look forward his brief therapy sessions. Sometimes he literally leaned on me, or, if I was sitting on the floor (a common occurrence during sessions); Daniel liked to lean into my side.

At times, Daniel's mother (who regularly participated in the morning sessions after she dropped Daniel off) contributed highly valued content and emotion to the briefing and debriefing process. Sometimes she stayed through entire mornings and when she was there, I would brief her as thoroughly as I briefed staff, and always in close proximity to Daniel so that he could hear what was being said about him and participate in the briefing if he wished. She often contributed relevant information about Daniel's behavior at home. In particular, she tended to focus on Daniel's displays of cruelty and his apparent meanness or indifference to the feelings of others, and how this contrasted with how much he wanted children and teachers to like him. During in-classroom debriefings, I often shared the interpretations I had made to Daniel concerning those cruelties, conveying the content with Daniel's help to the teachers and mother. In one such interpretation, I told him: *"Daniel, you are worried about breaking parts of toys, like this car, when you are worried about accidents hurting parts of yourself. You break the toys when you are worried about yourself. "*

In another instance, my interpretation was: *"Daniel, you want to be liked by Lonny, and you try hard to be his friend. But you are afraid he will not like you. So you take charge and make sure he does not like you. That way you are the boss of whether he likes you."*

Shortly after this last interpretation, his mother reported evidence of Daniel's increasingly friendly interest in his peers, including the fact that had begun to express this desire by inviting Lonny to his home and playing well with him there. She supported Daniel's socialization in many ways. She also reported Daniel's increasing affection toward her, his father, and, to some extent, toward his brother as well. During another in-class briefing to the teacher and me, Daniel's mother provided information about some recent anxiety-heightening events, including an injury to Daniel's father due to an accident involving use of a power tool. This information shed light on some of Daniel's play, in which he seemed to be taking on the role of the father in a household repair activity, and was quite worried about being hurt in the process.

With Reflective Network Therapy, as empathic capacity increases, peers can function as "co-therapists" as they develop the desire and some ability to imitate affective or relational behavior to other children which they have seen repeatedly exhibited by the network of adult helpers. Daniel benefited from this phenomenon. The fact that peers served as co-therapists for Daniel helped greatly because he was motivated to be friendly alongside his impulses to be cruel. Other children's protests about his cruelty helped him tame his aggressive impulses. As Daniels's aggressivity decreased, he became a valued friend to others in the classroom.

After a few weeks of treatment, Daniel willingly acceded to the primacy of the index child during other children's sessions, participating according to what that child was doing, rather than trying to interfere. In a memorable moment, he rose to the challenge of a crisis in Oscar's life. [See Oscar's case study, below.] Both children profited from their mentalizing of Oscar's domestic catastrophe, and Daniel developed an increased altruism. He displayed empathy, had reduced hyperactivity, a longer attention span, and showed greater frustration tolerance every month. Daniel literally urged Oscar to *"go to the doctor for help."* He became an expert co-therapist for several others at times.

Daniel's Treatment Outcome: Cognitive and Clinical Gains

Videos of his work show Daniel beginning to interact with teachers at length. Over time, he seemed to be only intermittently avoidant or intermittently frantic; he began gradually slowing down. (See Appendix A for information about viewing clinical tapes.) A longitudinal view of his treatment, as documented by video shows a marked slowing of his motor activity. Such slowing down of frenetic activity often happens quickly, within moments of beginning a therapy sessions, and reflects a long-term trend as well. This was true for Daniel. By the end of his eight months of work in Reflective Network Therapy, Daniel had an 18 point rise in his Full Scale IQ, from 74 to 92 points. His global assessment of functioning score rose from 45 to 60. Daniel moved into a mainstream, setting, with only part of his day and later none of his day in special education.

OSCAR: A FOUR YEAR OLD VICTIM OF DOMESTIC VIOLENCE

Problems and History: Oscar's treatment began when his special education team referred him because of combined receptive and expressive language disorder. He initially tested at an IQ of 74 and a CGAS (Children's Global Assessment Scale) score of 40. Among his presenting difficulties were frenetic, inattentive, impulsive and aggressive behaviors. Oscar was barely four when he entered, but he had already seen too much. His African American mother and father lived in near poverty and verbal and physical combat with each other. Oscar responded with many problems: psychological numbness, particularly following stressful events, loss of interest in play, failure to develop his receptive and expressive language skills beyond a very low level, seemed inattentive, had a short attention span, lack of empathy, immature social skills, oppositional and defiant behavior. He also had a speech articulation pathology (garbled his words), had shown no ability to learn to read or write and was hyperactive.

Oscar's Treatment

The extent of domestic violence he was witnessing did not become clear until Oscar's mother began to trust us enough to come in for most of her weekly parent guidance sessions. In Oscar's second month, she arrived in visible pain, her face badly scalded from coffee her husband had thrown at her a few

Figure 2.1. A child's drawing reflects fear, helplessness and powerlessness, perhaps death, following a traumatic event.

moments earlier. Oscar had witnessed this presumably traumatic event. She entered the classroom to brief the teacher and me (the therapist) on what had happened and tell us that she was moving herself and Oscar to a protective shelter. We supported in her decision. Oscar's entrance into the classroom on this day was very dramatic. He used his body and movement to express his profound feelings in response to the morning's traumatic events in behavioral metaphor. He ran in at high speed in front of his mother and suddenly deliberately fell face down onto a rug in the center of the classroom, lying still in a posture that suggested he was suddenly stuck down dead. He maintained the posture and attitude of pretending to be dead for a long moment until I began to work with him. (I informed the teacher that Oscar would be the first child treated, shifting the preplanned order.)

In a debriefing, the teacher mentioned that Oscar had an imaginary fight in the play kitchen, and had been cleaning it up. I realized that Oscar was enacting the moment of his mother being beaten on her face in his own kitchen.

I got close to Oscar and began chatting with him about Oscar acting dead, as if something has killed him. Oscar then pretended to attack me ominously using a rather harmless toy mop. He cursed me and then slowed down, visibly calmed. He looked for solace by moving to a section of the room where he sought out framed photographs of small groups of his peers in the classroom. I also appeared in some of these pictures. I interpreted this action and interest to Oscar, telling him: *"They are like a family right now, when you feel you need a family."*

Oscar responded by loudly cursing and moved away from me, frenetically pretending to be a flying witch. He soon moved into interactive play with Daniel who was working on building with Styrofoam blocks. Daniel allowed Oscar to become the center of this activity and became his helper, at first tossing Oscar a block when Oscar was looking for one and soon, tossing a series of blocks, one by one, in response to Oscar's asking him for more. Oscar repeatedly made constructions conspicuously tall and unstable, (obviously doomed to fall), stacking triangular blocks on top of curved blocks and trying to balance blocks on their corners and peaks instead of their bases.

As I discussed the deliberate shakiness of this construction process with him, Oscar became more quiet and calmer; he slowed down significantly and apparently became ready to think more deeply about his family circumstances and his feeling about them. I refrained from interpreting this to Oscar at that point, until the child showed me behavioral derivatives of the destructive events. He seemed to be telling me of his family and home as a structure falling apart using blocks hurling through space, which was connected to his feeling of being in danger earlier expressed by hurling his own body through space. After a few such metaphors, and with Daniel's encouragement, Oscar had talked straightforwardly about his puzzlement, I interpreted: *"Oscar, I see how tippy these buildings are that you are making. Today is a tippy day, and all the buildings are falling apart. It feels like your family feels."*

In response, Oscar muttered about his mother being beaten. Meanwhile, Oscar had been seeking and receiving help from Daniel with his building. Now Daniel offered advice, telling Oscar that he, Daniel, goes to the doctor when he needs help for trouble. Oscar replied, *"I got trouble. Black eyes. Why black eyes?"* Then, turning to me (the doctor), Oscar said: *"I need help."*

At this point, Oscar stopped making "tippy" buildings. He then proudly built several increasingly sturdy, tall towers, distinctly phallic in appearance but also apparently a sublimated expression of his desire for stability. He proudly displayed a successful tall tower to his teacher. She in turn admired the work, and Oscar's whole body language became all smiles and bowing. There was probably great unconscious significance to being able to show off to the female head of the classroom family on a day when the male head of his home family was so dangerous and angry. A phallic-oedipal progress in the form of his architectural showing off was possible for Oscar to continue in the safety of the classroom. He then thoughtfully told his teacher: *"I need help. My Mommy has to go to the doctor."*

This session was the first time Oscar sought or used intimate interaction in the form of verbalizing (rather than acting out) a fearful need. It was not the last.

Figure 2.2. Oscar's drawings increasingly reflect his interest in relating.

Oscar's Treatment Outcome

Videos of Oscar's treatment show a shift from behavioral enactments of his conflicts to mentalizing: making a mental map of his own or others' experience. This shift parallels his ultimately increasing IQ. Oscar's increasing ability to mentalize his situation and internal life relieved his need to act out through metaphorical falls, racing around, assaultive behavior, defiance and hyperactivity. While his mother and father dealt with their marriage difficulties, Oscar lived with his mother in a chaotic shelter, where he adapted surprisingly well, as he did later in foster care.

Oscar's IQ rose more than any other child in the uninterrupted series of ten consecutively studied preschoolers, rising 38 points from 74 to 112. He went on to regular schooling. He seemed bright and well related. His expressive and receptive language disorder had cleared, along with his articulation disorder and lack of interest in learning academic skills.

NEXT CHAPTER

In the next chapter, a "how to do it" manual presents all the basic elements of how to conduct Reflective Network Therapy and explains further the techniques which make this method unique. Actual though disguised case material is included in the manual in order to provide practical examples of how the method is applied.

Chapter Three

Reflective Network Therapy: How-To-Do-It Manual for Therapists, Teachers, and Parents

Gilbert Kliman, MD and Elissa Burian, MA

INTRODUCTION

This manual may be used as a stand-alone practical guide for use in train-ing. Therefore, some material from other chapters is repeated in a different context, for instructional value. By creating a how-to-do-it manual, we hope to encourage and increase the systematic replication of Reflective Network Therapy (RNT) and augment the comparability of work and research done at multiple sites-sites. Only when a team follows a manual can we compare the results of sites using therapeutic apples with the results of other sites us-ing hopefully the same therapeutic apples. The manual details the method's procedures, including reflective classroom techniques to help children see both themselves and others as full people. It presents concrete guidelines for helping children to heal their troubled emotions and developmental disor-ders using Reflective Network Therapy. Therapeutic concepts and processes are incorporated into the manual through real life examples of children's treatment. A series of excerpts from clinical and scientific papers about the method (included later in this book) supplements the manual. They are an adjunct for advanced training, with rich information about how the method has been used.

In most psychoanalytic therapies for preschoolers, children are pulled out of their classrooms into a private office with one person, a therapist (or thera-pist and parent) or work with a one-on-one behavioral aide. In contrast to a standard child analysis, DIR/Floortime psychotherapy or the Lovaas Method (ABA), a child treated with Reflective Network Therapy is never pulled out of the classroom. Instead, a whole network of attached and attuned helpers works with the child in a classroom group. Rather than having a two person interaction with an aide or therapist, the child learns to value and share the

RNT therapist with peers. The RNT therapist deliberately works with others individually in the child's presence, increasing the value of therapy to all of the children and stimulating a healthy desire for therapeutic time. There is identification of each child with each other child's socially discussed mental life and therapeutic process. A child in a Reflective Network Therapy classroom is always in a peer-inclusive process, which is therapeutically valuable as well as responsive to the philosophy and legal concerns of modern public special education.

We don't know yet how old a child can be and still benefit. Given outcome data showing that the method rapidly and usually produces IQ rises among testable children, and considering neurologic research suggesting more brain plasticity than previously thought, we suspect that particularly anxious, traumatized and many developmentally delayed children could benefit from this method at any point in childhood. It remains to be seen whether RNT is dependent on a narrow time window as a factor allowing substantial brain plasticity and growth. We believe the treatment produces positive effects on IQ through neuronal growth and connections. We know that neuronal growth is also stimulated in some animals by certain medications, (Lagace, Noonan and Eisch, 2007). Whether any interpersonal treatment can produce detectible brain changes is under consideration for more formal study even as we write. Stanford's Department of Psychiatry has a related project, hoping to determine whether individual autistic and other genetically compromised children's brains vary over time (Carrion, Weems and Reiss, (2007; Hoeft et al., 2010).

The Children's Psychological Health Center, Inc. provides Reflective Network Therapy training for professionals who treat preschool-age children within mental health clinics, and public preschool special education services. We give ongoing supervision with priority to nonprofit, governmentally assisted and potentially stable projects in well-established agencies. [See appendices A and B.]

Therapists need more start-up training help than parents or teachers with this method as detailed below. A professional child therapist who is new to the method needs several full days of initial training before starting, followed by weekly supervision for a year. Some teachers have succeeded in start-up just by using videotapes for training. As they progress, their own videotaped therapy sessions can assist the team and the supervisor in assuring quality control. Weekly conferences which include viewing and discussing videotapes of recent RNT psychotherapy sessions increasingly enable the team to monitor itself after a few months. When establishing a brand new service site, it is important to set up a systematic data collection system for measurable outcome data before starting treatment and to re-asses that system after several months of operating the new program to verify that the data collection method is working. In many communities a school psychologist could do the initial and follow up IQ testing and CGAS scoring on children in RNT classrooms.

Parents and teachers do not need prior specialized knowledge or experience with Reflective Network Therapy to participate. Inexperienced preschool teachers and day care workers, and even therapists with little prior experience in other forms of therapeutic education or special education have all successfully used the RNT method, often with very difficult children. Because RNT procedures are quite natural, many families and educators can create Reflective Network Therapy services or use the method with a particular child within their private preschools and public special education classes. For four decades, the method has helped keep troubled children in their schools and communities, helping them learn to relate lovingly to their families and socialize well with their peers. The method has generally been used with modest cost and high effectiveness. It has served as a social and educational bridge for hundreds of children, allowing most RNT graduates to continue mostly in regular elementary education classrooms in regular schools, and go on to become engaged, contributing members of their families and communities.

Many parents and therapists ask about medication and other supplemental treatments, such as nutritional therapy, speech therapy, and applied behavioral treatments for child patients. Concerns about medications are particularly important for the senior author as a medical doctor and psychiatrist working with very young children whose bodies and brains are developmentally evolving and are much more vulnerable to some side-effects than are adults. My team members and I are comfortable with psychotropic medication prescribed by pediatricians, so long as use is being monitored for side effects and general safety. RNT teams and I have recommended medication for only a very few of the 1500 RNT children treated so far. On the contrary, we are likely to recommend reducing or removing medications as children improve within the benevolent influence of their therapeutic human network. Children should continue any prescribed medication(s) when they first enter treatment. We prefer that children do not start new medications soon after starting RNT. We urge at least a trial of RNT before medication is changed.

It takes two or three months in the Reflective Network Therapy classroom to establish a baseline of observations which might support a recommendation to the child's pediatrician for the reduction or elimination of medication(s). Zelman's studies (1996) show that the worst IQ outcomes among his twice-tested cases were among children treated by another method who were also medicated. They actually declined in IQ, contrasting sharply with unmedicated RNT-treated children who experienced rises in IQ.

None of our 69 twice-tested IQ series) continued with ongoing Applied Behavioral Analysis (Lovaas method) treatment while in RNT. No child who started RNT treatment with an ABA aide has ever needed the aide in the Reflective Network Therapy classroom after a week or two. We do encourage continuing any dietary, speech therapy, occupational therapy or other appropriate treatments already in progress when children enter our program. We are particularly eager for autistic children to have speech therapy, which we prefer to go on right in our classroom.

COMPARING REFLECTIVE NETWORK THERAPY WITH OTHER INTERPERSONAL THERAPIES

So far, it appears that Reflective Network Therapy is the only psychotherapy method which reliably and regularly produces IQ gains as well as mental health gains among over 95% of its IQ testable patients. Individual psychodynamic psychotherapy and individual child psychoanalysis have not studied IQ outcomes very much and do not regularly produce IQ gains (Kliman, Schaeffer, Friedman and Pasquariell, 1982; Zelman, 1996). Therapeutic preschools which are psychoanalytically informed but function without an in-classroom therapist (Furman & Katan, 1969) have never reported such regularly occurring gains. We can't rule out that possibility until a few such schools have become psychometric data collectors, including initial and later IQ testing. When considering other interpersonal methods, which are particularly appropriate for comparison to RNT, we think often of Mahler's tripartite therapy (Mahler, 1968) which encouraged a parent, child and therapist to engage as a reflective team. RNT develops this aspect further. Some features and goals of later-developed two-person methods such as DIR /Floortime are identical with those of RNT, particularly the emphasis on promoting empathy and attunement with a caring, affectionate adult. Publications of our methods preceded Stanley Greenspan's valuable work (Greenspan, 1992) by decades. RNT psychotherapy sessions are the same length as later adopted by DIR/Floortime: fifteen to twenty minutes. The involvement of parents is absolutely central to both methods. With DIR/Floortime, educators are not used synergistically in the classroom (as they are in RNT treatment) but they certainly could be. DIR/Floortime used for multiple years with a responsive child has outcomes with resemblance to RNT's outcomes after eight months. A subgroup of 16 DIR/Floortime treated autistic patients was followed for ten years, selected because of their promising early response to that method. They did very well academically and socially, despite the ominous diagnosis received years earlier (Greenspan and Weider, 2005).

Almost all testable RNT treated children have IQ rises, averaging 12 to 28 Full Scale IQ points after 8 months of treatment. Greenspan reports that 20% of autistic preschoolers who are testable and treated have IQ gains with DIR/ Floortime treatment. But this treatment requires *two to five hours per day for 2 to 8 years* to achieve such gains. A key technique difference between RNT and Greenspan's method is that DIR is characteristically limited to influencing mother-child couples which is close to a one-on-one approach. In sharp contrast, making it appropriate as a school-based method, Reflective Network Therapy always uses the classroom network with multiple peers. RNT emphasizes systematic ways of multiple helping participants adding reflections, creating a social hall of peers with adult mirrors adding multiple caring attunements.

RNT systematically includes and depends on early childhood classroom education, classroom social processes and at the same time makes daily use of child analytic techniques. For those many children who can discuss or listen to a discussion of their own behavior even in the most limited way, we consistently use interpretive psychotherapy in the midst of real-life play and real-life interpersonal interaction within the classroom. A full range of dynamic and "defense-focused" interpretations are often appropriate to the growing abilities of a child. Defense-focused interpretations particularly concern a child's resistances to being taught and loved by the adults and peers. Sometimes it is possible to get a child to understand he is deeply fearful and defensive about intimacies such as receiving information and that he actually dreads the opportunity to learn new skills. When this information becomes conscious, such defenses can be significantly mitigated. Our work is unlike therapeutic nurseries run by teachers (Rosenblitt, 2005) which by design avoid the actual psychoanalytic process of making interpretations. The RNT method regularly uses in-the-classroom interpretations of in-school behavior to help children overcome arrests in development. The in-classroom therapist can often help a child understand connections between past and present and make connections between transference processes in school, which come from experiences with persons in the child's family life.

See Chapter 9 detailed comparisons of Reflective Network Therapy, DIR/ Floortime, ABA, TEACCH and individual "pull-out" psychotherapy in terms of clinical results, versatility, feasibility, replicability, cost benefits and time required for improvements.

REPLICATION TECHNIQUES, PROCESSES, PROCEDURES AND CLASSROOM STRUCTURE

Reflective Network Therapy is helpful for most seriously emotionally disordered (SED) preschoolers. The method is also appropriate and evidence-based for young children with pervasive developmental disorders (PDD) including autism (often referred to as autism spectrum disorders or ASD). Like any psychotherapy, the method is tailor-made for each patient. Thus it also helps children with some psychiatric diagnoses that do not neatly fit into broad categories. Reflective Network Therapy's spectrum of utility and its capacity to be tailored to an individual child's needs makes it effective for children with anxiety disorders, oppositionalism or attentional and hyperactive difficulties.

Normal children (children with no psychiatric diagnoses or severe disorders) including staff members' children as well as healthy preschool siblings of preschoolers with serious disorders have sometimes attended RNT classrooms. They have helped other children, grown in altruism and enjoyed their "expert player" status. Some of these children have received scholarships to attend, making the classroom population more diverse. Parents report that these children benefited from attending, though we have no systematic data about them yet.

There is very strong statistical evidence of the method's value for foster children (Kliman, 2006). It is no coincidence that the first Cornerstone therapeutic preschool where Reflective Network Therapy was applied was originally established as part of The Center for Preventive Psychiatry, to preventively help traumatized and orphaned children (Kliman, 1968). Our experience with the method leads us beyond treatment, to encourage preventive referral of bereaved children and foster children even if they presently have no diagnosable disorder.

Settings

This method works well as an enhancement to an ongoing special education service. It can also be a separate classroom service in a public school. Reflective Network Therapy works well in a part-day or full-day preschool, daycare service and in preschool programs in community based mental health facilities. The method also does well in an independent part or full time preschool. Inclusion of Reflective Network Therapy service for children into a larger public school special education class, Head Start, daycare center or similar agency is valuable for the purpose of achieving full mainstreaming of many of the children in one or two years. Inclusion in a larger public school is a means for encouraging social growth of the child patients within the larger community. It helps de-stigmatize the psychiatric problems of young patients. Ideally, in such comprehensive settings, the method can be offered as an enrichment or supplementary service, scheduled like a music class or physical education activity during part of every school day.

Frequent classroom sessions (five times a week for several hours each) work reliably and even better, as our outcome data shows. At a minimum, two or three in-classroom educational sessions at least two hours long are required each week, with psychotherapy occurring in the classroom each of the days for each child. The children served can also join in playground activities and classes with other children in the same school during part of the rest of the day with at least a teacher's assistant who is learning or is trained in Reflective Network Therapy close by. Cornerstone Argentina is using this mixed class model, having the children join with other classes during recesses, outdoor activities, and art classes. The tightly integrated peer functioning of the RNT therapeutic classroom participants as a network promotes a deep inclusiveness in the classroom group, in contrast to having an aide or other therapist always at the child's side. RNT nurtures nonverbal as well as verbal children and leads them to relate to each other and their families, to trust and love their teachers, to play and learn with other children and parents and become ready for fuller future mainstreaming. Most of our children go on to regular education in public schools by first grade.

Reflective Network Therapy is an inclusive method, deliberately treating children within their classrooms rather than pulling them out of class for behavioral modification or individual psychotherapy. RNT does not segregate or isolate children socially from inclusion within the therapeutic classroom group by having an adult aide constantly at a child's side. RNT treatment and education gives a child a gradual transitional preparation for entry and inclusion into the larger real world. It cushions children, protecting and limiting their actions and serves as a stimulating but protective half-way house en route to the more demanding larger community. It is a "holding environment" (Winnicott, 1965) giving children opportunities for soothing, impulse-containment and expression-supporting relationships, thus not only allowing growth but also correcting for developmental and behavioral difficulties, (Alpert, 1941, 1954; Alpert & Rapin, 1953). Children are contained by the thoughtful, understanding presence of teachers and a therapist who understand each child's developmental status, needs and individual impulse control limitations, and who encourage the evolution of his or her expressive skills.

This method differs from other psychotherapies and educational approaches in several ways. It is unique in the way it deliberately combines classroom education with interpersonal psychotherapy. Since children are not removed from the classroom, psychotherapy sessions are witnessed, shared and reflected on in the real life space of the classroom by all of the teachers and children in the group. Thus, Reflective Network Therapy makes therapeutic use of all the material and behavior which arises naturally in this setting.

The psychotherapy aspects of this method are based on interpersonal rather than behavioral conditioning influences. A complex network of interactive helpers (peers, therapist, teachers, teachers' aides and parents) works with the children as a team, supported by the principles and practices inherent in Reflective Network Therapy. In a reflective network, information (about behavior, expressed fantasies, perceived feelings, significant events and therapeutic themes) is all communicated openly among all adult and child persons in the classroom as well as shared directly with the index child. Thus, each child patient as well as adult helpers witness the index child through a set of social lenses and can access mirrors of others' views and feelings. Each child patient can come to perceive him or herself as richly understood in an empathic fashion by teachers, parents and therapist, and importantly, by other children.

Until now, there has been no systematic, replicable and inclusive method of deliberately applying individual interpersonal psychoanalytic therapy entirely within a preschool educational setting. Rather, children have been grouped for educational work and individuals have usually been removed from the classroom or even transported elsewhere for what psychotherapy the school believes is necessary. RNT has been successful in many settings: preschools, day care, homeless shelters, special education classes, and Head Start settings with children having multiple psychiatric diagnoses including pervasive developmental disorders and posttraumatic stress disorders.

The need for an in-classroom method of school-based psychotherapy literally combined with education is great. The purpose of this manual is to create a basis for carrying out such therapy in school classroom settings, using Reflective Network Therapy. This manual is data and theory driven. It selects features related to the way data has shaped how the author thinks of the method. It describes the techniques and procedures required to achieve the cognitive and clinical gains Reflective Network Therapy induces.

Reflective Network Therapy is distinctive in its cognitive and clinical gains combined. Other methods rarely produce combinations of the large clinical and IQ gains seen with RNT. One reason may be that other methods lack targeting of both emotional and cognitive achievements. Most lack simultaneous interdisciplinary aims and most lack real-life environment as an arena for therapy. The synergy between disciplines of teaching and therapy creates an emotionally and cognitively powerful reflective network in the classroom, which supports and nurtures, mentally enriches, and stimulates children's emotional and cognitive growth simultaneously—each discipline including and magnifying the effects of the other.

The multigenerational human network set up in RNT includes familiar but newly reinforced care-givers (parents), care-giving teachers and peers and is optimal for the purposes of meeting many treatment needs. Treatment using this method can open the child to receive nurturing, and at the same time to begin thinking about himself and others as a result of receiving multiple sources of reflection from others in the reflective network. Once the child begins to be able to think about himself and his feelings, he simultaneously begins to build a repertoire of how to think about and relate to others, developing both his empathic capacity and his communicative repertoire. The deliberate therapeutic and educational use of multiple human beings in the classroom allows for the modeling of thoughtful and affectionate interaction. Therefore, the method's technical emphasis is on verbalized emotions and thoughts—the mentalized forms of behavior (Fonagy & Target, 2003). The child's expressive behavior and perceived emotional states are reflected back to him or her semantically, with love, discipline and transmission of various forms of cognitive and insightful knowledge.

The development of thinking itself depends on interpersonal practice, as Fonagy profoundly expresses, in his presentation of the concept of "mentalizing" (Fonagy, 2000; Fonagy et al., 2002). Fonagy defines reflective function

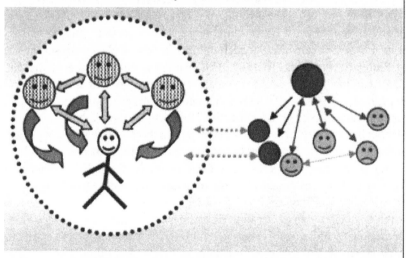

Diagram of a briefing in a therapeutic network scenario

Child, therapist, teacher and parent talk together while other children work with the assistant teacher nearby in the classroom.

☺ = [Left]   Adult helpers: therapist, head teacher and parent are sharing reflections among themselves and with the index child.

● = [Right] Assistant teacher is working with other children nearby. In this moment, two children are attending to the index child's briefing.

Figure 3.1.   Diagram of a therapeutic network scenario.

or mentalizing as the capacity to think about mental states in one's self and in others. He suggests that the capacity for reflective awareness occurs originally in the caregiver-infant dyad. The baby's relationship with the mind of a caregiver increases the likelihood of the child's secure attachment, which, in turn, facilitates the development of mentalizing in the child. Fonagy proposes that a secure attachment relationship offers an immature mind a chance to explore the mind of the caregiver, and in this way to learn about minds.

In this interpersonal and intersubjective model, the development of a self-concept could be rendered as a variant of Renee Descartes' "I think, therefore I am." The child's self-concept is dependent on a mutually regulated awareness of information and emotions experienced during relationships. Long before a child is a preschooler, he usually begins to experience complex reflections of how others feel about him and how they think of him. A child has concepts such as: "My caregivers have feelings about me and I have feelings about them. They have thoughts about me. I have thoughts about them. They think of me. They know I am thinking. I am living as a thinker." Fonagy (2000) argues persuasively that the therapeutic effect of psychoanalysis depends on its capacity to activate patients' ability to evolve an awareness of mental states and thus to find meaning in their own and other people's behavior.

Theory is important. But this how-to-do-it manual about Reflective Network Therapy is intended to go beyond theory, to give teachers and therapists a practical structure and specific guidelines for establishing a reflective network of treatment influences in their own RNT service. It will also be valuable for parents who wish to participate with professionals, joining them in a systematic collaboration to help their children using RNT. In addition to theory, data about clinical and cognitive improvements inspired and guided the manualization of the method.

CLASSROOM CLIMATE

In the classroom, we consciously develop, employ and strive to maintain a loving attitude and loving feelings for each child-patient, in each and every circumstance. We recognize the therapeutic functions of appropriate love as an essential therapeutic element and consciously cultivate it as a subtle but reliable, background emotional climate. Negative feelings which might arise within any of the adult participants in the therapeutic network are deliberately and openly acknowledged and worked through in structured interactions. These include weekly parent guidance sessions and staff meetings. The staff meetings include review of recent videotapes of the work, mutual supervision, with leadership by the classroom psychotherapist.

Angry or sociopathic teachers and therapists must be excluded from this work, during the hiring process. Excellent references are a great help in screening for talent rather than trouble. We've been fortunate in having been free of such limitations and difficulties within staff. Excessive fastidiousness and rigidity is another handicap we have not experienced with our staff. Team members should be empathic, receptive, flexible, imaginative, creative, and able to tolerate children's regressions and aggressions, as well as their tenderness. They need tolerance for their own positive and negative countertransferences. They need a rich ability to feel love for the children and parents, and to accept parents unconditionally without tolerating child abuse. They need to be able to cultivate the best in classroom colleagues and to accept as food for thought the observations of collaborating educators and therapists. To some extent, they have to able to learn to appropriately care about and love each other. It helps to be able to be playfully childlike in the classroom at times, without regressing in reality testing and impulse control.

In the interest of stability and minimizing influences extraneous to the natural classroom composition, visitors should be few. Observation for training is best done through video or one way mirror. More than one therapist in the classroom may be confusing. Lopez, Balter and Howard (1996) have reported successful use of multiple therapists with no teachers, but we have not been able to observe enough to confirm the finding nor do we have outcome data yet on that effort.

STANDARDS AND STRUCTURE

There is a range between ideal and well-tested or maximal standards and minimum standards. The maximal standards are very highly likely to produce cognitive and clinical gains. The minimum standards are less likely to be fully effective but are likely to be at least clinically positive and useful when practicing Reflective Network Therapy. Deliberately being repetitive, we will emphasize throughout the manual that some guidelines and aspects are considered essential, such as:

1. There should be at least three and no more than twelve children in a group.
2. Children are between ages two and six but classes of older children are being considered.
3. One child therapist is assigned to each classroom of up to twelve children.
4. Each psychotherapy session occurs only in the classroom.
5. If more than three children are present, two preschool educators are needed, to conduct educational activities while one child is treated at a time within the classroom.

6. Educational activities can occur daily for full classroom days which occur five days a week. They must occur at least two hours a day, at least two or three days a week, totaling at least six hours a week if there are eight patients.
7. In-classroom psychotherapy sessions must occur with each child at least two and preferably five times, each session on separate days of the week.
8. Each session should be preceded and followed by a "briefing" or "debriefing."
9. Insistence is required on a child's individual therapy taking place in the classroom in the presence of other children and teachers.
10. Weekly parent sessions must occur with a staff member, sharing what has happened in class and home, and most of those sessions should be parent-teacher sessions of at least 45 minute durations.
11. Weekly staff conferences are needed, sharing what has been going on with the treatment.
12. With parental permission, videotaping of psychotherapy sessions should be regularly used to assist at staff conferences, and for objective follow ups.

The method is based on a network of intersubjective influences, not just a therapist's, teacher's, parent's or aide's influence. In order to be sure that the RNT service is well set up, all the component pieces should be present and interconnected. If a certain piece of a network influence is lacking, a network's communication processes might go down or be weakened. We aren't sure why this is so. It may be analogous to an internet server's disconnect causing a widespread e-mail outage or a broken wire causing lights to go out in a larger but highly connected electrical grid. The most likely influence to be lost is teacher-parent conferencing, as parents are often avoidant and teachers are not accustomed to parent interactions of weekly intensity. Yet there is data showing this factor is extremely powerful in the cognitive and clinical results.

Any RNT service should start with a daily class or classroom group which regularly meets two to five days a week. The method does well with a considerable age span (between 2 and 7) in a single classroom, a flexibility and inclusiveness which is partly due to the differences in children's pathologies and developmental levels. Developmental and cognitive inclusiveness, providing a range of children's ages, executive skills, and cognitive and emotional developmental stages is very useful to the treatment. Having such a mix of children in the classroom is often revelatory to a therapist as she or he may notice behaviors which indicate the child's perception of his place in his family, including sibling relationships. (Kliman and Ronald, 1970)

STAFFING REQUIREMENTS

Each class usually needs at least two teachers per classroom group (head teacher and assistant teacher) and a third teacher assistant if there are four to twelve children in the group. It is possible to have a very small RNT group, with only three children and one therapist and one teacher. Each class requires a psychodynamically trained child therapist, who must be in the classroom for a couple of hours each school day. The child therapist must have enough time to work at least 15 minutes and preferably 20 or more minutes with each child during each RNT service day–usually three to five times a week. The same therapist should be prepared to meet with each child's caregiver or parent for 45 minutes once a month. The head teacher must be prepared to work with each group daily for at least two hours of each day classes occur, and to meet with each child's caregiver or parent, for 45 minutes weekly.

Every effort should be made to keep staff changes to a minimum in the interests of a stable environment. Even a school teacher turnover rate of one change per semester is potentially detrimental, and a tally of any changes should be kept as part of the clinical and educational record keeping effort. Use of substitutes should also be tallied. At least 80% of the RNT school year should be conducted by a stable team. Summer programs are valuable supplements, which require some substitutions of staff.

RNT staff often experience accelerated personal growth as a result of an in-service effect from participation in regular briefings, debriefings, and staff conferences. Some otherwise relatively rigid therapists who feel uncomfortable or frustrated with primitive children find they can nevertheless work well with the emotional and social support of teachers. Teachers who started out knowing little about severe childhood problems ultimately develop profound understandings. More specific information regarding the training and supervision of staff, their distinct roles and responsibilities, and their combined collaborative influence as network therapy is discussed below.

Essential Procedures Include:

1. In-classroom briefing just before a child's psychotherapy session.
2. In-classroom psychotherapy sessions for each child, multiple times a week.
3. In-classroom psychotherapy (15 minutes or more) each day the class meets.
4. In-classroom debriefing immediately after the child's psychotherapy session.
5. In-classroom educational activities.

6. Weekly parent conferences: A 45 minute duration, three times a month with a teacher and a monthly parent conference with the RNT therapist.
7. Weekly Team conferences (therapist and teaching staff).

Briefings are structured times of in-classroom communication among at least two adults (teacher and/or parent and therapist) and the child right before the child's in-classroom psychotherapy session. These communications involve the teacher and child jointly narrating a summary to the child's therapist about the child's day so far. This briefing serves several functions for the particular child who is about to have a psychotherapy session. It gives the child practice in experiencing being thought about by two important adults (teacher and therapist) at the same time. He processes the emotional expressions as well as words of the two adults who are collaborating about him. He develops a theory of multiple minds. He has a chance to practice learning how two (and up to a dozen classroom people) can have caring and detailed knowledge of his behavior and shared but individually varied theories about his mind. During the next fifteen or twenty minutes, his psychotherapy session is necessarily influenced by his knowledge that he is being thought about and his expectation that this experience will occur every time he is in the RNT classroom.

THE PRE-SESSION BRIEFING IS
FOLLOWED BY PLAY THERAPY

Fifteen to twenty minutes of in-classroom psychotherapy is provided to each child for as many days a week as the class meets. All of the play therapy sessions take place in the classroom so that the real-life behavioral confrontations and insights developed with the child are shared and verbalized immediately with him or her and the teachers, in the presence of other children and some parents. It is critical that this is done regularly and right on the spot, before connection and meaning is lost to the child's immature memory and limited attention span or buried by such defenses as avoidance, denial, repression, isolation, dissociation or projection.

THE INDIVIDUAL PSYCHOTHERAPY
SESSION MUST BE FOLLOWED BY A DEBRIEFING

The debriefing is an interpersonal event lasting a few minutes. It contains a structured effort to communicate. It provides the child with hundreds of opportunities in a school year to view, mirror and identify with others' feelings and behavior about him. The child and therapist endeavor together to speak to the teacher about the content and emotional tones of their session. When the child cannot or will not verbally narrate his or her own experience of the session, the therapist fills in the teacher, while in the child's presence. There is a deliberate recursiveness to this process, as each player has important input into the others' communications and other interactions and receives input about those which didn't directly include him or her. Other children in the classroom may be part of and listen to the index patient's psychotherapy and may hear and participate in the debriefing.

LOCATION

RNT child psychotherapy sessions should always take place exclusively in the real-life space of the classroom, never on a pull-out basis. The location is essential, as in-classroom psychotherapy draws heavily on the therapist's and the child's shared perception and experience of the events going on in the classroom. These events often include other children entering into the index child's therapeutic conversations, as well as therapist and child talking together about other children and events they see going on around them in the classroom.

CONTROL AND PARTICIPATION

The index child is the child who is therapist's primary focus during a therapy session. Other children will have their turns. They should be allowed to help the current index patient, but only to the extent they do not interfere with that child's play and opportunity for self expression. A participating peer must allow the index child to have his way in temporarily controlling the expressive process. Teachers and therapists unhesitatingly remove a disruptive child from the vicinity of the index child's session with the psychotherapist. In practice, most children are initially jealous of the classroom therapy time their peers receive with the therapist but usually become collaborative within a few days or weeks. Soon the children value the sessions so much for themselves that most children become altruistic, helping each other to have sessions, and becoming supportive of each other's efforts to play and talk during the classroom sessions. Videos show that children in a Reflective Network Therapy setting often help each other work at their highest level of abilities, and nurture each other. Within a few weeks, each child can be seen increasingly respecting the rhythms of the others and identifying with the helpfulness of the classroom adult helpers. The children's empathy, altruism and understanding of each other's minds are readily commented upon by the adults. Such commentary provides modeling as well as a behavioral reward for intrapsychic and interpersonal growth.

REFLECTIVE NETWORK EFFECTS

The network effect is enhanced on a peer level by allowing and encouraging children to hear one another's sessions, and to help the index patient play with others during his session in whatever fashion the index child chooses. This naturally multiplies opportunities for mirroring and mentalizing. Additionally, jealous or mean interference by peers tends to be remarkably infrequent once children settle into a new group. The network fosters a culture of kindness. Viewers of our treatment videos are often surprised by the altruism the children demonstrate. Because children learn to be reciprocally considerate of each other, collaborative and enriching behavior becomes self-sustaining.

THERAPEUTIC MATERIAL AND
FREQUENCY OF THERAPY SESSIONS

The content of therapeutic sessions must be as varied as the children themselves. Every child expresses different behavior, ideas and affects, and has different life experiences, developmental levels, and life challenges. Therefore, a child's psychotherapy sessions should be dominated by the play, thoughts, themes and words of that one child.

In-class psychotherapy sessions should take place two or three to five times a week; the duration of each child's individual session is 15 to 30 minutes. These sessions usually follow a fixed schedule. Children's names are posted in the sequence planned for their sessions on the classroom chalkboard. Many children quickly learn to read all the names. Each child in turn becomes an index patient within the real life space of the classroom. The norm is that on any given classroom day, every child receives a session. The total number of sessions has an orderly correlation with outcome, especially of IQ gains, so we encourage more rather than fewer sessions. Reports by Marianne Lester, M.A. (Kliman 1997) of successful twice a week treatment have been confirmed by work of Tish Teaford, MFT intern, as studied by third party evaluators (Hope 1999). We have found that Reflective Network Therapy treatment usually requires at least a school year before there are lasting good clinical and cognitive results although clinical changes have often been much more

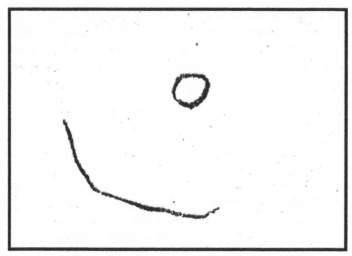

Figure 3.2. Child tells therapist about his drawing of a face without eyes: "That's you!"

rapid. The variation of clinical response velocity is immense, however. Linda Hirshfeld, PhD has treated a selectively mute girl, who never spoke in another school, yet she began to speak after a single day of Reflective Network Therapy! Other children keep growing emotionally and cognitively–slowly and steadily. A very few children have had two or more years of continuing RNT work. Zelman (1996) reports good clinical and cognitive results when preschoolers continue in after-school evening RNT treatment groups. The best documented success with a severely autistic child took three preschool years to accomplish, five times a week.

Essential Procedures Outside The Classroom Include:

1. Home visits before or at the start of classes.
2. Weekly parent guidance sessions.
3. Weekly staff conferences with review of videotaped sessions.

HOME VISITS DURING THE INITIAL EVALUATION PROCESS

Home visits add greatly to teachers' familiarity with parents and children as human beings who can be deeply understood and with whom the teacher can compassionately identify. The visiting process sets an expectation that the parent will participate, and will do so in a natural way. The home visit takes place early in the evaluation process, so that teachers can be perceived by the child as knowledgeable, friendly adults whom the child knows as part of the family's network. Sometimes parents are uncomfortable about behavior their child manifests during such a visit. The teacher is encouraged to let an uncomfortable mother know that the teacher appreciates her distress and that the teacher realizes there are many aspects of the child's behavior, only one of which is currently being shown.

The home visit is a good launching point for the first parent conference, when the parent can be encouraged to discuss differences in the child's home and out of home behavior. Teachers should engage in a home visit and all parent conferences with the assumption that the parents know a great deal about their child, and are the richest source of clinically and educationally useful information about the child's behavior. Should they find the parent's perception is distorted or unrealistic, this is an important concern to share with the child's RNT therapist. A team effort enhances a parent's observational skills, and supports a lifting of the parent's defenses against realistically perceiving certain aspects of the child's functioning. Sometimes the child is greatly underestimated or overestimated by a parent, or falls far short of expectations or ideals within the family, yet the child may have many undeveloped assets which the parent has not consciously attempted to cultivate. These are often easier to see during a home visit than in a strained new interaction with strangers on new turf such as a classroom presents to an anxious child.

While the home visit should occur early, it may often have to be delayed until parents have already visited a classroom and have decided to enroll the child. The parents are invited and welcomed into the classroom, just as warmly as is their child.

WEEKLY PARENT GUIDANCE SESSIONS

Weekly parent guidance sessions, 45 to 60 minutes in duration, are conducted mainly by the head teacher. Once a month, the parent guidance session with the teacher is replaced by an hour with the classroom therapist. Sessions usually occur in a private office within the school, but have often been effectively carried out in a corner of the classroom during classroom activities. Weekly parent guidance sessions start soon after the child's acceptance into the classroom, and the parent must be prepared to invest in the travel time and an hour a week with the teacher. Home or telephone visits for some homebound parents can to some extent replace a session in an office, as can Skype sessions. Resistance to parent guidance sessions is often not only the parent's problem but a product of teacher's unfamiliarity with relating so intimately to an adult rather than a child. Thus, a therapist can useful supervise the parent guidance, during staff meetings.

Communication to staff about personal matters in the family and in relation to the child is difficult for many parents. Naturally, as trust in the teachers is developed, frankness and straightforward talk by parents becomes easier. Teachers will recognize the importance of regular meetings and setting an expectation with parents that such will occur. Teachers tend to need a good deal of supervisory support in the guidance process and are surprised by the importance of their work. Supervision comes from the therapist, who is usually experienced in parent guidance concerning emotionally disordered children. Often, teachers' parent guidance provides a supportive psychotherapy for the parent, who may grow a great deal as a result of sharing home and school information in two directions at the weekly meetings. Some parents use the guidance as an opportunity for psychotherapy, often including a spouse and other children in a family therapy. Alicia Mallo, MD (Director of Cornerstone Argentina) has been doing the majority of parent guidance sessions, rather than the teachers. She is skilled at family therapy and the families tend to be seen as highly dysfunctional in the population she serves. However, we prefer the predominant use of teacher guidance, as it may significantly enhance the network's modeling process and may explain why a greater number of parent sessions lead to greater IQ gains for the children.

A helpful parental guidance concept is that Reflective Network Therapy will make children more gratifying to their parents. It allows love to flow in both generational directions. This view helps parents be motivated to participate in the treatment. It reduces premature terminations of treatment, which can occur when a child is making progress and becomes more demanding and expressive of developmentally advanced needs. Some parents wish their children to remain immature and dependent, and experience a sense of loss when the children grow. A good relationship with a supportive teacher growth-promoting helps compensate for this parental sense of loss. During parent guidance, some parents receive enough support and nurture from the teacher that they are helped to realize their own mental health needs and allow themselves to seek more in-depth psychotherapy by referral.

We are reluctant to accept and maintain a child in RNT treatment whose parent will not attend such meetings. That reluctance is explained before acceptance.

STAFF'S WEEKLY REVIEW OF VIDEOTAPED SESSIONS

It is enormously helpful to have a video camera and videographer available at least weekly. The videographer is often a parent, but lay volunteers, clinical or education students, and cinematography interns can do the job as well. Confidentiality agreements are required and legal requirements for working with children should be met by volunteers (fingerprinting and criminal record clearances included). The videos should be used regularly in weekly staff conferences. They provide a reflective stimulus which encourages professional understanding of the children, and to track the progress children make over the course of their treatment. Videotapes are extremely helpful for supervising teachers and therapists during their training. Videotaped records of work may also have many values for objective research purposes.

CLASSROOM ENVIRONMENT

The environment is cheerful, busy, colorful, at times noisy, but surprisingly quiet at many moments, and generally kept neat and orderly. There is a strong emphasis on early childhood education. A room 12 x 30 feet or larger is needed for eight children, two teachers and a therapist. Access to an adjacent outdoor play space is desirable. Even more than in most preschools, the RNT classroom must be well-equipped for expressive play as well as for formal learning of skills.

Classrooms should include the following items for expressive play: play dough, paints, clay, water, blocks, dolls and furnished doll houses, puppets, comforting stuffed animals, toy vehicles, blankets, and a variety of dress-up clothes and hats, as well as housekeeping supplies like toy dishes, tea sets, brooms, and the like. Designated areas should be set up for special activities such as dress-up or block building. Water play and sand tables are helpful.

These play and formal learning resources allow immature children much gratification and comfort, and allow more developed children to regress constructively. They stimulate imagination and encourage creativity. Developmentally progressive and advanced learning materials such as Lincoln logs, puzzles and games should be readily available to round out a good preschool environment. We have found that some overanxious and some autistic children, dislike their work to be permanent and enjoy using an Etch-a-Sketch apparatus, which they can erase at will. Some children benefit from learning programs on computers. Others cannot do art work on a computer, but can work with crayons or paint. A digital camera to preserve an image of quickly destroyed art work can be helpful in allowing a child to tolerate the viewing, and in showing him or her that the teachers and therapist are thinking about his products.

SAFETY CONSIDERATIONS

Staff screening by interview and reference-checking is not enough. We urge, whether or not local laws require, that all U.S. facilities staff and volunteers

Figure 3.3. Drawing by a severely traumatized child. The sublimative material in this drawing is not readily apparent: an example of why only the therapist should make interpretations to the child.

must be processed by fingerprinting by the U.S. Department of Justice, which will reveal disqualifying histories such as felonies.

The classroom should be safely and appropriately furnished and supplied, meeting the local licensing standards for a public or private preschool or day care center. If the classroom is in a mental health clinic, as a minimum, safety standards for a group therapy room in a mental health center may be used. Running a free-standing, non-public special education school may require sprinklers, fire alarms, special exit doors, and a certain square footage of outdoor space. Staff should have lockable doors on their toilets, but children are at hazard if they can be locked in a toilet stall. In facilities our agency developed we had "line of sight" access to the children at all times. There was supervision over the children's bathroom activities by having partly open child lavatories and child size toilets, visible from a corner of the largest area of our classroom. Line of sight policy—allowing children to be seen at all times in all places within the school—is a good insurance. It prevents a predatory visitor, parent or staff member taking sexual advantage of a child (something we fortunately have never had happen) and against a physical accident to a child occurring out of sight.

REFERRALS TO REFLECTIVE NETWORK THERAPY

Referrals may come from many sources: pediatricians, psychotherapists, parents, day care personnel, nursery school teachers, public school personnel, family therapists, private preschools, case workers, family friends and other parents. Within one public school system, we worked in one project for six consecutive years on an Individualized Education Plan (IEP) basis; that is, each and every one of about 40 children were sent to us by teams of public school personnel who recommended our special program to parents.

CLASS COMPOSITION

Social, racial and ethnic diversity should be valued. It has varied greatly in different sites. At times, the majority of our children in have been African-American offspring of single mothers who were socioeconomically stressed. Sometimes many children were in foster care when we treated them with RNT. At other times, the majority of our children have been from Caucasian, two-parent families whose financial circumstances were middle class or even very wealthy. Many successful applications of RNT have been in projects serving children from a wide range of ethnic backgrounds whose families were in various socioeconomic circumstances.

The diagnoses of the children receiving RNT has varied greatly. Zelman (1996) reported that 50% of the 42 twice-tested New York Cornerstone children about whom he wrote suffered pervasive developmental disorders. Therefore, we estimate conservatively that 25% of his cases (10) had PDD. Hope (1999) reported on a consecutive series of ten twice-tested children with pervasive developmental disorders. Most of the Cornerstone Argentina children treated by RNT and those treated at the Ann Martin Center (California) have pervasive developmental disorders. Only a few of the children treated so far at Wellspring (in Seattle) have that condition.

While the outer age limits are two and seven years, the younger the children are, the smaller the total number in the class should be. That is especially true if these very young children are seriously emotionally disordered or highly developmentally disordered such as children at the severe end of the autism spectrum. Small class sizes also work best for highly aggressive or destructive children, but introducing one such child at a time into a large well-functioning group is very feasible and often quickly calming for the child.

As for gender (as in the group of children discussed below) the majority of children referred to RNT services have been boys. Ordinarily, all sources of referrals (including referrals from private day care centers, preschools, kindergartens and pediatricians) tend to identify more young boys than young girls who are inattentive, difficult, aggressive, overactive, obstinate, highly withdrawn or on the autism spectrum. The same is true of children referred for RNT based on public school IEP's (individual educational plans) in public school preschool and kindergarten years. Children with autism spectrum disorders, are disproportionately male, are a growing population and are usually in need of special education. Although our ideal would be to have equal gender ratio, and a broad range of abilities, given the gender proportions of the difficulties RNT best treats, we accept and encourage all workable combinations of children into the RNT classroom.

THE ROLE OF PARENTS IN THE CLASSROOM

Parents are valued team members and participants who are absolutely essential to the network process that heals children treated with this method. In addition, parents are themselves fortified in the process, bolstered to continue their challenging parenting roles even more fully. Parents should always feel welcome in the classroom.

Parents are encouraged to stay with their children for several days at the beginning of a child's experience in RNT treatment, if at all possible. Later, parents may just drop the child off. The daily parent-teacher briefing which occurs when a parent drops off a child often takes just a minute but is an important structured opportunity for the parent and child to be impacted by witnessing reflective network therapy time and again. In addition, the content of those parent and teacher briefings are often used to accelerate the child's recovery. For instance, Oscar's mother (whose case is discussed in another chapter) provided critical information about specific family violence which immediately enhanced the therapist's ability to interpret the child's social difficulties and violent, frenetic behavior. During parent guidance sessions as well as in class, this contributed much information about Oscar's anxieties concerning body integrity in the face of family violence. Over time, she was also rewarded by the child's growing social abilities and ability to express tenderness.

PARENT INVOLVEMENT AT THE
BEGINNING OF TREATMENT

The acclimation process is structured to include the child's parent(s). Parents (or primary caregivers) should be prepared to do the following during the first week:

1. Come into the classroom and try to be themselves with the child.
2. Introduce the child to the staff and other children.
3. Get settled in the classroom for a few hours during each of the first days their child visits.
4. Observe what is going on.

In addition, we require every family to have (or to have recently had) a pediatric evaluation of their child in conjunction with the onset of a child's intake for RNT treatment. There is no point in treating a child without knowledge of the child having petit-mal epilepsy, metabolic cause for behavioral problems, Rett's Syndrome, Kleinfelter's syndrome, thyroid problem or brain tumor. Such important diagnostic omissions can usually be addressed by a good pediatric evaluation and medical treatment plan.

ONGOING PARENT INVOLVEMENT

After the initial period, the parent should expect to continue to communicate history to the teachers and therapist, including a history of their relationships to their children and their behaviors. This history goes back into pregnancy and previous generations, including genetic endowment, if known. Important physical influences or disorders the parent has or the child has developed have to be considered with the parent's help. These include prescription medications tobacco, alcohol or illegal drug exposure in utero, and metabolic disorders which may not have been known or disclosed before. Usually these have been well excluded by obstetricians and pediatricians, but the reflective network team will want to make doubly sure since parents sometimes only gradually disclose physical and environmental factors which contribute so much to childhood behavior or disorder(s). History of the parent's own traumatic childhood or psychiatric disorders may be late in being confided, but will help guide the child's treatment.

Each morning, parents are expected to come into the classroom and spend a few moments briefing the teachers about how the child has been feeling, behaving and verbalizing during the previous day and evening. These early morning briefings are often essential to the children's treatment and education. Parents routinely participate in the classroom at least periodically thereafter, frequently listening in and talking with the staff about their children during the course of classroom activities. Weekly parent guidance sessions must be attended. Parents should welcome routine home visits (usually by teachers) when indicated.

Parents are often invaluable classroom helpers with practical matters such as operating a video camera or assisting other families during family emergencies.

In some teams, monthly all-family meetings are held at the end of a school day, in the last 45 minutes of a class session. These meetings are usually quite popular, and involve all the children, with sharing of children's progress and problems, and often a sharing of family news and school news. Zelman (1996) held such evening groups weekly for years after the completion of the preschool programs, scheduling parent conferences for evenings, and found that these sessions were significantly associated with high degrees of IQ growth.

PARENT GUIDANCE CONFERENCES

Once a child has been evaluated, there is an ongoing parent guidance process in which both the teacher and therapist have roles. The staff finds it easier and easier, with experience, to be respectful of each parent's burdens and knowledge concerning their child. Parent-blaming and adultophobic attitudes that might be present, (and at one time were common in psychotherapeutic and educational professions) are easily lost with training and experience. Staff becomes increasingly sensitive to parents' attitudes toward living with a difficult and changing child, fluctuating mutual dependency needs, and often sudden shifts in aggressivity and affection. Staff develops a heightened awareness of the parent's ability to make critical contributions to the child's recovery.

The staff-parent meetings require sympathetic listening, sharing observations, helping parents to carry insights gained in the classroom into the home environment and supporting parental capacities and responsibilities. Since this method depends on a network influence, the teacher must model good communication skills during these meetings, conveying to parents much about how she/he thinks and feels about the child. Helping parents accept their child's perceptiveness about home adversities and changes is routine. Helping the child mentalize those experiences in child appropriate doses in the classroom occurs as it arises, and parental support of this process is essential. During parent conferences the teacher will try to convey information about the child's intersubjective life in the classroom to the parent, making a bridge between home and school. The teacher's verbalizing of this information to the parent places the child's functions in a developmental framework which a parent might find more difficult to conceptualize without help from the teacher. The Reflective Network Therapy classroom teacher's parent conferences (three conferences per month) have four main functions:

1. Receiving information from the parent about the child and current family events.
2. Sharing information with the parent about the child's classroom experience.
3. Giving educationally oriented developmental guidance.
4. Giving support to the parents or parent surrogates.

During conferences with RNT teachers and monthly conferences with their child's RNT therapist, parents receive deep emotional sustenance. That sustenance is often required to set up a constructive nurturing cycle of reciprocal love and caring with their children. The failure of a child's reciprocity is depressing and depletes many parents. The therapeutic team should assume that each parent needs and deserves such support in order to care for very troubled children. Each parent has the burden of living with a child whose emotional life is difficult to support, and whose relationships are layered with resistances and problematic neurobiological complexities. The child's special assets and deficits, as well as their communications, are often puzzling and quite different from what other families experience. Most parents of such children have been previously frustrated, disappointed and discouraged—and sometimes immobilized—in major aspects of their relationship with their children, no matter how much they love them. Parent guidance sessions go a long way to mitigate their resulting pain and confusion. Strengthening the child's primary support system in turn strengthens the possibilities for the child's home environment to be as nurturing as possible throughout the child's treatment.

Parent conferences are conducted in private if possible. Again, the teacher sees the parents or primary caregivers (both parents if feasible) three times a month for conference. The therapist meets with parents once a month and the teacher does not hold a parent conference on the week that this occurs. Current information, current events, and earlier events of importance are reported on this weekly basis to the teacher and are transmitted to the therapist for use in his or her daily work with the child and in the therapist's monthly sessions with the parents. The child knows that Mommy or Daddy, or whoever sees the teacher, sees the teacher regularly and that the teacher and therapist share information directly with the parents or caregivers. The teacher helps the parents understand the needs of the child, especially how to cope with the child's developmental process. Some parents must be helped to know the difference between what constitutes normal development and what is peculiar to their child. The parent is empowered to cope with the child's difficulties as well as changes on a day-to-day basis and acknowledged for doing so.

Changes in the child's affect or behavior which are actually changes toward health and recovery can be confusing to parents. Many parents often have a difficult time accepting changes which are actually positive movement toward recovery when the changes (which can be quite sudden) are not discussed and explained. After years of reacting to dysfunction, parents may experience temporary difficulty adjusting to healthy changes. Or, perhaps the parent needs help to move quickly from needing to be primitively needed to taking pleasure in developmental milestones which put new demands on them to change in response. This resistance can be a normal, brief adjustment period that parents can traverse quite easily with guidance. Sometimes parents may have other complex issues which manifest as resistance to changes in the child. In either case, conferences with the therapist support parents through the changes to achieve a healthy, joyful acceptance of their child's achievement which reverberates back to the child. Sadomasochistic and other parental complexities are sometimes confided, leading to constructive referrals to outside therapies for the parent (Kliman, 1970).

The child's ability to deal with his or her family members in a positive way is promoted through staff support of positive parental responses. Parents can verbally vent their feelings of frustration and anger at the child, during parent guidance, and these expressions are accepted and given an interpersonal reflection and perspective by the teacher. An important ramification of the teacher's role in such conferences is that helping parents understand and continue to participate in knowing about and informing their children's therapy supports the child's entire developmental process. The teacher is trained to accept the parent's feelings and work with the parents' concerns, including criticism of the therapist. Criticisms or concerns about the other children, or the program are also dealt with and accepted, thus helping insure continuity of the therapy.

Parent conferences aim to include and coordinate with mothers, fathers, grandparents, and any others directly involved in day to day dealings with the child (including social workers, and the like, if appropriate). Through daily contact with parents and surrogates who bring the child to school, as well as through weekly parent conferences, the teacher can model good parenting to worried parents with difficult, puzzling, atypical or slowly developing children. The teacher's acceptance, genuine affection and feeling for the child, and her ability to influence the child's behavior provide an important model for frightened, discouraged, and angry parents. Parents gain more realistic expectations and perceptions of the child through the eyes of an interested and concerned teacher.

Boundaries between generations are often a subject of teacher guidance with parents. Sleeping arrangements, viewing of parental sexual activities, perception of sexually explicit, disastrous, violent or frightening news and otherwise inappropriate television programs is often a shared concern constructively dealt with in weekly meetings. What the teacher learns about how the child gets along with other household members, pets and neighbors impacts the content of therapy in many cases, and provides parallels with classroom activities. Thus, the teacher can make a data-rich contribution to the team, enriching the child's therapists understanding of social disabilities and developmental lags in ways that are real and immediate for the child.

Although the parent guidance focus is on the child, in order to support the healthy changes for the child, the teacher must develop empathy for the parent. For example, a mother has a child who will not go to sleep, but the mother wants to watch an inappropriately sexy or violent TV program which would further make it difficult for the child to sleep. Guiding the mother or father with sensitivity to her/his own point of view, while considering her needs, is more helpful than guidance from a totally child-centered position. Sympathy for her interests and needs will help her delay her own gratifications when this is in the child's best interests. Unless a parent feels respected, appreciated, understood, and nurtured, she or he is unlikely to respond to guidance or make any lasting positive changes that might be needed.

ASSESSMENT AND TREATMENT PLANNING

Evaluations: Several forms of evaluation must precede a full RNT treatment planning for each child. Staff needs to determine a child's diagnosis, look for causal or contributing factors (such as genetic contributions, traumas and family adversities) and sources of strength and resilience, as well as family and child treatment needs. We conduct an examination of each child, usually right in the classroom, videotaping the interview and the child's behavior in the classroom. The parent is present during this initial interview. There is usually a class in progress, so we can assess interactions with other children. We review previous evaluations done by others, contact previous treating professionals and schools, and use several psychological and educational assessment and testing tools. Assessment tools include: The Achenbach

Child Behavior Checklist, standardized questionnaires, psychosocial and developmental history forms, Childhood Autism Rating Scales (CARS), and a questionnaire called "Your Child". If the child is capable of being IQ tested, the initial evaluation will include a baseline cognitive assessment using the Wechsler Intelligence test for Preschoolers (WPPSI-R or its latest iteration). In less cognitively competent children, a Vineland Inventory is helpful. The child's behavior in an ongoing RNT group may help a great deal to decide whether a child can be helped in the RNT classroom, or by what other means.

While important components of the evaluation take place during the initial home visit and within the classroom group setting, an initial and carefully detailed history taking from the primary caregiver(s) is usually better done with a degree of privacy more easily obtained in a side room. The evaluating therapist enlists the teacher to conduct part of the initial history taking and observation and gives the teacher clinical input as to the styles and needs of the adult caregivers and the child.

The therapist is more experienced diagnostically and is ultimately responsible for the intake evaluation, including history taking from parents, direct examination of the child, diagnosis, and consultation as needed with other professionals. For therapists who are conducting this work, we suggest the diagnoses used in initial and follow-up evaluations, including quarterly evaluations should closely follow the American Psychiatric Association's Diagnostic and Statistical Manual, version DSMIV-TR (2000).

CRITERIA FOR APPROPRIATE PLACEMENT
IN REFLECTIVE NETWORK THERAPY

The therapist is ultimately responsible for the final decision regarding appropriateness of accepting a child for a trial of treatment. If circumstances or evaluation results exclude participation, alternatives to RNT should be considered and recommended, such as referring for primarily psychopharmacologic treatment or other procedures. These procedures may be neurological, psychological, genetic or metabolic studies regarding possible reversible or irreversible disorders. The following inclusion (admission) and exclusion criteria are applied.

Inclusion Criteria

A mixture of developmental abilities and behavioral characteristics can be accommodated, including some children who are treated for preventive purposes—such as in response to bereavement or other presumably major traumas. Siblings of severely disturbed children have been also been helped by Reflective Network Therapy. Emotionally healthy foster children and children of staff have been welcomed. The following are suggested optimal but not absolute criteria:

1. Evaluation has been agreed to or already performed by a pediatrician, licensed psychologist, or child psychiatrist, or other clinician, or else an IEP (Individualized Education Plan) has been provided by a public school district. Evaluations optimally start soon after the first visit to the classroom and ideally soon include the Wechsler Preschool (WPPSI-R), and/or similar IQ testing.
2. Children can be accepted with a wide range of diagnoses. Commonly, one or more of the following has been diagnosed or broadly categorized: SED, PDD, an emotional, developmental, behavioral or psychiatric disorder, or an expressive or receptive language disorder.
3. Receptive and/or expressive language is (or was, before symptoms began) at least at the two year level. Exceptions can be made if the child appears related to other people. (Cornerstone Argentina and other sites are accepting children who do not meet this criterion, and we are following their preliminary results with appreciation.) Children with complete, selective or elective mutism are accepted.
4. Parents or guardians are willing to permit professional supervisory, educational and scientific use of closed circuit and videotaped study of the child's treatment.
5. At least one parent or caregiver agrees to participate in weekly guidance conferences concerning the child's needs and progress.

Exclusion Criteria Used by Most RNT Service Sites

The following exclusion criteria are best considered following several in-classroom observations of the child:

1. Severe autism, with the child having no useful language by age five, nearly constant occupation with stereotyped behavior such as whirling and twirling, little eye contact, little symbolic play *and* no sociability for the previous six months. (Cornerstone Argentina is accepting exceptions to this criterion and seeing important improvements in some children).
2. Persistent or severe dangerousness to others during the past few months and during in-classroom visits to the RNT group.
3. IQ or Developmental Quotient is or appears to be under 50 and the testing psychologist has the opinion that the child will probably not be testable

by Stanford Binet or WPPSI-R protocols within the next few months. [For examples of exceptions, see the complete recovery in the case of Dorian Tenore-Bartilucci in chapter 4 of *Reflective Network Therapy in the Pre-school Classroom* and the IQ rise and clinical progress in the case of "J." included in a report by Fran Morris in this manual.]

INDIVIDUALIZING THE TREATMENT PLAN

Planning for a predominance of social and cognitive education at one extreme versus predominance of dynamic and interpretive psychotherapy at another extreme requires asking oneself (as a therapist) "Can the child understand abstractions?" If so, can the child use interpretations?" Many children cannot even understand concrete words when they first start RNT treatment. They must be helped to learn to mentalize and form abstractions about their behavior. They need lots of practice in placing thoughts and emotions into words. Nurturant corrective relations work and the mentalizing functions of early childhood education as well as therapy will predominate over dynamic therapy for a long while in some cases. The therapist and teachers routinely and intentionally provide the children with modeling, practice and support for mentalizing.

STAFF PREREQUISITES

Therapists who are candidates for certification in Reflective Network Therapy should have already had some psychodynamic or psychoanalytic training. The value of interpersonal therapy should already be appreciated, as well as the value of insight. A prior experience with family therapy training or network therapy training would be valuable. Clinical licensure is required for RNT therapists, unless they are supervised by a clinically licensed person weekly. Appropriate licenses are MSW, LCSW, MFT, PhD or Psy.D., MD, or DMH. Psychology and MFT interns have been accepted into closely supervised use of RNT on field placement basis, and we see no reason why this could not extend to LSW interns.

A potential RNT therapist usually already knows the basic features of child psychopathology and family process, and has already done some child and family therapy. Ideally, the therapist is or is becoming an independent diagnostician capable of conducting several forms of psychotherapy. Some talented persons with insight about their own psychological processes can carry out the method with supervision, without having had psychotherapy themselves. A supervisor could best determine whether the particular therapist is achieving sufficient understanding to practice RNT on this basis. However, a beginning RNT therapist's prior training should ideally include psychotherapy or prior psychoanalysis for the therapist. This is desirable in order to achieve an adequate understanding of transference and countertransference processes, and it is preferable that the therapist have had such psychotherapy or psychoanalysis during a time when he or she was actually doing psychotherapy with children. Clinical licensure is not a guarantee of this experience.

In addition to selected readings, new therapists and their team's teachers are supported by the following tools and procedures for training:

1. A three-day intensive seminar in the RNT method is taught by a senior RNT therapist and teacher who have successful experience applying the method. A Reflective Network Therapy training seminar covers several diagnostic categories of treated children, the work of several different teams, illustrates adaptation of the method to different physical sites, and includes presentation and discussion and study of videotaped documentary of children's RNT psychotherapy sessions.

2. Studying and applying a spectrum of RNT techniques in the classroom under supervision. Primary source material for that purpose consists of an archive of training videotapes from the Children's Psychological Health Center, Inc. which illustrate those techniques with children treated in other Reflective Network Therapy classrooms who had a variety of diagnoses and disorders. Training tapes include portions of actual briefings, debriefings, and full therapy sessions with individual children in the classroom. Training videos demonstrate dynamic techniques, children's immediate responses, therapeutic turning points, and long term changes. These videotapes are selectively made available only to credentialed mental health and educational professionals and to interns and students who sign a binding confidentiality agreement.

3. Continuing supervision by an RNT therapist or teacher for the first year of practice. Supervisorial feedback and guidance is based on review and discussion of videotapes of RNT work with children performed by the trainee team member(s). A minimum of 10 video recorded hours of actual work performed by the trainee will be provided to the certifying supervisor for such review.

4. The therapist will be reviewed and guided to perform periodic assessment and record keeping. Therapists (or visiting consultants who are psychologists) will assess children's progress according to established clinical standards and will contribute to outcome studies, and follow-up studies (using IQ testing and other tools.) Minimally, a therapist will keep a problem/symptom checklist and rate changes quarterly, as well as making a DSMIV-TR axis 5 rating (Children's Global Assessment Score) based on behavioral

observations. Maximally, a well trained psychodynamic or psychoanalytic therapist may keep a Hampstead Profile, which is a complex description of many psychological functions (A. Freud, 1962; Nagera, 1963) on each child, as well as quarterly clinical summaries containing a problem/symptom checklist with ratings of change, and a consideration of changes in object relations (e.g., from narcissistic to altruistic), ego functions (e.g., degree of reality testing, which defenses are used and which predominate), superego functions, psychosexual theme levels, and transference processes. At the Center for Preventive Psychiatry, abbreviated Hampstead Profiles were designed and used quarterly, (Kliman, 1972).

5. The therapist will be guided in all aspects of her or his responsibility to provide clinical leadership of the team.
6. When additional or further services are needed, the child's RNT therapist should take the lead in that process. The supervisor will discuss any such referrals with the therapist during the training period.

During supervision of a new team, the supervising therapist is responsible for monitoring the work of other team members sufficiently to determine whether a team has replicated the method. This is important not only for quality control, but also for scientific purposes, as comparisons of results amongst methods depends upon careful replication criteria.

In general, we recommend that the therapist be trained to focus on a child's interpersonal relationships and communication of here-and-now play and emotional process. Ideally, with eight children in the group, the therapist would be responsible for 160 minutes or two hours and forty minutes of therapy per therapeutic day in the classroom. This calculation is based on:

1. Twenty minutes per child or 160 minutes in the classroom per day including briefings and debriefings with child and teachers. In five days a week there would be 800 minutes or 13.3 hours of in-classroom psychotherapy given to the eight children.
2. Two hours a week or eight hours a month of parent guidance and at least one and a half hours a week of leadership at a team conference.
3. An additional minimum of one hour a week for other patient related duties should be allotted as well as, and one hour for miscellany. At least one hour a week of clinical record keeping is necessary.

The total time demands on the therapist are approximately 18-20 hours per week to serve eight children, seen five times a week. A typical breakdown of the therapist's time for a class meeting 5 days each week with eight children is expressed in Table 3.1.

Minimally (in a classroom group of less than eight children seen daily), a therapist could do useful work for example with four children, meeting only three times a week. This minimal intensity and minimal case load would require a therapist position of at least 8.5 hours per week. Many doctoral candidates could usefully take on this level of work successfully. On a per child basis, the therapist's time in this scenario is just over two hours per child. This calculation is tabulated above as 80 minutes a day for three days per week in the classroom (4 hours/week). The difference between this small and less than daily case load of four children and a larger case load with daily treatment of eight children is 8.5 versus 19 hours. In the ten hour differential, much more intensive treatment and much more likely measurable progress is provided for four more children. The intensively (daily) treated children are more likely achieve more IQ growth as well as mental health improvements Therefore, we strongly recommend the four to five times a week model to realize maximum cost-benefits for a group of eight children. Multi-site outcome data provides evidence that the more intensive treatment plan is optimally effective for IQ growth and probably for clinical change as well.

CLARIFICATION OF ROLES AND RESPONSIBILITIES

The roles of the teacher in the RNT classroom are many. She or he has roles as a reality oriented educator, as communicator between the patient and the therapist, as a stimulator, receptor and observer of communications and behavior, and as an observer of responses to interpretations when those responses occur after the therapist has left the classroom. The synergistic division of roles is respected in Reflective Network Therapy. Therapists are not trained as educators in the formal sense. Therapists use a broad repertoire of psychotherapy techniques individualized to a particular child. Cognitive restructuring, dynamic interpretations, and transferential interpretations are feasible within RNT (Kliman, 1970). It is essential to the method that the respective roles of the teacher and the therapist are made clear for the children. The children learn that the therapist is there to talk about, interact with, interpret and clarify the child's behavior and thoughts. They know the teacher is there for educational tasks, in the broadest sense, as well as for discipline management. One child showed his clear understanding of teacher and therapists' different roles as he finished a block building and said to the teacher, "It's my turn to be with Dr. K." He pulled a rocking chair over to Dr. Kliman, who was sitting nearby and said to him, "Let's work," and began to talk about his dream of the previous night" (Kliman and Ronald, 1970). The children are also aware that the teacher and therapist share information about the child as equals in the reflective network. The child not only witnesses this but participates when this sharing occurs during briefings and debriefings.

The teacher is responsible for developing and implementing the curriculum and educational plan appropriate to each child's abilities and for supporting the expectation of progress in socialization. The teacher advances curriculum implementation by constantly adjusting to children's responses and performance. For example, most children are expected to and sit in circles for such activities as "dress the weather man" with weather-appropriate clothing each morning. If they can't do it, teachers will verbalize the expectation that the children will be able to succeed in this group activity some day.

The teacher prepares the children to adapt to transitions without emotional upset. For example, children are helped to learn about the calendar and time, and to anticipate the rhythms of weekends, vacations, and each other's absences. The teacher helps build ego strengths related to handling transitions involving gratification delay. She regularly helps a child learn how to wait or how to share. The therapist will not teach but will interpret a difficulty in sharing or waiting, the more so as the child becomes increasingly aware of the functions of sharing and waiting. The teacher models good reality testing and good communication about realities. There is much value in teachers talking to children in small groups the about the unavoidable upsets that inevitably occur, such as a teacher's illness, a pet's death, a birth in a family, or the hospitalization of a parent or grandparent. Such discussion psychologically immunizes children against being overwhelmed in the event of any future, more destabilizing events (Kliman, 1968). In their essay on this subject, Kliman and Ronald (1970) noted: "The educational program additionally consists of helping the child to explore the real world around him, with all the ramifications of learning to develop logic, order and problem solving ability as related to his world."

The teacher is responsible for providing a program designed to promote the social, emotional, physical and cognitive development of each child. In this setting the RNT therapeutic teacher also assumes the traditional educator's role of providing a socializing influence by managing children's disruptive or aggressive behavior. This management of classroom discipline frees the therapist to do his or her interpretive work without the complication of distractions irrelevant to the children's psychotherapy sessions. The teacher's opportunity to work daily in such tandem with the therapist in a preschool setting is a core part of this method. It resembles the use of life-space interviews in psychiatric hospitals. For example:

1. The teacher has primary responsibility for limiting the child who wants to challenge the safety of the group. The therapist interprets the motive for provocation and the associated fantasies of abandonment or injury.

2. For the borderline psychotic, immature or regressed child, the teacher verbalizes differences between fantasy and fact. The therapist is freed to interpret the child's feelings, fantasies, and reactions.

Minimally a teacher's record keeping includes maintaining daily attendance sheets, and writing several sentences about each child in daily educational logs. These records are kept in a child's private file along with summaries of meetings with the child's RNT therapist. In addition, Content of parent-teacher conferences are briefly noted and shared with the child's Cornerstone therapist. Maximally, in terms of record keeping, teachers will create educational progress reports which are curriculum-based and which include standardized achievement test data, socialization ratings, and behavioral standards achievements for the individual child.

Teachers (particularly head teachers) are expected to become familiar with and able to describe the psychological history of each child. Teachers must also be able to meet for three quarters of an hour with each child's family three times a month and for ninety minutes with the psychotherapist on a weekly basis. Teachers focus their parent guidance on developing a network effect in which the teacher and parent share essential new information about the child's life and behavior with every other member of the team. As detailed in the discussion of parent involvement above, the teacher has key responsibilities for supporting the parents/caregivers and expanding the therapeutic network's access to information during daily briefings and weekly private parent guidance conferences. The teacher also supports the role children can serve as peer helpers (co-therapists) for each other's healing and recovery, under the therapist's supervision.

Even children with low cognitive abilities are often aware of external catastrophes in the surrounding society, (Wolfenstein and Kliman, 1965; Kliman, 1968; Kliman et al 2001; Kliman, 2006, 2010). External catastrophes such as wars, major political events, acts of terrorism, and natural disasters should be discussed in with the children to the extent that teachers find it possible to introduce structured adult-led curriculum on those subjects. Children will often sense changes in the therapeutic milieu when the adults carry an emotional response to external events. They will also know when the team is experiencing distress or friction within itself, whether it is accepting of its members, or whether the team is in a conflicted state. Weekly team meetings provide an important opportunity to resolve such difficulties as well as to share new information about child patients.

If something terrible and perceptible happens to a team member, it will usually be necessary to communicate with the children about what they have perceived. For example, at the beginning of one school morning, a teacher learned of the sudden and unexpected death of her husband. The children witnessed her shock and weeping just before she left the classroom in distress. We found it useful to share that tragic event in child-appropriate doses. The psychotherapist cancelled previous appointments for later that day in order to be maximally available in the RNT classroom. Parents were briefed by phone and the event was discussed when they arrived at the school with their children. The second teacher immediately organized classroom discussion about the bereaved teacher's evident distress, which was helpful to the parents as well as the children, allowing them to understand why the teacher had been crying and then abruptly left for home. Numerous resonations occurred within the children's subsequent RNT therapy sessions, which were useful for each of them.

TEACHER TRAINING AND SUPERVISION

Head teachers must be licensed in their state or supervised by a state licensed teacher, and have training appropriate to the age levels of their pupils. Ideally, Special Education Certification is desirable for the head teacher, though we have had only three such head teachers among our teams. At first, new RNT teachers study actual treatments by viewing selected training videotapes. This is essential for understanding how the method is carried out. Ongoing in-staff training includes weekly review of current treatments, which have usually been videotaped, at least once a week, during team meetings.

The therapist supports and guides teachers to develop or deepen skills, to achieve performance expectations and to learn Reflective Network Therapy techniques and practices both explicitly and through modeling. Briefings and debriefings and working in tandem in the classroom provide opportunities for on-the-spot teacher training as do the weekly staff meetings. Most supervision of teachers by RNT therapists involves sharing information and keeping each other's knowledge synchronized in the sense of being up to date about the cognitive and therapeutic status of each child. The therapist has an important need to have each child's therapy informed by the teacher's observations during briefings prior to a psychotherapy session. Therefore, the therapist must help the teachers to put their observations into the therapist's sphere of knowledge during briefings and conferences, and, in turn, help the teachers increase their observational skills. Generally, teachers need very little supervisory help controlling children's impulses and promoting or assisting with the development of socialization. This actually may come more easily to teachers than to therapists. Teachers are already trained to be instruments of socializing through group education as well as individual cognitive development.

Often, the mere process of talking about and increasingly understanding a child opens the gates of tenderness, so that all parties can be more affectionate to the child and in turn the child becomes more responsive to classroom discipline. As indicated, some supervision occurs right in the classroom. For example, the therapist may discuss a child's problem behavior with him, right on the spot, and ask the teacher for help with the behavior, or suggest a way the teacher and child could enjoy each other in a manner more therapeutically beneficial to the child. During supervision, a therapist may support a teacher's efforts, and tactfully suggest any ways in which the teacher might be inhibited about containing a child's impulses.

Ideally, supervision is a two way process. The teachers learn from the therapist about the child's diagnosis, causal factors, and family influences, and the therapist gains from the teachers a broad view of the child's behavior which occurs when the therapist is not present, not observing or interacting with the child. The teachers know a great deal within a few school days concerning how the child relates to them, family and peers. However great their observational contributions are, teachers may need some support to be understanding and supportive with parents. The head teacher plans the curriculum and is usually best equipped to supervise other teachers and have an overview of what transpires in the classroom. The teacher's assistant (as well as any interns or students) can give one-to-one attention to creative projects with a designated child but must be carefully supervised as he or she may not have a sufficiently deep understanding of what is appropriate in a therapeutic classroom or skilled in supporting the child in returning to group activities.

It is extremely rare that a trained preschool educator might be assigned who is deficient in the level of empathy and understanding the therapeutic educational environment requires. We have encountered only one instance in which the therapist had to take the lead in replacing a teacher for a Cornerstone group.

INTERDISCIPLINARY TEAM COLLABORATION: TEACHER-THERAPIST SYNERGY

Maintaining rapport among all team members is crucial to the RNT process. In weekly conferences a candid look at the team process enables each member to gain understanding and support to correct for perceived deficits, in the network's functions. While optimal functioning and harmony preserves the appropriate Reflective Network Therapy classroom environment at its highest level, it is sobering and humbling to realize we cannot always live up to our highest standards. Humility adds to our flexibility. Thus, beginners need not fear RNT.

Communication between the teacher and therapist is continuous during classroom activities and all during the classroom week. The child knows (and witnesses) that whatever he tells the teacher will be communicated to the therapist and that the therapist continually keeps the teacher informed of general trends of his work. All this is integral to the therapeutic work with the child. Some children find it easier to talk to the teacher rather than to the therapist. One little girl sat on one side of the teacher with the therapist on the other side of the teacher. She said, "Don't tell him about my dream last night," knowing full well that the therapist would hear this. She thereby used the teacher as an acceptable and receptive intermediary. Another child was very fearful of the therapist and of what the therapist was going to talk about (feelings about the loss of her mother), but could use the therapist's interpretations well while sitting on the teacher's lap during her session.

The teacher provides the child with a model for reception of deep communications by being reliable, accepting, and honest and by setting a climate conductive to expressive play communication. In order to set the stage for communication, it is the teacher's responsibility to create a climate which is straightforward and free from ambiguity. It is important for this reason to acknowledge absences of classmates or staff members. It is important to say hello or goodbye to anyone coming in and to clarify the purpose for the visit. Similarly, it is valuable in the specific treatment of a particular child to acknowledge child-perceivable realities around him, such as the child being able to see his mother's car parked outside the classroom window. Refraining from veiled in-classroom staff communications, and refraining from covertness in drop-off and pick-up time communications with parents helps model adult willingness to help children understand their perceived worlds.

The teacher encourages and supports the child's sublimations when the child draws a picture or involves him or herself in dramatic play. She shows genuine interest and thus helps to elicit the child's ideas. This type of education enhances the therapeutic process while making the child aware that self-expression and gathering knowledge is an important part of his life as well as important to therapeutic work. (Kliman and Ronald, 1970)

While the interpretive therapist spends only fifteen or twenty minutes with each child on a given day, the teacher usually remains in the classroom an entire school day. During sessions with consecutive index children, although the therapist maintains peripheral awareness of the other children, his or her primary focus prevents him from observing significant behavior and expressions of the other children, whom the teacher, meanwhile, continues to observe. Because a child's treatment session themes often continue to emerge throughout the school day, the therapist will miss a lot of first-hand experience of any given child's behavior and expression when not engaged in individual sessions. Continuations of expressions of therapeutic themes are commonly presented by all of the children in the classrooms after their sessions. The teacher performs the extremely valuable function of greatly prolonging professional observation of highly treatment related expressions by communicating to the therapist in their next briefing any significant behaviors and expressions from children which occurred when the therapist was absent or occupied with other children. The teacher's observation and reporting literally multiplies the duration of observation by a factor of at least two or threefold on a daily basis, certainly well beyond that of private psychotherapy sessions which usually last 50 minutes. This contribution from the teacher is an important factor in the child's progress towards recovery as her observations often provide the therapist with rich material that is relevant to children's core issues and this material can confirm or help correct the therapist's interpretations.

Further, there is often a deepening of communication as the child's theme proceeds in expression during the class day. Children do more than express elaborations and derivatives of the same theme they communicated in the session. Greater frankness and consciousness of meaning is often developed by a child after a session. For example, a child who had been speaking in a symbolic way about masturbatory activity and castration anxiety with the classroom therapist proceeded an hour later to tell the teacher that he was worried about touching his own penis. He had earlier been unable to directly express this specific concern about his own body and had been doing so with the therapist in disguised ways involving buildings falling down and being broken by pinching lobsters. In that session, the teacher—having been made aware of the content of the psychotherapy session in a debriefing with the therapist immediately after the session—was able to communicate the material immediately to the therapist for his further understanding and future interpretation, (Kliman, 1970).

A method-specific collaboration between teacher and the interpretive therapist occurs in the treatment of intellectually inhibited children. Just as the therapist is interpretively releasing the child from inhibition, so that the child needn't release raw aggressive activity, the teacher may help the child to sublimate in a channeled way suitable to the individual needs of that child's newly available energy. An example involves the case of a child who was retarded to the point of seeming imbecility, but who responded to interpretations by showing marked eye contact and interest in other human beings. She began to scream for attention and became bullying. Teachers put this energy to work by utilizing her budding interest in the outer world, channeling it into creative and intellectual pursuits, particularly painting, storytelling and reading. The child became the best reader in her second grade class in a large metropolitan school system. Here the educational and interpretive processes had a clear synergistic effect. The therapist would have been handicapped in the interpretive process if he were simultaneously responsible for teaching the child to speak, read, and write. On the other hand, the teacher would have had no access to the necessary energies of the inhibited child were it not for the therapist's work with that child.

Because the teacher is constantly nearby during the child's interpretive therapy, she is able to observe and understand much of his play before and after the therapist's work with him. She can recognize many confirmative or responsive elaborations of particular interpretations through the child's play or words. She is usually far better able than the child's own parent to receive and communicate these observations succinctly to the therapist on the spot or before the next session. After the therapist leaves, the teacher often observes behavior that confirms or contradicts the therapist's interpretations. She is trained to always observe what the children do when the therapist leaves the classroom. In a traditional, pull-out analytic setting, a mother takes a child home at the end of fifty minutes (after an individual treatment) and there is scant opportunity to learn his reactions to interpretations or discussions. In Reflective Network Therapy, teachers have the opportunity to actually hear individual therapy sessions and make immediate follow up observations. The post-therapy themes are very often closely connected to the work that was done, so that there is a precise record of some of these confirmations and elaborations of themes or the continuity of theme, and the material is available daily, rather than during an occasional parent visit. The teacher becomes so attuned to the post-psychotherapy work that she or he is often useful to the therapist's memory and becomes an actively understanding observer of her or his work. Time and again the therapist is grateful to have the teacher pick up a lapse of his own observation, perception or memory. Equally, the therapist is very useful to the teacher in helping her to perceive herself and the way in which she works with the children, (Kliman and Ronald, 1970).

Thus, the teacher facilitates the child's work on clinical themes in a variety of ways, including her function as a stand-in observer for therapist while the therapist facilitates the child's ability to learn the curriculum as well as further cognitive development as a result of the therapy itself. We believe that the cumulative collaborative interplay inherent in the method is a factor in Cornerstone treatment outcomes showing surprising emotional as well as cognitive leaps over much shorter treatment periods, compared with our experience and data about other treatment methods such as ABA, (Sallows, 2005).

Therapists and teachers also collaborate to use simple criteria to monitor whether certain RNT processes are occurring as the method prescribes. Most commonly, there may be resistance to weekly parent guidance conferences.

Monitoring that dimension has proven to be a supervisory necessity. Use of alternate means of network influence with parents can be helpful remedies or enhancements to regularly occurring parent guidance sessions; group meetings, and telephone contacts on an individual basis can be helpful. After hours meetings are often realistically essential. The collaborative benefits resulting from the parent guidance sessions are described above, including the high value of parent input and observations which influence both educational and therapeutic interactions with the child.

EXPECTATIONS FOR TEACHER TIME INVESTMENT

Teachers should plan for at least two classroom hours a day with the children, at least two or three days a week and preferably a full five day school week. They should have coverage to allow an additional 90 minutes three times a week for parent conferences, team conferences, case related phone calls, and record-keeping. Classes which meet three mornings each week require 10.5 hours a week for the head teacher. Half day RNT classes convene five days a week with three hours in the class and 1.5 hours a day of other activities requiring 22 hours a week of the teacher's time. Teacher time spent on curriculum transmission will be planned to accommodate interruptions for individual child therapy sessions, to ensure participation in briefings and debriefings and to conduct weekly parent guidance sessions, except for once monthly when these sessions are replaced by parent conferences conducted by the therapist.

COORDINATING SERVICES AND
SHARING INFORMATION

Sometimes a child in RNT treatment on a part time basis is simultaneously enrolled in another educational program. When speech therapy is provided, we encourage this therapy to be given within RNT classroom and this is often practical for the provider. The teacher is the best person to coordinate schedules and communications with other educational or supplemental therapeutic programs.

Upon a child's graduation from RNT, the teacher and therapist together with parents should select what material is appropriate for transmission to later levels of service. Not all family material is appropriate for such transmission. A carefully selected compilation of material should be approved by the parent prior to transmission to public and/or private agencies. Control by

parents over such transmission is best accomplished during parent conferences; parental signature(s) indicating approval of the documents and consent
for transmission can also be obtained in this meeting.

REFLECTIVE NETWORK THERAPY:
COSTS AND STAFF TIME

Reflective Network Therapy is less expensive than most other methods for a
variety of reasons. Table 3.2 shows costs which result in an estimated annual
savings of $270,000 per eight autistic children served by RNT rather than
by ABA. For a large school system with 80 autistic preschoolers the savings
would be $2,700,000 using the peer-inclusive RNT method instead of one
aide per child.

Public Special Education programs in public schools or carried out elsewhere for public school children who cannot be served in mainstream settings
are, by definition, supported entirely by the school district. Federal and state
funding is potentially available to help local school districts with funding for
children who qualify for I.D.E.A. (Individuals with Disability Education Act)
resources.

Just as a portable oxygen tank might be necessary for a child to function
in school, combining therapy with education may be both educationally and
therapeutically necessary. Many children cannot be educated or reach their
educational and developmental potential without special treatment. Reflective Network Therapy is well suited to fill that special need. Working within
a public or private school or in collaboration with other preschool programs,
RNT can successfully replace a public special education class. Alternatively,
the method can be adapted to supplement an existing public school special
education program. As a supplemental program, Reflective Network Therapy
can be incorporated either in the mornings or afternoons to provide treatment
within the classroom. In other words, RNT can be managed as a full day or
partial day program in any of these scenarios.

Upon graduation from RNT with a planned transition to another setting,
there are very minimal short term additional costs associated with the need
for an RNT teacher or therapist to make several visits to the new setting
while the child is present. The RNT team member acts as an emotional
bridge, much as parental participation assists with initial acclimation to
the RNT setting. The new setting's teacher should also be invited (with
parental permission) into an RNT team conference, once before and once
after the transition is made.

Table 3.1 expresses the staff time required and the costs of enrichment of a public school special education system by the school adding a part time RNT service. This special program can be within an otherwise fully inclusive public school which has many preschool and kindergarten special education pupils. Eight children would be given half time enrichment through an on site Reflective Network Therapy service, as part of their parentally approved IEP's. The charted calculations of costs for use of teacher and therapist time in the RNT classroom are based on two and a half hours per day, five days a week for an educational therapeutic classroom operating under the auspices of a U.S. public school system or mental health agency. It is assumed that the classroom already exists, that a public school or public agency administration is in place, and that the children's families pay no treatment or tuition fees. No calculations are made for payroll taxes or other indirect costs. Before the first treatment year starts, several days should be set aside for staff training exercises.

When considering cost-effectiveness, we hope school and agency administrators study this chart which shows financial feasibility and provides motivation to use Reflective Network Therapy as an economy measure as well as an improvement in the lives of their pupils. This calculation employs an arbitrary figure for teachers' salaries which actually vary from community to community and from time to time, as do the conservatively stated salaries for ABA aides. Much of the ongoing cost of training of staff during the first year is incorporated into the weekly Team Conferences. Table 3.2 shows the overall cost advantage of using RNT in public school special education programs as opposed to the commonly used ABA supplement (Lovaas method).

SMALL PRIVATE SCHOOLS V. PUBLIC SCHOOLS AS SITES FOR REFLECTIVE NETWORK THERAPY

A freestanding private therapeutic school is an expensive route, with costs similar to those incurred when using Lovaas one-on-one behavioral analysis aides. When a free-standing private preschool using only Reflective Network Therapy (which met California special education standards) was created, costs for the first year of operation were in the range of $250,000 per year for eight children (over $60,000 per child). That sum allowed for brick and mortar, utilities, insurance, administration, and full state special education certification as a California state certified nonpublic special education school. We didn't find the private school setting financially sustainable. We discontinued that effort and recommend a different approach: keeping costs

RNT: TYPICAL STAFF TIME PER WEEK AND RELATED COSTS FOR A 45 WEEK SCHOOL YEAR

HOUR PER WEEK FOR 8 CHILDREN, FIVE DAYS/WEEK	HOURS CLASS TIME	HOURS PARENT CONFERENCES	TEAM MEETINGS	HRS MISC	RECORD KEEPING	HOURS PER WEEK
Head Teacher Already in place at most special education services	31	6	1.5	0.5	1.0	**40**
Asst. Teacher Already in place at most special education services	38	0	1.5	0	0.5	**40**
Therapist	13	2	1.5	0	1.5	**18**
ANNUAL COST FOR RNT THERAPIST After the second year an RNT team with a licensed therapist can be self-supervising.						
If a therapist on staff is deployed for training and use in the RNT classroom	NO ADDITIONAL SALARY EXPENSE					
If a therapist is added to staff	ESTIMATED ANNUAL COST: $40,500					
Basic Costs for first year, second year and subsequent years: Training and Supervision						
START UP COSTS FIRST YEAR in a school or agency which already employs a suitable therapist who can be trained to perform RNT in the classroom	INITIAL INTENSIVE TRAINING, ONGOING TRAINING AND SUPERVISION IN RNT FOR THERAPIST AND TEACHERS				$20,000	
SECOND YEAR	WITH REDUCED SUPERVISION				$10,000	
SUBSEQUENT YEARS	SELF SUSTAINING: No Additional Costs				N/A	
START UP COST PER CHILD:						
1) COST PER CHILD FIRST YEAR: IF A THERAPIST MUST BE HIRED					$ 7,562	
2) COST PER CHILD FIRST YEAR: IF AN EXISTING THERAPIST IS TRAINED					$ 2,500	

Table 3.1.   Typical RNT Staff Time and Related Costs per 45 Week Full Day Full School Year

down by partnering with existing mental health agencies. Such partnering is now occurring at The Ann Martin Agency, in Piedmont, CA, just east of our Agency's San Francisco headquarters and at Wellspring Family Services in Seattle. It can occur best through the addition of an RNT therapist to special education classes in existing preschools, (public or private) rather than through the creation of administratively independent RNT schools.

Application of Reflective Network Therapy makes the most fiscal sense in an existing public special education system or a community based mental health agency, where there is already brick, mortar, staff, administration, and a preschool or kindergarten population identified as in need. We demonstrated such projects were feasible in San Mateo and San Francisco Unified School Districts. All that was needed was to train and add a therapist! In one project we trained an existing school psychologist (already on staff) to conduct Reflective Network Therapy.

COMPARING COSTS OF TWO EARLY INTERVENTION METHODS: STAFF TIME AND SALARIES FOR SPECIAL EDUCATION ENHANCEMENTS

Enhancement for eight (8) difficult to educate children (ages two to seven) who have Serious Emotional Disturbances or Pervasive Developmental Disorders including Autism and Asperger's disorder.	
Method 1) ABA Applied Behavioral Analysis (Autistic and PDD children only)	Method 2) RNT Reflective Network Therapy (Autistic children, children with other forms of PDD, children with SED)
Requires a full time Aide for each child, added to existing special education classroom costs	Requires one in-classroom therapist added to existing special education classroom costs.
8 full time ABA Aides at the additional cost of 40,000 per Aide The children may be distributed among various special education classes or may all be in one larger class	50,000 for a half time RNT therapist The children may be distributed among various special education classes or may all be in one larger class
Total annual additional costs for 8 children's ABA aides = 320,000	Total annual additional costs for 8 children's RNT treatment = 50,000
TOTAL ANNUAL SAVINGS USING RNT RATHER THAN ABA	
Treating 8 children with RNT vs. using ABA: Savings = 270,000 Treating 80 children with RNT vs. using ABA: Savings = 2,700,000	

Table 3.2.　Comparing Costs of Two Special Education Enhancements

EMOTIONAL RECOVERIES AND INTELLECTUAL GAINS

Current scientific thinking related to the effectiveness of Reflective Network Therapy is explored and further developed in Chapter 10 of this book. Considering the years of unexpected successes with this treatment method, the emotional recoveries and intellectual gains experienced by a large proportion of child-patients certainly demand much further scrutiny for a satisfactory scientific explanation. Modern concepts of brain function (such as activation of the mirror neuron system) and connections between brain centers and hemispheres are literally in development and are important for us to bring

into our studies. Today, functional MRI, PET scans, magnetoencephalographic studies and other new forms of brain imaging are possible. Beginning in 1996, we approached some families concerning MRI studies of their
autistic children but were not encouraged by their initial response. We would
like to try again. We have yet not had the opportunity to explore these lines
of research with children treated with Reflective Network Therapy. We are
focusing on what we have found by psychometric and clinical means and analyzing our procedures in an effort to isolate out what is necessary and effica-
cious. We look forward to various physiological and psychological multi-site
random-assignment and controlled studies by others, independent researchers
who can help point to fuller answers.

LOVE AND OTHER ESSENTIAL CONDITIONS
FOR SUCCESSFUL TREATMENT

We are in the midst of teasing out the factors which contribute to successful treatment in a very careful way by including blindly rated videotapes of
RNT treatment sessions. We already have clues to what these factors might
be. We believe the method's effectiveness has something to do with creating therapeutically designed social networks for groups of children which
provide shared emotional and cognitive circumstances for the recapturing of
the ability to love and to feel loved. Many of the children were lovable and
loving when born and later became unresponsive to their families and to other
treatments. Love, in this classroom method, is active in caring, tender, and
nurturant in ways that are all too often left out of the equation or less fully
employed in other methods.

Other therapies and education have often become overly sterile, even
exclusively pharmaceutical and behavioral, or exclusively psychodynamic.
Children are not merely a set of chemicals, habits, conflicts or symptoms to
be metabolically altered, behaviorally retrained or psychoanalytically interpreted. Society—especially parents, caregivers and teachers of young children—can gain important psychological support, skills and wisdom by studying this method's network of reflective interaction and thought-encouraging,
nurturant and caring treatment.

Roy N. Aruffo, MD, a senior child analyst from Houston, noted for his
work with school consultation, made the following insightful comments in
a personal communication to me after reading an early draft of *Reflective
Network Therapy in the Preschool Classroom* in 2007. His words usefully
restate the importance of appropriate love as used in Reflective Network
Therapy:

The thrust of the whole method is to provide love (caring, tender, nurturant relationships) to children who born loving but who later became unresponsive to their parents. It creates "humane classroom networks, shared emotional and cognitive circumstances for the giving and recapturing of the ability to love." I think that this means understanding ways to love, ways that precisely fit the love needs of the child. Oedipal love is not of much use to an undifferentiated child who needs a large measure of one minded love in which the giver consciously and/or intuitively understands the helplessness and utter dependency of the child. The child must feel the fit between his needs and the giver's capacity to recognize and meet the needs. This means that the giver is of one-mind and one-feeling with the child.

I think that Reflective Network Therapy generates a more and more precise understanding of the child and the family through the continual family work and the discussions between the staff members. The parents too must be developing and restoring their capacity to understand the child. This thinking emphasizes the ego aspects (caregivers as auxiliary egos) of the giver-child relationship as opposed to the libidinal aspects—the love and nurturance. Caregivers must provide all the ego functions that the child has not yet acquired, judgment, memory, control of impulses, thinking, interpretation of sensation, tolerance of frustration, postponement of gratification, recognition of danger, etc. Without this the child is helpless in a hostile world and open to great pain. When the caregivers succeed the child seems to be calm, receptive of care, feels protected, safe, and connected. The child learns, is receptive to love and moves forward in its emotional development. When they fail enough the child withdraws, develops in an irregular fashion and becomes dysfunctional. This thinking puts one mindedness, one feelingness (empathy) as preconditions for growth.—*Roy N. Aruffo, MD*

Considering Aruffo concept, we can say that in the practice of RNT, we too often see children whose parents convey to the child an excessive sense of being alone rather than one with his parents. The child who needs oneness with the parent in order to feel secure and protected accepts the parent's distortions, is one minded in an unfortunate way with the parent, and applies the parent's distortion everywhere, including in school. Helping the parent see the distortions, even for a short period of time unleashes the child's pent up developmental thrust. We find that the most powerful growth effects of Reflective Network Therapy we have seen so far happen when:

1. A two-way transmission of observations and insights about the child occurs with each set of parents weekly; and
2. A psychodynamic therapist works in an RNT classroom four or five times a week.

Both of these factors have a direct statistical association with the IQ gains and clinical improvements (Zelman, 1985, 1996). We think each is probably essential in the network effect. Going further in our thinking about what is essential, we strongly suspect that missing any one of these or an even larger number of connecting links in the network among the team members, there is risk this method may not work so measurably well.

The clinical success of Reflective Network Therapy relies on the contribution of all these interacting factors: clinical evaluations, carefully getting to know the parents, parent involvement in the classrooms while children are and teachers are present, parent guidance, team conferences, briefings and debriefings before and after each child's daily fifteen to twenty minute session in the classroom, peer reflections on the child's treatment and behavior, high frequency of sessions, and long treatment duration. Similarly, without clear classroom instruction and modeling of empathy, without parental endorsement of the classroom rules, without boundaries of acceptable limits on child behavior, the children will not help each other.

Weekly all-staff conferences are essential for creating the network effect, and benefit from regular use of videotaped sessions as a focus for supervision. The study of videotapes helps ingrain mental representations of the children in the staff's minds. Since others may innovate and make changes or deletions in the proven method, we urge that any innovations or subtractions from the above ingredients be recorded and reported to The Children's Psychological Health Center.

GETTING HELP: STARTING A REFLECTIVE NETWORK THERAPY GROUP

As part of its mission, The Children's Psychological Health Center (CPHC) is actively engaged in providing assistance with wider use of the method and tracking results for ongoing scientific studies. It can contract to provide experienced RNT trainers, supervisors, and help a new site launch and carry out their program. We invite you to contact The Children's Psychological Health Center at www.childrenspsychological.org for training resources and supervisory support.

USE OF THE TERMS: REFLECTIVE NETWORK THERAPY AND CORNERSTONE THERAPY

The term "reflective network therapy" has the purpose of distinguishing this psychosocial and psychoanalytic method from other efforts which may incorporate some of its techniques and processes but not all. As Reflective Network Therapy was first well known as The Cornerstone Therapeutic Preschool Method and referred to as Cornerstone Therapy or the Cornerstone method, we respectfully ask others not to call their work either "Cornerstone Therapy" or "Reflective Network Therapy" *unless* they use all of the method's component procedures as detailed in this manual, obtain basic training from certified, Reflective Network Therapy training supervisors, and operate under appropriate guidance. This will help avoid confusion as ongoing scientific studies of work using RNT techniques and service procedures go forward. If a team is borrowing bits and pieces of the method, in that case, please refer to the work by another name. Please keep us in touch with the results of your efforts so we can understand what might be the essential features of your successes and failures and help others learn from your innovations.

WHAT OTHERS HAVE DONE YOU CAN DO

Lest this technique might seem too difficult, or that only very highly trained or unusually talented people can make it work, an appendix (not comprehensive) identifies more than thirty persons who have actually used the method as the sole treatment modality in classrooms in several US states (New York, California, Washington, Massachusetts, Oklahoma) and Argentina. Over twenty others on the list were intellectual, supervisory, testing or scientific contributors or researchers. At least twenty teachers have done excellent RNT work not only without prior special education training but also without prior psychoanalytic experience, or therapeutic training. They did so mainly by working closely with their classroom therapists and receiving supervision from senior educators who had already learned the method. A marriage and family intern, Molly Franklin, MFTi, was very effective in the San Francisco private Cornerstone Therapeutic Preschool, using RNT with autistic as well as anxious and traumatized children. Similarly, Jane Christmas, PhD who was then a graduate psychology student, Miquela Diaz Hope, PhD, then a pre-licensure psychological assistant, and Linda Hirshfeld, PhD, also a pre-licensure psychological assistant at the time of her first involvement with RNT patients, all have very good clinical results. Peggy Herzog, PhD, who was at first a recently licensed psychologist, worked well with the method in Yonkers, New York.

FRAN MORRIS DESCRIBES APPLICATIONS OF REFLECTIVE NETWORK THERAPY IN OKLAHOMA

Fran Morris, MA, Clinical Professor of Psychiatry and Behavioral Sciences, University of Oklahoma Health Sciences Center, independently performed what we consider equivalent to RNT treatment for several years in Oklahoma City, Oklahoma. She emailed this follow-up which describes the duration of her experience with the method and also includes her notes on a follow-up on a patient after 18 years. The young man ("J.") had clinical and IQ gains that were sustained. Morris provided this report in a 2007 personal communication to Gilbert Kliman:

We started using this method in 1969 when analyst Marshall Schechter, MD established the first Diagnostic-Therapeutic Nursery at OUHSC as a part of our child psychiatry training program. Dr. Schechter had nurtured this idea since his visit to Anna Freud's Hampstead Nursery in England during his own training. The full-time program closed in 1984 but a Diagnostic Nursery continues (now only 1/2 day a week) as part of child psychiatry training, under the supervision of Povl W. Toussieng, M.D. (1984-1997) and James R. Allen, M.D. (1997-present). Dr. Toussieng and I passed on many of the basic concepts to Community Mental Health Centers in Oklahoma through a network of Therapeutic Nurseries that began in 1990 and built to 31 locations by 1996 but due to funding changes have now dwindled to almost none. There are still many clinicians in Oklahoma who are aware of Dr. Kliman's work. There is an active and growing Analytic Society here, and I still use a Cornerstone [RNT] video tape in some of the training I do for the state Department of Mental Health.

J. came to our Diagnostic Nursery in February, 1978 at the age of four (DOB: 1-14-74). ...the initial report found a severe speech/language delay, developmental delay in all areas except gross motor (which was considerably advanced), delayed emotional and psychological development and autistic defenses...I have a report from July 3, 1981 from Central State University that states that WISC-R scores were: Verbal scale 45, Performance scale 58, Full Scale 47. Next, I have a WISC-R dated March 20, 1982 that shows Verbal Score 67, Performance Score 81, and Full Scale 72. This was after he had been in our Therapeutic Nursery for 2 1/2 years. He was thereafter also in a special public school program for 1 and 1/2 years with me, where I provided once-a-week individual follow-up therapy.

The initial diagnosis he was given at our Center was "Withdrawing Reaction of Childhood and Developmental Delays in Speech, Social and Psychosexual Development with Autistic Movements and Rituals.—*Fran Morris, MA*

Studying Dr. Morris' report, we note that, in infancy, the patient got a normal "Leiter IQ", using a test based on nonverbal tasks. For the present purpose, we are excluding that data, to use an "apples to apples" comparison approach to track the boy's overall IQ changes. We have created Table 3.3 to represent Professor Morris' findings, confined to the Wechsler IQ tests, since they are conservative about improvements with age, and comparable to each other. The findings she reports indicate a marked and sustained rise of Wechsler Full Scale IQ, a highly significant improvement which continued to increase for many years. It appears she kept this improvement going with a continued individual treatment relationship. Zelman (1999) has also reported that continuing psychotherapy adds power to the treatment. Strong IQ gains were made among preschool children who continued in treatment, within after-school groups conducted by Zelman on the Reflective Network Therapy model. (Similarly, Dorian Tenore-Bartilucci's continuously rising IQ was accompanied by several years of weekly psychotherapy after her Reflective Network Therapy.)

Of the dozens of therapists listed as contributors to this method, only Kliman, Lopez, Balter, Rosenfield, Harrison, Henderson and Mallo have had full psychoanalytic training, and most had none at all. All, however, were supervised by dynamically knowledgeable and experienced RNT clinicians, most of whom had great interest in interpersonal therapies and the importance of human relationships in overcoming childhood disturbances of development.

OUTCOME COMPARISONS: RNT VS. ABA

Reflective Network Therapy's data base concerning twice-tested and closely followed children is still modest, like that of Applied Behavioral Analysis. Both methods have reported on similar numbers of children. The RNT data is much more comprehensive in important ways than the ABA findings, however. We have found only several dozen twice-tested among the ABA

SUMMARY OF AN AUTISTIC CHILD'S IQ CHANGES:
OKLAHOMA CASE
Oklahoma case—Morris and Toussieng's
Therapeutic Preschool Service

Test Type	Age	Year	Notes	Full Scale IQ
DOB Jan 14, 1974	0	1974		
WISC-R	4	1981	Severe autistic regression. Referred for treatment	47
WISC-R	5	1982	Marked IQ rise	72
WISC-R	6	1983	Continued IQ rise	91
WAIS-III	24	2001	Continued IQ rise	125

Table 3.3. **Independent Uses of Techniques Equivalent to Reflective Network Therapy Included the Remarkable Case of a Child Who Started Treatment With an IQ of 47 and Emerged With an IQ of 125**

literature reports on IQ gains. Conclusions stemming from ABA baseline testing methods were scientifically flawed because they used developmental quotients for a first measure and IQ for follow-ups. Even an otherwise well designed effort retained this flaw (Sallows & Grauppner, 2005). As for functional recoveries and possible "cures", my RNT experience does not warrant a hard number. We await much more systematic data on failures and successes in both RNT and ABA methods. When pressed, Kliman estimates that 40 to 60% of the autism spectrum and pervasive developmental disorder preschool children he has known through Reflective Network Therapy services have gone on to be free of that diagnosis. That means that his thinking is that the remainder have residual signs and symptoms enough to make the diagnosis after RNT treatment and schooling. If correct (and more funding, time and study is needed to verify that this is correct) then this success and failure rate is the same as the Applied Behavioral Analysis method. What is more certain is that the IQ gains in RNT treated children were better studied among properly comparable baseline and follow up tests; and, that the RNT IQ gains were at least as large as the ABA gains, occurred among even more children, and had almost no exceptions to the IQ gain effect among testable children.

Reflective Network Therapy is clinical, by definition aimed at the mental health of seriously emotionally disordered children, autistic children and/ or children with other pervasive developmental disorders. ABA does not generally define itself as a mental health technique, and probably for that reason has not measured the overall mental health effects on autistic or other children.

CATEGORIES OF CHILDREN WELL SERVED BY REFLECTIVE NETWORK THERAPY AND OTHER CONSIDERATIONS

Regarding the diagnostic categories of children who can usually be well served by Reflective Network Therapy, over the past four decades the method's combination of education and therapy has resulted in substantial clinical and cognitive progress among children suffering from:

- Adjustment reaction disorders, such as reactions to sexual molestation, foster care placements, and domestic violence
- Asperger's Syndrome, including Asperger's children with overly aggressive behavior
- Attention deficit disorders, with and without hyperactivity
- Autism spectrum disorders (ASD)
- Behavior disorders

- Combinations of developmental and emotional disorders
- Combinations of overanxious and aggressive behaviors
- Conduct disorders
- Depressive disorders
- Early childhood depression
- Early childhood psychoses
- Elective and selective mutism
- Emotional effects of life-threatening illnesses in the child or close relative
- Oppositional defiant disorders
- Overanxious disorders of childhood
- Parent-child relationship problems
- Pathological bereavement reactions
- Pervasive developmental disorder (PDD)
- Physical disorders that are worsened by emotional stress, such as psychogenic aggravation of asthma
- Posttraumatic stress disorder (PTSD)
- Reactive attachment disorders
- School phobia
- Social phobia
- Traumatized children
- Children with multiple diagnoses

Although Reflective Network Therapy clearly helps children in many diagnostic categories, our studies to date are statistically weighted for two categories: preschoolers who are either autistic or traumatized. Detections of these same two categories of early childhood disorders (autism and posttraumatic disorders) are probably on the increase in the general population as well as among children referred to RNT services. Current estimates of the general population incidence of autism are 1 in 150. This number may even be low due to underreporting and inconsistencies in screening practices. Reported cases of early childhood forms of autism have risen at a startling rate in the US, Europe and Asia (Cunningham, 2006). No one is sure yet whether autistic children are being more effectively identified or whether little-understood genetic and environmental factors are at fault for their reported numbers increasing.

There is no clear and persuasive scientific understanding or consensus of investigators about causal factors in this increase, although certainly, autism is a disorder with a basis in brain and genetic abnormalities. Functional MRI studies (Just et al., 2004, 2007) show many well-functioning parts of autistic children's brains but a lack of their connections via white matter. Children with autism can be rehabilitated through cognitive, or emotional and social exercises (Sallows, 2005; Hope, 1999) which from our point of view may have their good effects by exercising and enhancing networks of neurons and neuronal connections.

There are very widely differing sets of brain and interpersonal problems addressed in child psychiatric treatments of children with the disorders we listed above. The problems of emotionally disordered children with attention deficits, hyperactivity, anxiety disorders, depression, post-traumatic disorders or oppositional-defiant behavior are very different from the problems of children with autism, Asperger's Syndrome, or other forms of PDD. Foster children have additional special needs, tending to suffer prior neglect and abuse, followed by discontinuities of care partly brought about by their own posttraumatic behaviors (Kliman and Schaeffer, 1990.) It is probably not a coincidence that traumatized children respond particularly well to the reflective network of "Cornerstone" therapy (Zelman, 1996). Unlike other therapies, Reflective Network Therapy is particularly well suited to and can be easily individualized for children suffering from all the pathologies listed above and can be delivered in an inclusive classroom. A contributing factor to the method's success is its corrective exercise approach to a factor common to all of the listed disorders: resistance to loving and learning in small social networks.

THE ALL IN ONE CLASSROOM

Few child psychotherapies or educational methods have documented that they can be tailored enough to help children with such widely varying problems, especially in the same classroom or group. Reflective Network Therapy's interdisciplinary combination can be reliably tailored to be inclusive and to help very different kinds of special needs children with emotional or developmental problems in the same classroom. It also works well with the social adaptive problems of children overwhelmed by or coping poorly with the loss of a parent or placement in foster care and with children suffering from posttraumatic stress disorder. The inclusion of children suffering object loss who may not be developmentally delayed is good for all the children. It promotes healthy empathy and altruism among the more advanced children, and gives an opportunity for the less socially advanced children to develop further. The more advanced children perform the function of "expert players." (Wolfberg, 2003)

Few child psychotherapies are versatile regarding the settings within which they can be carried out. Using Reflective Network Therapy, an agency with a therapy group, a private preschool group, or any public special education class serving multiple diagnostic categories of children can be the arena for helpful treatment and sometimes even recovery. Head Start programs, shelters for homeless families or recently homeless families in transitional housing, and private day care centers have all found the method feasible and effective, and it is in use within a regular private preschool.

Still fewer child psychotherapies or educational methods have documented that they substantially raise objectively measured intelligence quotients (Heinicke, 1966; Lovaas, 1987). RNT's in-classroom educational and psychotherapy does raise intelligence quotients, substantially and reliably.

Reflective Network Therapy offers new hope to several sets of parents. The first set is parents of emotionally disturbed children–including traumatized children or those with anxiety disorders, oppositionalism or attentional difficulties. The method offers special hope for such children. The hope comes at a time when prolonged chemical psychiatric treatments with medication may be helpful but (in the cases of Ritalin, Risperdal and Clozapine, for example) sometimes dangerous for preschool children with such emotional disturbances (Lagace, Noonan, and Eisch, 2007).

The second set of parents (growing in number) is those whose children have pervasive developmental disorders, including the autism spectrum, Asperger's Syndrome and full-blown autistic disorders. Expressive and receptive language problems are a regular part of pervasive developmental disorders. So are interpersonal avoidance, oddities of play, stereotypic movements, and hypersensitivity to sound and touch. In moderate to severe cases the children lack a loving interest in human beings. They have little empathy, understanding or theory of the mind of others. Many children with these disorders live and go to school in their communities, but often only with great distress and high economic cost to their families and taxpayers. For this set of parents, the publication of this book comes when the best known and most widely used behavioral method, Applied Behavioral Analysis (ABA) or Lovaas method is also showing cognitive benefits (Eikeseth 2007), though its findings based on shaky science and requires thousands of hours of treatment. These benefits include IQ gains similar to those achieved using RNT but the ABA has major relative drawbacks. The Lovaas method is, in our opinion coming close to being scientifically sound (except in its choice of baseline measures to compare with later measures) and is probably effective but is not clinically versatile. It is much more expensive than Reflective Network Therapy, requires thousands more hours per year for similar IQ gains, does not use trained psychotherapists, is deliberately less ambitious in its goals about personality growth among autistic children, and is less clinically documented and studied than what the reader will find here. Taxpayers and school administrators will be surprised at the large cost-benefit which can come from using the less expensive RNT method for autistic children, in comparison with the more customary and more expensive ABA approach. Chapter 9 of this book provides a fuller discussion of the advantages of Reflective Network Therapy in terms of cost-benefit analyses.

The third set of parents who are helped by Reflective Network Therapy is those who care for foster children. Youngsters who are placed in foster care because of neglect or abuse or the death of a parent or primary caregiver are numerous, and those children are likely to have a posttraumatic reenactment tendency to provoke further rejection, abuse or abandonment. Their placements with foster families often fail because of child behaviors which are well calculated to provoke or test the possibility of new rejections (bouncing). In a controlled study, we found that about 25% of first placement foster children bounce from foster home to home during their first year. Bouncing is known to be one of the most psychologically malignant experiences for foster children (Pardeck, 1983, 1984; Kliman, 2006). Not one of the thirty foster consecutive children treated by Reflective Network Therapy method bounced during the study year (Schaeffer and Kliman, 1990; Kliman, 1987, 2006).

OVERCOMING RESISTANCE TO LEARNING

As mentioned earlier, soon after the method was applied to treat bereaved preschoolers, the method was discovered to help many young children cognitively as well as emotionally. Countless disturbed preschool children profoundly resist their caregivers' loving efforts. They stop receiving constructive knowledge from their teachers, parents, and peers; they become unreceptive to learning. The following pages have been inspired by the opposite experience, the opening of tightly closed hearts and minds.

In keeping with the appropriateness of still wider use of Reflective Network Therapy, and since the method requires the participation of parents, this book is written in a style intended to introduce the method to parents as well as teachers and therapists. Public education of parents about the method has already begun, with the help of television news broadcasts. In late 2004, an eight-year-old Bay Area boy and his father were interviewed by John Fowler (KTVU channel 2 Health and Science news editor and reporter) in an evening news feature. Viewers could see that the formerly retarded, odd seeming and withdrawn boy was in a happy relationship with his father, attending a regular, mainstream school, sociably joking and laughing, looking the reporter in the eye, reading math homework aloud and figuring it out correctly in the midst of distractions.

What was newsworthy enough for the eight year old and his father to be interviewed on TV? At the time, California was experiencing the first reports of an epidemic of children with developmental delays, especially with autistic features. Three years earlier, the now vivacious and humorous child had been a developmental wreck. A school psychologist, pediatrician and a child psychiatrist had all diagnosed him as mentally retarded and autistic. Only six months before the TV broadcast, this boy had barely been able to take the math section of the IQ test with a very experienced University of California developmental psychologist. Yet, as documented by Fowler's broadcast, he no longer seemed autistic or retarded. His IQ had risen from a retarded level at the first testing to normal at a second testing two years later. The TV segment documented his continued growth in math, which had become a source of pride for the child and his family. What caused this life changing turnaround in this boy's condition? He had received two years of Reflective Network Therapy, beginning at age four years. The previously restrained forces of his development, which had literally retarded him mentally, had been unchained by that therapy. Within two years, the socially isolated, screaming, oppositional, angry, grim, and socially withdrawn, seemingly very dull boy had become loving, humorous and bright. A year after he left Cornerstone, he was in regular public school classes, doing reasonably good work and behaving well.

CAN THIS METHOD BE CARRIED OUT IN THE HOME?

We have been asked whether this method might be adapted for primary caregivers and families to carry out. Although any arrangement which sacrifices key elements of the method should not be expected to yield the same clinical results as a full application of Reflective Network Therapy in a classroom, families with resources and substantial guidance may be able to use the method to advantage. Some parents have actually done so by establishing reflective networks on their own, after prior personal treatment experience as children in RNT treatment. We need to follow such experiences more rigorously.

Christina Adams describes her adaptation of "Cornerstone" [RNT] to her son's multiple needs (Adams, 2005). She and her boy, Jonah, received some modeling in Reflective Network Therapy techniques from us at a Cornerstone preschool and directly from me as a visitor in her own home. The family was very successful with their distinctly autistic boy, and five years later she was able to report that Jonah appeared vivacious, humorous, possessed of a good theory of other minds and was well recovered and well developed. Kliman was impressed with how Ms. Adams went about using the method's briefing and debriefing techniques, creating a reflective network team by including speech and occupational therapists involved with her son. Her autobiographical book (Adams, 2005) deserves considerable research planning. We would like to see a test of feasibility, using Reflective Network Therapy at home, orchestrated by children's therapists and parents in a significant number of families, with tracking of cognitive and mental health gains using standardized initial and follow up testing. That project could be conceptualized as having many delivery advantages, particularly before a child is old enough or competent enough to be attending a group setting. Dorian Tenore-Bartilucci's account (How I Recovered from Autism) also includes mention of doing "Cornerstone" work later in life with her own autistic daughter. Tenore-Bartilucci and the Adams parents recruited small networks to help their own autistic children. These important private home and family projects require another set of studies and essays to do justice to the potentialities of harnessing reflective networks in systematic ways.

Finally, we want to welcome you as new users of Reflective Network Therapy, and hope you find this manual useful in your everyday therapeutic and educational work! Please stay in touch to better help others in need.

Chapter Four

How I Recovered from Autism

Dorian Tenore-Bartilucci
Introduction and Afterword by
Gilbert Kliman, MD

From 1967 to 1970, the author of the autobiographical account below was treated by most of the essential techniques practiced in Reflective Network Therapy as it fully evolved. Dorian knew her therapeutic preschool as her Cornerstone class. Dorian had lost most of her ability to love and be loved. I first met her at less than three years of age. Within the previous half year she had lost her vivacious interactions with family and peers, and almost all of her earlier large vocabulary. She was now an extremely withdrawn and difficult child, a preschooler who certainly appeared lost in an autistic state. Her parents and a prominent day care center considered her autistic. She had been diagnosed as autistic by two child psychiatrists and a pediatric neurologist. It strains belief to see how well she is doing four decades after her successful Reflective Network Therapy treatment. She has truly regained full ability to love and be loved, which some autistic persons (who have otherwise recovered and function well) say that they feel they do not have. (Grandin, 1996)

One may well ask, "Can there be even a partial recovery from autism?" Autism is almost certainly a genetic brain disorder, with a range of severity. Autism is the most severe form of pervasive developmental disorders (PDD). Severe autism, as presented by Dorian, generally has terrible outcomes. Many children with such forms of autism recover very minimally and some cannot ever live unassisted within the larger community. There are numerous exceptions—cases of children who do well. I have treated some whose cognitive development and mental health improvements were exceptional. While Dorian came into treatment with many pronounced symptoms of serious autism; she emerged on an upward trajectory toward no symptoms at all. When last tested, Dorian's IQ was 149, clearly a quantum leap from her dismal cognitive development prior to RNT treatment.

I encouraged Dorian (now in her forties) to tell her own story. Her account is an astonishing story, showing the evolution of a formerly autistic child into the healthy, empathic, expressive and vivacious person she is now. Her life is emotionally rich and intellectually satisfying. Her creativity is recognized and rewarded. She is a mother raising two children. She is happily married and enjoys her career as a successful writer and researcher specializing in modern music.

Some of my most distinguished colleagues have carefully studied video-tapes of Dorian's current condition. (With Dorian's permission, her follow up videotaped interview, is available on our agency's website.) Reviewers included Henry Massie, MD, a researcher in autism long term follow ups of child development and psychopathology, and a former faculty member of the University of California School of Medicine Department of Psychiatry. We have all concluded that Dorian is no longer in any way showing that she was autistic. As with some other autistic persons, Dorian's memories are unusually well retained and quite detailed. She has a marvelous recall of some classroom events which she helped me to reconstruct, such as some aspects of play in the school yard of the preschool she attended. She remembers some of her first sessions with me. Her recollections are indeed consistent with my progress notes from that time (as well as what I recall that I never wrote down). She describes in a compellingly credible fashion the appearance and actions of adults and children who were there, including accurate details of their childish bathroom play that are unlikely to be invented and about which her mother was probably not an informant. She retains the ability to think in pictures, and gives a cinematographic quality to her reminiscences, combined with a delicious sense of humor suggesting keen theory of the minds of others.

How did it happen that Dorian clearly made a full recovery? She was treated for three years, by a reflective network team of teachers, parents, peers. I was her therapist for most of her treatment. During one year of her treatment Myron Stein, MD (Child and Adolescent Psychiatrist) was Dorian's in-classroom therapist. Her treatment occurred in a therapeutic preschool that I had designed for children with a variety of emotional disorders. Reflective Network Therapy was easily modified to suit the needs of an autistic child like Dorian.

I remember our great concern over the severity of Dorian's condition when we accepted her into the preschool. Dorian was in a severely autistic state. Almost mute, she made little eye contact. Her behavior included excessive arm flapping, roaring, twirling and biting. She was a socially isolated child who preferred to stay in nursery corners, staring at the walls. She was very distressed by transitions of any kind, and agitated when separated from her usual environment. Like most autistic children, she appeared completely unable to process her emotional responses to interpersonal events and she desperately avoided play. Her mother reported that during the six months before she was able to enroll Dorian in our program, she had lost her previously accessible vocabulary of approximately one hundred-words. She was reduced to echoing, meaninglessly repeating only a few words spoken by others (a sign of autism called echolalia).

Dorian's history of loss of developmental achievements, her behaviors of whirling, twirling and echoing, and her lack of interpersonal contact other than with her mother were sufficient for me to make a medically certain diagnosis of autism. Two psychiatrists, a pediatric neurologist, and Kennedy Child Development Center staff where Dorian had recently been examined all had diagnosed her as autistic and postulated that she was probably severely retarded. They referred her to our preschool because there were no other facilities operating nearby at that time which could serve a preschooler who was so isolated, autistic and, by all appearances, retarded.

Careful history given by her mother gave revealed that Dorian probably came by some of her difficulties through at least two generations of genetic loading. Maternal grandparents and aunts had shown remarkable behaviors of social isolation, sometimes punitively not speaking to each other for years at a time. Dorian's older sister had very little social life and had multiple psychiatric diagnoses, with severe psychological immaturity and developmental problems, including motor awkwardness and lack of coordination. Dorian's older brother had shown a tendency toward interpersonal isolation at the time. He later dropped out of touch with the family for over a decade. Mother probably had a period of depression at the time of Dorian's birth and first year, aggravated by bereavements. The genetic trend continued, and Dorian's child was later diagnosed by third parties as having Asperger's syndrome.

Dorian's history (and so far her daughter's) is a success story. Despite her genetic disposition toward autism and isolation, she gradually recovered, beginning with the daily intensive Reflective Network Therapy (and the methodological practice of providing daily briefings and debriefings with teachers. Often her mother participated in the classroom, as well as in the guidance and support provided in parent conferences. Her father often participated also. Her course of recovery is conspicuous for her dramatic series of rises in IQ scores from the time she became testable at age six years. It is a success story not only because her cognitive development was such that she was able to progress through higher education (and graduate from college), not only because she became interpersonally adept enough to marry and enjoy a social life. Even more remarkably, over thirty years later, she was strong enough to help her own genetically vulnerable daughter recover from an alarming

regression of development at the same age. It is especially a success story because she became able to develop a complex and nuanced theory of her own
mind and of the minds of others, as evidenced by her perceptive presentation
of her own story. Dorian's recovery and intellectual growth were among the
first of many strong recoveries I witnessed over many years of applying Reflective Network Therapy to children with severe developmental disorders.
Such cases particularly inspire Reflective Network Therapy teams to continue
to be rigorous about outcome data collection.

Of the children treated by the method described in this book, Dorian has
been followed over the longest, period of time: over 40 years. My colleagues
and I have studied and published concerning dozens of other children (69
twice-tested patients are reported in other essays) who have benefited from
Reflective Network Therapy. I am delighted to publish the story of the resulting therapeutic, relational, and personal success she has achieved in Dorian's
own words. Dorian was helped when Reflective Network Therapy was
known as The Cornerstone Method and attended a "Cornerstone" school. Her
natural use of that term rather than RNT is preserved here.

DORIAN'S OWN STORY:
"HOW I RECOVERED FROM AUTISM"

Like many parents and their children, my seven year old daughter Maggie and
I share many traits. We have the same kind of curly hair, nose, fun-loving
personality—and history of being labeled autistic. At the age of 2, Maggie
was diagnosed with a form of autism—just as I was at the age of 3. Happily,
both of us had mothers savvy enough to seek help as soon as possible. Maggie's story is my story, over 30 years later.

As far back as I can remember I've never processed information in quite
the same way as other people: I've always thought in pictures. It's rather like
having movies going on in my brain all the time. When I think of things that
have happened in my life over the course of a day or week or whatever time
period, I see them in my head as if they're a series of jump cuts in a film. One
specific example of this thought process dates from when I was a preschooler:
mental images of a series of events from a given day, such as a birthday party,
ended in an image of myself as a baby in a crib, accompanied by a feminine
adult voiceover intoning "...and that's that I dreamed when I was a baby."
While I no longer have a voiceover in my head, my thoughts still flow in a
cinematic style. It comes in very handy when I'm writing, particularly fiction.
A friend from my writers' workshop says I have a "video mind."

Back in 1965, I am told by my mother, I inexplicably morphed from a cheerful, affectionate toddler into a child trapped in her own world. Two years old at the time, I began parroting back dialogue or commercials I'd heard on TV rather than talking about things happening in real life, until my speech dwindled down to silence. When I wasn't curled up in a corner of the room, rocking back and forth, pulling away when my family members tried to touch me, I was flapping my arms or walking up and down on my toes. This alarming situation continued for close to a year. I remember only some of it.

One's first instinct when learning of a child with my kind of problems is to look into what's going on in the family. While our clan had its share of problems, they don't seem especially catastrophic now, but that may be because I'm looking at them through adult eyes. When I was born, my mother was still grieving for her parents, who had died within 11 months of each other, less than a year earlier. The youngest of three children, I lived at that time with my parents, my brother Larry, then 11, and my sister Fran, then 7, in an upper middle class section of New York. Our two-family house also included my aunt and uncle and my four cousins, the youngest only a year older than I.

With my father's alcoholism and gambling addiction, not to mention his working hours (as a restaurant manager and bookie, Dad slept all day and worked all night) he wasn't the easiest person to live with. However, over my parents' 25-year marriage, Dad's various endeavors earned enough money to make him an exceptionally good provider. I still recall some of our family's resulting vacation trips later in my childhood—for example, Mom taught me my ABCs during a trip to the Bahamas—and overall luxurious standard of living. These were pleasant distractions from Dad's emotional difficulties, and certainly we kids had everything we wanted and needed—not just material possessions, but also love, since our family was affectionate despite our dysfunctional tendencies.

One might suggest that my video-like mental processing came from watching too much television. In fact, on average, my siblings and I actually spent more of our free time playing outdoors or going on outings with my mother, usually zoos, ice-skating, swimming and other fun, yet healthy, activities. The relatively small amount of TV watching we did as youngsters went on when my grandmother babysat us. Grandma Karina would turn on the TV and bring out the candy and baked goods that she hid in her overnight bags, knowing Mom would frown on us having too many sweets. It was like a little secret party—one that got a healthy makeover with fruit, crackers, and raw vegetables when I was eight years old, when a dental checkup revealed eight cavities, and not all in my baby teeth, either. "Secret parties" aside, Grandma Karina was the glue that held our family together, even after Mom and my aunt had a severe falling-out that led to Auntie and the rest of her family moving out of the two-family house.

In fact, one reason Mom tells me she stayed married to Dad so long, despite their problems, was because she loved Grandma Karina so much. The close-knit quality of our family was one of the few factors that kept my older sister Fran on anything remotely resembling an even keel. At that time and ever since, Fran has been plagued with various physical and mental problems, drastic weight gains and losses, eventually resulting in anorexia, and learning disabilities, including dyslexia. She went in and out of hospitals and on and off various anti-psychotic meds for years, with nobody able to pin down one distinct diagnosis. Home life was nerve-wracking at times, with Fran erupting into unexpected rages and trying to harm my mother. To one degree or another, taking care of Fran dominated our family life.

When I became silent and withdrawn as a child, Mom was worried that I might have the same problems as Fran. Fortunately, it turned out my problems were different and treatable without meds. The only medications I ever needed on a regular basis were migraine meds. Migraines run on Mom's side of the family, and I was no exception; I began getting the headaches periodically during my teens. I still suffer from migraines, but they become less frequent as I get older. Now I only get them once or twice a month on average; they're triggered primarily by barometric pressure (i.e., overcast or rainy days) or my menstrual cycle.

Once I reached adulthood, it became almost funny to tell people that I was once diagnosed as autistic. They would look at me incredulously: "You, autistic? What kind of quacks were these doctors?!" If they'd seen me back in my early Cornerstone days, however, they might very well have reached the same conclusions as the doctors. Two child psychiatrists (Gilbert Kliman, MD and Myron Stein, MD), a pediatric neurologist (Lawrence Taft, MD), and the Kennedy Child Development Center staff had not only diagnosed me with autism, but even seriously considered the possibility of my being mentally retarded. Fortunately for me, Dr. Kliman changed his mind about my being retarded after he and his Cornerstone School colleagues spent significant amounts of time with me.

I have a terrific memory about lots of things including parts of Cornerstone treatment. I still remember my first meeting with Dr. Kliman at The Cornerstone School in White Plains, NY. I was rocking in the corner and Dr. Kliman was sitting on the floor next to me saying, in his kind, gentle voice, "I know you're in there, Dorian. I know that you are not away, you're in there. You can't fool me." Not wanting me to get into a permanent habit of retreating that way and creating a self-fulfilling prophecy, Dr. Kliman told the teachers, "You mustn't let Dorian fool you into thinking she's not there. Dorian,

I know you're there." That's when I began treatment at The Cornerstone School in its very first preschool class—only 3 years old, and I was already a pioneer.

Mom, present during this testing, now says she regards that rocking incident with Dr. Kliman as a turning point in my recovery. Dr. Kliman has later told me that he had some optimism that I would stop withdrawing from the world sooner or later, since I had been in many ways, he said, "an intrinsically intact baby and there seemed to be family stressors making you withdraw." Nevertheless, Dr. Kliman added:

> I was very worried about you because you seemed so clearly autistic, so clearly without social life outside of with your mother. Your language was reduced to "Rinso White" and roaring like a lion, you had given up your toilet training, you twirled and flapped, and made little eye contact. You were intellectually so reduced that we could not give you standardized tests for a couple of more years. So the picture was very guarded and serious. It's not unusual for a child to stop developing at age 2 and become permanently autistic after initially developing well. Your family and your therapists were very appropriately very worried since this was not just a few days or a few weeks, but a long period of actual reversal of your intellectual, emotional, behavioral and social intelligence.

I'm glad and grateful that Mom was able to enroll me in The Cornerstone School so I wouldn't spend any more time than I had to inside this particularly tough shell I'd put myself into.

One of the exceptional—and, for that era, revolutionary—things about The Cornerstone School's therapy style was that Dr. Kliman, head teacher Mrs. Doris Gorin, and the other Cornerstone personnel were warm, friendly, and close enough to help us kids when we needed it, but without getting in our faces. I never felt coerced or browbeaten into complying with instructions or treatment, and as far as I could tell, neither did my Cornerstone classmates. The gentle, receptive Cornerstone staff talked one-on-one with each of my classmates and me, using play therapy with puppets and toys to draw us out. There was a rhythm to it. Each of us was a patient right in the classroom, one at a time, while others played around us.

Like any preschool, Cornerstone made learning fun. I remember many lighthearted Cornerstone moments. There was the time I teamed up with one of my classmates, Hank, to make insect soup. Don't worry, animal lovers, no insects were harmed in the making of this gourmet dish, just slightly water-logged. Hank and I gathered our ingredients, ants and worms, in the school's grassy back yard. Of course, we had no heat on our toy cooking range, so I guess the more adventurous gourmets reading this would classify our concoction as a cold summer soup—the insect equivalent of gazpacho, I suppose.

The large black ants that Hank and I went to such lengths to catch took a dim view of becoming soup ingredients, judging from the way they kept crawling out of our pot. Dr. Kliman got involved in the "cooking" process, getting a splash of water in his eye from our soup pot at one point.

According to Dr. Kliman, of all the children in that particular Cornerstone class, I had an unusually good outcome. One proof was that by age six, I attended kindergarten and then first grade at our neighborhood public school instead of a special education class. I made some friends and did very well in class. However, with Fran's and Dad's problems, Mom saw to it that we all attended weekly therapy sessions. This became especially important in 1971, when our beloved Grandma Karina died and my parents' marriage began crumbling. By the time I turned eleven, I had already had regular appointments with family therapist Audrey Harbor weekly for about 5 years.

Back in my preschool days, just turning age six, I'd had an IQ test by the gold standard for that era and I got what seems to me an alarmingly low score of 80. (Dr. Kliman tells me he was thrilled that I got that "high" a score, because I had come into Cornerstone essentially untestable for IQ and without any language, three years earlier.) Two years later, my IQ had risen to 100. When I was a sixth-grader, my IQ was re-tested by Betty Buchsbaum, PhD. She was then my mother's therapist, but also a child psychologist. Everyone was thrilled with the results: a genius-level 149 IQ. Not too shabby for a kid once diagnosed as autistic and retarded! From my preteen point of view, it was both a blessing and a burden. You see, my well-meaning mother was so delighted with the results that she never failed to tell everyone within earshot about my 149 IQ—including my teachers, who'd been very impressed with my B+ grades until Mom's revelation about my high IQ made me look like a slacker. Yes, I know—we should all have such problems! Still, it was nicer to have that 149 IQ rating than not, once I got used to the idea that I had to live up to it by working up to my potential instead of resting on my laurels and staying in my comfort zone.

I've been shy and insecure all my life, but as I reached adulthood, I was able to hide my shyness well—perhaps too well. People rarely believe me when I tell them I'm shy. They say, "Oh, come on, you're not shy," scoffing good-naturedly when I insist that I am. I can act outgoing when I want and need to be; it's almost as if I'm putting on a façade, my "game face," as Dad used to say. I really have to work myself up to being outgoing and talking to people, even personnel behind counters in stores, but I can bluff my way through it, and as I do so, I manage to temporarily convince myself that I'm not shy.

Despite my shyness, I still made friends in school, summer camp, and Girl Scouts. I've remained close with a number of friends I made back in my college days and in my writers' workshops. In fact, I met two of my closest longtime friends back in junior high school and high school, respectively. Come to think of it, they were as quiet as I was, but perhaps I was the least quiet in our little crowd; as my dad used to say, "In the valley of the blind, the one-eyed man is king." Perhaps as a result of battling shyness, I usually found myself drawn to people who were either outgoing and bubbly, or quiet and low-key but still warm. We were always going to each other's houses, and we considered ourselves each other's best friends.

I'm happy I've been able to make friends with the friends I do have, and most of my friends are people I've known for a long time. For that matter, back when I was a child, neighborhoods seemed to have more of a sense of community. While most families had more than one child, it seemed like there were enough children in each age group for every kid to have several friends his/her age, whether they were tots, "tweens," or teens. All the kids seemed to hang out together and were involved in more or less the same activities, so making friends was generally easier than it seems to be now. Moreover, the neighborhoods where I spent much of my childhood were closely knit Italian-American communities with lots of grandparents, aunts, uncles, and cousins who lived within walking distance or, at most, only a short drive away. There was always a place to go after school, or if your mom had to go out, there was always somebody you could be with. It was a different world back then, easier to make friends and keep friends. I'd like to think that's one reason there seemed to be fewer dysfunctional families and disaffected young people around, although the more cynical among us may feel people have been troubled all along and that we're simply better at diagnosing emotional problems nowadays.

While I've had problems and made missteps just like anybody else, I'm pleased to report that I've handled challenges productively and grown up to lead a responsible life. After I graduated from college with a B.A. in Communications in 1985, I held down a series of jobs, mostly media-related. My first job out of school was in sales and programming departments. After 2 years, I tried my hand at working in low-budget horror films with 2 freelance opportunities. In the first, I worked as the Production Coordinator; in the second, my job was in Craft Services (a.k.a. providing food for the cast and crew on the film set). While it didn't pay as well as the office-based Production Coordinator job, I nevertheless wanted the experience of actually working on the set.

The jobs I liked best usually involved writing and editing in some way, such as when I edited and occasionally wrote package copy and other marketing material copy for movies on home video. My boss remained my friend even after the company moved to California and occasionally employed me as a research assistant and interview transcriber for his articles and his non-fiction book, I also loved my work at the now-defunct comic book company where, in addition to working in the sales department, I also wrote weekly newsletters, as well as character profiles in a section of a dark urban fantasy comic. My long-term temp stint in the offices of several other trade publications was also rewarding, in terms of both experience and monetary gain.

I write fiction, too. I've done that since childhood, in fact, just for the fun of it. I've been published, but only paid in free copies. Lately I've begun submitting my stories for publication again, so we'll see if I can turn my source of enjoyment into a source of income as well. Another source of enjoyment for me is movies—writing about them as well as watching them. From 2000 to 2002, I ran many film reviews on a website which is no longer active. Even writing for pay isn't a gold mine (unless my fiction miraculously gets onto the best-seller lists someday) but with my combined freelancing and office work, I made $30,000 a year at my peak before I became Maggie's stay-at-home mom after her birth in October 1996.

Those who knew me as a preschooler at Cornerstone might not have imagined me having a child of my own someday, but our little Maggie is here, happy, and thriving. Whatever one's physical and emotional health history and capabilities, becoming a parent is a big responsibility and an even bigger adjustment. Having a child has its joys, to be sure, but there's no denying it also turns your life inside out. Parenthood is great, don't get me wrong, but prepare to work hard and change your priorities! As far as my husband and I are concerned, it's all been worthwhile; Maggie quickly became the center of our lives, and lifestyle adjustments aside, we wouldn't have had it any other way.

Even when Maggie turned out to have developmental challenges similar to my own, because of my experiences at Cornerstone, the situation wasn't as daunting to us as it might have been to a parent who hadn't dealt with such issues herself. My husband Vin and I were on high alert to signs of dysfunction in Maggie, as were our relatives. Maggie was a smart, quick baby, but when she was about 2½ years old, we all began to notice that she was having trouble listening and following instructions. Even more worrisome, when we had her around other children her age at playgrounds, we realized how far behind her speech development was. While other kids around her age were starting to make short sentences, Maggie was crying, grunting, and pointing to objects that had caught her eye, only forming an occasional word while other children chattered away. When excited or bored, she'd begin what I later learned was referred to by developmental specialists nowadays as "self-stimulating" movements, the same kind of unusual arm-flapping and toe-walking I'd done at Maggie's age.

When Maggie was in preschool, her problems were thrown into stark relief. She did fine when playing by herself, but when called upon to interact with the group, she never quite managed it. The teacher would ask her to "use your words" when she was trying to tell her something, but Maggie had no words to use. My mother noticed this, too, as did my brother Larry, who is now an engineer. My sister-in-law Rosalie, a nurse, also commented on Maggie's developmental delays. Larry and Rosalie suggested that Maggie be evaluated at, of all places, the Kennedy Child Study Center, where I'd had my own evaluation as a toddler. It was only about 20 minutes' drive from our home, and as a public school, Kennedy didn't cost anything, so we figured we had nothing to lose.

The Kennedy Child Study Center's test results were like a déjà vu experience. Maggie's scores showed her to be very bright in some ways, but she also showed autistic tendencies. As had been the case with my toddler self, Maggie's speech and comprehension were well below those of other children her age. The Kennedy staff assured Vin and me that once Maggie improved in those areas, her interaction with other children would get better as well. She began attending Kennedy's preschool program for five days a week. Before long, our little girl's speech and interaction showed marked improvement. At first she was parroting back dialogue or commercials she'd heard on TV rather than having actual conversations about real-life situations, but it was an improvement over whining and grunting. We gradually got Maggie saying more situation-appropriate things by continuing to talk with her face-to-face, gently but firmly steering her back when she got off-course verbally. We made it a point not only to attend every evaluation meeting, but also to take Maggie to and from school ourselves so we'd have more opportunities to talk in person with her teachers about her progress and find out what we could do at home to help.

To our joy and relief, our efforts began to pay off. Soon it became apparent that Maggie was the most high-functioning student in her Kennedy class. By the time she began kindergarten at a local public school, Maggie was doing so well that after one week, she was promoted from special education to the inclusion program, where mainstream students and high-functioning developmentally challenged children like Maggie were taught together in the same classroom by a team of mainstream teachers and inclusion aides, with a ratio of five children to each adult. Since Maggie is feistier and more forthright than I was as a child, I believe that this, in addition to updated approaches to therapy, has helped her to overcome her developmental challenges more readily.

Our experiences with Maggie were also helpful when, in 1998, Vin and I became the guardians of our then-15-year-old niece, Katie who joined our household as a kind of adopted second daughter. Katie had a big impact on our nuclear family because she had been abruptly bereaved when her adoptive mother (my husband's mother) died of complications from a stroke caused by an undiagnosed brain tumor. Until then, Katie had quite innocently become accustomed to being babied, and adding her to our household was a big adjustment for all of us. After all, in addition to losing her mother figure, Katie had gone from being the only child still at home to becoming part of a household with two parents and a toddler who needed extra attention; once the star of the show, Katie was now another member of the ensemble. As a result, Katie had to become accustomed to helping out around the house and applying herself at school, we had to get used to having a teenager under our roof years before we expected to, and thanks to the magic of drywall, our one-bedroom apartment suddenly had a small second bedroom where our dining area had been. The new living situation had good aspects, too. Katie got along great with Maggie and was an excellent babysitter when the need arose, her grades improved exponentially when she moved in with us, and she went on to business school and got a part-time job and income of her own. By the time our family moved to Pennsylvania in 2001 as a result of Vin's company relocating, Katie was a more mature, responsible girl than she'd been when we first took her under our wing. Today Katie lives in California and is happily married.

My parents had already been divorced for about 20 years and both were married to other people by the time my father died of cancer in 1994. While I wasn't as close to my father as I was to my mother, I got along well with him, particularly once I reached adulthood. I'd also had a warm, affectionate relationship with my brother, Larry, until one day, out of the clear blue sky, he and his wife Rosalie simply cut off all contact with his friends and with our side of the family (they remained close to Rosalie's family, however). It wasn't as if some kind of argument or dramatic event occurred that you could point to as the reason for the rift; it was simply that one day he was in touch with us, the next day he wasn't returning calls. For 11 years, my brother Larry ignored all attempts to contact him, including my wedding invitation, emerging only to visit my father in the hospital and attend his funeral; he continued to be distant and unresponsive with family and friends he ran into at these functions. Larry continued to avoid us until shortly after Maggie's birth.

This makes me wonder if there's a genetic predisposition (or as Dr. Kliman has described it, "a negative talent") in our family towards extreme social withdrawal and tendencies towards autism-like symptoms. These tendencies seem especially pronounced on Mom's side of the family. Some of our cousins' children have had developmental challenges similar to Maggie's, particularly regarding speech. Happily, they are responding to treatment as splendidly as Maggie has. To help my daughter continue her great progress,

I want to pick up on any of her potential trouble spots the way my mom and therapists did with me when I was a child.

I enjoy happy, constructive relationships with my husband, friends, and most family members. Having met in New York City at improvisational comedy classes in 1985, Vin and I were simpatico from the start. We quickly began dating and became engaged on our third date, although we didn't actually marry until 1989, since we wanted to finish school and save up money to start a household. Throughout our marriage, Vin and I have boosted each other's self-esteem and made it a point to plan things and solve problems together. Vin and I have become more responsible since Maggie came into our lives—of course, if having a child doesn't make you responsible, nothing will! I think we've grown up a lot and we're basically happy and content with each other. We've both been very active, attentive and emotionally involved with Maggie's life, always making it a point to get to know her teachers and friends and their parents.

I felt a kinship with Maggie from the start, beyond the usual parent-child bond. Perhaps it was because she reminded me of my young self in so many ways. Maggie even looks like I did when I was her age; of course, being hopelessly biased, I think she's even prettier than I was. She's such a charming child that it's hard not to love her—and bless her, she's starting to realize it. Even people who claim they're not "child people" always take a shine to Maggie, perhaps because she is as outgoing and affectionate as she is beautiful—and such a ham! Maggie enjoys singing, dancing (her own improvisations—she doesn't follow instructions well enough yet to take formal dancing lessons), and acting out stories she's seen in movies and on TV. Maggie's tendency to imitate what we call "TV talk" was worrisome to therapists until she began using it in situations where it was actually appropriate, selling it in a deliberate attempt to make people laugh. When they do, Maggie claps her hands and chirps, "See! I made you happy!

It was Maggie's outgoing nature that made the physicians and therapists who examined her decide to change her diagnosis from full-tilt autism to Asperger's Syndrome, and recently downgraded further to ADHD. Maggie's intelligence and inquisitive nature made them sit up and take notice, too. She'll happily sit for hours and tinker with items, putting them in their places, trying to figure out what makes them work. Maggie also likes to act out stories with her dolls and plush toys, and these stories let me know she's very aware of what goes on around her. Maggie doesn't miss a beat; she's like a one-woman entertainment center. In fact, life is more fun for all of us now that we've learned how to deal positively and productively with problems instead of merely dwelling on them.

It's a privilege to tell you this true story and give encouragement to other families. Maggie's splendid adaptation and my own four decades of a productive and happy life, shows how far we have come in the treatment of autism spectrum disorders. Rather than merely dwelling on our problems, I trust my story can help show the way to actually solving them.

AFTERWORD BY GILBERT KLIMAN, MD:
A DISCUSSION OF DORIAN'S RECOVERY

Looking back on my case treatment notes, I think both Dorian and her mother came back to life with Reflective Network Therapy. Her depressed mother was at first ill-equipped to deal with an autistic child, but became emotionally stronger, richer and frank with supportive guidance. Dorian in turn became interactive and playful. Examples are of Dorian's lively fantasies of ant and worm soup, pretending with another girl to pee like a boy, identifying herself anatomically, developing an interest in getting married, and practicing stories of being a bride. I am led to wonder: Could Dorian have recovered from symptoms of serious autism and apparent mental retardation just as well as a result of an individual psychotherapy? If so, why doesn't it happen more often with children suffering from severe developmental interferences?

Reflective Network Therapy is a cognitively and clinically effective method for some children with autism. The method's particular effectiveness with Pervasive Developmental Disorders is shown by case histories and consecutively studied series of children like that of Dorian. Autism is a disorder of interpersonal relations and cognition. It is etiologically, almost certainly, a brain disorder. It has probable genetic origins, as in Dorian's case, and tends to show up in family histories. It is markedly male chromosome related, occurring predominantly and usually most severely in males. Dorian and her daughter probably had a less severe form than they might have had they been

History of IQ Changes: Dorian Tenore-Bartilucci			
Test Type	Age	Notes	Full Scale IQ
Untestable	2.75	Severe Autism, with apparent retardation at beginning of treatment.	Untestable
WISC	6		80
WISC	10		100
WISC	12	No symptoms of Autism, Superior IQ	149

Table 4.1. Other Children Treated with RNT Have Rapid Leaps in Cognitive Development. RNT's Averages 14 to 28 Points (Full Scale IQ Scores) Upon Retesting. Dorian's Rise from Presumed Retardation and Multiple Symptoms of Very Severe Autism to a Full Scale IQ Score of 149 Following Early Intervention with RNT Treatment was an Astounding Development

male.There is some homology (a distant similarity) between autism and cerebral palsy. In autism there are affective neuronal processing and mainly affect modulating brain system defects and abnormalities. In cerebral palsy there are mainly motor neuronal processing and brain system defects deficiencies. In cerebral palsy the affective modulating systems are mainly spared, although there are some affective system aspects. In autism the motor systems are mainly spared, although there are some motor aspects of the disorder. The most disabling autistic pathologies probably are in dysfunctions of the limbic system, the hippocampus and the connections between hemispheres (Just et al., 2004, 2007).

The role of deficient mirror neurons (Iacoboni, 2005) must also be considered, as their activities are a substrate for one person learning about the minds of others. Their influence is a lead to identification of one human being with another. Identificatory processes require mirror neuronal richness and intactness. From the motor identifications children build with adults and peers, and for which mirror neurons are required, a subtle representation of facial and bodily manifestations of emotion is built. Without learning and representing how other people feel and behave under affective stimuli, the autistic child has little representation of emotional models, no templates for their production and comprehension, and no empathy. The child cannot have a theory of the mind of others unless that theory begins with his viewing and mirroring in her or his own brain neuronal systems what is going on in the interpersonal world. Rehabilitation of both brain based disorders—cerebral palsy and autism—is to some extent possible and in some vigorously treated cases can be remarkably good. Significant rehabilitation of cerebral palsy, in its motor spheres, is commonplace.

As vividly demonstrated in Dorian's story, significant early rehabilitation of the affective processing systems of autistic children is possible, especially in preschool years. With a bereaved, depressed mother, processing of positive affective relationships in school was life-saving for Dorian. Such recoveries could become more common. We have several videotaped examples of such rehabilitation. In milder cases these can sometimes occur in as little as eight months of intensive analytically oriented in-classroom treatment, combined with parent role modeling and frequent guidance, all occurring without medication. Reflective Network Therapy yields IQ and clinical gains for children in several diagnostic categories as well as for children with pervasive developmental disorders. Elsewhere in this book I have detailed the cognitive and CGAS data from a prospective and controlled study of 10 consecutive Cornerstone treated preschoolers with autism spectrum disorders. The lack of IQ gains in six consecutive control children with this brain-based disorder who were untreated is very significant statistically.

All the differential data outcomes suggest to us that the underlying brain functions as well as personalities of children treated with Reflective Network Therapy may now be very different from those of the comparable untreated children. That's what Dorian's recovery also suggests to us.

Chapter Five

An Aggressive, Cruel Boy Becomes an Empathic, Socialized Learner

INTRODUCTION TO THE CASE STUDY OF "JAY"

This early case study shows the use of many basic features of Reflective Network Therapy's in-classroom treatment process as it is applied today. In-depth illustrations of classroom events as well as the detailed case history make it a rich clinical source for current practitioners. Examples of dynamic, historic, and transference interpretations are given. The differentiated role of therapeutic teachers and therapists is evident, as is the role of teachers as recipients of children's emotions. Here we present Jay's case history (first published in *The Psychoanalytic Study of the Child* (Kliman 1970). It was the second peer-reviewed publication and the first methodologically comprehensive article focusing entirely on the use of Reflective Network Therapy. The method was then called and written about as The Cornerstone Method, so, for simplicity's sake so I will generally retain that term in this iteration.

Several criteria for judging the existence of an insight directed classroom process are explained in this essay. The originally unexpected clinical effectiveness of Reflective Network Therapy becomes evident in the case of Jay who presented as a severely anxious, hostile, behaviorally disturbed and multiply traumatized boy.

Jay arrived as a Cornerstone patient in our first year of operating a Cornerstone Preschool in New York. Jay [name disguised] was a Cornerstone classmate of Charles whose story is told in chapter 7. At times, Jay feared the head teacher much as he feared his mother. He developed very useful fantasies about the teachers, and some of those fantasies were the subject of interpretation. By the time he finished one year of treatment, formerly dangerous Jay was able to attend a regular school for half the day and Cornerstone therapeutic preschool for the other half. Jay eventually went on to experience academic success beginning in elementary school which he sustained throughout high school. I stayed in touch and know that he also did well in college and with his graduate studies. Many children treated by the method described here experience significant gains which support rapid transitions such as Jay was able to make. Jay's case is presented in detail below as "One Child's Cornerstone Treatment."

Questions a therapist might ask while reading this account are numerous. For example, considering that the child's therapist spent only 15-20 minutes a day with the patient for two years, one might ask whether the material was as rich and whether the treatment as effective as a classical child analysis conducted daily for two years. I thought the answer was "Yes", as did my supervisor, Marianne Kris, M.D. She was also supervising me in other more orthodox methods of analyzing children one on one.

At the time Jay came for treatment, there were already daily sessions going on in our therapeutic preschool, with a therapist in the classroom at least an hour and a half each day. Two teachers were present. The teachers did the bulk of weekly parent guidance, and the classroom therapist saw parents once a month. As is essential for Reflective Network Therapy, all the children's individual psychotherapy sessions occurred only in the midst of classroom activities, with child patient peers witnessing and sometimes contributing to the index child's sessions. As happened with Jay's complex and deep interactions with his classmate, Charles, the children are often invaluable to one another as receptacles for each other's projections, fantasies, and as stimulators of verbal and play expression. I wonder if I could have understood and helped these two boys as well without the help each gave the other and me.

Children of several diagnostic categories were being treated together in Jay's classroom. The aggressive impulsivity of some unusually dangerous and aggressive children, (like Jay) could be readily contained by the teachers as they gained experience working with disturbed pupil-patients. The children's real life assaultiveness was visible to the classroom therapist who could deal with it interpretively on-the-spot rather than hours, days or a week after an event (as is usual in dyadic psychoanalytic therapy).

The Andrus Children's Center in White Plains, New York eventually took over operation of what was formerly The Center for Preventive Psychiatry, where Jay was treated by our method. The "Cornerstone" project is still ongoing there in a less than full form. The original "Cornerstone" service we conducted at this location was probably the first application of daily psychoanalytically oriented treatment conducted for hundreds of sessions, over as long as one, two or three years per child patient, conducted entirely within a classroom group. When we treated Jay, some procedural elements of the Reflective Network Therapy method were not yet fully developed. Not yet fully deliberate and systematic aspects of the Cornerstone method at that time were: (1) structured total regularity of network briefings and debriefings before and after each child's individual session; (2) regular use of interpretation of a child's resistance to analytic work, including his or her avoidance of proximity to the analyst; and (3) full appreciation of the entire classroom interpersonal network of peers as well as teachers and parents as a mentalizing influence, associated with cognitive growth and rises in IQ scores,

In retrospect, we think Anna Freud noticed an aspect of the improvement we only later were convinced was happening in the children's cognitive development. Ms. Freud read a draft of my essay on Jay before its publication in 1975 in the volume of which she was then editor. She commented to her co-editor Lottie Newman (Newman, personal communication, 1969) that the child patient used extraordinarily grown up language and concepts. Newman conveyed that observation to me as a possible criticism of the accuracy of the quotations I attributed to the child. Thus, Anna Freud's comment challenged us to document the accuracy of our reportage. As a fortunate result, we soon began videotaping the Cornerstone work. A wealthy grandfather, grateful for improvements he saw, donated our first video apparatus. It was a remote controlled. helical scan black-and-white recorder using large and quite fragile cellulose tapes. Though almost all of those tapes have turned to iron oxide powder, a few bits survived. The modern color video equipment which followed has permitted The Children's Psychological Health Center to develop an archive of over 300 hours of RNT treatments to be preserved and transferred to long-lived digital video disks. (See Appendix A for information about authorized access to our videotaped treatment session archives; see Appendix B for more information about training and visit the training section our agency's website for more information.)

The material below is presented here almost in its original form as published under the title "Analyst in The Nursery: Experimental Application of Child Analytic Techniques in a Therapeutic Nursery: The Cornerstone Method" (Kliman, 1970). The original case study has been minimally edited for the purposes of this book, including clarity for the general reader with some information which is fully detailed elsewhere in the book omitted. Some sections which might appear repetitious of material presented elsewhere in the book actually include additional information; other information remains intact as it presents specific aspects of the Cornerstone classroom context as it impacted Jay's successful therapy.

In this essay, I discuss one of the modalities employed at The Center for Preventive Psychiatry, emphasizing how certain child analytic techniques are used right in the classroom.

THE ANALYTICALLY SUPERVISED NURSERY:
EARLY CORNERSTONE METHOD DEVELOPMENT

When the Center for Preventive Psychiatry was established in 1965, an analytically supervised nursery was developed. Called the Cornerstone School, the nursery provided (1) primary preventive service as a fortifying milieu for highly stressed healthy preschool children, particularly those suffering from recent bereavement; and (2) secondary preventive service through early life treatment of emotionally disturbed preschool children. I extensively evaluated each child and family before admission to the nursery. Thus, each patient and family had some rapport with me from the beginning. In addition, the children regularly had individual sessions with me in the classroom where I observed them each day.

Within the first few weeks of treatment in the Cornerstone classroom, each child persistently related to me intensely. Several children talked regularly to me about their symptoms. Several had marked reactions to my arrival and departure. They spoke of me after I had left, both in school and at home. Some children told me their dreams in the classroom. Soon a marked thematic continuity in each child's communications became evident. After a few weeks I cautiously began to respond with interpretive comments akin to my usual analytic work with young children. The experiment was then pursued not only for its clinical value, but also for the scientific value of learning what phenomena would occur.

The early experiences eventually led to the development of a clinical method which combines child analysis and early childhood education. It is a technique with precedents in analytic work with residential and hospitalized patients, in life-space interviews on wards, diagnostic observation within nurseries, and in much collaboration between educators and analysts. (Redl, 1959; Gratton, LaFrontaine, and Guibeault, 1966; Speers, 1965; A. Freud, 1966; Neubauer and Beller, 1958 and Foulkes, 1964) Yet in none of these precedents did an analyst's work with young children evolve into a persistent, daily, systematic effort to use analytic techniques synergistically within the preschool educational process. In the Cornerstone method, treatment is performed only in the classroom. Two early childhood educators are in charge of the classroom educational activities. The teachers conduct a full-scale educational program, encouraging learning in all forms appropriate to the children's abilities and developmental level, with a warm socializing process very much in the foreground. Parents are given guidance by the head teacher each week, individually, and the therapist meets with each parent at least once a month.

As in a regular preschool, the teacher makes no interpretations to the child. Whatever insight she may have into the unconscious sources or connections of his behavior, she does not verbally convey it to the child. That role is left strictly to the Cornerstone analyst. The teacher has a clearly defined educational role, channeling impulses into useful activities and creating and maintaining discipline. In the midst of a treatment situation which liberates children's impulses, this is indeed a very demanding role, and one which the analyst is glad to have performed by an expert. The analyst (or analytically oriented therapist) is relieved of the many educational functions he exercises when alone with a young child in his office. When necessary, teachers immediately find appropriate outlets for or restrict a child's energies. Previously defended-against impulses can be harnessed by peer activities, or channeled into healthy curiosities and ardent desires to acquire skills. The teachers are on hand when a child is ready to learn, to build, to create, to grow emotionally by the numerous routes which good education provides.

Although the time the therapist spends individually with each child is short, the daily frequency seems to speed up the process of accruing mental health gains. Fifteen to twenty hours a week of carefully observed classroom communicative play and fantasy process, combined with social and educational activities of many dimensions, also enable the therapist to observe and understand unconscious trends over a period of time and in depth. It then becomes feasible to validate or discard lines of interpretation and clinical hypotheses. The analyst is present in the classroom 90 minutes to 2 hours daily when school is in session. [See Chapter 3 for requirements and exceptions regarding the therapist's professional qualifications.]

What goes on after the therapist leaves is in a sense "extra-analytic," but is nevertheless a clear continuation of treatment. The analyst has knowledge of those many hours a week which the child spends with his teachers after the analyst has left as a result of daily briefings and weekly staff conferences. Even when the analyst is in the classroom, there is much that he cannot observe about all the children. But the teachers funnel a great deal of immediate information to the analyst. A particularly "ripe" or "clear" bit of play observed by a teacher is often conveyed to the analyst within a few moments. Such communications often are made after the analyst has worked with a particular child. His understanding fortified with this additional information, the analyst can deepen the previous work in subsequent therapy sessions with that child. Thus, nothing which occurs in the classroom is truly "extra-analytic." In addition to the on-the-spot messages, the teachers and analyst confer about each child's behavior several times a week, so each can use the other's observational powers in a very fresh way—often to sharpen thinking rather than for direct use with the child. Cultivation of the teachers' observational and receptive abilities is crucial for the method, which requires close supportive supervision by the analyst, and a deep sense of "teamness."

The teachers have an educational and guiding role with parents as well as with children. As with the children, they multiply the usefulness of the therapist's time in the parental communication and guidance process—by being his eyes and ears, and working under his supervision. Meeting weekly with each parent or family, the teacher gives educator-appropriate guidance, learns about current family events, expands her knowledge of the child's past development, and shares this information with the therapist, who meets only once a month with each family.

What of a child's need for privacy? We have found that a child rarely requires privacy with the therapist in order to convey a fantasy, behavior, or concern. All children understand that each child in the class is in treatment. They also know that the teachers will bring their own observations about the children to the therapist's attention. Occasionally, a child will ask to speak to the therapist privately. This happened, for example, in the case of a child who was soiling, and with another little boy who (because of his relationship with his younger brother) wanted exclusive contact with the therapist. Sufficient privacy can be achieved in a corner of the room. Once the child has seen that privacy can be obtained, it is interesting how rarely he utilizes it. Nor is there much sustained intrusiveness of one child into another's work. Intrusions and interferences are dealt with by education, often by interpretation, and by the children themselves. The fact that all the children are in treatment facilitates tolerance, acceptance, and respect for each other's treatment. (Any behavior which is seriously disruptive to individual session or to any classroom activity is generally managed by a teacher.)

Children who must retreat, withdraw, avoid, or otherwise resist dealing with processes stirred up by the treatment often do so by turning to educational and social activities. These activities, in turn, are not purely resistant by any means as they increase the therapist's understanding of each child. In older Cornerstone-treated children, emerging into latency, the use of educational and social means as retreats from the therapist is seen more frequently. The Cornerstone nursery classroom is set up in a standard form, and regular preschool classroom activities go on constantly. As in other preschools, activities are often structured to follow and take educational advantage of the child's interest. Toys and creative materials such as paint or play dough are generally available, as are other creative materials. Music may be playing, and cookies and juice are available when the children want them although we tend to have regularly scheduled times for snacks.

Through their observations of what children do before and after a therapeutic session, the teachers multiply a therapist's knowledge of the details of each child's mental life. Through exchanges of information with the child's therapist and parents, the teachers in turn are deepened in their understanding of each child's needs and abilities. Thus the efficiency with which teachers and therapist use their time with a child is increased—most notably for the child therapist—who could not see so many children as effectively without the help of the Cornerstone teachers.

When children interact erotically or aggressively with each other, this interaction may promote growth as well as being equivalent to acting out in the regular child analysis situation. On occasion there will be a synchronized similarity of resistances or defenses on the part of several children, especially when there is much separation anxiety, or in response to shared external factors such as the illness of a teacher or classmate, or a vacation. At these times we can interpret to several children almost simultaneously, but still in-dividualize the remarks so as to keep clear to each child the individual nature of the work he is doing with the analyst. Generally, however, there is a clear individuality of communicative styles and themes.

Within the classroom, using this method, the child resistant to direct, con-tinuous work with the therapist can pursue treatment work alone, internally, or in social play, or with a receptive and non-interpreting educator. Then the child can return for still deeper work at some mutually agreeable time later in the same session. Resistance is interpreted whenever possible—and therefore frequently. But the ready availability of social action and conversation with teachers and peers is developmentally syntonic with the low tension-binding capacity and low frustration tolerance of preschoolers.

A CROSS-SECTIONAL VIEW OF THE REFLECTIVE
NETWORK THERAPY (CORNERSTONE) METHOD

Having given a schematic description of this new application of child analytic techniques, I turn first to illustrative moments in a classroom of six children before describing Jay's treatment. The following examples are from 20 min-utes of an ordinary day in Cornerstone, in its second year, when the method already incorporated most of its basic current features. [Still missing from our functions in Reflective Network Therapy at this time was an appreciation of the importance of the network effect on cognition and IQ scores. Nor was there as much regularity of structuring of briefings and debriefings. Further, the analyst did not yet notice as much as in later years how much he was deal-ing with children's resistances to education and socialization interpretively.]

The children, 3 to 5 years of age, belonged to several diagnostic catego-ries. Leon, a 3-year-old, had been referred because of a behavior disorder manifested by frenetic, negativistic destructive acts. Charles, 4¼ years old, suffered from leukemia and a variety of neurotic manifestations such as clinging, enuresis and separation anxiety. Ted, at 3¾ years of age, was a bright, pathologically obstinate, adopted boy. At age 3, Keith was a pseudo-retarded mute and autistic child of severely unhappy parents. Anthony was a depressed foster child, a 3½-year-old insomniac.

Jay, an assaultive 4½-year-old with numerous problems including persistent cross-dressing behavior was a member of this classroom. As in Charles's case, presented in this book, Jay's cross-dressing lessened of its own accord when he dealt with underlying disturbances. In both cases, cross-dressing tendencies were symbolic expressions of conflict and pain arising from their inner and interpersonal lives. In an unstressed and emotionally healthy boy such cross-dressing behavior might be simply one expression of early childhood gender preference.

Cornerstone "morning group" children arrived at 9:00 A.M. and stayed until noon. Each child was brought to class by a primary caregiver, usually his mother. The opening moments of interaction with a primary caregiver are invaluable for ascertaining a child's mood. We note the way each child leaves his mother and greets his teachers, analyst, and fellow patients. Parents often say a brief word to the staff about current events or behavior changes before leaving.

This day Leon was surly. His father brought him and, in the doorway, mentioned to me that Leon had wet his bed the previous night. The information reverberated in my mind with earlier episodes of bed wetting, usually connected with arguments between Leon's strife-ridden parents. Earlier that morning the teacher had had her weekly conference with Leon's parents and learned of a furious quarrel which Leon had witnessed. She had already informed me briefly of these events. At first Leon refused to enter the classroom, but the teacher coaxed him in.

I had been chatting with Teddy about a birdhouse on which Teddy had worked for the third session in a row. I commented on the care Teddy took to make the house strong, and how Keith, who also had carefully fed some birds outdoors on the previous day, was like a parent who took very good care of a family of children. Ted and I discussed how much the birdhouse feeding and caring for the birds were related to Ted's father's temporary absence, Ted's previous fantasies of abandonment, and an episode of nightmares Ted had had during another paternal absence. For five minutes Ted glued the roof quietly and did not otherwise spontaneously express his thoughts.

As I began working with Leon, I remarked to him, his father (and the class in general): "It's another one of those upset days, Leon, when you can hardly face being with us. Maybe I can help you because now you and I know more about your troubles." Leon interrupted here and told me, "Come to the fireplace, Dr. Kliman." Going with Leon to the fireplace, I helped the child light some wooden sticks to make pretend fire, and then listened to Leon's story of the "people" (play-dough figures) he was "melting" and "killing" in the pretend fire. Leon imagined how very hot the people must be, and I commented on how horribly filled with hot feelings they must be. After a while, I made a gentle allusion to how somebody might even think of cooling the hot feelings with water, like a fireman, and later also alluded to the fact that the fire might be special for a boy whose father, like Leon's, was a fireman. Leon said the people were arguing, and he hated them.

As the people "burned, died, and melted", I mentioned the parents' argument of the night before. Leon responded by saying that once his mommy had beat up his daddy, but then Leon could not proceed any further. He wandered about the classroom so restlessly that I suggested the upset feelings and ideas could be talked about some more in a little while or whenever Leon was ready. Later in the session, Leon resumed the theme of parental fighting. He spontaneously added that the fight he remembered had taken place when the family moved. (I already knew that this move had occurred over a year ago.) Leon then gave an association related to the morning of the day of this session. He had "scared Natalie" (his baby sister) this morning—put a blanket over her head when she was in the crib. I interpreted:

> *That made her feel lost She didn't know where she was. And on the day your parents were fighting a year ago, you felt lost because your family was moving to a strange place. When your parents screamed at each other last night that made you feel lost again. You wanted to feel like the boss of that lost feeling, so you made Natalie feel lost.*

Leon listened with rapt attention, and then played at covering a girl doll with a blanket. He offered no further verbalizations. In the next few days, however, he progressed in his intellectual functioning—an important step for this child, who presented with problems of intellectual inhibitions. He questioned his parents probingly about the death of his grandmother, amazing them with his curiosity.

In the early weeks of working with the group, the analyst's transition from one child to another often led to resentful feelings being vented by the child who was left. These responses were interpreted as they arose. Still later, it was often possible to interpret resistances and regularly have long periods of deep work with each child. Moreover, as we gained experience in the use of the Cornerstone method, periods of resistance were no longer sufficient cause for turning to another patient, and the analytic work correspondingly profited. Many transitions were actively induced by the children themselves, as the following episode shows:

Jay, an intellectually precocious boy who verbalized far more elaborately than most 4 1/2-year-olds, announced that he saw a lobster on a recent vacation. The lobster tried to pinch a child's behind. I said, "A child could have many thoughts about what happens if a lobster pinches his behind." Jay responded gravely that he thought the lobster would "pinch off his peenie and then he would have to make a pee-pee from his poo-poo." I reminded Jay that recently his worries about a boy losing his penis had frequently shown up in ideas about dangerous cracks in the floor that "pinch people" and doors that pinch people's fingers. Thereupon Jay walked away from me, apparently feeling a need for distance. He did not abandon the theme, however. He walked to the block corner and began to construct a "lobster" out of blocks, in full view of the analyst. I took Jay's walking away and the cessation of direct communication as a signal for momentarily easing my direct activity with the patient. I said to Jay, "It must be hard to continue now because the pinching lobster thoughts are upsetting." Jay then persisted in constructing a lobster. I later heard Jay's remarkable verbalization of the fantasy: Jay pensively wished he "could be a lady, because the lobster would give the boy's peenie away to a lady. So then if I was a lady, I would get my own peenie back."

This sequence shows that in respecting the child's defenses, but pointing them out to the child, the therapist had opened the way to a further elaboration of the warded-off fantasy.

ONE CHILD'S CORNERSTONE TREATMENT

The purpose of this section on one child's treatment is limited to describing some aspects of Cornerstone work which are like a regular child analysis. In addition to those analytic features, many other processes also occur in Cornerstone treatment—social, educational, supportive and corrective object relations, and the creation of an artificial family, to mention a few. The following brief definition of a child's analysis is useful when considering the phenomena to be described in Jay's Cornerstone treatment. If successfully established, a child's analysis will elicit unconscious material; produce insight into major current and past problems or symptoms; produce transference phenomena; produce a transference neurosis; give the child marked increase of behavioral repertoire; and produce symptomatic, behavioral, and characterological improvement in correlation with insight and working through themes. With this definition in mind, I proceed with the special purpose of the case presentation that follows: to describe the child analytic features of the treatment. It will then be possible to discuss what happens when a psychoanalytic process occurs simultaneously with social, educational, and other therapeutic parameters.

Jay's treatment is chosen for several reasons. Jay was one of the first children treated by our method. His father died suddenly, 6 weeks after Jay entered our school, so that his treatment had both preventive and therapeutic features. Jay had an unusual ability to play in a symbolically expressive way, verbalize his ideas and memories, and collaborate affectively and to employ self observation, all of which facilitated his mourning and an exploration of unconscious aspects of his difficulties. [Now, still further weight is given to his successful treatment because we were able to follow Jay's development until age 13. Then, at age 40, Jay contacted me, reporting that he remembered me and Cornerstone. Jay reported that he was having a satisfying personal life, and was professionally productive in a creative field.]

Jay's Case: Background

Jay was 4½ years old when his mother first sought help. Jay's regular nursery school teachers reported that he attacked other children wildly, endangering them by hitting them with sticks and rocks. In class he persistently costumed himself as a woman, swishing his hips femininely. He also exposed his genitals and tried to undress other children. He had no friends, and often said that other children hated him. Consultation revealed that dressing up in feminine clothes began at home with an intense interest in his mother's high-heeled shoes at age 2½. His father became angry upon seeing Jay in women's shoes, and Jay would caution his more tolerant mother, "Don't tell Daddy." Jay also wore his mother's pearl necklaces. His body movements often took on a feminine quality when, draped in towels or sheets, he pretended to be a queen, princess, or witch. Jay frequently harmed himself and was often harmed by his mother. He sometimes ran outdoors in cold weather wearing only his pajamas. Once while he had an upper respiratory infection and was warned that he might get much sicker, he ran out in the freezing rain right after a bath. Since early infancy the mother had been unable to restrain herself from hurting Jay. At home, Jay's mother often pinched or squeezed Jay's buttocks so hard that they were black and blue. While pinching Jay, his mother would squeal, "Mine, mine!" Jay also squeezed his own buttocks while saying emphatically, "Mine, mine!"

During his mother's pregnancy with his brother (born when Jay was 3½years), Jay became notably destructive. He jumped onto a small table, which obviously could not bear his weight, and broke through it. Quite deliberately, he crayoned an entire terrace floor. On one occasion he punched 15 neat holes in a porch screen and 24 in another; and he could be relied upon to destroy household equipment whenever he was left alone with a maid. After his brother's birth, he was at first cuddly and affectionate with the baby, but soon cruelly hit, poked, and threw hard objects at him. He developed difficulty falling asleep, needed a night light, and early each morning would get into the father's side of the parental bed. His speech was marked by misarticulation of the sibilant "s" for which he substituted the "th" sound. Otherwise, his speech was clear, often pedantic, poetic, and pseudo-mature. He had an extraordinary vocabulary and syntax for his age. His social skills were contrastingly very poor. He had failed to develop any social play free of pushing, poking, and bullying other children—most of whom he towered over.

Jay was the product of an uneventful pregnancy during his mother's undergraduate years. His delivery interrupted her final examinations, but she quickly returned to them and managed to breast feed Jay until he was 3 months old. He was then weaned and left in the care of a succession of nannies. During his fourth month, the mother left on a vacation for several weeks. The nurse said that Jay was uncomplaining and smiled when smiled at. The mother recalled no stranger or separation anxiety during his first year. His motor development and other landmarks were unremarkable. Although he quickly was able to climb very well, Jay was kept in a small crib and a small playpen until he was 2½ years old. Family friends pressed the parents to give Jay a youth bed and let him have free run of the house.

A wrestler in college, Jay's father ran an enterprise related to feminine fashions. He was alternately gentle and rough with his boy. Although sometimes coy with friends, according to his wife, Jay's father nevertheless impressed me as an overtly masculine, serious, friendly, and as a genuinely concerned parent. Early in Jay's treatment the father decided that Jay was too excited by their bedtime ritual of wrestling and kissing bouts. He recalled that Jay once begged, "Please, let's not wrestle before I go to bed, because then I have bad dreams." Except for wrestling and vigorous morning cuddling in bed, father and son shared mostly quiet activities. Jay frequently asked his father to read Swiss Family Robinson. The two would go over a chapter and then tirelessly add stories of their own. Jay loved to use his father's carpentry tools, often assisting in house repairs and projects.

The father was filled with realistic plans for business expansions and personal growth. Shortly after Jay's treatment began, he undertook psychotherapy on his own, seeking to improve his relationship to the boy. He felt he had become too impatient with Jay, and that his anger was making the transvestite behavior worse. The weekend before his death in a plane crash, he told his wife that he had succeeded in thoroughly enjoying his two children's company even though they fought each other noisily. He began to speak gently to Jay, urging him to talk to me about the problem of dressing up as a girl, and impressed the mother with his new freedom from rancor. There was, however, a frightening carelessness on the father's part after one of the first sessions with his own therapist. While lighting a bonfire in the backyard, in view of his wife and Jay, he poured kerosene directly on the flames.

Jay's mother was a bright, attractive, earnest woman who inspired a benevolent, mildly parental feeling in both teachers and in me. Her intermittently harsh treatment and neglect of her first child were partly understood as resulting from preoccupation with her own needs and her identification with an older sibling who had been cruel to her. Her late childhood was marked by her mother's severe illness, aggravating her difficulty in achieving maternal maturity a few years later. She seemed determined to overcome many of her present difficulties, and entered analysis at our urging about a year after her child entered Cornerstone. The history of her pinching Jay was not entirely clear. She definitely pinched him black and blue during the first six months of his life, causing her husband to be very angry at her. Apparently the pinching continued, with somewhat diminished intensity, right up until the beginning of Jay's treatment. While pinching him, she would grind her teeth so hard that she actually chipped several teeth. At the same time she would exclaim, "I love you! I could eat you up! I eat boys. I think I'll eat your foot first."

Jay's First Treatment Session

My first session with Jay was an individual one. [In later years all Cornerstone evaluations occurred in the classroom.] He was a charming, serious, reflective child with an excellent vocabulary and a high level of information. He easily left his mother in the waiting room, where she was in severe conflict over whether to tell me something. Finally (when Jay ran ahead) she whispered to me, "Jay wanted you to know that he touches his penis a lot because it itches. But then he said for me *not* to tell you."

After Jay's mother left the room, Jay concentrated on crafts material, especially finger painting. He was quite proud of the multicolored cheerful blots he made by folding the paper over onto the thick paint. Although he seemed generally at ease, he was quite concerned about dropping finger paint on my Formica table and on his clothes. He claimed that he was going to a party soon and his mother would not like his clothes messed. On the other hand, he went out of his way to drop globs of paint on the floor and did not seem distressed. He did not mention his concern over his penis at all, but told me his trouble was that other children hated him. He thought that his mother hated him because he hit children. He thought that I might hate him too.

Treatment Progresses: Themes Continue to Emerge and Develop

After a few days in the classroom, Jay frankly communicated his feminine wishes. He told me he had waked with a "mermaid feeling ... wanting to be a mermaid," and also wanting to catch a mermaid and give one to his father. He believed his father would like to have a mermaid, while his mother would like to have a regular fish, a perch. I pointed out to Jay that he felt like the kind of fish he knew would please his father. He was already apparently conveying fantasies symbolically communicative of his sexual problems, and beginning a substantial dialogue with the analyst.

Soon, an intriguing new fear emerged, which I began to suspect was part of the onset of a transference neurosis. Jay took special trouble telling me that he disliked cracks in floors and would like the whole school floor to be smooth. Something about the cracks made him feel upset at school. He clearly understood the analyst's task to help with such a problem. Simultaneously, he was showing me that his block buildings were very "tippy". When I pointed out that Jay was talking about tippy buildings just after talking about cracks that upset him, construction of tippy buildings became a long-continuing theme. When I suggested to Jay that perhaps he felt he was kind of tippy himself and not as strong as he would like to be, Jay became more aggressive with other children and adults in school and at home. Within 48 hours he caught two persons' hands in the cracks of doors which he slammed on their fingers. Jay also showed me that he wanted to catch another child's head in a crack between two tables. I interpreted that Jay was trying to make himself feel better by being in charge of this new trouble of frightening cracks, making other people afraid of cracks.

Jay's therapeutic alliance vacillated markedly at first, from positive to negative. He repeatedly told his parents he hoped I would help him stop "itching" his penis, and actually reduced the frequency of his genital masturbation. This reduction of autoerotic impulse discharge was an early indication that the treatment process could alter Jay's behavior into more frustration-tolerant states at home even while he was increasingly and impulsively discharging aggression in school. At the very least, the treatment process was beginning to shift Jay's most turbulent mental processes into the treatment situation and out of his home life. Whether the reduction of masturbation he hoped for was otherwise desirable is a separate question. At times he would seek me out for long sessions of quiet play with building blocks and serious talking. At other times the transference was so impulsively hostile or his love for me so defended against that Jay became assaultive. A conspicuous assault followed his discussion of feeling like a mermaid; about twenty minutes later he tried to kick me fiercely.

After a few weeks, Jay showed the treatment team an assortment of ways by which he caused other children to hate him. He was told that the teachers would help him control himself, while the analyst would try to help him understand himself, so that he could play with other children in a way that made them friendly. It was suggested to him that his way of acting with other children might not yet be completely under his control. For example, he would ask a child, "Do you like me?" and then hit the child with a block a few minutes later. Still later he would complain that the child hated him. He listened attentively when I pointed out that he seemed to be doing just the opposite of what he wanted to do. I consistently transformed Jay's behavior into narrative in order to help Jay transform his own behavior into thought and emotion rather than action that both endangered other children and kept him from getting a positive, desired benefit.

Before his father's sudden death (after which treatment continued) both his parents had become regular contributors to Jay's Cornerstone treatment, providing much extra-analytic information during interviews with me and the teachers. They reported that two cross-dressing episodes had occurred in close connection with seeing his mother undressed. After one observation, he immediately put on her pajamas. On another occasion he dressed in her high-heeled shoes after being kissed by her. Thinly disguised sexual longing for his father was expressed when he asked his father if he could make Jay float to the ceiling.

The day after his father's dangerous behavior with the fire and kerosene in the family's backyard, Jay confided in me about the event, but he was unable to talk about his father's part in the matter. In direct sequence he spoke of his own trouble that night, having pains in his legs and difficulty falling asleep. I was able to point out to him that there was probably some connection between these upsetting things and the upset in his legs, but did not try to interpret further.

As a baseline, it is important to note Jay's state of mind and the state of treatment just before his father died. Over a period of several weeks I had interpreted Jay's efforts to make other children afraid of cracks, which he himself feared. Some work had been done on that subject, in terms of a fear of female genitalia, only a few hours before his father's fatal crash. When I left the nursery school, Jay seemed to be responding to the interpretation of his classroom violence as a defense against his own dread of cracks. He took several cans of paint and made an awesome mess by spilling them about, then worked very hard helping to clean up, fearing the teacher would be angry and tell his parents. He soon spat a whole mouthful of water on the floor. A little while later, Jay abruptly jumped on another child, banging the child's head on the floor and had to be restrained by the teacher. Jay looked very worried, and was told by the teacher that he could not be allowed to hurt other children, and that this was the kind of trouble that Dr. Kliman and she had been trying to help him with.

Jay then took off his sweater very deliberately, hung it carefully in his cubby, walked backward a few steps, then ran hard and fast straight into the far concrete wall, ramming it with his forehead. His teacher was horrified. Jay fell to the floor and sobbed. While being comforted, he allowed himself to be held close. After a long spate of perspiring profusely, he calmed down, looked up at his teacher, and said, "I love you, Mrs. Gorin," remaining tranquil for the rest of the morning. This was the first time a furiously self-hurting tendency had been apparent.

The interpretive work concerning his fear of female genitalia had led to many rapid shifts of a turbulent nature. His use of identification with the aggressor changed to an alternation of that defense with aggression turned against the self. Object relations moved to testing of the teacher as a possible transference object for his oedipal love. A shift of symbolic focus regarding cracks had also occurred, with displacement upward from genitalia to the head. From the anxiety-stimulating phallic impulses with regard to cracks he regressed libidinally to the predominantly anal-sadistic impulse level of enraged attacking and messing. From an ego point of view he shifted momentarily to reaction formation against the liberated sadistic impulses, briefly being clean and compliant. He soon returned once more, libidinally and symbolically, to a phallic concern with heads, but then turned aggression against himself. This was followed by an earlier kind of impulse expression—cuddling the teacher during story time, perhaps taking in the teacher's story reading as if it were comforting at an oral level, while also allowing an oedipal gratification.

Treatment Focuses on Jay's Responses to His Father's Sudden Death

Jay had been in Cornerstone treatment for six weeks when his father went on a business trip which ended in an instantly fatal airliner crash. The loss occurred at a phase of Jay's life when tolerance for painful affects was naturally poor. The work of mourning, aided by therapy though it was, had to go on at a slow pace and with low intensity of sadness and yearning for the lost father. After a brief initial phase of overt protest, ("I want my Daddy back!"), gross identificatory mechanisms dominated Jay's behavior. He played intently and intricately at being a daddy, far beyond the level and frequency of his prior play. Yet sadness was a definite, conscious, and persistent affect. Rapid, intense expressions also occurred of the need to cathect (emotionally invest in) new objects (including the analyst and teachers) far more quickly than would be expected with an older patient in mourning. The reality-testing aspects of mourning also went on piecemeal and were appropriate to his age.

Other post-bereavement trends observed were an increase in the frequency of the self-directed aggression, which had begun to emerge just prior to the loss. There was increased expression of magical thinking. Sublimatory activities, especially artistic expressions, deteriorated. His oedipal strivings became more gross and grandiose. Fantasy themes and play activities became heavily centered about the death, with details about smoke, fire, mystery, and searching. Both instinctual and ego regressive phenomena were evident, with increased greed for supplies, inability to share, and loss of achievements in frustration tolerance and object relations. Although gender identification with the mother had already been in evidence prior to the bereavement, increasing identification with some of her pathological defense mechanisms now emerged, especially in regard to her post-bereavement magical thinking about clairvoyant processes and the power of thoughts.

We wondered whether Jay would develop a permanent split in reality testing and retain a powerful fantasy of father still being alive. The mother's magical thinking and difficulties in impulse control seemed of great importance. They might further restrain the child's already weak functioning in the same areas. At this point it was not possible to say what the short-term and ultimate bereavement effects would be. We could predict, however, that without treatment, a phallic-phase child with transvestite tendencies would do much worse in the absence of his father's protective influence. Further, the partial coming true of his natural wish to possess his mother exclusively would burden him with extra guilt. Thus the task of assisting this much damaged boy to deal with the new insults to his development was formidable.

Our negative prognostic views were balanced by the vigor with which Jay pursued his therapeutic work. He showed great continuity of themes and a remarkable persistence in working them through despite the intervening bereavement. Continuing work on his female-identified thoughts, he expressed a complicated fantasy when he painted a girl with her head cracked open. He then accused me: "You cracked my little girl's head open!" A strange epithet which had rarely been used by him in the past, "Your head!" was now voiced rather frequently, angrily, and energetically. Three weeks after his father's death, angrily objecting to my efforts to interpret his aggressions against other children as a way of mastering his own fears, Jay threatened me: "Mrs. Gorin [the teacher] is going to come and kill you. She'll chop your head off with an axe!"

Following this, Jay stuck a small twig in a crack in the wooden side of the sandbox. He then wondered "who was the boss in school"—the teacher or the analyst? This was an exact parallel to his conscious concerns several weeks pre-bereavement over mother-versus-father dominance at home. His psychological life was increasingly becoming centered on the school, and, as happens often with the Cornerstone method, the child was using the personnel and his peers in the process of working through his conflicts. His fears of female genitalia and mother were being translated into fears of cracks and fears of what teachers could do to penises and men. As he gained some insight into his fears, a transformation of the related psychological processes became apparent. Instead of raw manifestations of catastrophic anxieties and discharge of impulsive behavior, more structured and more neutral states appeared. There were changes in his relations with people, particularly in the classroom. He began to appreciate other persons as complicated whole objects rather than need-satisfying or terrifying part objects.

Jay's Treatment Deepens

I shall now skip forward to a time when Jay's relationship to the reflective network team of helping adults was very well established. In the intervening half year much work had been done to reveal to Jay the origins of his intense castration anxiety as well as to facilitate his mourning. When Jay re-entered the Cornerstone School after the summer, his disruptive, poking, and scratching behavior had cleared sufficiently so that he could also attend a regular public kindergarten in the afternoons. At that time, three other children were entering his Cornerstone group—two for the first time. There was immediate evidence that Jay had elaborate, intense fantasies involving the Cornerstone School.

Jay believed he had seen a certain former Cornerstone child in public school, and seriously considered that the former classmate was using a disguise. The disguise theme was already understood by me as part of Jay's cross-dressing. I responded by reminding Jay that being in disguise, like disguising himself as a woman, was a familiar thought in Jay's mind. Then I dealt with the theme of an old friend being in Jay's public school class as a wish, interpreting that having an old Cornerstone friend in public school with him would make Jay feel happier and less lonely.

The next day Jay entered a fierce verbal competition with Charles, claiming, "I'm very smart," and trying to overwhelm Charles with an explanation of what happens "when two chemicals get together." I remarked that Jay had a lot of feelings about being smarter and knowing things about chemicals getting together, which were all very important to him. Jay responded by telling Charles and me that he had a collection of his deceased father's valuables, and in a few minutes added that he wished to "be" a certain uncle. This was

Jay's first expression of desire to be a particular grown man, and represented significant progress.

After I left the classroom the teachers (as usual) continued working with the children for an additional hour. They served as recipients, elicitors, and observers of a fantasy which apparently continued and deepened the masculine identification theme Jay had expressed earlier. He lay down on the floor, saying, *"I am dead."* Although the teachers were aware of the connection of this play to the earlier talk Jay had had with me about his dead father, in keeping with the method, they made no interpretation. They encouraged the expression of his concern in dramatic play and reported it to me before the next session. They also took note of the fact that Jay again lay on the floor and claimed to be "dead" when his mother arrived to pick him up and go home.

The next day Jay told me that he was not feeling well; he had a stomachache which had started on his way to school. Asked if he thought it could be because there was something on his mind which came up when he "thought about school and the things we work on together here," Jay said, *"That's right, there are a lot of things on my mind all night and I don't want to talk about them, but they bother me."* Jay soon revealed that, on the previous night, he had heard a loud noise when falling asleep and gradually unfolded the fantasy that creatures from outer space had come into his backyard. Perhaps they had come from Venus. If he could have gone out to see, maybe he would have found them, and they would have "antennae on their heads and be mean." I made an interpretation which was confirmed by Jay:

Therapist: *Although they were scary creatures and you thought they were mean, too. When a boy thinks his father is in outer space, a boy is lonely at night and even lonely at school during the day.*

Jay: *Like in heaven.*

Therapist: *A boy like that might sort of hope and sort of fear that a man from outer space would visit his backyard.*

In response, Jay expressed considerable interest in a male classmate's behind, which he tried to smear with play dough, and kicked a lady teacher in the behind (rather tentatively). He then wondered whether a certain toy rhinoceros would break easily.

Jay's drawing (Figure 5.1) is a good example of symbolic expressions which the therapist can interpret in the light of treatment themes. I spoke to Jay about the rhinoceros thoughts and the thoughts about the boy's behind, saying that Jay was worried about the boy getting hurt in his behind and the rhinoceros getting hurt in front. Perhaps Jay was "worried about a boy who wanted to stop being lonely and wanted to do things closer to other people

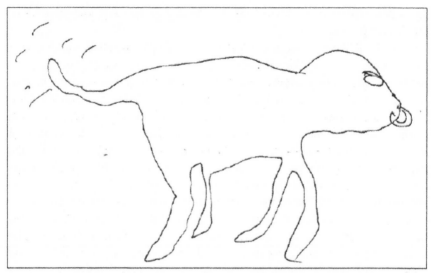

Figure 5.1. "Fighting rhino with nose ring." Jay's drawing is an example of symbolic expressions which the therapist can interpret in the light of treatment themes.

by putting fronts and behinds together, and who worried about what would happen then, and whether fronts and behinds could get hurt that way." This interpretation also used knowledge gained in the prior nine months of treatment during which Jay's poking of other children in the anal region had in part been understood as a wish for and fear of penile penetration of his anus. Apparently in response to the interpretation concerning the rhinoceros front and the boy's behind, Jay made an entirely new kind of block construction which differed essentially from his earlier block play in Cornerstone. He made a building which was sturdy, instead of shaky, solid instead of slender and easily toppled. [A similar sequence in the case of Oscar is described in Chapter 2.] Jay insisted that it must be "very strong and very tall" and wanted help whenever he felt uncertain that he could accomplish these goals. Giving Jay a minimal amount of help, and keeping up a "patter" of discourse with him, I commented on how this building was the opposite of a rhinoceros which could break easily. The building then became a kind of garage to which a truck brought cement. The matter of the right-size opening for the truck absorbed Jay for several reflective minutes. He called a teacher to admire the building, "See how big it is. It's taller than the chair."

The next day, Jay drew what appeared to be a man with a large penis, but he could neither talk about the drawing, nor even acknowledge that what he had drawn looked like a person. He soon became involved in breaking a felt-tipped marking pen, and had to be restrained by one teacher from a rather vigorous attempt to smash it. I observed, but did not physically intervene, having the advantage of the teacher's availability. I could thus preserve my purely analytic, non-disciplinary function. I commented that Jay was trying to tell us something about his troubles and that these must be connected with what he told us about yesterday: things which break. I then remarked sympathetically to Jay about a walkie-talkie antenna which, upon entering the classroom, he had told the teacher his younger brother had broken. I said that I hoped Jay could talk more about problems that were really very hard to talk about.

Jay then used a crocheting needle which was in the classroom, demonstrating some crocheting tricks to other children, who were duly impressed. He complained that his mother did not permit him to crochet because she said only girls should do it. Jay's competitiveness with Charles was now less evident than it had been the previous few days, and he confined himself to disputing one of Charles's remarks. It was a remark of considerable significance to Jay, for Charles had said, "People don't go away forever." Jay said, "People can go away forever." He not only insisted that Charles admit the error, but he was also upset to the point that he became unable to tolerate his own failure in gluing together a three-sided wooden structure whose purpose and nature he had not yet verbalized.

I now engaged Jay in a discussion of how nice it would be if people did not go away forever, acknowledging that Jay knew that sometimes people did not come back. I mentioned a maid—one of a string of "missing maids"—who had most recently departed from his home. Jay agitatedly expressed his belief that this particular maid would come back, taking the same view about another maid who had been gone even longer. I wondered "if sometimes a child whose father had died might hope that the father would come back somehow." Jay replied with sadness, "No, that can't happen ...once he's dead." He seemed relaxed at this point, although an agitated state immediately preceded these remarks. Jay's customary agitation was absent during the remainder of the hour and a half.

On the following day, Jay played a game of "killing" Charles, his closest companion in class. Then he made up a story about Charles's ghost and his own ghost playing together. His own ghost was "a very angry and scary ghost." I left the classroom, but the teachers were able to observe the continuation of Jay's expressive fantasy. This information was communicated to me the next day in a routine pre-session briefing prior to Jay's individual psychotherapy session.

Jay went outside to join a teacher and another child, Mary, who were playing in the yard while other children were having juice indoors. Jay played in a deep hole for about ten minutes by himself and then he called to the teacher, "Please stay here." She sat a short distance from him, while he lined up some flexible dolls which he draped with colored straws. Having established the identities of the dolls as members of a family, Jay described the father as a very kindly man. The boy doll would say to him: *"May I go horseback riding, Daddy?"* *"Certainly"* was the reply. *"Oh, thank you."* *"May I fly a plane?"* *"Yes. Certainly."* *"Oh, thank you."* *"May I drive an automobile?"* *"Yes. Certainly."* *"Oh, thank you."* Suddenly the colored straws became atomic rays. The father doll came forth to save other dolls, which were being *"attacked by atomic monsters."* Jay then noticed a worm, which seemed to be dead. He shrieked, *"It's a cobra! Mommy, look, it's a cobra!"*

The two figures next to the mother doll were now designated as "a nurse" and "a magical sister." The nurse also had a "little girl." Jay exhorted the father doll, "Daddy, Daddy, it's a cobra! Save us!" Daddy was able to kill the cobra, even though it bit him. Several dolls were bitten by the cobra, and buried one by one—all except the father. Jay then attached sticks attached to each leg of the father doll and the father became an airplane which flew around trying to slay atomic monsters. The atomic monsters were dropping dust on the figures below; then the monsters attacked the father-plane. He was wounded, fell to the ground, but was all right and got up again. The father-plane flew around attacking atomic monsters and managed to kill them all, although he was struck and fell crashing to the ground several times. Finally, the father doll went over to Jay's burial ground and unburied every one of the dolls. As he unburied the last one, he pulled the dirt off it and announced emphatically: *"EVEN YOU [are saved], YOU WITCH MOTHER!"*

Thus, by the end of five days after his return, it became clear, with the help of teacher observations, that Jay regarded his mother as a witch, magically responsible for the father's death.

He seemed ready to "go deeper". I would not have expected more of a 5½-year old child's therapeutic work in a comparable ninth month period of intensive treatment. I also had the impression that some of the above material might not have been so readily available in analysis conducted in a traditional playroom setting, especially the poking and smearing of other persons' anal regions, the discussion with Charles about people who do not come back, the visible display of competitiveness with a peer, and the intense, creative reactions to my departures. The high frequency with which interpretations could be made and their useful consequences for Jay's therapy suggested to me that an effective analytic process was indeed in progress. The patient had verbalized a fantasy (a child in disguise) which enabled me to interpret his defended-against affect of transference-related loneliness. He responded to interpretation by further elaborating the dominant theme (in terms of an unidentified flying object fantasy), thus enabling me to link the associated affect of loneliness to the death of father and the child's wish for father's return. Some connections between his play activities and his sexual identity concerns were also clarified for him. The fear of breaking the toy rhino's horn was connected with the fear of what happens to boys' fronts and backs. And there was an associated change in ego functions toward improved executive skills and sublimative activity (building sturdier buildings).

Middle Phase of Jay's Treatment

Material from early in Jay's second year of Cornerstone treatment illustrates the continuing thrust of the child's fantasy themes, and their ready emergence in the reflective network therapy setting. It also demonstrates some of the special split quality of transference in that situation, and the regularity with which major communications are made to Cornerstone teachers. Verbalized reflections among the helping adults which are made in the child's presence are an important feature of the method which we think partially explains the acceleration of treatment generally.

As an apparent reaction to my walking to another part of the room, Jay started talking to a teacher about fantasized visitors from outer space. I observed to Jay that the monster-visitors idea was connected with wanting me to stay nearby. Jay then asked me to pretend to be afraid while he pretended to be a monster following me. A further aspect of the loneliness theme emerged when Jay mentioned that his mother had been ill for two days, and shortly thereafter put his head down to rest in a teacher's lap. I interpreted to him that a child whose loneliness gets bigger when his mother is not well enough to take care of him could get so lonely that he could even want a monster for company.

A few sessions later, frantic needy behavior appeared, with panicky demands for food and crafts equipment. The teachers helped Jay with his wild behavior while I watched from a short distance. Soon he invited me to use some carpenter's tools with him, especially one. I reminded Jay that this particular tool was one he and his father had used together, and his thought about it was connected with loneliness for father and the good feeling he had had when he did tool things together with father. Jay then asked Mrs. Gorin, "Are you smarter than my mommy?"

When Jay's mother once forgot to give him a lunch to take to school, Jay brought this problem to our attention so that a lunch was provided. Jay then pretended to be a robot-monster, frightening some of the other child patients. In outdoor play, he asked other children to bury him in leaves and they cooperated. His identification with his longed-for father was not interpreted by the teachers, and I had already left.

The next day Jay brought in a tool kit belonging to his father and some of his father's coins. He had begged his mother for permission to do so. Again, he buried himself in leaves. He was very anxious, and furtively tried to look under a teacher's skirt. Then he unexpectedly urinated on the classroom floor, under an easel.

We soon learned one reason for Jay's newly heightened anxiety. He was threatened by a tonsillectomy because of tonsil and associated middle-ear infection. His mother was determined to proceed with the operation, and announced the plan in the classroom, although the entire matter was news to the staff. Jay then wildly wielded a knife which had been used for cutting a face from a Halloween pumpkin. I interpreted to him that he was once more turning his own fear around by making other people afraid. The surgeon scaring Jay was now Jay frightening us with a knife. Simultaneously, the dangerous action was stopped by Mrs. Herzog, our assistant teacher, before Jay came near anyone else.

Jay settled down with Mrs. Herzog, and after I left he told her how to make a genie by a secret formula of flour, salt, and chemicals. It would last a long time. He had a genie of his own, he told her, and would use it to get the teacher all sorts of things, especially a wood-burning set. He would also like lots of money to buy a private plane. My understanding was that the genie was a magic helper-father, creatively evolved from the child's wishes like the visitors from outer space. It appeared when I left the classroom, at a time of extra need. Jay felt threatened by his mother's recent inattentiveness due to her illness, a threat much aggravated by the planned tonsillectomy. It was powerfully over-determined because the time of the first anniversary of his father's death was now only a week away. A report from his public kindergarten, which he attended half days, confirmed the ascendancy of thoughts about his father. He cried in the other school, the same day, telling the teacher his father was dead, adding in the same breath that he was going to have his tonsils out.

Another bit of work with Mrs. Herzog further indicated that Jay's mourning was now transference-linked. He mistakenly believed her purse was "made of cobra skin." I told him that perhaps it was the same cobra that inhabited Jay's magic mountain dream. Shortly after his father's death Jay had dreamed that he would have a reunion with his father and a maid in this cobra-inhabited magic mountain.

Two days later the tonsillectomy was averted by my guidance of the mother and pediatrician. Jay had told a story about a bad robot and a bad plane. Both characters had begun their development in my presence. There was a hospital, an overt reference to the preoccupation with current medical matters, which Jay had discussed an hour earlier with me. The hospital was under threat from the bad plane. Apparently the father-plane had returned, angrily, to wreak vengeance on the hospital. Again, the classroom situation had provided means for continuing and elaborating themes in Jay's analytic work after I left. I had the advantage of the additional material, as usual, in time for inclusion in my thinking before the next day's session.

I told Jay that his wish for an outer space robot was connected to the hospital bombing because he wanted his outer space dead father to protect him from the tonsil operation. Jay listened very seriously. I added that it was like the way he wanted me to protect him from his mother's anger. Jay responded elaborately:

> *I wish there could be a machine that would make all the other children bad at Christmas time. There would be a bad man who would make that machine and all the children would get into trouble because of that machine. Then Santa Claus would find out about it and he would get a special dart gun and he would shoot that bad man in the behind with the darts.*

Jay then detailed the story further while sitting down on the ground next to me and later while he played on the outdoor climbing structure. He explained that the darts would be very sharp and there would be lots of them going into the man's behind. Santa Claus would shoot at the bad man's penis and the darts would go right in the man's penis. He would holler. There would be a special dye in the needle. It would be helium. It would make the man go high in the air.

I interpreted, telling Jay that this idea was connected with feelings boys and men have in their penis, which does go up in the air sometimes, by pointing upward.

In the following days, the theme of building airplanes occupied Jay profoundly. He spent weeks constructing a huge model glider from sheets of balsa wood, making an excellent original design. He believed this might be the largest model airplane I had ever seen, and the largest a child had ever built. It actually was able to fly. Of considerable concern to Jay was whether it would survive crashes, which I related to his wish to have saved his father.

Once, upon entering the classroom, Jay commented both about a minor leg injury he had just suffered and about his father's death a year ago. He spontaneously noted he was finding it hard to remember what was going on in school then, showing a remarkable degree of self-observation and interest in his mental processes. I interpreted both his leg injury and his efforts to remember as connected with his father's death. After I left he apparently responded to this association. He composed the following song (captured on tape) which he sang "for Mrs. Gorin":

> *On the planet, Mars*
> *Where the people smoke cigars,*
> *Each puff they make is enough to*
> *Kill a snake.*
>
> *When the snakes are dead*
> *They put roses in their heads.*
> *When the roses die,*
> *They put tulips in their eyes.*
>
> *When the tulips die it is 1965.*
> *Oh, this land is my land,*
> *It's only my land.*
> *If you don't get off,*
> *I'll blow your head off.*
>
> *I had a shotgun*
> *And it is loaded.*
> *This land is made only for me.*

After this song, with its message of guilt and triumph, of anal-sadistic and phallic-oedipal dreads, his further work was marked by an increased mourning through remembering as much as he could of previous work with teachers and me. Often this went on in counterpoint with sadly remembering bits of play with his father. It seemed there was a blurring and linking between father-memories and treatment-memories. The reality-testing and affect-discharging work of mourning was facilitated by the transference. He was able to think a good deal about how people's bodies were after burial, and made up songs about *"worms eating your bones"*. In association with thoughts about decomposition of a body, he begged his mother to allow him to visit the attic where his father had kept tools. Other children assisted Jay at times by saying in a matter-of-fact way, *"Your daddy is dead, Jay."* Jay would reply, also matter-of-factly, *"Yes"* or *"Yes, my daddy is certainly dead."*

Contiguous to Jay's increasingly testing the reality of his father's death was his increasingly verbalized insistence that his mother had a penis inside her vagina, and Mrs. Gorin had a bucketful of penises in the school basement. He often put phallic-shaped objects inside vagina-shaped ones, shouting, "Penis!" as an epithet to the lady teachers. Much work was done with related fantasies of women having a penis inside the vagina. Jay worked through several memories of observations he had made about female relatives. For example, he had seen one woman give herself an enema and described the procedure in some detail. Jay recalled having had the idea that she had retained the nozzle and was now able to correct this misunderstanding spontaneously.

Fantasies of immortality and rescue by supernatural means occurred intermittently, particularly one of an "eternal lighthouse" which "keeps young people from dying in planes and boats." The link between his longing for his father and the anxiety about his own anatomy became very clear on the anniversary of his father's death, when the eternal lighthouse fantasy merged with a suggestion Jay made to another child that they both go into the bathroom and take their pants off. He soon made remarks about Mrs. Gorin's penis having been taken off, and Dr. Kliman's head having been chopped off. Although he was still working with me on a model of exactly the same airplane in which his father had died, he whispered to Mrs. Gorin: *"I want to tell you a secret, but I don't want you to tell Dr. Kliman or anybody. My secret is I believe in God."* He soon confided further to Mrs. Gorin that he did not really want to have a penis.

By the 16th month, Jay became more relaxed and comfortably warm with the teachers and me. He often joked in a husbandly way with Mrs. Gorin, telling her that she looked funny. Once he amused her and said, *"I wish I had a camera so I could take a picture of you laughing like that."* At the same time he was able to speak sadly and seriously with his mother about her feelings toward his dead father, *"Mommy, you didn't always love daddy. You wanted him to die."* Jay seemed relieved to be able to express these ideas, and other children began responding to him with greater friendliness.

Shortly after this, Jay was able to let his mother know that he blamed her for his father's death and also expressed thoughts that his father himself was to blame emerged. Jay began calling me stupid in connection with his wish to spray paint near the school furnace. I was able to point out to Jay that his father had been killed in a burning plane and that his father had been spraying a dangerous fluid near a fire a few days before the plane crashed. Calling me stupid was a way of criticizing his father for dying. In response, Jay complained that he might die himself from choking on wet crackers, and seriously urged Mrs. Gorin to be good to him.

Jay's Cornerstone Treatment Ends Successfully

While much could be learned regarding childhood mourning and cross-dressing behavior from a further delineation of Jay's Cornerstone treatment, these are not the focus of my presentation of Jay's case. I am also aware of the fact that a thorough evaluation of the case would require the narration of a full treatment record, but for the purposes of this essay I will only make a few additional points.

One day, elaborating on much of the preceding work (while playing a game in which he pretended to be a crab) Jay told me:

Dr. Kliman, the reason I pretend to be a lady is that the lady and the pinching crab are connected in my mind. If the crab pinches off the boy's penis, then I want to be a lady because the crab gives the penis to the lady. And if I am the lady, I would have my own penis. And I don't have to go without a penis.

This intricate, spontaneously verbalized insight followed many earlier dialogues and interpretations concerning his feminine and cross-dressing behavior. He had begun to understand his intense fear of cracks in the floor as originating in his fear of and identification with the female aggressor and her genitalia. He had become clearly conscious of current and past fears of his mother, including the specific fear that she would pinch off his penis. This fear had been interpreted to him as being in part a product of his mother's former custom of pinching his behind black and blue.

Interpretations produced several lines of historical material that were highly relevant to Jay's current problems. When I noticed that Jay was making increasing demands for more and more supplies from the teachers, I told him that he was acting "hungry" to get supplies in a big hurry; that he seemed "hungrier" than at other times; and that seeing other children get supplies from the teachers made him "even hungrier." I then added that it must also be hard for him to watch his mother being nice to his younger brother Eric (who was then 2 years old). In response, Jay became reflective, and said he could remember when Eric was born, and that Mommy was very nice to Eric. He had a faraway look in his eyes, and I surmised that a process of reminiscence had been set in motion. Encouraging Jay to communicate, I learned that Eric had been breast fed and Jay now recalled watching his mother breast feeding Eric: *"I always wished she would let me do that. But you know what my Mommy would do if I tried? She would have killed me!"*

Jay was gradually helped to understand the naturalness of his desire to try the breast, and simultaneously to work through and moderate both his classroom competitiveness for attention and his dread of his mother's ferocity at home. I also acknowledged that his mother did at times act fiercely. As an apparent result of these endeavors, his aggressive acts toward his younger brother diminished further and he showed increasingly tranquil behavior in the classroom.

Jay's aggressive, destructive behavior had begun in the months before the birth of his baby brother. The reconstruction of the historical bases for his animosity in the classroom gave vital impetus to his treatment. Interpretations connecting his classroom behavior to those jealousies were not only helpful in showing Jay the continuity of his emotional life between school and home and past and present. They also helped him correct and work through his tendency to project envy and rage and to perceive others as hating him.

An encouraging development throughout the second year of treatment had been Jay's attachment to the school staff and children. We became a second family, for whom he cared deeply, and of whom he spoke often at home. His mother shared this positive attitude, which helped her immensely in the difficult task of controlling her verbal and physical onslaughts, and also helped her to identify with our attitudes toward her son. Caring for Jay many hours each week made the teachers particularly important real objects, a force magnified by Mrs. Gorin's weekly meeting with Jay's mother. Although I met with her only once a month, she knew I was available in any emergency and responded well to my confidence in her ability to grow into successful motherhood with our team's help. The rich reality of the Cornerstone School had made this mother's participation and growth possible, and a thinner diet of realistic help, as a less supportive nursery and a more emotionally isolated analysis would have provided, could not have sufficed.

After graduation from Cornerstone, Jay remained in treatment with me on an individual basis. He was seen several times a week for a few months, but then only once a week for a few more months, and finally every few months for several years. My wish to analyze him further was not realizable. The results satisfied his mother and Jay for the most part. His dangerous assaults on brother and other children had ceased. His transvestite behavior had not returned. He was no longer shunned or complained about by other families, and he developed friendships. The disruptive school behavior of prior years and in Cornerstone itself was not present during his first grade in public school.

Therefore, we judged that major treatment goals had been fulfilled in the Cornerstone classroom: favorable, progressive alterations of character had emerged with improved flexibility of adaptation to existing social tasks, frustrations, and discharge opportunities. On the other hand, at age 7, he retained a mild phobia of darkness and moderately excessive magical thinking, together with a diffident attitude toward formal learning.

Follow-Ups into Early Adolescence Verify Jay's Sustained Mental Health Gains

Follow-ups to age 13 showed Jay comfortably masculine. He was not interested in being analyzed further, regarding it as a financial extravagance; but in situational crises, usually involving his mother's discipline, he returned to me for occasional private (dyadic) sessions. It is evident that Jay sustained important mental health improvements he achieved during his course of

Reflective Network Therapy in our therapeutic classroom at a young age. Although he retained a critic's interest in women's fashions, his interest in cross-dressing had disappeared. He never again injured another child, despite an early history of near-murderous assaults. Far from being intellectually diffident (as he had been in first grade) he now vigorously employed his intelligence in school, where his reading, math, and artwork were outstanding. He was quite logical, and free of floridly magical ideas, using primary process thinking only in well-sublimated story writing, poetry, and gifted painting. He survived several further life strains of major proportions, with sparing use of my help. His mild phobic tendency was gone, and he appeared ready to enter puberty in good condition. Mourning for his father proceeded quietly, with frequent small doses of sad remembering, and shifting of paternal attachment toward his grandfather and toward his mother's male friends. His transferences to and conscious memory of the teachers and Cornerstone children gradually receded, as did his memory of the analytic work.

At a recent community meeting where I saw Jay functioning with warmth and poise among his friends and family, he took me aside and said with the seriousness and clarity which had characterized much of his early childhood treatment: *"I don't know what you did for me. I can't even remember what we did. But I'm sure that without you I wouldn't be here today."*

DISCUSSION

Jay's treatment, as well as that of over 100 children treated in The Cornerstone Preschool between 1965 and 1969 using Reflective Network Therapy, was not only based on psychoanalytic thinking. It also showed many of the essential features that are characteristic of the processes occurring in a regular child analysis. In considering the question of whether or not a method of treatment is analytic, I developed a set of criteria as guidelines for judging the existence of a psychoanalytic process. They underlie the definition of child analysis which I stated at the beginning of my presentation of Jay's treatment, and the remarks that follow are based on them.

There was evidence that Jay understood the nature of the analyst's work. He collaborated in exploration of, and communicated about, his inner life. He brought fantasies, dreams, and problem-related mental contents. There was marked thematic continuity and considerable dialogue about psychological functions and he clearly manifested transference phenomena, which were subject to systematic interpretation. He responded to interpretations with elaborations and new, illuminating themes. Often, interpretation of a conflict led on the one hand to oscillation in the psychosexual level of Jay's behavior, and on the other to increased awareness of the relationship between his current anxieties and defenses against impulses. Symbolic representations of his present and past conflicts were understood by him. Progressive growth of character was evident, with increasing flexibility in social tasks and increasing maturity of object relationships as well as insight into and working through of the transference neurosis.

An interesting feature of Reflective Network Therapy is the regularity with which not only profound transference phenomena occur, but with which certain features of transference neuroses are manifested. These correlate closely with the favorable outcome of many of our cases. In Jay's case, there was no doubt he loved and hated the teachers and analyst intensely, and this was not surprising. He also progressed from his perverse, primitive, impulsive state to a more advanced condition in which he created new symptoms—an artificial neurosis in the treatment situation. He expressed many anxious fantasies which crystallized around the Cornerstone personnel. Some of these fantasies were neither currently nor previously experienced consciously as concerning his family. For example, he not only wished to marry the teacher; he feared her and fantasized she had a bucketful of cut-off penises in the basement, collected from many Cornerstone boys. Further, he fantasized that she would "slip" off Jay's penis or chop off the analyst's head with an axe. He tried to involve other children in sadistic sexual acts, while his behavior was sedate and free of erotic assaults at home and in public school. Meeting one operational criterion of transference neurosis, his neurotic behavior, actions, fantasies, and accompanying distress were largely confined for long periods to the treatment situation.

The ultimate establishment of harmonious relations between Jay and his Cornerstone "family" was accompanied by many positive oedipal fantasies. These in turn permitted working through of his transference neurosis, with its castration anxieties and underlying separation anxieties. Again, by transference neurosis, I mean the phenomenon of symptoms and behavioral problems previously expressed in home-based relationships disappearing but reappearing in the therapeutic context where they can be worked through. As insights developed, their broadening was wrought in a vivid, real-life situation, syntonic with the child's developmental needs and capacities. The analyst then became primarily a benevolent, accepting father-in-transference and the teachers accepting, nurturing, educating, and safe mothers-in-transference.

As the techniques used and the observed phenomena in Jay's treatment demonstrate, the method of Reflective Network Therapy is child analysis conducted within a synergistic educational process. This treatment method can be accomplished using psychodynamic child therapists who do not have a full psychoanalytic training from a psychoanalytic institute. They can conduct the method if given orientation and receive required training under qualified supervision as described in Chapter 3.

Chapter Six

A Traumatized Child
Emerges from Chaos

Thomas Lopez, PhD and
Gilbert Kliman, MD

THE CASE OF MONROE

The current essay is an in depth case study of a child who was treated in his classroom by Thomas Lopez, using Reflective Network Therapy. Lopez is a very well trained and particularly gifted child psychoanalyst, but we have learned that the techniques and practices of Reflective Network Therapy are often successfully carried out by RNT trained psychotherapists who have no prior experience of psychoanalysis per se (see chapter 3). Monroe's case presents an example of Reflective Network Therapy as an application of child analytic techniques integrated synergistically with therapeutic education.

Dr. Lopez treated Monroe in The Cornerstone Therapeutic Preschool in White Plains, New York. I believe that the multi-layered and poignant flow of Monroe's treatment will be more accessible without significant updating. Therefore, in this chapter, I have kept references to the older term, "Cornerstone" from the original published case report, particularly in the larger part of this discussion which is preserved in Thomas Lopez' voice. The account was first published in The Psychoanalytic Study of the Child, (Lopez and Kliman, 1980). It shows the effectiveness of Reflective Network Therapy for a neglected, emotionally starved and economically disadvantaged minority child. He had what many clinicians would now call a pervasive developmental disorder (a term not in use at that time). Monroe also had many features of a posttraumatic stress disorder. Monroe was treated at the Cornerstone therapeutic preschool in the mornings and went to a day care center in the afternoons. (This combination of schools is similar to the use of Reflective Network Therapy class in the morning followed by public school kindergarten, mentioned in chapter 5). Other SED and PDD children have benefitted from half day classrooms using Reflective Network Therapy, which helps them to succeed in regular classes.

Introduction

Monroe presented with marked intellectual retardation and nearly psychotic degrees of withdrawal, impoverished affect and episodic difficulties with impulse control. The child had experienced major life discontinuities including placement in foster care. A member of an ethnic and racial minority, Monroe lived in the poverty of a big-city slum ghetto. All factors combined, some might have expected little meaningful progress therapeutically (Meers, 1970, 1973). The fact that his treatment ran dramatically counter to the usual pessimistic expectations makes the fascinating adventure it turned out to be especially worth reporting. Monroe's case also serves as an example of scores of children in similar situations who were treated successfully by the RNT method.

With Reflective Network Therapy, the child's cognitive gains became very evident. Within less than a year, Monroe's Full Scale IQ rose from a baseline of 53 (a mentally retarded level) to a normal range, 73, on retesting. The difference between the first and the second test results are sufficient to make a child seem likely to become employable and less likely that he would need a special education class. In fact, with RNT treatment, Monroe continued to progress well after transitioning into a regular public school classroom.

Not all therapists would have been as comfortable as Lopez was with Monroe. Dr. Lopez brings richness and clarity to his description of interactions Monroe had with his "Cornerstone family," more than sufficiently justifying the interpretations Lopez made of Monroe's past losses and traumas. The links of the prior life experiences to present day themes and behaviors are made clear. Briefings and debriefings in the classroom are well described, such as a teacher's description to Dr. Lopez of how Monroe's demands for food were strident when the analyst was out for a week. The network effect of teamness is emphasized, including the advantage to Monroe of the process of mentalizing which provided him with crucial experiences of being thought about and cared about. The collaborative nature of the adult helper participants in the reflective network are shown to have had effects on the adults themselves, fostering their growth in knowledge about the child and improving their skill in working with the child.

A particularly compelling aspect of Monroe's treatment is its contrast with the previously ineffective work it replaced. Before his work in the Cornerstone school began, Monroe had been paralyzed and withdrawn emotionally and cognitively. Educational therapy, daycare and therapeutic companionship had all failed to help Monroe significantly prior to his Reflective Network Therapy in the "Cornerstone" classroom. The method released a lot of Monroe's energy. He soon ceased his previous behaviors of crying, howling and begging. He not only became receptive to learning, he also developed a vigorous thirst for learning which propelled him to experience more and more successes, and to heal.

Case Report (Lopez and Kliman)

Monroe was the second of three sons born to an impoverished African American couple. When he was 2½ years old, his mother suffered a psychosis following the birth of her third child, who was born with a defect requiring a chronic tracheotomy. The mother's psychosis (about which no more than the most fragmentary information was ever gained) included delusional fears a man would enter her window and attack her. She was hospitalized for nine months and then treated by drugs, the dosage level of which induced her face to take on a mask-like appearance and caused her to become grossly obese and slow in her movements. While she was in the hospital, Monroe and his brother, older by two years, were cared for by their father and paternal grandmother. The baby was placed in permanent foster care. When Monroe's mother returned home, his father moved out for good, and remained out of contact with the family, except for occasional visits. Throughout Monroe's treatment, neither his mother nor anyone associated with the case knew where his father lived, nor were they able to meet with him. The combination of father's absence and mother's condition made it impossible to gain full information about Monroe's early life and development.

Monroe was referred by a daycare center as a result of his obvious profound developmental lags and grossly atypical behavior. He had little ability to relate to peers and adults and very sparse use of language (limited to occasional phrases such as, "I don't know" or "Thomas hit me"). He also had a grossly deficient capacity to learn; a withdrawn, detached appearance, interrupted only by occasional outbursts of obstreperousness; and overall, a joyless lack of vitality. On intake, he was described in terms of wandering gaze, lax facial musculature, paucity of expressive interchange, impoverished affect, and scored a Full Scale IQ (WISC) of 53. However, I, as the examining psychiatrist, noted some positive features. Monroe's receptive comprehension of verbal communication was at a higher level than his active linguistic expression. He readily brought a toy elephant and a yellow truck when asked to do so, easily finding them in the middle of a cluttered floor. On request he built an excellent tower of blocks with some 25 pieces and he seemed very pleased with the therapist's admiration and encouragement for this accomplishment.

Monroe began what were to be two years of Cornerstone [RNT] treatment at age four. Prior to Cornerstone, he had been seen individually by Mrs. H. Baskerville of The Center for Preventive Psychiatry in educational psychotherapy (Stein and Ronald, 1974)—an approach similar to that discussed by Weil (1973) Three sessions weekly of educational psychotherapy for ten months brought about no appreciable improvement in his functioning. A "homemaker," a woman employed by the county, spent eight hours of each weekday with the family to help care for itself. In addition, a "therapeutic companion," a female graduate student, had been provided by the Center for Preventive Psychiatry to spend time with the family, one day of each weekend. The balance of this report is preserved in Dr. Lopez' voice.—*G. Kliman*

The First Year of Monroe's Treatment, with Thomas Lopez

When Monroe arrived at Cornerstone, accompanied by his seemingly barely ambulatory mother and homemaker, he fully fit the description of him at intake. His eyes appeared glazed; his visage, like that of many institutionalized patients, blank; his affect flat.

However, in the very first session, when, in an attempt to make emotional contact with him, I cautiously rolled a toy truck to him, a somewhat livelier facial expression immediately developed. More important, Monroe rolled the truck back! I suggested we were getting to know each other. Monroe managed to smile through his sad vacant look and actually seemed delighted. Then he smiled broadly and rolled the truck to other people in the room: to the teachers, to his mother, and to other mothers who were present because it was the first day of school. He responded to my remarking on his discovering other people eager to play with him with an almost uncanny show of ecstasy: he squirmed about the floor, seemingly trying to rub as much as he could of his body on it. A thing as good as this, I commented, ought to be made contact with by as much of one's being as possible.

Monroe quickly became more active. In the second session, he jumped off a table into my arms, declaring he was a baby and I his mother, and assigning to me the task of his caretaker. By the end of the first week, when another child was in possession of something or someone he coveted, or when the day's class session had come to an end, Monroe shrieked in a deeply pained, almost unearthly manner, though without tears. At the end of one session, he attempted to destroy the watch on a teacher's wrist, seemingly in an effort to halt the passing of time. Within two months, Monroe cried and wept continuously during the greater part of three sessions immediately following each three-day interruption of school.

Within a month of entering Cornerstone, Monroe became very difficult to cope with. He would kick, bite, spit, punch, scratch, and make a shambles of the classroom, create chaos and drive the teachers to near despair. He would ingest great quantities of food, storming the cupboard where it was kept or attempting to appropriate all of what had been set out for the entire class. When he was stopped and scolded, his frenetic activity often dissolved in a flood of tears, following which he would fervently hug and kiss his scolder, ask to sit on her lap and be cuddled by her. As infuriating as Monroe might be one moment, he became as lovable the next. In one session, he bit a very attractive female psychologist who had come to administer tests. Then he stuffed himself with pretzels and potato chips. My verbalizing that the recipient of his bite was a "yum-yum" brought forth ecstatic nods of agreement from Monroe. He then declared a wish to go camping with her in a nearby forest.

Despite the turmoil, there was a general feeling that Monroe's condition was improving. Following his morning session in Cornerstone, he continued to attend the daycare center, where he was functioning better; he was following his teachers' instructions and getting on better with the other children. It appeared that the attention, tolerance, and affection, and, of course, the food Monroe was receiving from the Cornerstone nursery were enabling him to feel more nourished and intact outside of it. (Kohut, 1971, 1977). Confirmation came from a most unexpected source and for reasons that were astonishing: Monroe's mother, her pitiable appearance unchanged, volunteered that her son was improved because he seemed more lively and troublesome at home! While it was difficult to know to what extent she was suffering from mental illness, and to what extent from her drug treatment, it was clear that she was no longer actively psychotic. We failed in our efforts to prevent continuing overmedication to which she was subjected by a nearby aftercare clinic, but we were able to engage her in nearly weekly parent guidance.

Within three months, Monroe was affectionately feeding a dog outside the school; playing at being a fireman at the local fire station which we often visited at his request; proudly presenting Ms. Balter, one of his teachers, with splendid phallic structures made of blocks; affectionately hugging her while wearing a mask he had cut out of paper to disguise himself as a grown man; and once playfully urinating on her hand when she helped him with his trousers in the toilet. He emerged as the most competent among the children at cutting designs from paper, and radiated a charisma which made him very popular among his peers.

Nevertheless, Monroe's limitations were glaring. His thinking was so stimulus or context-bound (Goldstein, 1939; Werner, 1940/1926, 1957), that he was unable to engage in much conversation because he could not, at will, call up relevant ideas within himself. For example, to deal with the fact that waiting for him to produce material relevant to therapy invariably resulted in little more than his ignoring me, I would at times begin work with Monroe either by throwing him in the air and catching him, or by holding him by his feet upside-down—activities which delighted Monroe. When asked which he preferred, however, Monroe was unable to verbalize his choice, simply saying "yes" when I did so.

His affects had an unmodulated, all-or-none quality (Fenichel, 1941; Rapaport, 1953). Rage, anxiety, despair, affection, happiness would emerge, dominate his entire being, and then recede only after they had seemingly exhausted themselves or in response to a dramatic change in the environment, such as a scolding, a cuddling, a frustration, or, at times, an interpretation.

By the middle of the fourth month of treatment, Monroe's entire demeanor—the sound of his crying; the clinging torturing manner by which he related; his preference for drinking from a baby bottle; his occasionally becoming incontinent with regard to urine; the manner in which he sought adults' laps for "refueling"—increasingly took on the qualities of a toddler, frequently of a desperately grieved toddler. Time and again, on little or no pretext (or on one he had largely manufactured himself) he spent long periods crying pitiably on a teacher's lap. Gradually I had changed my approach and stopped the game of throwing him in the air and catching him so that we might work on "ideas." In response, Monroe clawed and hit at my watch. When I verbalized how terrible it was that good things, like our playing, come to an end, Monroe became desperate, pleaded to be given a baby bottle, and calmed only after he had received it.

But when I verbalized the hurt "baby feelings" that had been stirred in him, Monroe again broke down into desperate crying and continued uninterruptedly for some 20 minutes. During this time Monroe repeatedly called for his mother and cuddled close to me while sitting on my lap. Presently, he picked up a plastic shell shaped like an egg split in half (a container for pantyhose), placed it on my chest, and mouthed and sucked it as a baby would a breast. At that time I attempted an interpretation that related his behavior to his mother's current psychically impoverished condition and past breakdown. I reconstructed: long ago, his mother became sick, and had to leave him to go to a hospital. He could not be with her, sit on her lap, or get "good feeling" from her. She still was very sad, slow, and difficult to feel close to. Now, when he is unable to get something he wants, the terrible pain of being unable to feel close to his mother comes up.

For the next four months this was the main line of interpretation. The results were dramatic. A way had become available for making sense of Monroe's internal chaos and desperation. Although the reconstruction may have been valid only in a "hazy way" (Valenstein, 1975, p. 63), and though they surely made use of much that Monroe had since pieced together from discussions with his mother and perhaps from other sources, dialogue became possible where previously only comforting and restraint could be resorted to. Material became accessible for understanding and mastery which otherwise almost surely would have remained out of reach. Settlage and Spielman (1975, p. 46) offer a similar formulation.

In one session, after having become furious at me for working with other children before working with him, Monroe ostentatiously ignored me when his own turn came. I verbalized Monroe's rejecting me as a retaliation, and said how difficult it was to wait for someone one wanted to be close to and how often Monroe must have felt and still felt rejected at home by his mother. He continued to ignore me. I then became more concrete. I first enacted Monroe's feeling rejected when I worked with other children, playing both Monroe's and my own role, and verbalizing his pain and anger. Then I enacted Monroe's trying to gain his mother's attention, imitating Monroe's and his mother's mannerisms and vocal qualities.

Monroe abandoned his withdrawal. He alternated between furiously attacking me with spit, bites, kicks, and punches, on the one hand, and desperate crying, on the other. Finally, with great venom, he loudly accused me of being crazy. I pointed out that Monroe's mother had been crazy when he lost her, and might still seem crazy to him. Moreover, her withdrawn state might often make Monroe feel crazy. He sobered, went to a doll representing a woman, undressed it and caressed it. Then he twisted its movable limbs so that they became hopelessly tangled. I interjected that Monroe's mother had become all mixed up. Monroe dressed the doll and again caressed it. "How you love your mother and want to care for her," I commented. Again Monroe began to cry, but this time, instead of striking out, he hugged and kissed me.

In many of the ensuing sessions, Monroe continued variously to hug and claw me while crying desperately. I in turn attempted to facilitate Monroe's expressing his emotions. I verbally elaborated on the persistence in Monroe of "bottled up" feelings, which originally had been evoked by his mother's disappearance, and were still aroused by her withdrawn state. I imitated Monroe's and his mother's manner of speaking to dramatize their mode of interacting: Monroe seeking; mother unable to respond; Monroe becoming frantic. After a period of intense crying, Monroe usually became calm and sat quietly for a time, often continuing his sobbing with a teacher. During this period other material emerged.

Monroe ran out of the classroom, as if to escape. However, he quickly ran back into the classroom, said he was scared and sought refuge in the arms of one of the teachers. In response to my comments on how frightening it must be to live with his unresponsive mother, how often he must want to run away, and then how terrifying the prospect of being totally alone must become, Monroe volunteered a considerable amount of information about the baby whose birth had apparently precipitated his mother's breakdown. He said his mother had told him about and had shown him pictures of the baby. He described the hole in the baby's throat and told of his currently living with another family. In this interchange the concretistic quality of Monroe's thinking (concrete representation of abstractions of a type indicating confusion between thoughts and reality) was not as evident. Invariably when he described matters which deeply engaged him, his thinking was less concretistic.

Monroe walked about aimlessly, seemed terribly sad, and said he was scared. He turned to me and asked in a pleading tone, "Who took my Mommy away?" When I questioned him about who he thought had done so, Monroe answered that he himself had. Then, extremely sad, he fetched a teacher's sweater and her apron. He went to a corner of the room, curled up on the floor, held them to his face and sobbed. Relying on dramatization, I elaborated the idea that in his mother's absence, a child may try to hold onto things that belong to her, like her clothes. Perhaps Monroe had done so when his mother was away, and, to help tolerate her emotional absence, still did so. Monroe's crying became almost unbearably desperate. At times he literally clawed the walls. Several times he came to hug me, only to push me away as if I were not the person he was looking for. I commented that there are other people who care about us, but they do not easily replace the mother we love. Finally, tired from crying, Monroe hugged the teacher whose garments he had gathered. "It's so good to have a woman to hold and love," I said.

I took up Monroe's rejecting another child's efforts to befriend him in terms of his identification with his mother in her past and present rejection of him. He responded by asking who took care of him in her absence. I gave a completely factual answer to his question, feeling that such an answer would be the most helpful to Monroe's efforts to organize his experience (Buxbaum, 1954).

I related Monroe's crying at not gaining the attention of a teacher occupied with another child to the pain he felt when a person he loved was unavailable to him. He responded by crawling under my chair and declaring he wished to eat my feces. I then elaborated on the terrible drop in self-esteem and immense hunger Monroe felt when the person whose attention he was seeking was unavailable; on how lonely and hungry for his withdrawn mother Monroe must often feel. Next I used Monroe's wish to eat my feces to reconstruct that such a wish would have been a natural reaction on his part to the loss of his mother at the age of 2. Monroe emerged from beneath the chair and sobbed quietly while sitting on my lap.

I took up Monroe's ignoring me in terms of retaliation for my ignoring him while I was working with other children. Monroe fetched a set of keys from the teacher's desk and attempted to unlock the door to a closet. He claimed he was trying to release his mother from the hospital. In response to my saying how much Monroe had missed her, he sat on my lap, sucking and biting my chest. Then smiling, he tenderly combed my hair. Understanding Monroe's actions in terms of displacement, I acknowledged Monroe's love for his mother and his wish to care for her. I also underscored that although she no longer was in the hospital, she still seemed very much locked up—not in an institution, as she had been, but within herself. I acknowledged that Monroe must often want to unlock the barrier that separates them and sink his teeth into her.

Monroe kicked me in the stomach and vehemently called me a "fucker" in response to my having interpreted his obstreperousness as a defense against painful affect. I linked his outburst to rage at his mother for having left him to "fuck"—to have intercourse—and have the baby whose birth precipitated her breakdown. He furiously grabbed at my throat, thus enabling me to take up Monroe's rage as it related to the throat-damaged baby. Monroe sobered and became calm.

Seemingly in response to my having missed a week due to illness, Monroe again hit me in the stomach and called me "fucker." He also howled "Mommy" time and again while crying desperately. Again I acknowledged that Monroe understood that his mother's breakdown had been precipitated by the birth of his brother. I also pointed out that my own absence had aroused in Monroe feelings similar to those he had experienced when his mother was absent

After this last exchange, Monroe stared out of a window for a time, in an effort, he said, to find ambulances among cars he saw in the street. He then set himself to draw a face which he called "the Easter bunny monster." For the eyes, mouth, and nose, he drew holes. Asked to tell me about the drawing, he said the picture reminded him of his little brother and the hole in the baby's throat. He elaborated the similarity further with one of the teachers, after his time with me had ended.

Monroe's fixedness to a prephallic position was loosened considerably by this line of work. The four months during which it had been central were followed by nearly a month during which remarkably conflict-free phallic material and behavior were dominant. Monroe's despair and his obstreperous, provocative, sadomasochistic ways receded. They were replaced by his strutting about wearing a fireman's hat or an Indian headdress; demonstrating expertise in riding a tricycle; building handsome towers of blocks which he delighted in presenting to his teachers; proudly waving a flag at the end of a sizable stick; and lifting cardboard boxes by inserting the same stick into their handles. He often assumed a very "manly," responsible role in the nursery: he eagerly volunteered to do chores, such as serving food during snack time, or cleaning up. Frequently, he assisted smaller or less able children. Once he stopped a fight involving two other children.

A clear yearning for a paternal figure he might love and admire—in whose strength he might participate—began to emerge. He frequently requested that we take walks and on these occasions displayed great skill in attracting the notice of the neighborhood "father figures." At the fire station, firemen patiently demonstrated their fire-fighting equipment to him. Construction workers similarly displayed their shovel-wielding techniques. A guard at a nearby museum we occasionally visited allowed himself to be placed under arrest by Monroe, who had dressed himself to look like Batman. Often, following an interaction in which his self-esteem had been raised by participation in the manly strength he attributed to me, Monroe made romantic overtures to one of the teachers. In addition to employing his impressive displays of phallic prowess to woo them, on one occasion he shyly presented a teacher with a necklace he had patiently constructed from beads and thread.

Then a shift in Monroe's behavior occurred. What had been an ebullient seeking of association with men to gain a feeling of strength became rigid, compelling, and clearly defensive in character. It became a means of escaping from closeness to women—in the nursery, from closeness to the teachers. When I became aware of this shift, I began to frustrate Monroe's desire to go into the neighborhood to seek men and focused on his need to take flight. Monroe's reaction was dramatic. Outbursts of chaotic ambivalence returned full force: hitting, throwing, spitting, and biting on the one hand, desperate clinging and crying on the other. He fell frequently, on occasion hurting himself. Once he threatened to jump from a balcony in the school's stairwell, and was convincing enough to cause the teacher accompanying him to become quite frightened.

The turn of events was, at first, puzzling. My focusing on Monroe's longing for a father to rescue him, and on guilt causing him to turn aggression against himself, as manifested by his suicidal gesture, was probably at least partially valid, but it seemed not truly to hit the mark. Finally, information conveyed by Monroe's therapeutic companion shed light on what was happening. His mother's condition had deteriorated. She had become even more inert and less involved with her children. This information was now made use of in working with Monroe, and care was taken that his home was visited weekly. (The therapeutic companion had missed a week, leading to the delay in my gaining this information.) A closer tie with the homemaker was established.

For the next two months, the further deterioration of his mother's condition was the main focus of my work with Monroe. His experience and expression of pain became more intense, but our work appeared to be effective in helping him to cope. I shall describe in detail three sessions from this period. They illustrate that despite the dreadful grimness of the situation, Monroe's grip on it actually improved.

Illustrative Treatment Session 1

Following a day when I had been absent, Monroe frenetically insisted that we leave the classroom and visit the fire station. Ms. Schnall, the head teacher, reported nonjudgmentally that prior to my arrival that morning, Monroe had been demanding all manner of food he knew he was not permitted and creating chaos when refused. As Ms. Schnall spoke, he became even more insistent that we go out. When I linked the behavior his teacher reported to his yearning for the emotional nourishment his mother's involvement might provide him, and which she now was even less able to give, Monroe became truly beside himself. He hit, bit, spit, and attempted to turn the classroom upside down. I caught him and placed him atop a countertop where I could maintain him relatively immobile without actually sitting on him. Ms. Schnall now added that on the previous day Monroe had cried frequently and had asked for his mother. I commented that Monroe must also have missed me, whereupon Monroe broke down in a flood of tears. I verbalized how painful it was for Monroe to live with a mother as unresponsive as his, and to be a whole day without a person, like myself, with whom Monroe was able to have good feelings. I also commented that if only his father were with the family, Monroe might gain some relief from his mother's emotional absence. For a time Monroe's crying did not decrease; then, perhaps as a result of fatigue and discharge, it abated, and he asked for a baby bottle. He spent the next half hour sucking on it, while cuddled on Ms. Schnall's lap.

Illustrative Treatment Session 2

This session, from the middle of this period, illustrates Monroe's increasing symbolic elaboration. He again began by requesting that we visit the fire station, but he was no longer frantic. I reiterated the importance of our staying in the classroom to work on issues we might otherwise avoid. Seemingly appreciating my position, Monroe began to play with a baby doll. He declared he was its mother, and alternated between affectionately bathing and caressing it and blandly throwing it about the room; carefully applying talcum powder to it, and bizarrely burying it in the powder. I wondered aloud whether Monroe could trust his mother to care for him, not to hurt him, even not to kill him. Monroe, very serious, looked up and said, "Don't take my Mommy away." I focused on Monroe's fear that if he told me what his mother was like, this might well cause her to be taken away. I then linked these fears to Monroe's angry wishes to be rid of her, which his mother's withdrawn, frightening state aroused in him. Monroe walked about aimlessly for a while. Then he wandered to where clothes used by the children as costumes were kept. He dressed in women's garments—a hat, high- heeled shoes, a shawl—but in such a way as to make himself look ridiculous, accentuating this appearance by the manner in which he carried himself. I interpreted that Monroe was conveying how mixed up his mother seemed to him. Again, Monroe dissolved into tears, and this time pleaded that I be his mother. While holding him, I elaborated on the pain of his situation.

Illustrative Treatment Session 3

The next session is taken from the latter part of this period. In what had by then become almost a ritual, Monroe began by requesting that we visit the fire station. My usual refusal, for the usual reasons, brought on demands for cookies and, when these were refused, another of Monroe's colossal storms of obstreperousness. Again, I contained him by placing him atop the countertop. While crying desperately, Monroe positioned himself on my shoulder, much as a baby might when being burped by his mother. As Monroe cried, he dribbled saliva down my back. I said he seemed like a baby, and asked him why he was crying. Through sobs Monroe answered, "I'm crying for my Mommy." He gradually calmed down as I focused on the baby feelings stimulated in him by his mother's worsened condition, then he asked to get off the closet, and returned to ground level with the other children. Behaving more maturely, Monroe appeared to create a family of his own. He protected a smaller boy, whom he called his brother, from attack by a larger boy. Then he rested his head on a teacher's shoulder, and "jokingly" called her "Mommy." I verbalized his enactment and enumerated the terrible things that had happened to his own family. As I spoke, Monroe once again was unable to maintain his composure. He broke into tears and ran to raid the food cupboard. When he was prevented by a teacher, he furiously hurled everything he could lay his hands on at her. His fury, however, soon gave way to fear and then to a desperate affection, as he hugged and kissed her when she succeeded in holding him. He then hugged and kissed the other teacher, several of the children, and me. I reflected aloud on how painfully empty it makes a little boy feel to love his mother so and have her to unable to return his love.

Presently new stresses burdened Monroe's beleaguered ego. The Cornerstone Therapeutic Nursery was in operation 12 months a year. When summer came, there were vacations and substitutions of the nursery's teaching
staff. Ms. Balter announced she would be leaving permanently in early July.
Despite these losses and changes, Monroe did not substantially deteriorate,
though his dramatic storms recurred. Previous work clearly had provided him
with an enhanced capacity to cope. Monroe had learned to use the nursery as
a family which was fluctuant but generally reliable and enduring. He clearly
came to understand that in it he could safely express and experience the
agony within. As his affects remained accessible to his ego, mastery of his
inner life continued to progress.

A few days prior to my own one-month summer holiday, and about one
month following Ms. Balter's departure, Monroe began a session by telling
me explicitly that his mother had seemed very sad that day. He then played
with a toy ambulance, aimlessly rolling it about. I verbalized both Monroe's
sadness and his recurrent fear that his mother would again be hospitalized.
Monroe responded by placing a toy sheep in a small rectangular wooden box,
the lid of which he shut. The resemblance of the box to a coffin led me to take
up Monroe's fear both for his own and his mother's life. Monroe began to cry
softly, but he did not fall to pieces. He hugged and kissed two teachers; then
sat quietly sucking a baby bottle and listening to a story. I commented only
that Monroe was bearing his terrible situation better all the time.

In another session, just after the children had been informed of the nursery
team's summer vacation schedule, I began working with Monroe while sitting on a wooden ladder laid horizontally between and bridging two climbing
frames. Monroe ran under me, shouting, "Move your big butt!" I did not, instead suggesting to Monroe that we examine the ideas that emerged. Monroe
responded by poking his head up into my buttocks. He said that he wished to
pull down my trousers so that he could go into my "butt" and get my "doo."
I stopped Monroe from undressing me, and with great formality indicated to
Monroe that children of his age were able to use words in place of actions. I
then drew a pair of large buttocks on the blackboard and offered him a board
eraser in place of feces. Monroe refused it, insisting it stank.

To elicit more material, I cried pitiably at his refusal of my fecal gift, and
loudly protested that Monroe did not care for me at all. Monroe, sensing vic-
tory, now refused my gift even more strenuously, declaring for all to hear
that its stench was horrible. As my crying achieved "uncontrollable" intensity, Monroe ran behind Ms. Herzog, the teacher who had taken Ms. Balter's
place, hugged her around the hips, and stuck his tongue out at me.

I commented that Monroe seemed to be saying he did not need my buttocks. Ms. Herzog's were softer, warmer, bigger, and in every way superior,

more like his mother's. Ms. Herzog gently stroked Monroe's head and showed absolutely no sign of discomfort. I elaborated my understanding of what Monroe was communicating: Monroe was experiencing the coming vacation of the nursery's team, on the one hand, as an anal rejection of him, as if he were feces, causing him to try to "re-enter" my anus, and, on the other, as a rejection at the anal level of his own gifts of love, of his fecal products. Moreover, he was defensively turning passive into active by becoming the rejecter. I also linked this material to its roots in the anal phase of Monroe's development and to his mother's illness, which had occurred during that phase. Monroe listened quietly, his receptiveness greatly enhanced, I felt convinced, by his identification with his teacher's comfort with what was being said.

The Second Year of Monroe's Treatment

When I returned from vacation, Monroe at first withdrew emotionally, but by the second day became angry, tearful, obstreperous, and difficult to manage. Several times he lost control of his urine in class, something he had not done for some time. However, within a week and a half, his behavior indicated that he had in fact not deteriorated in my absence, but rather was reacting to my return. The following session marked a turning point: Monroe was supplied with a fresh pair of trousers after he had urinated in his own. Embarrassed, he sat sullenly, staring straight ahead. When I sat next to him, he looked up and called me "stinky." I accepted Monroe's externalization, pretended to cry, and wailed that Monroe did not like me. No longer withdrawn, Monroe railed at me, insisting that he did not like my smelly feces, and inducing other children to join him. My pretending to be further driven to despair made Monroe wild with power. As was his wont, he proceeded to wreak havoc in the classroom, knocking furniture and toys about. I caught him and held on to him. I interpreted his having felt discarded like feces by me during my absence, and again related these feelings to similar ones he had when his mother was withdrawn and therefore absent. As I spoke (and dramatized to improve my communicativeness) Monroe broke into tears and cried terribly for some ten minutes. Seemingly spent, he became quiet. Then he fetched a stick and furiously tried to hit first me and then a child with it. When I again contained him and urged him to express himself verbally, Monroe asked to be taken to the toilet.

On the way he stumbled and had a painful fall down the stairs. I comforted him, and interpreted his rage at having been left, his guilt over his own aggression, and his turning this aggression against himself by hurting himself. Monroe hugged me and again cried pitiably, to which I responded by once more emphasizing how much Monroe had missed me.

After the toilet, at Monroe's request, we went outside and came upon a group of physically impressive workmen digging a large hole. Monroe looked longingly at them for some time. At intervals, he whispered to me that he wanted to handle one of their shovels. Finally, a workman noticed him, and Monroe had his wish fulfilled. As we walked back to the classroom, Monroe asked me to carry him, and again cried, this time softly and sadly. I verbalized Monroe's desperate longing for a man to help him feel strong and good about himself, and I related this longing to his having missed me.

Once Monroe's relationship with me had been re-established, this session turned out to be the beginning of a period of progress, sustained throughout the year. Monroe achieved a level of functioning far superior to what had been possible for him previously. Soon after this session, it became commonplace for Monroe to strut about the classroom waving a flag; wearing masks he had cut out of paper, representing children's current superheroes, and imitating the shovel-wielding men at whom he had so movingly stared. It became especially commonplace for him to eat great quantities of food in an effort, he said, to make himself big; and insatiably to ask me to throw him in the air and catch him.

Monroe turned to women for support of his emerging phallic self. On one occasion when Ms. Solomon, the teacher who had permanently replaced Ms. Balter, failed to attend him, he impulsively kicked her in the face. Shocked and hurt, she responded first with anger, then with withdrawal. Monroe was shaken and frightened, until my verbalizing of what had happened helped his teacher regain her composure and again relate to her charge. Greatly relieved, Monroe hugged her and apologized. Then after sucking from the barrel of a toy gun, he delivered a dramatized rendition of Superman to his now attentive teacher. On other occasions, when women observers were present, Monroe cavorted exhibitionistically before them in ways that ranged from demonstrations of athletic prowess to ogling at them like a grossly undersized King Kong.

Sexual wishes manifested themselves in other ways. Monroe invented a way of making bow and arrows from plastic drinking straws, and affectionately shot these at the teachers and children. He delighted in my drawing a Valentine heart with an arrow through it, as an aid in interpreting the loving connotation of his activity, and also in my underscoring Monroe's getting people to "fall for him," as they often playfully did when hit by one of his arrows.

Monroe created family groups and situations, assigning roles of mother, father, and son to himself and to the adults and children whose participation he enlisted. For example, Monroe had been playing family with two other boys, assigning himself the role of "baby," to one of the boys the role of father, and to the other boy that of mother. When his turn came to work with me, he asked to visit the fire station, but stipulated that he and I be accompanied by Ms. Solomon. Monroe walked between us, holding hands with each, contentment on his face—an obvious continuation of his play with the boys. He proudly told us that his father was planning to buy him a tricycle. This was the first hint we had of his father's reappearance.

After a very successful visit to the fire station, Monroe set about digging for a "brown snake," which he said lived in the ground outside the classroom. He declared he wished to bite the snake, and also to keep and hide it. When it did not materialize, he angrily beat the ground with his spade. I suggested that he was searching for his father, the man with the brown penis, who was so hard to find. Monroe was serious for a time and then said he wished Ms. Solomon would come to live at his home. I interpreted that Monroe's thought might be: if Ms. Solomon lived at his home, his father might be persuaded to live there too. He must feel it was his mother's illness that had caused his father to leave. Monroe nodded sadly.

After some quiet contemplation, Monroe noted that Ms. Solomon, now with another boy, lacked a spade with which to dig. He lent her his. Then, almost manly in his demeanor, he demonstrated his prowess at running up and down a nearby hill. I verbalized my interpretation for Monroe: Although Monroe could not have his father be with him, he could act in fatherly ways toward others.

At about midyear, Monroe scored 73 on an IQ test (WISC), 20 points higher than on intake. As the year progressed, his intelligence appeared steadily to improve; he probably would have scored even higher by the end of the year, had it been possible to re-test him. He displayed leadership qualities as he organized other children for dramatic play, or to hunt for insects and worms which he placed in paper cups after capturing. He exuded an air of competence.

Monroe became so helpful with less able children and teachers, that he earned the title, "Dr. Macher" (vernacular for "big shot"). The classroom took on the quality of home for him. He even set himself the responsibility of keeping the grounds immediately outside of it free of debris. Late in the year, he conveyed a clear recognition of his parents' intellectual retardation. Wearing a mask he had cut from paper, Monroe enacted robbing a bank. He planned to use the money, he said, to buy food with which to fill his refrigerator. However, he planned to hide whatever money remained from his parents. He feared his mother would either burn it or wash it down the sink, and his father might leave it on the street where it could be stolen. I underscored Monroe's belief that he was the cleverest person in his family. He responded by hugging me affectionately, in clear appreciation of having been understood.

In the latter part of November, unexpectedly, Monroe's father emphatically entered the scene. By way of the therapeutic companion, we learned that he had come unannounced, without a word had taken Monroe and his brother with him, and had kept them at his home for the four-day Thanksgiving weekend.

The stay with his father truly moved Monroe. He described it with delight in the immediately following sessions, conveying affection for the woman who was living with his father and telling of outings the four of them had had together. Guilt over his pleasure soon intruded, however: Monroe began calling himself a "bad boy"; enacted a thief attempting to evade the police; took prohibited food from the cupboard, clearly in order to be caught at it; and once hurled himself headlong into a large garbage can. In the course of several sessions, I took up Monroe's guilt in terms of his feeling disloyal toward his mother for wanting to leave her and live with his father. Monroe met my attempts at first with protest and avoidance, but then with a kind of resigned, sad acceptance.

A new spurt in the direction of positive development followed. During the next three weeks, Monroe showed a greater seriousness about his schoolwork and again made use of me (e.g., rides on my shoulders) as a fueling base for his phallic forays.

Then, as unexpectedly and unannounced as the first time, Monroe and his brother were once more taken by their father to spend time with him—this time for ten days, including Christmas. On this occasion, however, it was possible to elaborate his experience considerably, because material relating to it remained central for two months. Monroe talked of what had occurred at greater length than he had after his first visit. He described the appearance of his father's apartment and of the room he and his brother had slept in. He told of how kind the woman living with his father had been: she read bedtime stories, gave them medicine when he and his brother's tummies hurt, and cooked tasty meals for them. He told of the four of them having gone fishing. In class he rendered elaborate and sustained dramatizations of family groups and situations, enlisting both adults and children for the purpose—clearly efforts to recreate the family-like situation he had enjoyed with his father.

However, as had been true after his first stay with his father, Monroe's good feeling frequently gave way to painful affect and outbursts of crying. He often hurt himself by falling and mishandling toys. Repeatedly he would be overcome by a depressive mood. At the core of his pain was the conflict over his wish to leave his mother and be with his father. In one session he called me, in another, one of his teachers, "Mom." On each occasion, as if to escape, he then ran to the telephone and frantically but randomly dialed it, in an effort, he said, to reach his father. Each time, when there was no answer,

Monroe lapsed into helpless crying, allowing me to put my understanding of what he was saying into words. I was also painfully moved by Monroe's enacting the part of my son, after he had disguised himself as Caucasian with the help of a mask he had cut out from paper.

Monroe's efforts to separate psychologically from his mother manifested themselves in another striking way. The final nine months of his treatment were marked by good progress interspersed with episodes in which he would call desperately for her—at times insisting that her hospitalization or even her death was imminent. Vomiting, complaints of stomachaches and head pains, painful minor accidents, and another threat to jump from the balcony on the stairwell outside the classroom accompanied his tears. However, no relationship between these episodes and his mother's actual condition could be discerned from home visits and interviews with her.

It dawned on the nursery team that the key to understanding these episodes lay in Monroe's concretistic mode of thinking, causing intensely experienced ideas to become confused with reality. Thenceforth I related these episodes interpretively, not to Monroe's mother's imminent departure, but rather to Monroe's own efforts to detach himself psychologically from her both by functioning independently and by going beyond her inadequate mentation. In each instance my efforts were rewarded. Monroe regained his composure rather quickly and resumed his progressive development. For example, Monroe was carrying on in his all-too-familiar provocative, obstreperous, sadomasochistic manner in a session which followed one in which he had responded to an attractive female observer by being stimulated to ecstatic heights of phallic exhibitionism. When I focused on this shift in his material, Monroe sobered, turned to me, and said, "My brother killed my Mommy and sent her to the hospital." I verbalized Monroe's wish to be rid of his mother, especially after having been exposed to the visitor of the previous day, his guilt over his implicit wish, and his displacing responsibility for it onto his brother. Monroe stopped and nodded sadly. He then engaged in a variety of activities, including instructing a boy with a tested IQ of more than 130 on how to make bow and arrows out of drinking straws; hugging a teacher and two children affectionately; and playing at being an Indian warrior battling imaginary adversaries on the nearby hill.

In early May, Ms. Solomon announced that she would be leaving the nursery within a month. Monroe's coping with her departure conveys something of the progress he had made. He acknowledged the fact and pain of it and at the same time demonstrated a readiness to seek and accept substitutes. Initially, he responded by stuffing himself with food and by angrily shouting obscenities. Soon, however, a more complex response emerged. In one session, I attributed Monroe's being especially difficult with Ms. Solomon to her leaving.

Monroe responded by hugging and kissing her and then by proposing that I marry her. I interpreted: "Since I was not leaving, if Ms. Solomon and I were married to one another, she would not be leaving either." Monroe developed a surprising variation on this theme in the following week. When his turn came to work with me, he hurled obscenities first at Ms. Schnall and then at me, but he ostentatiously ignored Ms. Solomon. When I became the target of Monroe's abuse, I gradually moved closer to Ms. Solomon in an attempt to undo the displacement. The strategy worked as Ms. Solomon soon became the unequivocal focus of Monroe's rage. Monroe loudly declared he hated her for leaving him. But when I interpreted the pain underlying Monroe's anger, he melted, cried, and hugged his beloved teacher—and more! He proposed another solution. He would marry Ms. Solomon, and I would be his and his bride's child. Accepting this child role, I focused on the dilemma that small boys find themselves in. Because they are not able to marry, they repeatedly lose the women they love so dearly. Monroe sadly agreed, but that did not stop him from further elaborating his solution. He enacted being caring and affectionate to the family he had created and set up a home for it. He took me, as his son, for a walk, gave me pretend money, and bought gifts for me. Finally, he built a handsome phallic structure of blocks for Ms. Solomon, his wife.

In a later session, Monroe submitted yet another solution. He had been withdrawn and in a melancholy mood, but intermittently he launched into angry verbal tirades against his teacher for leaving him. When I verbalized his grief and anger, Monroe stuffed rags under his shirt in the region of his chest and announced elatedly that he had breasts just as Ms. Solomon did. I focused on Monroe's identification with his soon-to-be-lost love object, and took the opportunity further to explicate Monroe's depleted state prior to treatment by stressing his earlier identification with his barely available, depleted, intellectually retarded mother.

On Ms. Solomon's last day, Monroe loudly proclaimed he wanted nothing to do with her because she was leaving. Then the teacher who was to replace her entered the classroom for a visit. Monroe already knew her from several occasions on which she had substituted for a temporarily absent teacher. Ascertaining that Ms. Solomon was aware of him, he flamboyantly presented the new teacher with a plant he had taken from the windowsill. When I verbalized that though he was losing a person he loved, he was looking forward to a new relationship, Monroe became very sad. He placed a chair in front of a window, sat on it and stared into the distance. I focused on Monroe's not wanting to look into the room where Ms. Solomon would no longer be, and on his staring far away where she would shortly go. Monroe turned to Ms. Solomon, tried to smile, but, finding the effort beyond him, ran and enclosed himself in a large metal box. I did no more than put into words the pain of it all.

In the session that followed, Monroe openly and soberly verbalized how much he missed Ms. Solomon. Then in appreciation of love objects still present, he went around the room kissing each of the children, the teachers, and me. Smiling, he announced that he had "other friends."

Monroe's treatment ended shortly thereafter. In August, without warning, his mother moved with him and his brother to a rural area in the South to be with her own mother. A letter sent them by registered mail was received, but there was no reply. A half year later, however, another letter was sent, and this time there was a reply! Monroe's grandmother wrote, stating simply that the family was doing well. Perhaps more important, Monroe wrote back! In his letter he demonstrated that he could spell his first and last names and write the numbers from 1 to 20.

Three and one half years later, just prior to publication, we reached Monroe's mother by phone and, through her, his school and teacher. Though she did not have a recent IQ score available, his teacher said: "If you treated him, you must have cured him. He's a most wonderful, outgoing little boy. He talks like a cricket, and is most enthused about learning. Though he was placed in a learning disabilities class, and left back one grade, we're going to move him up to grade level. He's too smart to be left back. If he keeps up his enthusiasm, he should easily keep up." His mother, in a very lively voice, said that she and the children were "happier than ever" and doing well. She added that she had wanted to visit Cornerstone for some time, but had not had the money. Our hope that his grandmother and rural life—perhaps less stressful than the urban ghetto he left—would be good for Monroe and his mother, it seemed, was being fulfilled. The team also suspected that the move was a successful escape on the mother's part from her previously debilitating psychotropic drug therapy.

DISCUSSION OF MONROE'S SUCCESSFUL TREATMENT

Contrary to what might have been assumed all too easily, Monroe's treatment established that he was not a child who had been catastrophically deprived and unalterably damaged by life with a mother whose personality had been profoundly impoverished throughout. Rather it showed him to be a child, living in the dismal conditions of a big-city slum (Meers, 1970, 1973, 1975), who in addition was impinged upon by three monumental interferences with his early development (Nagera, 1966): (1) at the age of 2, he lost his mother for nearly a year due to her psychosis and during her hospitalization, he lost his younger brother to a permanent foster care placement; (2) then he was forced to live with the barely recognizable shell of her former self who returned to him; (3) on her return he lost his father, his older brother and his paternal grandmother, leaving his heavily sedated, pitifully inert mother as sole caretaker.

The detachment, passivity, and flat affect he manifested on intake became clarified as states into which he had to withdraw in order to survive in the grimly unsupportive circumstances in which he lived (Kliman, 1977). Joffe and Sandler (1965), discussing detachment, the third of three phases described by Bowlby (1960) as children's reactions to prolonged separation from love objects (protest, despair, and detachment), aptly state:

> Whereas in the phase of despair we can discern a general inhibition of both id and ego functions, in the phase of detachment we can postulate a partial lifting of the generalized inhibition which is characteristic of the depressive response. This is made possible by a form of ego restriction, in particular a restriction of attention and a flattening of feelings. It shows itself in a devaluation of the affective importance of the mother or indeed of any object. The child settles, so to speak, for its actual state of the self. It is a type of resignation which can be seen as an attempt to do away with the awareness of the discrepancy between actual self and ideal self, and in this sense it is a form of adaptation which stands in contrast to the process of mourning. [It] is not an inherent response to a separation experience but rather one fostered by deficiencies in the supporting environment. "Detachment" may occur even in situations where there is no actual separation, but rather chronically inadequate mothering (p. 409f).

The gross interferences which impinged on Monroe's development, in combination with his environment's failure to compensate for them, caused the basic integrity of his very young personality to be profoundly undermined. His ego became inundated and overwhelmed by diffuse anxiety, the pain of narcissistic collapse, and unintegrated, raw libidinal and aggressive strivings. It could do little more than capitulate and retreat into lost specialization in form or function—a dedifferentiated state in which substantial detachment from his mother and from the object world were central. The alternative surely would have been even greater psychic disintegration and damage (A. Freud, 1967; Kohut, 1971, 1977). Stultifying of his capacity for life though it was, Monroe's detached state also performed a protective function. It acted to diminish and to dull the amount of stress his environment could inflict upon him.

In Cornerstone, Monroe's pathology began to reverse itself. Efforts on the part of teachers and analyst to gain access to the "person within" Monroe resulted in his forming increasingly strong attachments to them. Nurtured, sustained, and enhanced by interpretive work and by analytically informed acceptance, these new ties began to provide him with the empathic, caring objects of which his life was so starkly devoid. Detachment began to lift. Aided by the presence of a supportive environment (Aichhorn, 1935/1925), he began to re-experience his despair and thereby to diminish it. As hopelessness lessened, for the first time in more than one year, Monroe became able to protest, and protest he did! Potentials for interacting with the world about him (Erikson, 1950) were stirred from dormancy. Since he had been so little exposed to the taming effects of participation in social life for so long, their awakening was accompanied by repeated storms of intense affect (Fenichel, 1941; Rapaport, 1953).

Time and again Monroe ran rampant, made a shambles of the classroom, and became generally very difficult to control. But he had come to life! The beauty of his rebirth helped the nursery team to endure.

With Monroe's self revitalized, the social world (Erikson, 1950)—the world of love objects beyond that of his depleted mother–also became revitalized (A. Freud, 1951). Incentives to "improve his relationship" to it (Hartmann, 1958/1939), to resume development (Aichhorn, 1935/1925; A. Freud and Burlingham, 1943; A. Freud, 1960), were activated. For only by so doing could he hope to reside in this more vital world he was becoming increasingly aware of, and increasingly able to love.

Neurotic conflict, the pain of narcissistic injury (indeed, Monroe's whole inner world, largely inactive behind the wall of detachment) now became vividly reactivated (Meers, 1970, 1973). Kept consistently in contact with this revived inner world by therapy, Monroe's ego was stimulated to efforts to master its chaotic state. Thereby his ego also was stimulated to greater differentiation and development (A. Freud, 1936).

The treatment which Monroe underwent in Cornerstone can be thought of as having two distinct, though highly related foci: one, its basically nonanalytic, "upbringing," educational aspect; the other, its more specifically psychoanalytic aspect.

With regard to the nonanalytic aspect, it became commonplace for Monroe to use teachers, analyst, and children to create family like situations and relationships, in an effort to compensate, however partially, for the terrible deficiencies of his home environment. Spurred and sustained by the teachers' and analyst's pride in him (Mannoni, 1972; Berger and Kennedy, 1975), Monroe strove to become more adept in the realms of language, cognition, and social interaction. He became, in a sense, "addicted" to his new love objects, nourished more and more preferentially through them, and increasingly reactive to them as objects for identification and as auxiliaries to his own ego functions.

This ability to use objects for identification was substantially enhanced, we believe, by the concerned, nonjudgmental way in which teachers and analyst routinely discuss each child, right in the child's presence, immediately before and after the child works therapeutically with the analyst. These interchanges give the child, often for the first time in his or her life, an experience of being thought and cared about by two or more collaborating adults. Further, they promote verbalization and self-observation in the child by contributing to a group-supported atmosphere in which talking about one's feelings and about what motivates one's behavior is the accepted norm. The team discussions, at the same time, give the analyst the advantage of broad knowledge about recent events or behavior and often about themes the child has been developing with one of the teachers immediately after or before working with the analyst. Never, in our experience, has a child objected to these discussions.

There are many values in the "teamness" of the therapy, not only for the children, but also for the analyst and teachers. The team members support and provide narcissistic supplies for one another. This helps counter the development of "burnout," emotional fatigue, and depletion, which are otherwise likely to occur when therapists deal for years with large numbers of depleted patients.

We would like to underscore a special feature of the Cornerstone method, one amply illustrated by this case. The analyst's interpretations, as they do in individual treatment, appear to release in the patient considerable quantities of libido and aggression. But instead of becoming available only for further analytic work, as these energies are in individual treatment, in Cornerstone child patients are provided with a therapeutically novel opportunity. They can immediately become employed in intense relating to the teachers and other children. These relationships in turn, provide the child with myriad opportunities for sublimation and structure building, both in the social and in the cognitive realms (Rapaport, 1960; Lustman, 1970). The value of these opportunities for Monroe is strongly implied in the way in which he explored the environment in and around Cornerstone, took pride in and tended to its upkeep; charmingly and skillfully courted his teachers; constructed head-dress, bow and arrows, and necklaces; and in the end vigorously asserted himself as rational, social, and dignified, rather than remaining the depleted, dull, unsocialized, almost "feral" child he started out as.

We are convinced, however, that the non-analytic aspects of the Cornerstone method could not by themselves have accounted for Monroe's coming to life in the way he did. Otherwise, the educational therapy offered him during the previous year, together with the provision of daycare, homemaker, and therapeutic companion, should have had more evident value than it did. In our opinion, the crucial difference lay in the analytic approach enhanced by opportunities presented by the real life environment and events of the classroom. Indeed, we believe it was the analytic work which permitted the non-analytic aspects of the treatment to be effective at all.

Our reasoning is as follows. By the time Monroe began treatment, the stress and deprivation to which he had been subjected had rendered his capacities to make use of empathic understanding and narcissistic supplies defensively inoperative. We mean by this that under ordinary, i.e., non-analytic circumstances, Monroe could no longer "open up" to people. He could no longer benefit from people's affection, support, or generosity, however well intentioned. Analytic work was required to lift Monroe's pathogenic defenses so that his needs and capacities could again become operative and available to him. Once these were operative and available, analytic work was required to maintain them against persisting resistances, to permit working through.

Consistent with this view is the experience one of us gained in supervising Monroe's very dedicated educational therapist during the year prior to his entering Cornerstone. Two factors seemed central in the minimal impact educational therapy made on Monroe's pathology. One was the educational therapist's inability—unequipped as she was with the tools of analytic understanding—to deal with Monroe's primitive chaotic material without herself withdrawing emotionally. The other was educational therapy's inability as a method to cultivate and work through a transference illness.

A transference illness was, however, in our opinion, activated and cultivated in Monroe to his benefit. His analytic treatment evoked in him a condition in which all of the basic elements of his previous pathogenic experiences and pathology were repeated, though in a form which was entirely new. From at least the age of 2, Monroe was chronically subjected to object loss and deprivation as a result of his caretaker's emotional withdrawals and absences. These losses and deprivations were, in the treatment situation, replicated both in reality (though, of course, in highly muted forms) and, most importantly, in Monroe's imagination. In Cornerstone, however, (and in all likelihood for the first time in his life) on experiencing his desolate aloneness, Monroe was responded to in a consistently empathic way. This, in our view, made it possible for him to develop a transference illness in the only form he could: in the form of affect storms and intense, persistent crying, or at times in the form of violent, destructive, and near-suicidal behavior.

The illness, in turn, was responded to neither with emotional withdrawal nor with efforts to tone it down. Rather, teachers and analyst worked to help Monroe tolerate, understand, and conquer it. They made themselves affectively and physically available to provide Monroe with a holding environment (Winnicott, 1965) that would enable him to express and experience his illness. Further, his transference illness was analytically interpreted to him, in order to help him gain insights into its topographic, economic, dynamic, genetic, and adaptive aspects. As far as we know, Monroe's stormy behavior in Cornerstone was unprecedented in his life prior to treatment. We believe it had the quality of what Blos (1972) referred to as a latent infantile disorder, which for the neurotic patient is an infantile neurosis. According to Blos, this infantile disorder or illness is activated only by analysis, is a product of analysis, and is not to be equated with an actual preceding childhood illness. It is an iatrogenic illness, but one which seemed essential to accept in order to help Monroe.

The view that his crying, storms of affect, and his pain placed a therapeutically unfruitful strain on his already all-too-fragile ego has been put forth by some who know our work with Monroe. In our view, however, the center of Monroe's pathology was not a precarious balance between ego and id which could easily be overthrown by a large influx of affect. Rather, we saw as central to it a psychic apparatus massively depleted of libidinal and aggressive energies. Amelioration was possible only through Monroe's suffering the pangs of love and hate aroused by the transference and "real object" ties fostered and maintained by the Cornerstone personnel and treatment situation. It is well to remember that Monroe's tearless shrieking of the early sessions turned into tearful crying only after he had become emotionally attached to the Cornerstone personnel. Thus, it was his ability to experience himself and others as more fully human that made the communicative, discharge, and self-soothing functions of tears relevant and active (Greenacre, 1965; Lofgren, 1966; Kliman, 1978). A related view has been put forth, that Monroe's affect storms and intense crying were little more than ways on his part to protest against the agonies being stirred in him by the analytic work. We regarded them, however, as indicative of revivals in the transference of past agonies, which earlier in his life had led to despair and detachment. They were consistently interpreted accordingly. Monroe's response to these interpretations with steady improvement in his condition seems to lend support to our view.

We believe that the affective intensity which accompanied Monroe's crying actually had an enlivening effect on his psyche, and that its pain was more than compensated for by the positive experience it gave him in causing him to feel more alive. This is attested to by the fact that throughout treatment Monroe made no prolonged effort to avoid analytic work. He was generally enthusiastic about his sessions with the analyst, usually clamoring loudly for his turn to come. He also produced ever more elaborate material in the course of his episodes of crying, which in turn permitted consistently more elaborate interpretations. A period of intense crying during a session with the analyst was usually followed by a period of calm, during which Monroe often cuddled with one of the teachers, and his appearance took on a more "normal," affectively richer quality.

In this regard, it also was striking that we received no complaints from his mother, homemaker, or therapeutic companion about Monroe having become especially difficult to manage at home, as might be expected from his opening up in Cornerstone. On the contrary, his mother expressed being pleased by his greater liveliness which contrasted so sharply with his dull, numbed affect prior to Cornerstone treatment. It is possible that Monroe's long experience of living with a withdrawn mother had taught him to expect and demand very little from her. It is also possible that once his condition had improved, he knew better than to put extra pressure on her, and he turned to others or even to himself for comforting and gratification.

Interpretation as a therapeutic tool played a key role in Monroe's treatment throughout. At the beginning it was instrumental in setting therapy in motion by helping to overcome his resistances to relating and by helping to overcome his defensive flight taking. Dynamic, genetic, economic, as well as transference elements entered the interpretive work. Genetic reconstruction, especially of his mother's breakdown, was of great importance in helping Monroe to achieve increased mastery over the archaic affective chaos, narcissistic injury, and conflicts rooted in his chronic deprivation. It was of great importance in making explicit and thereby promoting his efforts to compensate for the gross deficiencies of his early environment, at the same time making more understandable to him the gross deficiencies of his current environment.

Nonverbal indicators (changes in affect and symbolic play) had to be relied on to a greater extent than is usually the case, to determine whether or not interpretations were reaching Monroe, given his initially limited intellectual and verbal capacities. During the first period in which the analyst heavily relied upon reconstructive interpretation, the extremely dramatic, affective discharge responses were considered the main indicator of its effectiveness. Monroe almost immediately changed from acting obstreperously in the service of maintaining emotional distance from objects or driving them into states of helplessness. Instead he became a boy experiencing profound pain, pain which motivated the very opposite kind of behavior. Instead of trying to keep distance from human objects, Monroe began turning to them in desperation, to gain comfort, affection, and support. At times the analyst could now infer the correctness of interpretations on the basis of Monroe's responses in symbolic play. For example, Monroe twisted a female doll's arms in every which way, in a "crazy" manner, in response to the analyst's interpretively linking his chaotic behavior in the classroom to his mother's formerly psychotic, currently withdrawn, "crazy" states. At other times the analyst inferred that Monroe understood his interpretation on the basis of affective responses. For example, following an interpretation Monroe might calm down and take on a sober appearance; or the opposite, he might become aroused or agitated as a result of affect released by the interpretation.

Modifications in the basic technique of child analysis were required by Monroe's pronounced tendency to defensive flight from intimacy, and by his stimulus-bound mode of thinking (Werner, 1940/1926, 1957). The analyst's persistent, highly active, indeed stubbornly intrusive refusal to be "shut out" by Monroe; the analyst's relying heavily on dramatization to bring Monroe's material concretely to life; and the analyst's allowing, indeed encouraging Monroe to hug and claw at him as the inner chaos emerged—these were, in our opinion, of greatest importance as parameters.

The analyst's intense activity—which the context of the nursery classroom made less threatening than it might have been had he and Monroe been meeting in individual therapy (perhaps to them both)—was necessary in countering Monroe's overriding tendency to detachment. Without it, we believe, it would have been impossible to gain his attention and to involve him in a significant relationship. Monroe's detachment, like that of so many other pseudo-retarded children, constituted a "Maginot line" of resistance which had to be circumvented, in part even overwhelmed, before he could utilize interpretations. The analyst's use of parameters such as initiation of play, employing dramatization, and accepting, at times even encouraging, physical contact are not unlike those used by many child analysts to reach psychotic or withdrawn children.

The high degree of dramatization employed by the analyst also helped to compensate for Monroe's concretistic thinking. It acted to provide a cognitive framework in which Monroe's emerging material could "fit," much as Goldstein's (1939) brain-damaged patients could conceive of a phenomenon such as rain only if it actually was raining. The dramatization also enhanced dialogue and gave boosts to Monroe's self-esteem. On the one hand, it provided him with relief, albeit at first only temporary, from his stultifying inability to communicate with other people, relief to which he reacted early with grateful elation (Freud, 1905) and increased responsiveness. On the other hand, it provided him with the privilege of seeing his thoughts and ideas spur other people (adults and often children) into lively, fascinating enactments. In these, the existence and value of his inner life were graphically mirrored.

The analyst's physical availability in the classroom ten hours each week concretely diminished Monroe's sense of being alone and overwhelmed by inner chaos. It provided his overtaxed ego with the auxiliary it needed in the palpable way he needed it. Without it, we believe, mastery by means of repetition, interpretation, and working through could not have occurred. Though, at the end of two years, Monroe was clearly far from being a "normal" child, during no appreciable period in the time he was in Cornerstone did his functioning fail to show continual improvement and, a few years later, his regular education teacher in a public school reported him to be "cured...a wonderful, outgoing boy" whose cognitive development was so improved that he was about to be moved "up to grade level."

In our approach we were fortified by our previous successful experience with detached and seemingly retarded blind children who appeared to be unlikely candidates for any form of psychoanalysis (Lopez, 1974) and by previous successful Cornerstone work with pseudo-retarded ghetto children (Kliman, 1969, 1970) who ordinarily would not be treated analytically, whether from prejudicial labels or from economic constraints, or both. We hope that this report will in turn fortify others who work with the far too many children in circumstances similar to Monroe's.

Chapter Seven

Helping a Child with a Serious Emotional Disorder (SED) and a Serious Physical Disorder

INTRODUCTION

I originally published this material as a chapter in Psychological Emergencies of Childhood (Kliman, 1968). The work described here is another example of how the power of Reflective Network Therapy emerged early on, soon after it was conceived. I have edited the original paper to update some particulars. I kept some references to the method's earlier nomenclature "Cornerstone," but substituted "Reflective Network Therapy" where the more precise term adds clarity.

The focus here is on a physically ill child (disguised as Charles) whose psychological development was profoundly disordered. The case report shows the flexibility of Reflective Network Therapy, individualizing the method for children with different diagnoses and different needs. I don't think I could have treated Charles nearly as well and as effectively with individual therapy. Honesty of communication, so vital to potential end of life communications with children, was easier for me with a network's support (Auvrignon, Leverger and Lasfargues, 2008). My report demonstrates how the method helped a physically very ill boy to grow psychologically stronger. Charles and Jay (introduced in chapter 5) were treated in the same classroom group. Charles recovered from a gender identity disturbance which appeared to be part of his extreme and reality-based anxiety about body integrity. His anxiety was not the only theme of his treatment. Charles' projected short life span (cure of leukemia was not common in 1968) and his awareness of it, make his in-classroom psychotherapy and his mother's parent guidance poignant, as it might be with a child in 2010 suffering from AIDS. With Reflective Network Therapy, Charles became more curious and less devious in his thinking, and more straightforward about expressing his needs. His IQ was not studied as we did not yet have an awareness of how regularly IQ would be improved. We did know that countertransference tenderness was a major ingredient in our effectiveness.

Loving Charles (rather than reacting to his bed-wetting, self-injuring behaviors, incontinence or twists of gender identification) was vital. Parent guidance for his mother was also crucial. Charles seemed to realize the importance of his mother's role in overcoming in his emotional disorder, as he initially chose to talk to me incisively and straightforwardly about his core issue of anticipated death precisely at those times that his mother entered our therapeutic space. Thus, because Reflective Network Therapy occurs in this real life space, she could participate in the process, not only through our guidance sessions but also in the here and now, with the opportunity to witness the child's therapeutic session in the midst of his peers and teachers. (Kliman, 1968)

Rather than describe further what has been well-documented about sick children in other works (a good example being Bergmann and Freud's Children in the Hospital, 1965), I have extracted some general principles from a dire situation: terminal illness. This area is poorly documented, despite the clear needs of many dying children for assistance with their emotional burdens. The lack of data may be attributed partly to the almost unbearable quality of adult experience when confronted by a dying child; this adult pain places severe limitations on psychological investigation.

Listening to Maurice Ravel's Pavanne for a Dead Infant allows one to feel a manageable dose of the painful emotions elicited by the event of premature death. Poets, including Wordsworth and Goethe, have struggled with the theme, sometimes with marked efforts to deny the reality of a child's death. Ruckert, a poet of nineteenth-century Germany, wrote a series of over four hundred poems, entitled Kindertotenlieder, in response to the death of his own two youngsters. A translation of Pavanne for a Dead Infant (Planck, 1964) conveys the initial need an adult feels to postpone and negate the awesome truth:

The Servant comes to tell the children their sister has died. They hear it said,
And yet with one voice say the brothers: It is not true, she is not dead.

They see her white, they see her lying, her lip so pale that was so red,
And whisper softly as replying: It is not true, she is not dead.

They see the mother weeping, waning, the father's tears his heart has bled,
And yet their chorus is remaining: It is not true, she is not dead.

And when the day came and the hours to lay her in her final bed,
To lower her beneath the flowers: It is not true, she is not dead.

May she remain your sister longer. May every year her beauty spread,
And may your love grow ever stronger.—It is not true, she is not dead.

The difficulties adult investigators and therapists encounter when dealing with dying children are not made any easier by the children themselves.
Childhood communications about death in general are understandably faulty.
Young children, when faced by the death of another person, especially a parent or sibling, usually find it difficult to express openly their sad feelings.
Such expressions are often momentary and small in quantity compared to
adult outpourings. Children who are unable to express their fear and grief
may be thought of as lacking in feeling, although careful investigation reveals that their emotions are profound and often more fatefully long-lasting
than those of more quickly-mourning adults. This expressive difficulty must
be considered when thinking of children's emotions in the face of their own
impending death. Much may be underground, waiting for the careful listener
to hear.

Further, children's intellectual comprehension of death is quite faulty
throughout the first ten (or more) years of life. It would be desirable, but
beyond the limits of this presentation, to do more than mention the findings
of Piaget and Nagy about the developmental features of healthy children's
understanding of death. Briefly, it has been fairly well-established that preschoolers have little understanding of the finality of death. No matter how
clearly informed by adults, they tend to persist in regarding death as reversible. There is a strong tendency for children up to age five to believe life is
equated with movement. Soon thereafter a tendency develops to personify
death as a malevolent person who pursues the living (Piaget, 1928; Nagy,
1948). Similar obstacles to comprehension are those parents encounter when
trying to inform their children how a seed is planted inside the mother's
womb. As they are taught a new understanding of the process, preschoolers
tend to maintain their phase-appropriate and individually varying fantasies of
oral and anal impregnation in tandem with or even in lieu of the new information they receive.

In reviewing Eissler's classic *Psychiatrist and the Dying Patient* (1955),
no reference to a dying child could be found. Indeed the relevant literature is
still quite sparse in 2010. This is especially true of investigations conducted in
an unstructured manner, giving opportunity for fatally ill children to express
their fantasies and knowledge. Such investigations are almost completely
lacking. Even when an effort to listen to a child is made, skilled and thoughtful therapists such as Emma Planck tended to approach the child's statements
with preconceived ideas and prohibition of full communication. In presenting
a case, Planck (1964) injects the thought:

> Life but not death is children's business. When a child who may conceivably die
> during hospitalization brings up the question of the possibility of his own death,
> we reassure him with great conviction and help him to deny the possibility. We

would not reconcile the child with thoughts of his own death or feel a need to prepare him for it." Bergmann (1965) indicates the same tendency.

The child about whom Planck's preliminary remarks were made was later described playing with a doll that is fantasized to be sick. "She's got to stay in bed and get an I.V., and then she can get up and play.... She's not gonna die...." Reviewing the description, it seems likely that the little girl was occupied with thoughts that the female doll, representing herself, was going to die. The child was in need of communication with an adult in some child-appropriate way about her fear that she would die. She was apparently not given an opportunity to share such fears.

Friedman, Chodoff, Mason and Hamburg (1963) state: "Some acknowledgment of the illness is often helpful, especially in the older child, in preventing the child from feeling isolated, believing that others are not aware of what he is experiencing, or feeling that his disease is 'too awful' to talk about."

Vernick and Karon at the National Cancer Institute have done an extensive study of 150 children, ranging in age from three to twenty years (1965). Forty years later (Kreitler, 2004) their work is still acknowledged as solid and compelling Even with the youngest children, as soon as the physician gives the news of a diagnosis of leukemia, a child immediately "knows" he has something very serious. The child's entire environment changes. The child quickly notices that the people whom he had previously trusted and loved are now keeping something frightening from him. Their silence is as if they were saying, "Please don't ask me about this for it is too terrible." A nine-year-old girl in Vernick's care remarked, "I knew it was leukemia. I knew I had something serious and leukemia is serious." An eleven-year-old said, "I know there is no cure for leukemia. But at least I'm glad you told me what I have." A sixteen-year-old who was not told the diagnosis by his mother for six months until twelve hours before his death, lamented, "Mother, I knew I had it all along." He had, in effect, been out of forthright communication with her for half a year.

Vernick and Karon also note that failure to discuss the diagnosis with the child contributes to behavior problems. The patient may be told the diagnosis and other truths by strangers and especially neighborhood children. Vernick believes the best way to strengthen the child against "the thoughtless barbs of his peer group" is to discuss the diagnosis with him beforehand. An illustration of the practical value of Vernick's hospital work is the case of a ten-year-old who was uncooperative on admission, frightened, withdrawn, whining, crying and refusing medication. He revealed he did not know his diagnosis but, while in the office of his family doctor, his parents were called and he was left alone. He knew nothing of what they had been told, but knew his parents had some knowledge not shared with him, about which he was worried. When the medical staff guided his parents to discuss "the great mystery surrounding his hospitalization," his parents gave the doctor permission to speak to the child about his diagnosis. The patient became more open, cheerful, relaxed, and problems about refusing medications practically disappeared. Other children on the ward noticed this change and called it amazing.

Among other findings of the National Cancer Institute group is that children often will not ask questions of the staff or their parents. Instead they wait for adults to show a readiness to anticipate and deal with their serious concerns. Only then will they reveal the pre-existing worry. Vernick and Karon also caution that the child who is gravely ill is "worrying about dying and is eager to have someone help him talk about it. If he is passive, it may only be a reflection of how little the environment helps him to express his concerns." A nine-year-old girl described how frightened she was when nobody talked to her about her downhill course: "It was like they were getting ready for me to die."

In "Death Anxiety in Children with a Fatal Illness," James Morrissey (1964) reports on his study of fifty children, sixteen of whom he judged to be aware or suspicious of the fatal nature of their illness. A three-and-one-half-year-old child had considerable anxiety about her own death. Shortly after the onset of her lymphocytic leukemia she remarked that "Jesus" was "coming down from Heaven" to take her there. She wondered if Jesus had toys in heaven. She seemed quite worried and upset that she would die, and did not want to go to heaven. Instead she wanted to stay at home and be with her mother. On one occasion while being prepared for sleep she asked, "Am I going to die?" adding, after a moment, "You know, God is going to come down from heaven and God is going to take me back with Him." After searching the literature, I believe that this child and one other child (mentioned below) are the only fatally ill preschoolers about whose cases detailed psychological observations were made prior to 1968.

Solnit and Provence (1963) assert in *Modern Perspectives in Child Development* that it has become apparent that:

> "...a more systematic investigation of a child's psychological reactions to his own dying will have to take into account the adults' tendency not to perceive the dying child's behavioral and verbal communications about his own fears because of the anxiety evoked in the adult by the dying child."

With this open, caring approach, among the cases described is that of four-year-old Larry, who was aware of his impending death although this was never discussed with him. Larry was dying from a widely metastasized neuroblastoma. He became quite attached to a young intern caring for him. Once in a panic before the induction of anesthesia for a diagnostic operation,

Larry asked the intern to sing a certain lullaby which his mother always sang before she tucked him in. His relationship with the doctor grew and Larry confided more. On the day before Larry died, he asked the intern to hold him and said he was afraid to die. His doctor should "promise to come anytime" Larry "needed" him. The intern was amazed, and wondered how long Larry had known of his impending death. Unaware of this, when the child died in a coma the next day, his parents reassured each other by saying that Larry never knew he was dying. The authors quote several other children as having even more clear awareness of their impending death, far beyond that acknowledged by their parents and physicians.

CASE REPORT: CHARLES, A FATALLY ILL, FOUR YEAR OLD BOY

A psychoanalytic approach can provide a clear view of a dying child's fantasies and concerns, as well as information regarding the extent of his realistic appraisal of his physical situation. The rare opportunity to gain such understanding was presented by the presence of a leukemic child in a Reflective Network Therapy service with psychoanalysis conducted in the classroom supported by an engaged reflective network team. The first two-month's of Charles' treatment in that environment reveals some general principles useful in therapeutic management of fatally ill as well as Seriously Emotionally Disturbed preschoolers.

Charles was four years and seven months old when he entered nursery school and simultaneously began analytic treatment in the Reflective Network Therapy modality. Charles' leukemia had been diagnosed seven months previously, close to his fourth birthday. Having been hospitalized for two weeks (during which he received a sternal puncture, blood transfusion and numerous finger punctures) Charles emerged from the hospital with daytime urinary incontinence, occasional soiling, marked whining and clinging behavior. All of these were new troubles, although he had previously been incontinent of urine at night—a behavior which continued after hospitalization. Charles slept in his mother's bedroom (in a separate bed) for two weeks after coming home from the hospital. When he enrolled in a regular nursery-school program he was unable to separate from his mother in order to attend and grew worse in regard to both enuresis and daytime urinary incontinence. Before Charles joined our therapeutic preschool group, his play activities tended to be more and more with girls, less and less with boys, and he generally confined his activities to playing house. He usually preferred to be the baby or the mother, and liked to wear girls' clothes during such play. His mother complained that he was becoming increasingly "identified" with her and with his sisters and that this was expressed in his imitative mannerisms and speech.

Nonetheless, Charles could be alert, charming, and almost always playful. Charles was especially interested in music. His "cultural" activities continued to progress during the seven months following diagnosis of his leukemic disease. He picked out tunes on the piano, demonstrated good pitch in his frequent singing, spoke in a coy, girlish way with a precocious vocabulary. Charles also loved to draw and paint; many of his drawings demonstrate advanced skills for his age. Charles' leukemia was by no means the only burden in his early life. Charles and his sisters (two and four years older) witnessed many quarrels between their parents. From the time he was two years and six months old until he was four years old, there was almost no period of marital harmony. After several separations and reconciliations, permanent separation of the parents occurred when Charles was three, followed by a divorce which was finalized only two weeks before the diagnosis of leukemia was made, right before Charles' fourth birthday.

In the context of this report, it should be pointed out that Charles had apparently experienced deprivation of paternal affection, certainly beginning no later than age two. Not only was paternal presence lacking, but it became clear that, during increasingly infrequent weekend visits to his children, the father began to show a marked preference for the company of his daughters. Charles mother reported that he had complained of this jealousy causing experience for a few months, but by age four had stopped complaining. Paternal attention diminished more conspicuously following the divorce and then the diagnosis of leukemia. Charles' mother reported that the father moved to another city. He was unwilling to come in for medical conferences following the onset of weakness and anemia which precipitated Charles' hospitalization. When psychoanalysis began seven months later, the father made frequent trips to the local area but never accepted the analyst's requests for conferences regarding his son.

Charles' father was known to us mainly through his mother. She described him as an emotionally detached, intellectually absorbed executive. Charles' description of his father centered about a pattern of his father first inviting Charles to come along and then ignoring him; in situations such as an outing where the father played tennis with adults while Charles grew impatient and finally wandered off by himself. Throughout the experience of his parents' quarrels, separation and divorce, Charles received no direct communication of the reasons for the marital difficulty. Lack of clarity and incompleteness was also the analyst's experience when trying to gain understanding of the marital circumstances which preceded the divorce.

Charles' mother presented herself to the analyst as a sad, weary, harassed young woman who found it impossible to honor appointments at all, or else could not arrive on time for the first few months. She spent much time complaining of the mechanical disrepair of her automobile, and derived numerous gallows-humor examples from "the contraption" and its hazards. A graduate of a fine college, she took a medical technician's course after Charles became ill. She hoped to contribute to research in leukemia through this latter endeavor. A few days after being given a rather ambiguous explanation of Charles' illness, her oldest child began to steal. She received prompt brief psychotherapy with a rapid favorable response.

Relevant family history includes the death of the mother's sister when the mother was fifteen. The sister was about four years old at the time (approximately Charles' age). A peculiar feature of the history is that the mother recalls that her sister's death was "due to 'osteomyelitis' associated with a very high white count." (There is a form of leukemia which sometimes becomes manifest as an osteomyelitis.) The osteomyelitis was of one leg. One of the first manifestations of Charles' leukemia was a complaint of fatigue with leg pain. Prior to diagnosis, particularly while walking upstairs, he would say, "My legs hurt too much to walk." The mother looks back ruefully to those early days of his illness—when she tended to underestimate his complaints. Perhaps a residue of her own sibling bereavement inhibited her response to Charles' leg pains.

Initial Examination

Charles was quite friendly, overly ingratiating, and surprisingly spontaneous in discussing his hospitalization—which had taken place over half a year prior to the first interview. Charles' first mention of his illness was in connection with my being a doctor, and his having been in a hospital where he "had a wonderful time and watched a lot of TV." After discussing the supposed "good time" and helping Charles with his efforts to draw some of the TV characters he had in mind, I pointed out that what he said was a kind of "opposite talk." He readily agreed that it hadn't all been "a good time. Just some of it was a good time."

Not only was a denial of the painful and fearful experience involved, but also a reversal of affect—recounting memories of events and affects as if they were a story about "Mickey Mouse from TV." At the child's request I started to draw Mickey Mouse and he finished it. I only drew the outline of the head and he filled it in. This drawing was a complicated communication. Mickey Mouse had some extra fingers and toes. Charles made a very distinct effort to be sure that I put in an extra foot for Mickey (shown protruding from Mickey's head). This was very important to him. I tried to resist for a minute, frustrating the effort by asking what this was about. Charles wouldn't be frustrated. Mickey Mouse had to have a third foot at once, (see Figure 7.1). I interpreted to him that a child might make this kind of drawing if he had a sickness that he was worried about. The child might feel it would be very good to have some extra parts around in case he might have some trouble with his body and might need those extra parts. I was impressed by how ready Charles was to accept this kind of talk.

Following two individual evaluation sessions, Charles became the fourth pupil-patient in a small therapeutic classroom group. Nowadays I would do such evaluations right in the classroom to begin with. It was our first Cornerstone Therapeutic Preschool class. I came to the class as therapist for 90 minutes a day, with each of the four children in turn becoming the index child (the focus of therapy) for therapy sessions each time the class met. Two teachers assisted and provided regular age appropriate preschool educational activities on a half day basis each day of the week.

Figure 7.1. "Mickey Mouse with Extra Parts." Charles made this drawing in seven colors, using crayons.—Previously published in *Psychological Emergencies of Childhood*, (Kliman, G., 1968).

Working with Charles' Mother

It soon became apparent that certain parallels of distortion of facts in their daily life existed in the views of both mother and child. An example arose when Charles told me the name of his summer-school teacher. It wasn't really his teacher's name that he gave me. His real teacher was an entirely different woman. When I asked the mother for permission to speak to his summer-school teacher, the mother gave me the same wrong name. It turned out that both child and mother had wanted to have that "wrong-named" teacher and were very disappointed when they got another who was not so much in tune with their personalities.

Charles revealed another sort of distortion when he insisted that his pediatrician, whom he had been seeing every few weeks for seven months, was his sister's doctor. In a multiply-determined distortion of reality, Charles once more preferred to be female. His distortion equated him with one of his lively, healthy sisters who would outlive him and also avoided the unpleasant doctor who gives him bad news and pain. (Similarly, the teacher whom he didn't want to have for a teacher would not "be" his teacher. Let the nice one be his teacher.)

In early months of applying analysis in the Charles' classroom, an effort was made to undo some distortions by interpretation, choosing them because they were not in themselves vital to the child's psychological economy. Approaching from the periphery, the distortions were used as examples to test the possibility that Charles could make a better adaptation by sharing the realities than by sharing adult avoidances of realities. Gradually his mother was helped to undo some distortions, beginning with the teacher's name. Then we began to talk with his mother about her avoidance of discussing with Charles some of the grim facts in his life. At that point, Charles began to spontaneously refer to his doctor appropriately.

Our educational director, Mrs. Doris Gorin, who was the head teacher of Charles' class, had the responsibility of conducting weekly guidance sessions with Charles' mother and three other mothers of children then in the small class. (The analyst conducted the parent conference once a month, as is usual in a Cornerstone classroom.) We gently began to ask Charles' mother what it was like from the boy's point of view to go to the doctor and to the hospital for frequent tests, to be in a hospital, to take medicine every day, and not to have one thing said about why he was taking the medicine, why he was getting the tests, why he had been in the hospital, why he had a blood transfusion or why he had a painful puncture of his breastbone. Charles' mother gradually began to see that it was really burdensome to her child to have no explanation of these procedures. She re-entered therapy herself and learned that her avoidance of communication had some relationship to her previous experience of the death of her sister. Her work on the crisis in Charles' illness appeared to have some value in reorganizing her attitude toward the previous adaptive crisis.

We began guiding Charles' mother on the subject of other current illnesses in her family. Her own mother was then seriously ill. Another grandparent was dying. We suggested that these somewhat more distant illnesses might be used by some children to initiate discussions about sickness and death, feelings about death, and fears about death.

Staff Attitudes and Challenges

We soon came to be very empathetic with the mother and sympathetic to her difficulties. Unlike Charles' mother, we did not often avoid issues. However, the analyst found himself suffering from a small amnesia about some of the data at one point. One of our staff members was in tears upon learning Charles' diagnosis. The educational director discovered and reported to me that she found herself in a mild, but still uncharacteristic, deviousness with this little boy. She had gone to the child's home for the home visit (a proce- dure always done prior to the opening of class) and said to him—knowing full well that both of his sisters were in school—"Where are your sisters today?" Consciously she felt she was trying to make conversation. But upon reflection, she reported the conversation in her daily supervisory conference with me, so that I could discuss it with her. It was an avoidance of knowl- edge. Charles had known that the teacher knew where his sisters were. She acknowledged her error about the sisters with Charles at the first opportunity. We let the mother know about some of our own difficulties and shared some of our own pain with her so she would not feel alone.

One day Charles told me that he had an ache in his eye. Another day this same eye ached him. Meanwhile, he had a facial rash which evoked in me a fantasy of leukemic invasion of his skin. Another difficulty then arose. I was supervising the educational director and on the previous day had given her a lengthy account of my analytic work with Charles so that she would be up to date. I said, "There's something else I want to tell you but I just can't think what it is except that I know it's important. It will come to me in a while, but how did you get that mark on your eye?" She told me about her eye, but I still didn't remember that I was worried about Charles' eye-ache and the rash on his face. It was only when I went back in to the schoolroom and saw Charles' face that my associations began to flow.

We learned that the mother had told all the other families on the street about Charles' leukemia. One of the other parents in the school came in one day and said, "I understand Charles is in hematologic or clinical remission."

He said this in Charles' presence. During an interview (conducted by Ann Kliman as part of the Center's study of family crises) concerning Charles' siblings, his mother made a slip about a dog that had died—a dog which had already become a focus in our interest. She explained, as she had to the head teacher, that she couldn't bear to tell the children of the death of this dog which had occurred now a week before. Then she said: "The day Charles died I just couldn't bear to tell the children that they had suffered another loss." She became aware of her slip spontaneously.

Charles' First Two Months in Reflective Network Therapy

These early months are described in detail because they contain work which was particularly related to Charles' latest psychological emergencies: his terminal illness and geographic separation from his father. One of Charles' first communications to me in the classroom was about pleasurable aggression against himself. "I just love to hit my own thumb." Charles then gave some hints of connections between his feminine identity and his stay in the hospital. He pretended to be Cinderella and dressed up as a girl, saying, "I watched that [story on TV] in the hospital." He began to invent deviously aggressive methods of getting even with other children in the class when they hit him or were mean. He wouldn't hit back, but would say, "I'm going to get even with you. I'm going to give you a present that'll be the worst present you ever had!" He said to one child at whom he was angry: "You like trucks. I'm going to give you one, but it'll be so rusty you can't play with it." Charles told another child: "You like dolls. I'm going to give you one that's no good."

About the middle of the first month of in-classroom analysis he indicated some hopes for the future. No doubt they were denials, but also some evidence of what might be phallic strivings such as, "When I grow up I'm going to have a car." (A few months later he was going to be a jet pilot.) But he now spoke of being scared by TV shows, about being lost in space, and about one-eyed robots. Perhaps his distress about one-eyed robots was a way of telling us of his fears about his eyes which ached very much. He began to try to master these fears in a forthright fashion. He took some plasticene (his own facial skin was speckled with an alarming rash) and made a mold of the teacher's hand, saying, "This (clay) is skin. I'm a doctor. I'm going to find out what's the matter with the skin." He took a knife, like a good pathologist, sliced the "skin", studied a section, held it up, and very slowly gave his opinion, "It's going to be all right." He put it down and went about other play activities. He soon began to be open about more intimate expressions of curiosity and fantasy, imaginatively stating. "Teacher doesn't have any underwear." While he was on the floor, he tried to look up the teacher's skirt and said, "I can see her behind."

In the third week of analysis Charles fantasized about little lost lambs, lonely and in need of protection. He brought some toy lambs into a block shelter, built a great fortress around them, and when it was all enclosed, he said, "You have to be careful to leave some windows open because they can die from no air." This was his first analytic expression of fear about death. He explained that people can die from no air, too, ". . . but in my house it's all right to have all the windows shut. We have water, and from the water we get air when the water dries up. So we can always breathe."

At this point came a dramatic turn in Charles' analysis and in his clinical progress. His mother had decided to "level" with her children ten days after the death of the dog. By now Charles had been well-established in our application of child analysis, and had made the communications already described. Five minutes before class started, his mother chose to tell him about the dog. Upon entering class behind his mother, he came to me. Then he sat down and had his mother sit next to me in the nursery school room. Very seriously, and with appropriate sadness he said, "You know, Spot was sick and he died." Then he added, "You know, I'm sick and I'm going to die." This was said with calm sadness.

Despite and because of the work I had done with Charles up to that point, this was a distressing communication which evoked sadness and anxiety in me. Perhaps it was helpful to the child to feel my distress and particularly my sadness. Perhaps one has to be prepared to die a little with the patient, as Eissler advises (1955).

I drew him out about his illness and the dog's death. Step by step I shared with him my serious views and elicited from him his serious views. I agreed with him, "Yes," that "Spot had died, and that it was a serious sickness that must have made Spot die. But wasn't his serious sickness a different matter? ...Spot's a dog nobody knew was sick and you're a child whose family knows he is sick. ...Spot never even went to a dog doctor or hospital, and nobody even knew that Spot was sick. Nobody could help Spot. Spot never got dog medicine, never got dog blood, didn't take dog pills every day, like you do—even two different kinds. They didn't take dog blood tests every two weeks. It's different for you even though you do have a serious sickness and you might die from it, because children do die from the serious sickness you have." This statement of his possible death did not remove Charles from his attention to me.

My lengthy response was a "dose" of reality. It was a pediatric dose of bitter truth contained in sweetened syrup of hope. It seemed appropriate to the child's developmental status and intellectual abilities.

Charles proceeded well in his analysis. He persistently used a toy telephone to communicate with me. Much discussion and fantasy emerged about how to fix things, such as kitchen parts. He wanted to make a magic stove with a button which, if pressed, would fix all the other parts of the stove so it would never break again. He expressed denial and hopefulness in this omnipotent fixer-button fantasy, which I was able to interpret as related to his wish that he could get well forever by being fixed in a magic way. I supported this wish by saying, "Wouldn't it be wonderful if you could?" I never said to him, "Charles, you'll never get well."

A difficult time arose when another child's father died quite unexpectedly in a car crash. This child was in Charles' class. The complexities of that experience were enormous, but included Charles' desire to avoid coming to class and analysis. This was dealt with by permitting him to come but not forcing him to speak about whatever he didn't wish to speak about. Nevertheless, he managed to speak somewhat about the dead father. Following a discussion about the dead father, he put on a cloth and called it a skirt, indicating his use of feminine identification as a defense against massive anxiety. He then disclosed a fantasy that his mother had a husband who had died, and he had a father who was divorced.

Charles was quite an original child. Among his original songs were: "If I were an orange I'd eat me," and "If I were a tooth I'd scrunch me." He was still quite orally occupied in many ways, but it was remarkable that in the midst of his fear and conscious knowledge about his own impending death, he was able to deal somewhat with his oedipal problems and sexual confusions. He told me about a bull. The bull was called "daddy cow" and had a baby cow inside which gets born. The daddy and baby cow get lassoed by a cowboy. The daddy cow gets squeezed so hard that he dies, but the baby cow lives still inside the daddy. Later the daddy cow comes back to life. The dying and coming back to life are repeated several times. Then came a story of a boy who got so angry at his daddy that he tried to kill the daddy. Why? Because the daddy kissed the mommy!

The story carries a communication about the reversibility of death, which any child his age might believe. There is also a linkage between that reversibility of death and the reversibility of sexual roles—daddy cow being pregnant and giving birth. After these linked confusions were pointed out to him, Charles came out with another positive oedipal triangular story in which he, in a fit of jealousy, kills the father. This again indicated more strength than I had anticipated in this dying child. The underestimation stemmed from my own denial of the dying child's strength, suggesting a reason why therapists avoid the treatment as well as investigation of such children's psychological processes.

During the second month of analysis Charles proceeded with stories about how a parent deceives a child in a hospital by telling him that the food will be good when it is really terrible. By now the analytic and therapeutic relationships to me and the teachers were so firm that at Thanksgiving time he said, "Damn, I wish there weren't any turkeys. I don't want to have Thanksgiving with no school." Analysts and teachers alike are accustomed to denial and reversal of emotional response at such times, as children try to convince themselves and adults of cheerfulness or brazenness rather than sadness at the moment of departure.

During the first two months of analysis in the classroom, Charles revealed he shared with other four and five-year-olds the idea that a dead person cannot move and cannot breathe. But being so attached to school and his analyst, he added an idiosyncratic detail about death: "A dead person can't breathe and can't move, but he can learn." This detail apparently signified that Charles wished to continue being with his teachers and analyst even when he was dead. Blindness soon was mentioned by Charles as if it were equated with death. "Blind people are dead, even though they can move." For Charles, some of the separation problems of death and blindness were similar: not being able to see people whom he loved. Now that he was lonely for his dead dog, Spot, Charles drew pictures of him, saying, "I wish you could see Spot's face. It's so nice."

Varieties of oedipal fantasies came forth more and more in Charles' analytic material. He would drive a car for the purpose of saving his mother. He would take the wheel when she had an accident. He would save her. He would fly an airplane. He would swoop down from his jet airplane, pick up the damaged car, repair it, and return it for mother to use.

By the end of his second month, Charles' clinical progress was definite. He no longer wet his bed at night, nor dampened his pants during the day and he did not soil any more. He separated readily from his mother, came to school willingly and went freely outdoors to play with friends after school. He played well with other children, was as creative as ever, and eager to learn from the books his mother and teachers read to him at his request. Charles was overheard speaking to his classmates occasionally about his illness, and defined for them one aspect of its effect on his life: "I have a sickness, but it's the kind where I can go to school most of the time." He did not speak to the children about dying, but spoke of it to the analyst when other children could hear. Charles was now open about certain resentments. "Why should I have to go to take blood tests every two weeks? My sisters don't have to go except once in a while." He hit his sisters when they were mean to him. He hit his mother a great deal, rather unprecedentedly, but under circumstances which the mother felt were justifying. He hit other children in the class when annoyed or hurt by them, a contrast to his intellectual revenges of the first month. Occasionally he would give the analyst a moderate blow, either in a jealous moment or as an act of defiance directed against the teachers as well as the analyst. He would occasionally knock over classroom equipment when angry, and—interesting in view of his thoughts about blindness and death—would pull down window shades and turn out lights in bursts of mischievous glee.

Ever-continuing preoccupation with deterioration of his body was suggested by Charles' response while watching another child punch holes in a paper cup: "That's like punching holes in skin. If you really did that to a person, they would bleed. The blood would come out of the holes." He stopped, thought, got very tense, saying, "Then the bones would come out, and then the eyes would come out, and then the person would die."

Medical Evaluation of Charles' Physical Status in the First Two Months of Analysis

Charles was under the regular care of a pediatrician and hematologist, who—like his therapist at school—worked to some extent as a coordinated team. They reported Charles to be in good hematologic remission, with no evidence of active disease during this period. He was judged capable of participating fully in all physical activities. His medication consisted of two forms of antimitotic agents (which help block leukemic cell growth) given in series. Two weeks with one agent were followed by two weeks with the other agent. His facial rash was possibly allergic but never well-understood. Occasional anorexia and nausea were thought to be effects of one antimitotic agent, but in time was noted to appear while the other was being received.

The pediatrician and hematologist advised us that physical prognosis could not be given in a definitive fashion. (In the mid 1960's) some children had been known to live as long as five years with remissions and exacerbations of leukemia treated by the methods which were being applied in Charles' case. The mean life expectancy was one year, of which nine months had passed at this point. With passage of each month there was statistical reason to expect survival even longer than one year, but no special criteria could be applied for such predictions in any given child.

DISCUSSION OF THE FIRST TWO MONTHS' THERAPEUTIC MATERIAL

By the end of the first two months, the analyst and, through him, the child's teachers and mother had confronted Charles with a multidirectional effort to correct and compensate for his multiple pathogenic experiences. Pathogenic deprivations, also multiple, had been approached as follows:

Deprivation of emotional investment from the mother was partly corrected by helping the mother overcome her avoidance of communication with the dying child. This reduced a major obstacle to healthy influx of maternal emotional supplies.

Deprivation of paternal affection and investment was partly corrected by establishing an intense relationship with an adult male, the analyst, who was with the child six hours each week in the classroom. Deprivation of emotional experience with heterosexual "teams" of adults was partly corrected by the establishment of intense relationships with the analyst-teachers team.

Charles' experience with sensations of weakness, fatigue, subtle experiences of body-image change, and perception of painful medical procedures all were made worse by a "fear experience." That fear experience was potentially, if not actually, pathogenic, compounded, as it was, by an absence of information from his parents concerning the purpose and meaning of what was being done to help him.

The fear experience was approached by: (1) Helping the patient's mother to share with the child her own emotional resources in dealing with the realistic danger to him; and (2) Offering the analyst as an object with whom the patient could share fears and discuss both the realistic danger and reverberations with neurotic anxiety and conflicts related to Charles' fantasies and underlying problems.

In some ways, Charles' thoughts about death were met much as a child's thoughts about sexual behavior could be met at this age in the midst of an analysis. The family was helped to deal with what the child observed or had already asked or spoken about–notably the death of his pet, about which his perceptions and feelings were presumably highly accessible. Just as it probably would not be useful to explain to a child of this age aspects of adult sexual activity which had not come to his attention, it was not considered desirable for the child to be confronted with aspects of his illness and the process of dying which would be incomprehensible and perplexing to him (provided there was no evidence that the child was already trying to cope with these aspects). It was considered essential that the patient should be allowed to know that death can occur at his age. He was brought back into the channel of communication on this matter, rather than separated from his mother, whose own emotional life was perceptibly reverberating with the knowledge of her child's impending death.

Vernick and Karon (1965) concluded their study of leukemic children in a hospital by asking, "Who's afraid of death in a leukemia ward?" They answered "Everyone." The resolution of that fear was everyone's problem on the ward. In an atmosphere of complete freedom for their child patients to express their concerns, Vernick and Karon found that most of the children already knew of their illness, and some knew exactly what was wrong. Their staff was able to abandon traditional tactics of protecting children by being secretive, and as a consequence became actively and constructively involved in helping their patients cope with the realistic experience of fear. They reported marked diminution in withdrawal, depression and behavior disorder which are so frequent on leukemia wards.

Up to this point, Charles' treatment tended to confirm the findings of Vernick and Karon (1965). Charles was capable of verbalizing his own incurability and impending death. His comprehension of these matters was appropriately immature and faulty, as were his sexual ideas. He believed in the incompleteness and reversibility of death in a way comparable to his belief in the ability of a bull to bear a baby cow. He appeared to feel much better when he communicated about his illness, fears and fantasies. His improvements were by no means simply the result of improved communication about illness and death. He was a paternally deprived child, and to some extent a maternally deprived child. Partial corrections of those deprivations had been distinctly helpful. Each relationship involved in such corrections had a common and basic feature. That feature was not only warmth, but a combination of warmth with persistent truthfulness and willingness to listen.

Emerging from Charles' analysis was a process I call "psychological immunization" (Kliman 1968), which requires a "pediatric dosage of reality." As with all powerful medicines, there are a few patients who should never receive doses of certain realities for special reasons. As with all medicines, the smallest doses should be given to the smallest children. The capacity to usefully absorb is smaller and the toxic dose might be more easily exceeded in the exposure of young children to painful reality. The necessity for containing the pediatric dose within a suitable vehicle has become clear, and the desirable vehicle appears to be reliable human relationships in this case, including reliable medical care.

Also emerging from the analysis in the first two months were indications of special problems in the assisting adults. Not only Charles' mother and father, but also his analyst and teachers, were clearly distressed and to some extent conflicted about Charles' experiences. These distresses and conflicts tended to interfere with treatment of the child. Recognition of staff difficulties occurred early enough to permit greater empathy for the mother's experience, which supported her in dealing more responsively with the child's own experiences.

POSTSCRIPT

After going into a marked psychological remission by the end of a school year, Charles did not require further psychoanalysis. But he did not go into a full remission of his leukemia. Those were days when cures were rare. Three years later, Charles died. I had occasional sessions with him after he left our therapeutic preschool, and I was able to visit him in the hospital several times, when he was close to death.

Charles' dying years were characterized by a steady masculine identification, constant developmental progress, freedom from regressions of executive skills and sphincter control, and increasing intellectual curiosity. In his dying hours he was glad to see me. He told me he knew he was dying. He questioned the hospital staff as to whether they were giving him enough oxygen. While I was with him, he succeeded in getting nurses to provide him with the right to personally control his oxygen tank valve and use an oxygen mask, which he felt cleared his thinking. It was my countertransference feeling that Charles died with dignity. He showed activity and realistic awareness of his impending death, using a commanding strength—dying "with his boots on."

Chapter Eight

Bereaved Preschoolers with Serious Emotional Disorders (SED)

Sections of this chapter previously appeared in a chapter by Kliman in *Perspectives on Bereavement* (I. Gerber, A. Wiener, A. H. Kutscher, D. Battin, A. Arkin, & I. Goldberg (Eds.), 1979).

Here you will meet several children who had suffered tragic losses and were helped by Reflective Network Therapy. This chapter is essentially practical in its orientation to technique, describing several forms of treatment of bereaved children, with a minimum of theoretical essay. Probably the best definition of "mourning" for our current purposes is, "the totality of reaction to the loss of a loved object." We omit from this definition any immediate consideration of whether mourning can occur at various stages in childhood, and if so, to what extent one or another investigator judges that it has occurred, although such consideration is worthy of volumes. To simplify the task somewhat, because it is actually of extreme complexity, Freud's definition of the work of mourning will be used, (1957/1917). Important background scientific contributions we do not detail here include the work of Altschul, (1988), Bowlby, (1960, 1980), Eth and Pynoos (1985), Furman (1964,1981), Kliman (1968, 1980), Terr (1991), Kranzler et al. (1990), Melhem, et al. (2007) and Brown et al. (2008). Never a momentary injury, childhood loss of a loved person is often a long-enduring pathogenic influence. It deserves preventive intervention whenever the loss has occurred early in life, and especially when the early loss is that of a parent. The children discussed in this chapter were treated at The Center for Preventive Psychiatry. From its inception, that agency was concerned with developing techniques of primary prevention to help orphans who might otherwise develop mental illness as a consequence of unresolved issues related to bereavement. Data concerning a series of 18 untreated orphans show that few orphans are free of newly arising neurotic symptoms.

The original mission of that agency was to help adults and children dealing with severe emotional burdens, particularly those related to crises precipitated by situational stresses and traumas. Among the thousands who came the Center during its first 12 years of operation were many victims of severe, traumatic sudden crises other than the loss of a loved one (object loss). Some were children who were sexually molested, or who had been badly beaten or who had witnessed murders in their families. Some were suffering adverse effects of their involvement in highly over-stimulating experiences, or incestuous relations within their own families. Some were severely physically ill. Some had sustained psychological trauma, developmental derailment and loss of home and property due to sudden, mass disasters such as floods or tornados. No patients however, attracted more of our systematic professional interest or consumed more of our professional energies than adults and children who suffered the sudden and then chronic strains of bereavement.

Often we found that even orphans referred to us very soon after bereavement, specifically for preventive support, already presented important neurotic symptoms. In fact, the majority of recently bereaved children suffered recognizable symptoms of neurosis, and in some cases, psychosis. On the other hand, children often became able to express their deep loss and longing creatively, giving voice to the seemingly inexpressible. We strongly disagree with Wolfenstein (1966) concerning her view that mourning only becomes possible with adolescence.

The Cornerstone team practicing Reflective Network Therapy who worked with Ellie (an orphaned child) will never forget her mournful singing. She sang roughly in the cadence and melody of Kumbaya, an old spiritual by Reverend Marvin Frey (popularized by Joan Baez in the 60's). Fortunately, Ellie sang directly into a tape recorder so that we were able to transcribe her creative expression. She repeated the first few lines *many* times before continuing her song:

> *Where, oh where is my mother?*
> *She's down in the ground—*
> *Graveyard and deep asleep.*

> *Where, oh where is my mother?*
> *She's down in the ground—*
> *Graveyard and deep asleep.*

> *Where, oh where is my aunt Eliza?*
> *She's down in the graveyard dead asleep.*
> *I want to be with my mother in the grave.*

Oh, Lord! Where oh where is my mother?
My mother hit her head on the stove.
And then she died. God, please—

Bring my mother back.
Please, Lord. Please, Lord. Please Lordy.
We put a plant on her grave. We put a plant on her grave.
Aunt Eliza is in a grave next to my mother.
O Lord—I want to be there too.

O Lord, O Lord—Please O Lord.
Bring my mother back to me.
Bring her back, O Lord! Bring her back.
O Lordy bring her back.

In an extraordinary demonstration of resilience, Ellie showed us her readiness and willingness to transfer her needs for mothering and nourishment to an appropriate and available love object, her Granny, almost immediately after singing this dirge. After a brief hesitation, she sang these new verses into the tape recorder with marked energy:

Where's my Granny, Lord?
She's at home cooking.
O Lordy, Kumbaya.

Hello, Granny. Hello Granny!
What are you doing there?
Hey, Granny, what are you doing there?

You home cookin'. Hey, Granny!
Hey, Granny, can I have some Cheerios?
Oh, my goodness—man. Man, I want it!

It is interesting to me in retrospect that Ellie sang her verses in a tune that so closely resembled that of Kumbaya. In its language of origin "kumbaya" is three words meaning come by here *("O Lord, come by here")* from Mende, used by the Gullah people, a language called "The Language You Cry In" in a 1998 documentary film by that title. Specific feedback on this child's engagement with the present, including her current primary caretaker, "Granny," reinforced her recognition of present time love and support.

It is the task of caregivers to create and cherish opportunities for children to express their grief and do the work of mourning in order to release the child's otherwise potentially arrested development. Doing so in the therapeutic context of Reflective Network Therapy classroom affords children an adult network which magnifies beneficial emotional resonance by verbalizing (mentalizing), reinforcing or interpreting the emotional content of creative expressions. This gives the child an acknowledged place to stand where she feels that she is understood and from which she can be encouraged to move forward. Just as bone fractures are a categorical damage from which children may successfully recover untreated, the same is also theoretically true of orphans. But a break in a love relationship early in childhood usually needs help in healing. It is our position that means for healing such fractures in a child's love-life are extraordinarily undeveloped, little used and, indeed, sometimes shunned. The RNT Method is particularly well suited to fill this void in the treatment of childhood bereavement and its related neuroses.

The major and often statistically significant works of Beck (1963), Barry (1960), Kliman (1968), Gregory (1965), Bowlby, (1980), Furman (1964), Krantzler, (1996) and others amply demonstrate the long standing, common-sense impression of many clinicians working with children that death of a parent is a severe insult to psychological health. Especially when bereavement occurs during early childhood, there is an excessive incidence of psychopathology within a few months, and it endures noticeably throughout adult life when left untreated. Terr (1991) has correctly noted that both loss and trauma are involved in various combinations in the production of serious psychiatric disorders. Terr puts it in terms of the long term effects of experiences like the set of children described in this chapter have gone through:

> Childhood psychic trauma appears to be a crucial etiological factor in the development of a number of serious disorders both in childhood and in adulthood. Like childhood rheumatic fever, psychic trauma sets a number of different problems into motion, any of which may lead to a definable mental condition. There are four characteristics related to childhood trauma that appear to last for long periods of life, no matter what diagnosis the patient eventually receives. These are visualized or otherwise repeatedly perceived memories of the traumatic event, repetitive behaviors, trauma-specific fears, and changed attitudes about people, life, and the future. (Terr, 1991)

Terr divides childhood trauma into two basic types and defines the findings that can be used to characterize each of these types. Type I trauma includes full, detailed memories, "omens," and misperceptions. "Type II trauma includes denial and numbing, self-hypnosis and dissociation, and rage. Crossover conditions often occur after sudden, shocking deaths... In these instances, characteristics of both type I and type II childhood traumas exist side by side..."

The above opinions about bereavement have been well established, especially by Gregory's (1965), Kliman's (1968) and Krantzler's (1996) various controlled, anterospective and retrospective series of bereaved and non-bereaved children from comparable social, ethnic, racial and economic strata. Society has much to gain by carefully attending to the problems of each orphan in the adaptation to his or her loss. Furthermore, the readily detected nature of this pathogenic factor makes it a prime target for the too often neglected field of preventive psychiatry.

Deutsch's studies (1937) suggest that the problem, amidst all its kaleidoscopic complexities, includes excessive childhood defensiveness against the painful emotions of grief. This is especially pernicious when the child's grief is for a dead parent. Defensiveness against affective charge may become a life-long pathogenic style for some bereaved children. To the extent that Deutsch has correctly discerned a major etiologic component in the emotional disorders following bereavement, one major part of the preventive task is to facilitate mourning by helping release a bereaved child's grief, including sad, yearning feelings and associated memories in a situation providing perspective, insight and corrective experience. This must be done in a fashion compatible with the child's defensive repertoire, his developmental state, and his life framework. Then he or she can experience further development and avoid fixation or arrest at the developmental stage at which the damaging loss occurred.

The illustrations of mourning facilitation provided in this chapter are gathered mainly from orphaned children treated with varying degrees of intensity at the Center for Preventive Psychiatry, especially in the Cornerstone School. The Center has a busy situational crisis service, to which many recently traumatized children come every month. By the early 1970's it had become the nation's largest situational crisis service. There was preventive value in the community's recognition that bereaved children need special help right away and that a place exists where appropriate help can be obtained. The children referred have ranged in age from infancy to 18 years and were bereaved for periods of a few hours to as long as five years before coming to the Center. Some of the children were known to the therapist before the parental death occurred, so that some baseline knowledge was available at the outset of treatment. We also drew upon a deep source of information about childhood bereavement—our in-classroom Reflective Network Therapy treatment of dying children.

THE SPECIAL PROBLEMS OF DOUBLE ORPHANS

Proceeding further into seldom explored areas of bereavement research, our experience with children who have lost both parents is illuminating. Their immediate grief tends to be more open than with other bereaved children who have lost one parent, in the literal sense of prolonged anguished crying. Conscious feelings of grief also attend later remembering of the dead parents, more openly and more frequently than with orphans bereaved of one parent. Although causally different, the phenomenological situation of double orphans is like that of Bender's psychotic orphans, who grieved profusely and even wildly. Double orphans, like psychotic children, lack adequate defenses. But the lack is in proportion to the great quantity of affect being stimulated by the double loss rather than because of an intrinsic deficiency of defense. Or, we could say the proportional relationship of affect to defense is disturbed by excess over the "average expectable" life of stress rather than by the inadequacy of their defenses due to any disease. But double orphans may also have suffered some actual weakening or exhaustion of defense due to the first loss, on which the second loss is now heaped. The task with double orphans is, therefore, how to facilitate the management of extraordinary quantities of affect becoming detached from two major love objects, and specifically how to manage this task without the development of gross deformities and breaches in the testing of perception and in the children's adaptation to new love objects.

One of the double orphans whom we treated frequently hallucinated. This was a major presenting problem. In follow-ups after treatment he was not apparently psychotic. One task with this four-year-old boy was to provide interpretations to produce a framework of insight, so that he could understand the nature of his hallucinations, especially their wishful, loneliness-induced origin.

In another case where we treated a twelve-year-old boy who was a double orphan, a main accomplishment was to allow more boldness in his adaptation to peer social objects. His high dose of affectively charged conscious memories of both parents became more manageable. In-session catharsis occurred repeatedly but was placed in perspective of how much his parents would—if they were alive—want him to develop friendships. This work was done twice weekly and successfully concluded in only ten weeks. For an entire year, his love-life had been previously been confined to going over memories of his parents, obsessively and morbidly pouring over photo albums. Before treatment he had also suffered prolonged bouts of silent weeping with regret over the lost and then idealized life he and his parents had had together. After catharsis in treatment, these mournful ruminations diminished and the child's social life became rich. Apparently the child became able to use the energy released from unhealthy preoccupations for making new attachments. (Energy available for making new attachments lovingly is sometimes technically called "libido".)

Elsewhere (Feinberg 1970), Kliman 1979) Feinberg (a Cornerstone colleague) and I have described related work: the task of preparing two older sisters for the impending death of "Charles" (see chapter 7) and facilitation of their adaptation to the actual loss when their brother died. Special attention is given by me to therapeutic support for feminine identity development in the case of a maternally bereaved girl in another report (Kliman 1979, p. 86). Still another report (Kliman, 1968) discusses a boy who lost his father; this report provides data concerning the relationships between mourning and multiply-determined symptoms of unusual (microptic or tiny) hallucinations as well as perceptual and memory impairment.

The following brief survey of techniques used in treatments of bereaved children will move from customary techniques to those less customary.

PARENT GUIDANCE ISSUES

Nothing can be more critical to a child's mourning than the mourning work of the adults around him and their attitudes toward the child's work. A major part of the preventive and therapeutic task can often be efficiently focused on parent guidance. Because such guidance techniques are widely practiced and well-known (Novick and Novick 2000 is an excellent introduction to the importance of parent guidance), we will not dwell on them except for some insufficiently appreciated and essential points.

Parent guidance in cases of childhood bereavement should include at least some check on the possibility that a remaining parent may be out of synchrony with the very difficult mourning rhythms of his or her child. For example, forceful evidence of lack of synchrony within a family is often found when a widow is ready to remarry, particularly if her remarriage is planned for a year or less after bereavement. She may need assistance to realize that her children are much slower than she to give up the lost love object, because of their greater defensiveness against permitting the work of mourning to proceed. During latency, mourning is apt to be particularly silent and slow. Throughout childhood, the tardy pace with which the old object is decathected is one cause of poor acceptance of substitute parents. It also accounts for the otherwise surprisingly higher incidence of certain psychopathology, as Gregory's large-scale study reports (1965) and is modestly confirmed by smaller scale reports by Kliman (1968) and Kranzler (1987). Among families where the surviving parent has remarried, there is actually a higher incidence of truancy, school failure and school dropout than among families where the surviving parent remains single. We must take these unpleasant facts very seriously, as they come from indisputable anterospective study made over a decade with several hundred orphans among 10,000 school children. The implication is that we must guide parents preventively to help their bereaved children with utmost tact when a remarriage is impending. However, our sketch of technique need not dwell greatly on that already common practice.

The surviving parent also needs guidance and support to avoid surprisingly regular tendencies to use the child as a partial replacement for the lost spouse. Our series of 18 consecutive non-patient orphans (Kliman, 1968) showed that seven out of eight families had one child who was chosen as bed companion for the surviving parent. Nine out of these 18 untreated orphans began a pattern of bed-sharing with the surviving parent. This occurred in families which had no previous pattern of inter-generation bed-sharing. A six-year follow-up showed that the tendency, generally manifest within a few weeks after bereavement, continued to be a major one. It is unquestionably an obstacle to full mourning, in the sense of moving on to healthy substitutes for the lost object. One of the initial study's bed sharers (then age 11) was over six feet tall by age 17. He had an active adolescent heterosexual life, but still shared the mother's bed several times a week!

Since a large fraction of bereaved children become parent bed-sharers, we can speculate reasonably that the incestuous impulses of many bereaved children—particularly when the bereavement is of the same sex parent—are a major obstacle to the progress of mourning. To mourn—and be thereby freed for the loving of other persons—is dangerous when the most available other person is the surviving opposite sex parent who is also a tempting bed partner. Bed sharing is, of course, only one form of erotically tinged distortion of parent-child interaction after a death in the family.

Timeless Interviews and Reflective Network Therapy for Bereaved Children

Before discussing techniques of the Reflective Network Therapy as it serves bereaved preschool children, I call attention to a fascinating technique for mourning facilitation developed and used with adults in Mexico. Remus-Araico (1965) reported excellent results with a series of 12 adult analysands orphaned during childhood. These patients generally suffered from repressed sad affect and fixation to developmental stages at which the childhood bereavements had occurred, with evidence of a "'traumatic neurotic'" process. Remus-Araico's data confirm and enrich the finding of Fleming and her co-workers (1963) in Chicago and provide an interesting innovative contribution to the facilitation of mourning techniques. That contribution is in the form of what Remus-Araico calls "timeless interviews." He found it very useful to arrange that several times during the course of analysis he would meet with the patient for an interview of a duration limited only by the interest and willingness of the patient and analyst. These interviews, which frequently endured several hours, often induced a state of remembering with extremely intense detail and high emotional charge. Remus-Araico frequently felt that the analyst and patient "were standing at the side of the grave together." We believe that such cathartic remembering is indeed difficult to facilitate in adults as well as in children. Yet, to some extent, it appears feasible even in children of preschool age, as well as those who are older. A necessary condition is a positive transference and ample time in which to set the mental stage. Such time may be provided by the many hours of school work which surround a preschool child's Reflective Network Therapy.

Reflective Network Therapy techniques regularly used by the Center for Preventive Psychiatry involved working 15 hours a week with small groups orphans (and other young patients) in a prevention-oriented nursery school with the analyst present in the classroom for six or more of those hours. RNT techniques appear powerful for orphans of preschool age with serious emotional disorders (SED) and pervasive developmental disorders (PDD) just as it has been for neurotic and psychotic children. This summary of RNT techniques used to help bereaved children is essentially the same as for treating children in other categories but includes explanations specific to children with mourning problems and presents in some detail the case of "Quentin".

QUENTIN AND OTHER CHILDREN IN MOURNING

Some of the children discussed below appear in other chapters of this book. This section summarizes techniques and treatments of children carried out at The Center for Preventive Psychiatry. While the teachers conduct educational activities, the analyst works right in the congenial and communication-evocative classroom setting. He or she transacts with one child and then moves on to work with another, and then another. In this setting, he is able to interpret material the children express to teachers or to each other, as well as the play and verbal communications made directly to him. When the analyst leaves the classroom after an hour and a half or two of work each morning, the six or eight child patients who constitute the class remain at work with their teachers. The teachers are early childhood educators, working under the analyst's supervision, as well as the supervision of an educational director. They observe and cultivate, but do not interpret the communications of the children made after the analyst leaves. Thus, while educational activities continue for the remaining hours of the morning, many fantasies and playful expressions set in motion by the interpretive work of the first 90 minutes continue to emerge and are observed and cultivated for long periods of school time, and are later reported to the children's analyst. At the same time, these expressions are channeled into ego-building social and educational activities.

Many essential features of a regular child analysis tend to occur despite the unorthodox setting. With the orphans among our Cornerstone patients, a considerable amount of vivid, affectively expressive and ideationally rich energetic mourning work takes place. We mean to include in this emphatic statement all elements included in Freud 's Mourning and Melancholia (1917) definition: the working over of ideas and affects associated with the lost object, the cathecting and decathecting (investing emotionally and removing investment) regarding the mental representative of that object, testing for the reality of the object's permanent absence, increased identification with the lost object, and use of liberated cathexis (psychological energy) for investment in new objects (Freud, 1917).

Time and time again, in the daily classroom treatment sessions with orphans, we find that the orphaned child's feelings and thoughts about the analyst are transferences, clearly and continuously linked to thoughts, memories and feelings about the dead parent. Even thoughts about extremely frightening and shocking experiences in the past can emerge in the classroom setting, as part of the transference-linked working over. An example is provided by Quentin, a five-year-old who was alone with his father in a car when the father had a heart attack and died. Quentin entered a Cornerstone RNT Project about six months later. The following excerpt from his work shows some of the interplay between the pathogenic past and the transference present.

Quentin went to a great deal of trouble to pull the analyst's beard, and made a drawing of the analyst with a very long beard. The analyst was required to help, and to draw Quentin going for a ride on the analyst's beard, straddling the beard. Quentin then began playing automobile riding games and speaking of his father. He placed some paint in a bowl of water and said it reminded him of blood, saying, *"This is very dangerous. It's my daddy's blood."* Continuing to develop the blood theme, Quentin thought about how the blood in a person's heart could stop moving and then a scientist could stick the person in the heart to make it work again. He spoke of good and bad scientists and whether other things besides caterpillars could go into a cocoon and come out butterflies.

Up to this point, we can see that the analyst's person, particularly his beard, was transitional in the series that led to his father and thoughts of his father's death and fantasies of metamorphosis or reincarnation. Quentin proceeded to thoughts about cars crashing, wondering if his now late school bus had been in a crash, and what that would sound like. He grew tired, wanted to nap, and draped some play jewels over his head. They were *"the flowers you put on a dead person."* Lying very quietly he then said, *"Would you be sad if a friend died?"* and hastened to explain, *"I thought my daddy was fooling. I asked the man who came if Daddy was alive or dead, but I thought he was just fooling, but he wasn't."*

The next day, Quentin demonstrated a marked continuity of theme in his Cornerstone work. He approached the teacher with the same colored beads, this time announcing, *"I'm an angel."* The analyst briefly recapitulated the work of the previous day for Quentin, to point out the relevance of this remark. Quentin then offered further details of the fatal episode: *"A man came and pulled me by the shoulders and I cried."* The analyst interpreted that Quentin must have wanted to stay with his daddy, and was still hoping that his daddy was just fooling.

The child responded with some further ideas about needles that could start a heart working again, which the analyst interpreted as thoughts which come because it would have been wonderful if Quentin could still have his father living, and Quentin would like to be a person who saved his father. In response, Quentin had two sets of thoughts. First, he asked if the school could get him an oxygen gauge, which he wanted to keep in the doll house he was now furnishing. Then he spoke of houses which are nice and houses which are not nice and scientists who are good and scientists who are bad. Scientists who are good save people and scientists who are bad keep people tied up.

In later work, this theme of goodness and badness was interpretable in terms of his anger at the father for having left him by dying, and his dread that if the father knew how angry Quentin was, the father would be angry at Quentin. The Reflective Network Therapy work proceeded, with increasing clarity of linkage and equation between the father and the male analyst, who was openly loved and died many times in the child's fantasies.

EVOCATION OF YEARNINGS FOR AN
UNKNOWN FATHER

The opportunity to work with a posthumous child, born after the father's death, is rare. At the Center, it was approximated by the presence in the school of David, a child whose father had died when he was several weeks old. Since David never actually knew his father in narrative or episodic memory, and it is of some interest to note the special vicissitudes of his work, by means of which he arrived at a useful awareness of what was missing in his life. The presence of a male therapist (Myron Stein, M.D.), within a heterosexual team of constructively collaborating adults, was probably a facilitator of his yearnings. In that emotionally nourishing setting, where his need for a father was to some extent actually met by the frequent presence of the analyst, he could dare to let the desire for a father emerge. The procedure is, of course, not strictly the 'same as the work of helping a child mourn for a loved person he has actually known, but is reported because of its relevance to the general problem of childhood bereavement.

David entered the Cornerstone Therapeutic Nursery at the age of three years, five months. Not only had he been paternally bereaved several weeks after birth, but his mother also had a chronic, presumably fatal illness. His two brothers were two and five years older than he. This was a family in which a great deal of high drama went on, but always in terms of actions, veiled hints, without direct acceptance, recognition of or communication about these matters.

Issues regarding separation, being left behind and death came up rapidly and in many ways during the first year of David's treatment. Initially, the matter of separation from the mother arose. This was a mother who wanted to leave the classroom immediately, who found it an intolerable burden to have to put in time staying with David in school. She was constantly referring to the issues of being there or not being there, and separation, but always in a displaced fashion, not directly relating it to the bereavement or to her own illness. She would do this with jokes. When David was shy one day, hiding behind his mother's skirts rather than relating directly to the teachers, she made the joke, *"I think I left David at home today."* This reference to his not being there, being elsewhere, or being lost, was repeated in many ways.

We did insist that the mother stay on with David a bit for several weeks, rather than abruptly leaving him in class. During that time, he focused repeatedly on his fear of her leaving. It was possible to point out to him his sadness, his fearfulness, his sudden noninvolvement when she left the classroom. This was sufficiently helpful that soon, when his mother did separate, he was able to stand it. David's concern about people being sick or away was expressed by a shocked reaction whenever anyone was ill or absent. If a teacher, a therapist or other children were away, David was very upset, and this upset was also pointed out to him in terms of his being worried about something happening to loved people. When his mother went for a periodic examination at the hospital, he was also upset and focused on the fear that something bad would happen to the mother. The therapist discussed the child's awareness of the mother being followed in the hospital because of an illness, and where she was being treated and cared for as much as possible. David's concern about his own body integrity came up in terms of his worries about his own physical examinations, linked to thoughts of his seriously ill mother.

The actual fact of David's father's absence and of his missing his father came up for the first time some months after he had been in the nursery. This was previously a completely avoided subject, and when the patient finally brought it up at home, his older brother's reaction was to turn to the mother and say, *"Mom, this kid's nuts."* In school, David made a magic potion of mud, water and paint. He was able to express exactly what the magic potion was in terms of "magic to bring a father back." Thus he was able to express his loneliness for his father and his wish for a father as expressed in his magic potion. He built a snowman outside and when a few of the children broke it down, he showed real despondency. He said that this was a real man. The analyst pointed out to David that he wished so much that he could have a real man, like a father, that when his substitute for the real man, namely the snowman, was destroyed, he missed it badly. He was able to agree with and seemed relieved by the interpretation.

After this work, there was a distinct change in David's typical way of functioning, Previously he behaved in imitation of a big man, puffed up, talking in a loud voice, denying anxiety and depression, instigating fights, and generally behaving like a little sheriff in the classroom. After admitting his sadness and his missing having a father, he was able to be more of a little boy, feeling and expressing a little boy's need of his father, missing his father, and sadness about not having his father. He initiated games with the therapist in which they would prepare meals together, eat together and trade gold. Much of the work seemed related to his deep longing for identification with a father or a valued male.

Vacations from the therapeutic classroom were difficult for all of the children, as were holidays, and David also found these separations difficult, in line with material discussed above. Transference interpretations were made in terms of David having to be tougher, more abusive, and less communicative just before and immediately following vacations and holidays. In response, David initially showed minimal changes, but then became able to demand the therapist's attention more directly and less directly avoided it.

For a long time, this rough, tough little man had needed to deny positive feelings towards the analyst. He referred to the analyst as stupid or "dootie." After the interpretations about missing the father, wanting to make a father through the magic potion or the snowman, when David became able to become more of a little boy, he was also able to directly express his positive feelings towards the analyst and became more receptive to the therapist's nurturing support.

TECHNICAL SEPARATION REACTIONS AS FACILITATORS OF MOURNING

The case of Jay's Cornerstone recovery, discussed in detail in a previous chapter of this book is useful to review briefly here, in terms of therapeutic

facilitation of mourning in children. The necessity to help this child deal with
the death of his father was unexpected as the death was the sudden result of
a commercial airplane crash weeks after Jay began Cornerstone treatment. A
feature of his immediate reactions to the death of his father was a combination of heightened positive transference to the male analyst, with considerable
expression of sad affect and yearning for the return of his father. The child
made steady clinical progress. Overcoming his difficulties with male identification and aggressive behavior, he experienced a rather vigorous mourning
process, including conscious and unconscious identifications with his father,
much remembering associated with sad affect, and a gradual surrender of
hopes for the father's return. Throughout the treatment process, a major feature was close attachment to the male analyst, Dr. Kliman, as well as female
teachers. In retrospect, it seems that the prolonged presence of a heterosexual
team, and especially the many hours of intersubjective relationship with a
real male substitute for the lost male parent, permitted the expression of what
might otherwise have been an unbearable yearning and sense of emptiness
in his life.

Jay expressed his sadness upon the death of his father both overtly at a conscious level and in multiform unconscious expressions at a level of symbolic,
verbal, playful, creative and dream activities. The father's death appeared to
increase the intensity of transference to both teachers and the analyst. Simultaneous with passionate attachments to the therapeutic team members, Jay
dwelled on thoughts of his lost father, experiencing powerful sadness and increasing identification with the father's traits. His clinical progress was excellent after two years in the school, and he continued working with the analyst
twice a week on a regular individual basis thereafter. When his recovery had
progressed so far that his treatment was about to be reduced still further, he
gave dramatic evidence of how a bereaved child can experience resonance
of the loss of a parent when confronted with treatment separations and loss.

At the end of three years treatment, Jay and the analyst discussed his progress. Jay talked about how well he was doing socially and in his school work.
Together they then made plans to reduce his treatment to once a week after a
vacation. At that point, Jay experienced a momentary loss of balance, while
reaching up to a high shelf from his perch on the table. He became frightened
that he was about to fall, and the analyst moved over toward him, saying that
this was a way of letting us know that he still needed help with his accident
trouble, which he had been talking about quite a bit lately. Jay said that it
sure was a trouble that he needed help with. In a few moments, Jay said he
was frightened because he was seeing "a dark shadow man" in the doorway,
adding, *"I think I'm having hallucinations. I get this feeling when I look into
a dark room or a closet, or I walk by a doorway, the feeling that I'm seeing a*

dark shadow man in there—a scary man. " Jay and the analyst then discussed the way this "hallucination" had come up when talking about something that would make Jay lonely for the analyst (not seeing him for office visits). At first, Jay denied there was any connection, but then further elaborated his fearfulness, saying that he also was afraid that he was having hallucinations sometimes because on a couple of occasions he thought he was seeing flying saucers—once at night and once in the middle of a foggy day, he recalled. Again the analyst reminded Jay of the connection previously established to lonely feelings and outer space monsters, a connection which at first Jay denied by saying that the fears had started before his father died, and they also came on when he did not feel lonely. Later he said it was funny though, that such feelings came over him when talking about not seeing the analyst as often. He would not like that. He wanted to come more often, three times a week, at least twice a week, and not just once a week.

This appears to be an example of a childhood transference neurotic process. The hallucinatory experience was precipitated by a separation pending in the form of a vacation to be followed by a reduction in frequency of sessions. There was technical utility in the separation, which could be analyzed in the light of the transference from father to analyst. The symptom of flying saucer and outer space men fears was transferred into the analytic process and appeared specifically in relation to the separation experience, which could thus be better understood by the child because of its narrow framework.

The session ended with Jay's feeling much more relaxed and clearly aware that he feared and resented the reduction in treatment but could tolerate it.

CASE STUDY OF MARVIN: A DOUBLE ORPHAN

Marvin, age four years and six months at onset of treatment, was from a severely impoverished African American family; both parents were physically very ill for several years. His mother died of chronic hypertension and a cardiac failure when Marvin was three years and eleven months. His father, who had been an invalid due to kidney disease and homebound most of Marvin's life, died only one month after the mother. Severe prior stress compounded the tragic fracturing of Marvin's life. Especially pathogenic had been his mother's insidious dementia as she succumbed to hypertension. Becoming a recluse, suspicious of visitors to her sad and increasingly unkempt home, she was unable to toilet train her children, who often ran naked and excreted on the floor. When able to shop, she would leave the children in the care of their weakening, bed-ridden and finally blind father. On one such dreary occasion, Marvin and his one year older sister played with matches under the stove and set a blaze which, however, brought the fire department before any serious damage occurred. Neighbors and firemen who rescued the helpless father and children called the New York Society for the Prevention of Cruelty to Children on finding the floors strewn with old feces. The parents' deaths occurred a few months later.

Marvin's maternal grandmother, freed from the prohibiting and demented suspicions of her now deceased daughter, came to assume the care of the two children. Marvin was almost without useful language and still not toilet trained. Soon enrolled in a day-care center, he was disruptive, restless, and unmanageably aggressive, Marvin was referred to Cornerstone Therapeutic Preschool for treatment. His initial examination revealed him to be agitated, incoherent, and very anxiously responding to hallucinations seen on the classroom ceiling.

In his first five months at Cornerstone, Marvin continued to hallucinate, and spoke of fire in the ceiling. He gradually became very attached to the analyst, the teachers, and the handyman. The hallucinations cleared concurrently with completion of the first major interpretative work. The handyman happened to be African American and Marvin began to misidentify the handyman as his father. When the therapist was able gradually to interpret the lonely, wishful quality of the delusion for Marvin, a significant change occurred. Marvin was then able to cling physically to the teachers, whom he called "Mother," in contrast to his formerly hostile and disruptive relations to teachers. The availability of new people on whom Marvin could transfer some of his old investments of love appeared highly useful.

After five months with his first therapist (Myron Stein, M.D.), the project's financial necessities required that two groups be reduced to one. The remaining group had a different analyst (Gilbert Kliman, M.D.). The transition was used with surprising advantage. Marvin insisted that the new analyst was really the first one. It was feasible to point out the similarity of this delusion to the handyman-father delusion. Thereupon Marvin began to speak to his grandmother and sister about how the first doctor "wasn't coming back anymore," and for the first time spoke of his mother and father in this same realistic way. It thus appeared that Marvin was able to assimilate the loss of the first doctor; because this dose of loss was moderated by the immediate availability of a replacement. Improved reality testing was feasible and further growth occurred.

With the second analyst, obvious questing for the analyst as father occurred, with open anger, sadness and weeping on many days when the analyst would end his 90-minute participation in the classroom procedures. The small daily dose of loss was digestible with the sweetening vehicle of two maternal teachers who remained in the classroom during Marvin's sessions and after the analyst left each day. Genetic interpretation of the transference expressions of protests and sadness led to many relevant memories being evoked of Marvin's life with his parents, charged with protest and anguished grief over their absence. The process of identification with some of their now remembered activities and traits was clear. For a while, a feminine identity trend began to hold sway (dressing in ladies clothes) along with a powerful yearning to learn to cook in school associated with talk of the wonderful pies, cakes and pancakes his mother used to make for him.

At this point a synergism of educational and analytic techniques occurred, as often happens in the Reflective Network Therapy situation. The teachers helped Marvin to learn to cook, while the analyst helped him understand his wish to become a cook like his mother so that he would not be lonely for her. This work led to his falling in love with the teachers, his sister and grandmother, all of whom he wished to marry. He then became very focused on one teacher and one girl in the Cornerstone group, making many gentlemanly and some not so refined romantic overtures and voyeuristic approaches.

Marvin's intellectual development then proceeded vigorously, as he reached the oedipal phase. He appeared non-psychotic and of good intelligence. After 14 months, he went into a public school No aspects of his treatment were as important as the dynamic and genetic interpretations of transference separation reactions. Therapeutic induction of mourning occurred through analysis of transference.

DISCUSSION AND CONCLUSION

There is general agreement that the process of mourning is much more difficult and often much less complete for young children than it is for adolescents and adults. Some believe that successful or complete mourning is not possible until adolescence. We have in this essay documented reasons for an opposite, optimistic view when intervention occurs to facilitate the process—even in preschool years.

We also view optimistically the immediate testability and analyzability of bereaved children. In contrast, Freud emphatically stated in his Analysis Terminable and Interminable that psychoanalysis proceeds most effectively "if the patient's pathogenic experiences belong to the past, so that his ego can stand at a distance from them. In states of acute crisis analysis is to all intents and purposes unusable. The ego's whole interests are taken up by the painful reality and it withholds itself from analysis, which is attempting to go below the surface and uncover the influences of the past" (Freud, S., 1964/1937). Many analysts today still believe that adults should not be taken into analysis in the midst of an ongoing love affair, or after the death of a loved person, especially during the period of acute mourning. Anna Freud goes further and suggests that child analysis will be less effective than ordinarily to the degree that "the threat, the attacker or the seducer is a real person, in contrast to situations where the child's fears, fights, crises and conflicts are the product of his inner world" (Freud, A.,1968). Our conclusion differs entirely with that of the Freuds, although based upon reasoning and experience which is similar up to a point.

It is our experience with children of a very young age (as well as with adults and adolescents in acute bereavement situations) that the crisis itself often forces or facilitates the tendency of a person to go below the surface of his daily conscious life and deal inexorably and regressively with influences of the past. The particular crisis of bereavement is an exceptionally strong potentiator of the emergence of the past, and therefore, we submit, makes the patient (adult and child alike) unusually available if the therapist is willing to accept the full range of communications brought to him and deal with them unflinchingly as material for scrutiny rather than as reasons to reject the task. Indeed, crisis patients generally have an exceptionally strong disposition to form strong, rapidly developing transferences which can facilitate analytic treatment and are best handled with analytic technique.

The flow of love and hate in transference provides an exceptional opportunity for a patient to experience manageable doses of the same emotions he experienced with loved and hated objects in real life outside of treatment. The therapeutic situation, whether by design or not, usually imposes new demands for reaction to loss. When the loss reactions occurring in treatment are deliberately scrutinized and focused upon, a bereaved child has a new chance to work through the reaction to the death of a parent, because the end of transferred reaction is more easily bearable than the original end of the life of the person for whom the child grieves. Because the transferred reaction is subjected to the therapist's interpretation, the child is provided with an increased repertoire of means at his disposal for mastery, including mourning and going forward with life's new loves and tasks.

In other respects, we are in agreement with Anna Freud, who stated (1968) that we still cannot know how far the neglect of developmental needs can be undone by treatment. She apparently includes in this suspension of judgment how far the absence of a parent and its myriad consequences may be undone by treatment. She points out that in a situation such as parent loss, therapists may be (wisely) unwilling to restrict themselves to analysis and may find other avenues of approach. One such approach, incorporated into the Reflective Network Therapy Method is to turn the treatment situation itself into an "improved version of the child's initial environment and within this framework aim at the belated fulfillment of the neglected developmental needs." Another approach is an endeavor to share the work with parents, who may be able to undo some of the harm they or circumstances outside their control have caused. With some cases, we have added considerable effort to induce a change in the surviving parent's behavior, using parent guidance, particularly where fresh pathogenic insult was added to the previous loss. This is true, for example, when a parent begins a dangerously seductive custom.

After so much technical detail, we would like to close this chapter on a missionary note. Any early-age group which suffers from a common variable likely to increase the incidence of psychopathology is a prime target for the development of preventive mental health services. Such a group can readily be found among bereaved or disaster stricken or foster care preschool children. For such children, we emphasize the Reflective Therapy method as a means to multiply efficiency in the use of psychiatric hours, making preventive efforts practical.

In addition, we think that parent guidance for the surviving parent has not received adequate scientific opportunity for assessment of effectiveness. Programs of even more superficial approach, such as parent education without guidance, also have been prematurely written off as hopelessly weak and ineffective. Parent guidance has much to offer, (Furman and Katan, 1969). It should be assessed in situations likely to yield a very high incidence of pathology in untreated states. Although parental involvement is almost universally touted as desirable and beneficial, we are still wanting in studies which support their structured inclusion in therapeutic work with young children as a critically valued necessity.

To date, fewer resources are available for prevention than for remediation. Unless we systematically explore, control and assess the effectiveness of applied psychoanalytically oriented means for large-scale prevention, we shall have defaulted in using the most obvious measures while immersing ourselves mainly in matters of great professional fascination without great hope of social yield.

POSTSCRIPT

After this essay was first published, I mounted several preventive intervention studies among populations of another form of bereaved children: foster children. There are significant and encouraging findings concerning the measurable effects (Kliman, 2006).

Part II

BENEFITS AND COST-BENEFIT COMPARISONS TO OTHER METHODS: THEORY OF WHAT HAPPENS IN REFLECTIVE NETWORK THERAPY

Chapter Nine

Benefits and Cost-Benefit Comparisons to Other Methods: The RNT Advantage for Special Needs Preschoolers and the People Who Care about Them

INTRODUCTION

I hope this essay reaches administrators responsible for school budgets, as well as those school psychologists, therapists and teachers with responsibility for the mental health and classroom care of preschoolers. Many preschoolers nowadays qualify for special education due to serious psychiatric needs, including pervasive developmental disorders (PDD). James McCracken, a child psychiatrist at the UCLA Center for Autism Research and Treatment, reported (2010) that families often have to fight with state bureaucracies to be deemed eligible for services, and some spend thousands of dollars for private evaluations to establish their child's needs. The demand for clinically effective and cost effective treatment of preschoolers with serious emotional disturbances (SED), autism spectrum disorders (ASD) or PDD is already great and growing. It is by now a much publicized and very worrisome public health statistic that between one in 90 and one in 150 children born in the United States in the past decade have been diagnosed with autism, (Kogan et al., 2009). Identification of children with pervasive developmental disorders, including autism, has increased markedly throughout the U.S. and Europe since 1988 and has been growing steadily since. The increasing incidence was noticed even earlier in Japan (McDonald and Paul, 2010). Additionally, it is widely suspected that still more young children with autism spectrum disorders go undiagnosed before they get to kindergarten. There are almost overwhelming challenges for public special education systems to respond with appropriate and early intervention to this public health crisis, which is both acute and long-term, (Chakrabarti and Fombonne, 2001; 2005; McDonald and Paul, 2010; US Department of Health, Children's Bureau 2010).

Further, Lavigne et al. (1998, 2001, 2009) and Achenbach and Howell (1993) report an incidence increase over time for other child psychiatric disorders.

Most children with PDD or SED enter the public school system, where their education often requires special attention dependent upon resources which regularly incur high taxpayer costs. Throughout western societies, billions of tax dollars—as well as the futures of tens of thousands of children and their families—are at stake in deciding what to provide for autistic children, children with other pervasive developmental disorders, children who are seriously emotionally disturbed and children with a range of other psychiatric disorders. As children enter financially overwhelmed public special education systems, hope for reduction of the incidence of autism, in particular, has not yet been realized by any preventive means. The good news is that several evidence-based methods are very helpful for some autistic preschool children and there are some evidence-based means for helping SED pupils during or after school hours. More bad news is the fact that school boards and public school administrators have little scientific basis collected in one place for deciding how to deploy scant resources. In this essay we consider how autistic and other special needs children can be helped in a way that reliably yields strong outcomes for cognitive and mental health while remaining cost effective within limited special education budgets.

We will present a conclusion that Reflective Network Therapy, better than the other methods reviewed, meets all of these requirements:

Early Intervention for Special Needs Children—Optimal Features

1. Clear psychometric evidence of good outcomes
2. Clinically versatile across diagnostic categories
3. Socially inclusive—inclusion of peers
4. Adaptability—readily individualized
5. Includes, utilizes and supports existing staff
6. Effectively includes and supports parents
7. Reliably delivers early intervention
8. Low amount of time needed to induce cognitive and clinical gains
9. High percentage of children become able to mainstream
10. Has a manual for consistent replicability
11. Feasible in a variety of settings
12. Training videos are on hand
13. Sustainable
14. Low Cost

For the benefit of administrators as well as parents and parent associations, I offer a summary of cost-benefit data regarding not only Reflective Network

Therapy but data for other methods widely applied for treating special needs children. Such data are increasingly useful when faced with the huge numbers of children in special education status, and the tasks required by United States Individuals with Disabilities Education Act (IDEA) and state laws. Those laws concern the millions of children whose conditions interfere with their education or who cannot be accommodated in regular classrooms without interfering with the education of other children. I will lay out the evidence for Reflective Network Therapy's and other methods' clinical and cognitive outcomes. There is enough evidence to permit objective comparison of the strengths and weaknesses of the methods, including their costs. The methods considered are RNT (Reflective Network Therapy) ABA (Applied Behavioral Analysis), DIR/Floortime, TEACCH and intensive "Pull-Out" psychotherapy in a school or office setting.

My review and tabular summations are a step toward filling an information vacuum, presenting information needed for decision-making not only by legislatures considering allocation of funds and government agencies but also by families, parent associations, local schools and administrators of unified school districts. I include sources and tables with criteria such as dollar costs, hours and school years needed for measurable benefits. The emphasis is on data showing objectively measurable benefits that are evident on widely used standardized scales, particularly IQ gain and improvements in global assessments of children's mental health (CGAS).

METHODOLOGICAL FEATURES: OPTIMAL INTERVENTIONS FOR SPECIAL NEEDS CHILDREN

For unreceptive, unexpressive and often uncomprehending children with PDD or SED precious developmental time continues to slip away. It is generally thought that an autistic child is best treated early in life (National Institute of Mental Health, 2010). Faced with largely unmet needs for psychotherapies to make education of developmentally delayed children possible, in-classroom treatment methods aimed at preschoolers are most desirable. Yet there was not much development in that regard until 1965 when Reflective Network Therapy was invented and at first called "The Cornerstone Therapeutic Preschool Method". Since special mental health needs children are so individually different, methods must be readily capable of tailor-made individualization. To prevent the chronicity of disorders, a method should be deliverable early in school life. Early treatment could prevent or reduce the severity of fundamental cognitive and social deficits. A method which can be delivered in the children's own real-life spaces without disrupting the ecology of the children's families and schooling is logistically preferable. Such delivery within a classroom is also preferable for therapeutic as well as economic reasons.

More restrictive and socially isolating alternative methods may add to the length of a child's day, require complex family or public transportation schedules, pull the child out of school for therapy or require the school to provide individual aides for each child (Lovaas, 1997). Such methods are stigmatizing, isolative and restrictive compared to Reflective Network Therapy's interactive method which places high emphasis on relationships with school peers. Also logistically burdensome and less likely to be therapeutically intensive are during or after-school appointments in one-on-one relationships with providers treating severely disturbed or autistic children. The numbers of qualified providers is limited. When psychotherapy or behavioral modification is given outside of class, much time passes from a child's point of view between a classroom problem behavior (such as a tantrum or prolonged inattentiveness) and the discussion of it days or a week later. Psychotropic medication treatment is commonly used at preschool ages, but so far there is no report of medication increasing cognitive abilities in PDD, and we have seen no substantial comparison studies where interpersonal methods are contrasted with medication.

In the data compilations presented below, children are often referred to as "Cornerstone" RNT treated subjects as their data comes from therapeutic preschool classrooms using the original name of the method. Some data presented in this chapter was presented in part in earlier chapters, as well as a modicum of related discussion of the evidence. However, discussion here is considerably more detailed and consolidated. This chapter permits me to provide a more comprehensive reference in one place for those who may wish to benefit from that organization.

RNT RESULTS: CONSISTENT, SUSTAINED IQ RISES AND MENTAL HEALTH GAINS

Our first prospective study of IQ as an outcome of an in-classroom psychotherapy was reported (Kliman 1978) on a series of 11 consecutive RNT treated children in White Plains, New York. The children were IQ tested twice, beginning in 1967, usually with at least a year's interval. Psychological testers included Miriam Siegel, PhD, Michael Harris, PhD and later on psychology interns under licensed psychologists' supervision of Harold Chorney, PhD and Steven Tuber, PhD. Dorian, whose autobiographical account is in chapter 4, was part of that study. Three of the children had pervasive developmental disorders with autistic features. The others had serious emotional disorders (SED) such as posttraumatic stress disorder, depression, and psychoses. All eleven showed full-scale IQ gains, with a range of gain from 6 points to 69 points. Two children had intervening psychological traumas with depressive symptoms. Showing a yo-yo effect, the two children with intervening traumas had transient drops of IQ, which they then surmounted for a gain in a subsequent year. The average was a 24 point IQ gain on last follow up. Therapists were Gilbert Kliman, MD, Myron Stein, MD, Daniel Feinberg, MD, Marianne Lester, PhD and Ruth Rosenfield. Teachers included Elissa Burian, Doris Gorin Ronald, Florence Herzog, Renata Rossmere, Susan Mandel and Marianne Schnall, The 1967-1978 data on IQ rise findings was so impressive that I began applying IQ as an outcome measure in larger studies of other psychotherapies. One was an NIMH supported project with 104 foster children administered two quantities (15 or 40 sessions) of individual psychotherapy. But we found little IQ change without the Cornerstone RNT modality (Kliman et al., 1982).

The Children's Global Assessment Scale was not available to us in the New York project for measuring children's behavioral, emotional and social functioning as Shaffer et al. didn't invent the CGAS until 1983.

The second prospective study was more sophisticated. In 1999 Miquela Diaz Hope completed a study of IQ and mental health changes in ten consecutive IQ testable and then retested children with PDD treated by the Reflective Network Therapy method within their public school special education classes, in San Mateo, California 1995 through 1997. Hope used a blinded independent rater to score IQ and re-evaluate the children's initial and later mental health using the CGAS scale Changes in the CGAS scores of these children with moderate and severe psychiatric impairments across all groups, show a significant difference between the lumped Cornerstone groups treated by RNT and the lumped Control/Comparison group. In the RNT treated group, CGAS measures of children with the most problematic behaviors improved significantly. Children in the control group (not treated by RNT) in special education in the same school system did not show improvements.

The children treated with Reflective Network Therapy also improved cognitively, having significant rises of IQ (discussed below) measured by WPPSI-R. Thus the study demonstrated that the RNT method resulted in meaningful cognitive gain as well as marked improvement in social, emotional and behavioral dimensions. (See tables 9.1, 9.2 and 9.3) CGAS improvements in the RNT treated group were greater by far and more robust than in the comparison and control groups (Hope, 1999). Unlike all testings of PDD children we have found among reports below using other methods, the RNT study used completely comparable IQ test methods at baseline and follow up. Apples were compared with apples. In other method studies, initial developmental quotients were compared with later IQ, a distinctly unreliable way of tracking outcomes.

A most significant finding was the positive influence of a high number of Reflective Network Therapy sessions on IQ outcome. For children in RNT treatment, IQ rises occurred in an orderly manner, in proportion to the number of Reflective Network Therapy sessions they received. Initially, the RNT treated children in the San Mateo study had IQs between 45 and 108. RNT treatment produced Full Scale IQ gains which were significant at the p < .01 level. RNT was clearly more cognitively effective. Full Scale IQ rose with p = .005. RNT was also more behaviorally effective. With Reflective Network Therapy, CGAS rose with p = .01 and most markedly for children who had more than one major psychiatric diagnosis, such as a combination of PDD with Oppositional-Defiant Disorder or Posttraumatic Stress Disorder.

The most intensive application of RNT in this project was treatment fifteen minutes at a time at least four times a week, with each child in the group getting brief psychotherapy sessions each day of class and benefiting from reflective network effects throughout their classroom work. Outcome data revealed that the higher frequency of RNT sessions produced *almost twice the amount of cognitive improvement* as less intensive uses of the method (once or twice a week). The *average* intensive therapy result from providing Reflective Network Therapy four times a week was a Full Scale IQ gain of 28.75 points. Children who received RNT less intensive treatment (once or twice weekly had an average Full Scale IQ gain of 14.7, also a very positive and statistically significant result, (Hope, 1999). We can contrast this generally one school year duration which far larger numbers of years and hours used by ABA and DIR to achieve similar IQ gains.

The CGAS distinction between RNT treated and control/comparison subjects was also significant. CGAS rose with p = .01 for RNT treated children who had more than one major psychiatric diagnosis. CGAS scores did not rise in children with control or comparison status. We could not distinguish the CGAS effects of two versus four Cornerstone sessions a week. However, both IQ rise and CGAS gains occurred without exception among the Hope study of ten consecutive children treated by RNT. (See Table 9.1)

The lack of exception to the phenomenon of IQ rise in children treated by Reflective Network Therapy is highly persuasive that the treatment is causing the effect.

It appears to be highly significant that the nine California control and comparison treatment children (also blindly rated) had no IQ or CGAS gains. (See Table 9.2) Regular special education in an excellent and well-funded school system program, did not improve IQ or mental health scores in this

MULTI-SITE STUDY: IQ AND CGAS CHANGES FOR RNT TREATED, IQ TESTABLE AND IQ RE-TESTED CHILDREN

MULTISITE STUDY: IQ AND CGAS CHANGES FOR RNT TREATED, IQ TESTABLE AND IQ RE-TESTED CHILDREN				
Source	Description	Average IQ Change	N	CGAS Change
Center for Preventive Psychiatry, NY (Cases of Kliman, Stein, Lester, Feinberg and Rosenfield) reported by Kliman, 1978)	Prospective study, 2-5 sessions/wk (Cornerstone) RNT	24	11	
Center for Preventive Psychiatry, NY (Zelman 1985,1996) Multiple teams	Archival study, 2-5 sessions/wk (Cornerstone) RNT	12	42	
Public School Special Education, San Mateo, CA (Diaz Hope 1999) Therapist Teaford	Prospective study, public special education preschool, 2 sessions/wk, (Cornerstone) RNT	15	6	15
Public School Special Education, San Mateo, CA (Diaz Hope 1999) Therapist Kliman	Prospective study, public special education preschool, 4-5 sessions/wk (Cornerstone) RNT	29	4	15
Oklahoma RNT (Fran Morris Report 2008)	Prospective study, Oklahoma Cornerstone using RNT techniques	80	1	
Ann Martin, Argentina and San Francisco (2008)	Prospective study of IQ testable children, in progress (incomplete)	15	5	
ALL TWICE TESTED RNT TREATED CHILDREN	**Pooled studies above**	15	69	

Table 9.1. Multi-site Study: RNT IQ and CGAS Changes

study. Similarly, there was little or no IQ effect from other comparison treatment studies.

Since Reflective Network Therapy has been shown to achieve twice the level of its own superior outcomes when children are provided this treatment at least four days a week, it is particularly compelling as a special education enhancement. Existing classroom staff can be trained economically and quickly to work with reflective network techniques along with an appropriate therapist to create a reflective network team. No extra teacher staff was needed.

MULTISITE STUDY: CONTROL AND COMPARISON IQ FOLLOWED CHILDREN		IQ Change	N	CGAS Change
Diaz Hope 1999 San Mateo, California	CONTROLS: San Mateo CA, Special Ed PDD. No treatment other than special education in a class of no more than 8 children.	-1	6	0.5
Diaz Hope 1999 San Mateo, California	San Francisco CA, Shelter Daycare. Supportive-Expressive in-classroom sessions 3-4/week. Therapist used no interpretations.	-2	3	3.0
Kliman et al. 1982 NIMH Project Center for Preventive Psychiatry, New York	White Plains, NY. Individual Supportive-Expressive. Foster Children (ages 3-13) received 15 unstructured individual psychotherapy sessions.	-4	30	
Kliman et al 1982 NIMH Project Center for Preventive Psychiatry, New York	White Plains, NY. Individual Supportive-Expressive. Foster Children (ages 3-13) received 40 unstructured individual psychotherapy sessions.	2	15	
Zelman 1996 Archival Report, Center for Preventive Psychiatry, New York	White Plains, New York. Comparison Preschoolers received individual educational psychotherapy	4	9	
ALL CONTROL AND COMPARISON CHILDREN FROM ALL SITES		-1	63	

Table 9.2.   Multi-site Study: Control and Comparison IQ Followed Children

The IQ and CGAS findings are highly significant and orderly data. There is almost no possibility the results are due to chance. (P is less than .001 for significance of differences between 69 treated and 63 control and comparison untreated children's IQ changes.) CGAS differences on a much smaller number of children are similar. Not only the type of treatment but the quantity of treatment has a strong association with IQ outcomes. The material from these multisite studies was subjected to a statistical meta-analysis, literally a statistical assembly of an accumulation of comparable studies. The data collected so far over a 45 year span leads us to state that RNT is an evidence-based method for cognitive and clinical outcomes. It has been delivered very effectively to preschool children with pervasive developmental disorders, as well as to SED diagnostic categories. Zelman first pointed this out (1966) in his

MULTISITE STUDY: SUMMARY OF FINDINGS	IQ CHANGE	N
ALL TWICE TESTED CHILDREN TREATED BY REFLECTIVE NETWORK THERAPY	15	69
ALL TWICE TESTED CONTROL AND COMPARISON CHILDREN TREATED BY OTHER METHODS	-1	63
TOTAL RNT AND OTHER CHILDREN TWICE TESTED FOR IQ		132

Table 9.3.   Multi-site Study: Summary of Findings Regarding IQ Changes

series of 42 children where no distinction was found between IQ responses in his 17 PDD versus 15 SED children.

The method can work in public and private special education preschool classes. After only eight months of treatment in Reflective Network Therapy within their public special education preschool classes, a series of ten consecutive RNT-treated children with PDD showed marked rise of Full Scale IQ, without exception, in orderly correlation with the quantity (total dose) of sessions. CGAS rise was also without exception but did not show orderly correlation with dose. Once or twice a week RNT psychotherapy sessions with PDD children produced a one standard deviation rise of IQ. RNT psychotherapy sessions conducted four or five times a week produced a two standard deviation IQ rise. We can see that Heinicke's (1996) and Fonagy's (1996) retrospective findings on quantity of child psychoanalytic treatment as a correlate of CGAS outcome are now paralleled by Reflective Network Therapy's IQ outcomes retrospectively and prospectively studied. Major differences from Fonagy's landmark study are that Fonagy had a much larger number of children, showed no effects of child analysis on pervasive developmental disorders, and did his study retrospectively, without control or comparison cases.

EXTRAORDINARY IQ RISES

Forty years ago, Dorian was almost three years old, carrying a diagnosis and a full array of symptoms of autism and had a diagnosis of autism from more than one qualified professional when she started RNT treatment. In addition, pervious professionals thought she was retarded and so she appeared to me. Dorian recovered from all symptoms which could be associated with those diagnostic labels following Reflective Network Therapy treatment. She gained

68 points between her first testable Full Scale IQ of 80 (at age six years) and her last retest (at age 12) when her Full Scale IQ was 149, Dorian is socially and emotionally very well. (See chapter 4.)

In 2007 Fran Morris, MA personally conveyed to me a report on a long-term follow-up on the results of an Oklahoma team performing intensive psychoanalytically oriented therapy in the classroom. (See chapter 1.) During 1976 Morris and her colleagues independently began using an equivalent of the original Cornerstone (RNT) method, establishing in-classroom intensive therapy programs integrated into therapeutic preschool classroom work in several state and federally supported Community Mental Health Centers. At my request, Ms. Morris arranged a retesting of an autistic preschooler she selectively recalled had improved markedly. She had treated him by an independently created variation of the Cornerstone Method (RNT). The boy was difficult to test early in life. He had a starting Full Scale IQ of 47 at age four. His Full Scale IQ at age eight, two years after finishing his therapeutic nursery time, was 72. At age nine years, 2 months, the child scored 91. At age 27 his Full Scale IQ was 125 and he was completing his university studies, where he earned a BA. We are hoping that archives of the Oklahoma treatments will yield data regarding more retested children.

Our data collection through 2008 from several current service site applications of Reflective Network Therapy is still in under review as we go to press and a percentage of our more recent data (from multiple RNT service sites) awaits retesting by independent raters. Nonetheless, there are a few points we can already make:

1. Rise from mental retardation in some child patients is feasible with Reflective Network Therapy.

   As with the more remarkable result in the Morris report on an Oklahoma child, a Cornerstone program in San Francisco tested and years later retested a mentally retarded child with pervasive developmental disorder who rose from an IQ level of 58 to a low but normal level of 71 (Full Scale IQ). The Buenos Aires Cornerstone has completed re-testing of two RNT treated children who started treatment with Full Scale IQs in the retarded range. One had pervasive developmental disorder, with mental retardation and prominent autistic features. The other was a girl with post-traumatic stress disorder as well as pervasive developmental delays. Both had a Full Scale WPPSI-R IQ rise of 12 points, one rising from a mentally retarded level to normal. Such results with even a few formerly retarded children are of great importance to the children's schools as well as to the children and their families. Additionally, one recent San Francisco cure of an autistic child has been reported, and two probable cures of children with Asperger's disorder (one in San Mateo and one in Piedmont). Conspicuous to me among those very few children over the years who failed to show robust improvement is a severely autistic child who was never testable, had almost no language development by age five, and almost no interest in interpersonal relations. Another autistic child who improved but was not IQ testable had hyperbilirubinemia, a brain disorder, beginning at birth. Still another had Rett's syndrome, an uncommon autism spectrum disorder with marked brain pathology.

2. Reflective Network Therapy among children in a homeless shelter preschool is very feasible.

   Feasibility in this venue is currently being demonstrated by Wellspring Family Services in Seattle and was previously demonstrated by our agency in San Francisco. (We also developed a specialized, psychoanalytically informed guided activity workbook for use with some children being served at Wellspring, available to other such applications as might be initiated: *My Story about Being Homeless*".) Laura Ahn reported on behalf of Wellspring (in an early 2010 update to Gilbert Kliman) that children treated at Wellspring have been measured with an average 15 point Full Scale IQ rise among five twice tested children *within five months of study*.

3. Some severely autistic children treated by Reflective Network Therapy have outcomes of significantly reduced symptoms of autism.

   The Cornerstone Argentina team practicing RNT in Buenos Aires, in particular, has produced Childhood Autism Rating Scale (CARS) data showing a substantial improvement within one year among all but one of 13 twice-studied preschoolers with severe autism.

RELIABILITY AND SUSTAINABILITY OF REFLECTIVE NETWORK THERAPY SERVICE APPLICATIONS

The Center for Preventive Psychiatry project was by far the longest application in which I was personally involved: about 25 years, first as a therapist applying the method and later as a supervisor and principal investigator for various research projects, and then as a consultant and contributing editor of the *Journal of Preventive Psychiatry and Allied Disciplines*. These tasks spanned the years from 1965 to 1990. Some aspects of Reflective Network Therapy continue to be used in New York by some practitioners, including services provided by The Andrus Children's Center.

At this writing, Wellspring Family Services is in its third year of providing RNT services. The Ann Martin Center in the San Francisco Bay Area is in its fifth year with experienced therapist Linda Hirshfeld, PhD supervising the reflective network team. Cornerstone Argentina in Buenos Aires, under the direction of Alicia Asman Mallo, MD is also in its fifth year of delivering Reflective Network Therapy services. Alexandra Harrison, MD continues into her second year of an innovative application of Reflective Network Therapy in Boston. Five years or greater longevity of the method in various preschool applications occurred in: White Plains, New York. San Francisco and San Mateo, California applications include six consecutive years in a public special education program and four years in a private therapeutic preschool. Various service sites in Oklahoma also have more than five years experience.

CLINICAL VERSATILITY: RNT WORKS FOR A BROAD SPECTRUM OF DIAGNOSES

A large number of diagnostic categories of children have been helped, including children with diagnoses of the following disorders who have consistently responded very well to RNT treatment: Expressive and Receptive Language Disorder, Attention Deficit Disorder, Oppositional Defiant Disorder, Posttraumatic Stress Disorder, Reactive Attachment Disorder and Overanxious Disorder, Depressive Disorders, Serious Emotional Disorders, Autism (especially mild to moderate autism) and other Pervasive Developmental Disorders.

Documented IQ rises in RNT treated children have occurred in culturally, linguistically, geographically and administratively diverse places and programs at service sites having different therapeutic teams and testers. Both retrospective and prospective studies concur in findings regarding this method's production of IQ gains. Data from public school cases, the Morris case from Oklahoma added together with the original 11 Kliman cases and 42 archival cases from New York, plus five new twice-tested children all seem a coherent whole. The findings show the ability of more than twenty separate Reflective Network Therapy teams to carry out the method with similarly robust clinical and cognitive effects in both public schools and private agencies in entirely different socioeconomic, administrative and geographic settings (on the east coast, west coast, in middle America and in Argentina).

STUDY OF REFLECTIVE NETWORK THERAPY BY MIQUELA DIAZ HOPE: A METHODOLOGICAL ADVANCE

The prospective and controlled research by Hope (1999) reported here is a small controlled study of 19 child subjects but is a substantial methodological advance. It improves on the significance of the earlier retrospective and uncontrolled studies of the method as carried out by Zelman, Samuels and Abrams (1985, 1994). As with Skeels and Dye's work with institutionalized children (1939), the earlier reporters on Reflective Network Therapy outcomes generally found an average Full Scale IQ rise of one or two standard deviations. Some children gained much more, as reported in two long-followed cases of Kliman and Morris. Skeels' experiment, which encouraged close-attachment within an institution for adolescent mothers and their babies, showed an average gain of 27.5 points above control cases for the IQ of institutionalized mothers' offspring, (n=13) versus a decline of 26.2 points in the control group (n=12). Skeels' and my own early RNT reports of the magnitude of IQ rises averaging up to two standard deviations are consistent with our findings decades later in public and private school Cornerstone / RNT data. Similarly, reports of mental health and cognitive gains in children treated with RNT at Wellspring Family Services (Seattle) are now being reviewed and so far look similar. In Boston, Dr. Harrison (who wrote the introduction for this book) remarks with enthusiasm about autistic children benefiting markedly from her work, but she has not reported on IQ outcomes.

Among the RNT treated children treated in New York (Center for Preventive Psychiatry): Zelman's archival report found a similar average rise of two standard deviations or 29.8 Full Scale IQ point rises with intensive (3 to 5 times a week) RNT treatment while there was an average rise of one standard deviation or 11.7 points with less intensive treatment. In Zelman's comparison group of 9 children who received only individual educational psychotherapy, without psychoanalytic work, there was a rise of only 4.22 points in IQ. This small gain was statistically almost the same as in Hope's 3 comparison and 6 control children, who had no IQ rise, (1999) and similar to Freeman, Holzinger and Mitchell's (1928) and Kliman's (1980) studies showing a 4 point rise among foster children assigned to middle class foster parents.

PROBLEM: HOW TO REACH THE CHILDREN?

The equal or superior cognitive and clinical results of Reflective Network Therapy compared to other methods are not yet familiar to many school administrators and decision makers. It is not well known that Reflective Network Therapy can be easily added to public school special education programs at considerably reduced cost compared to methods currently widely used. Public policy is often politically sensitive and resistant to change, but economic factors favor a change to increasing use of Reflective Network

Therapy. A major question then is whether public school systems will make the administrative commitment to create the sufficient stability required to reliably ensure RNT's advantages for their children. It is difficult for educational and therapeutic teams and systems to sustain an emotionally intensive effort. RNT requires it. Schools do not usually have administrative resources for cultivating a mental health process. Their missions are often consciously seen as cognitive objectives rather than for building children's interpersonal strengths. School systems may find that in many ways it is psychologically easier to avoid interpersonal involvement with children and their families. They sometimes end up getting too little for more money.

Here is a good example of just such a misguided use of funds, one which is in fact quite common. A great number of special education programs employ a large contingent of individual behavioral aides. One-on-one behavioral aides are not inclined to nor are they trained to use attunement with the painful inner lives of children and deep engagement with parents. Their business is not to comprehend and help transform persistent emotional disorder, nor to affect disordered processes with symptoms such as frantic fear, emotional withdrawal, inability to communicate, or persistent rage of unknown origin, for example. They certainly are neither trained nor expected to interpret symbolic behavior nor to recognize an opportunity for intervention in a chronically disordered or missing cognitive process nor to make use of issue or trauma based elaboration or repetition of themes and themes. In short, behavioral aides exist to help change behaviors. They are regularly very good at doing that. Unfortunately children with serious disturbances and disorders require and deserve much more. ABA does not give a cost-effective approach for that broad need.

Many schools inefficiently and irretrievably lose much of the precious developmental time of young children with PDD and SED by settling for minimal clinical results. The reasons for this are likely a combination of elements such as the inertia inherent in all systems and an assumption that all reasonable options have already been thoroughly vetted by disinterested parties or an erroneous belief that they cannot expect a whole lot more for children with such serious disorders. We believe that most educators care deeply about children's emotional lives and cognitive development. They deserve the opportunity to discover how their staff can easily incorporate and participate in a reflective network (in which teachers themselves are also supported) and why they can and should have greater expectations for the children in their charge.

We know that Reflective Network Therapy substantially reduces costs for helping special needs children. We know that the children benefit greatly. We know that Reflective Network Therapy induces improved sociability, development of empathy, regular rises in IQ which are significant and sustained, rapid improvements in mental health, increased understanding of the mental lives of others, increased vocabulary, increasingly elaborate communication over time, reduces anxiety and hyperactivity; increases receptivity to learning, and, of course, results in transformation of behavioral symptoms into dialogue and play. We know that the method, with its psychoanalytically informed procedures and techniques, works and yields more positive results for more children for less money. We also know that the prerequisite for any successful special education enhancement is the informed commitment of program administrators.

Sadly, even when a program is fully operational and remarkably successful, a lack of school system commitment can abruptly shut it down. This happened to a Reflective Network Therapy project in California. As soon as the responsible special administrator retired, the six years of "Cornerstone" RNT service was suddenly ended by a new administrator's decision made over a summer, without communication or even notification by the new administrator to participants (including parents!). After the fact of the program's termination, the new administrator informed us by phone that she (incorrectly) thought that the program was designed exclusively for psychologically traumatized children. She told me that she had no idea that most of the children served had pervasive developmental disorders. The new administrator, a young woman, tragically died suddenly (only weeks later), and before we were able to meet her in person. All the prospective beneficiary children had already been reassigned.

A similar administrative lapse ended a Reflective Network Therapy program in a special education classroom at a San Francisco public school, when a collaborative, knowledgeable and enthusiastic administrator left for other pursuits. A rapid turnover of school superintendents (for reasons unrelated to our project) created additional obstructive conditions. The most crucial remaining administrator was unresponsive and unavailable for six months: literally unreachable by phone, email, fax, or post. As a result, a thriving program benefiting eight children with serious disorders—contributed to the school system by our agency as a zero-cost program—came to an end, despite its no-cost status for taxpayers.

Though we were shocked, as an agency we landed on our clinical and educational feet. We did so by creating our own private non-profit special education preschool where we treated classroom groups of children from 2000 to 2004. The State of California certified and praised our school. Yet it was terribly difficult to overcome obstructive bureaucratic guidelines then in place at our local level. The attorney for the local city school system advised the Board of Education that the district was unable to contract with us to send seriously disturbed or autism spectrum children *until they would reach age nine*. From a legal point of view, SED and PDD children were erroneously (from our clinical point of view) considered already being served well enough until that age.

We eventually found that we could not sustain operations of a private special education preschool without a local community school system contract. We sorely needed and could not find a nearby system willing to seriously discuss contracting for our help with preschool SED and PDD children. Thus we began to train teams of staff in far-flung agencies which recognized the need and value of our method for their troubled and disordered preschoolers. Because the remote sites had their own brick and mortar as well as staff, the decision to shift to training new Reflective Network Therapy teams spared us much expense in helping children, and allowed us to help far greater numbers than we could on our own.

LOWER COSTS AND HIGHER BENEFITS FOR SCHOOLS WITH AUTISTIC PRESCHOOLERS

"There are still relatively few economic evaluations in this field (of treating autistic preschoolers)... In general, the quality of economic evaluations was limited by small sample sizes, constrained measurement of costs, narrow perspectives and over-simple statistical and econometric methods." (Knapp, Romeo and Beecham, 2009)

Six years of Cornerstone RNT service and research in a San Mateo public school serving special needs preschoolers, mostly with pervasive developmental disorders is described above. It was not only clinically and cognitive effective but also resulted in marked cost benefits summarized by the school's then senior special education administrator, Jay S. Parnes, Ed.D (who became a Scientific Advisory Board Member of our nonprofit agency after his retirement). Parnes wrote:

This is to report that the San Mateo County Office of Education, Special Education programs, has benefited from the services of The Children's Psychological Health Center, specifically its Cornerstone Therapeutic School Project. We have worked together for the past six years. Under the leadership of Gilbert Kliman, M.D., the Center has trained members of our teaching and school psychology staff to carry out a mental health service on our premises. We now have a collaborative project in its sixth year for our special education preschool children with Pervasive Developmental Disorders (PDD) and for those with Serious Emotional Disorders (SED) which interfere with their education. As an alternative to sending children to a private nonpublic special education school for extremely intensive mental health services at significant cost, this project has created and provides just such intensive service within a public preschool special class program at 65 Tower Road, San Mateo.

To my knowledge, among the 30 children served so far under the collaborative project, we are seeing cognitive, social and human gains which have decreased the gap between these children and their typically developing peers. Several families and children are thriving with less intensive special education service or returned to regular education class. Not only has the family and child suffering been reduced, the burden to taxpayers is also reduced. The children have been able to remain in the community, and some who were functioning as severely autistic and retarded now appear to be developing within a somewhat normal range. We are pleased with the quality of special education services our County provides for preschoolers with PDD or SED. We are also gratified with the research results provided by The Children's Psychological Health Center.

We recommend the Cornerstone project to other school systems, so that they consider it an important opportunity should they be able to collaborate similarly with The Children's Psychological Health Center. At California's common cost of $15,000 to $40,000 or more a year, for a special education child who needs full time special education services and auxiliary intensive help, the savings for even one child's 12-year career of intensive services in special education can be substantial. The savings from one of the successes we have seen may equal the costs of the entire Cornerstone project with the 30 children helped so far.

We have not yet seen any failures. The agency is showing measurable cognitive gains for our collaborative work which, according to their research, averages 20 to 28 points in independent WPPSI testing of the children in the Cornerstone program. The techniques are far more economical to use than we have found with the Lovaas method, which we also implement for some students. We have also seen the techniques transmitted to special education teachers as well as inexperienced therapists.

—*Jay S. Parnes, Ed.D, Senior Administrator, Special Education*

COMPARING RNT RESULTS WITH THOSE OF OTHER METHODS

All the methods used to treat PDD and SED preschoolers (Reflective Network Therapy included) suffer from a great deal of originator-bias in their implementation. Only RNT and ABA have manuals which set forth exactly how their methods should be carried out. Other methods have no manuals or lack manuals which are clear and sufficiently comprehensive for independent clinicians to accurately replicate the work. Those methods are still entirely dependent on training and supervision by originators or second or third-generation trainers.

Most methods lack scientifically sound multi-site and multi-method controlled and comparison studies, where there are random assignments to various forms of treatment and special education. The use of standardized psychometric measures such as IQ and CGAS is a necessity widely overlooked. For over 15 years we have been encouraging cooperation of various independent parties to collaborate in such studies, so that the flaws of originator-based replication of treatments can be overcome. We have sometimes found a marked resistance to objective studies by practitioners and proponents of other methods. For example, 12 years ago our agency provided a grant for IQ and CGAS studies to a prestigious independent therapeutic preschool center at a psychoanalytic institute in the United States. But results of the grant's use have never been reported! The prominent and influential head of another therapeutic preschool flatly refused to have her children tested as she regarded the IQ testing process and its results as too difficult for parents to accept. This kind of foot-dragging avoidance and outright refusal to be responsible for data collection and objective study is unfortunately typical of many data-poor mental health facilities nationwide.

We are not satisfied yet with the size and quality of any study of autism treatment, including our own, using a random assignment control series. We can nevertheless point to important facts which should inform and guide decision makers. In the socially natural, peer-engaging environment of public and private special education classroom, Reflective Network Therapy yields excellent IQ and CGAS results with large dollar savings compared to other methods. RNT delivers educational, clinical and cognitive results which are more heartening than the best of other methods we have personally used, seen or whose systematic reports we have studied. We make this statement not only after reviewing the data concerning other methods; the statement is also based on 45 years of experience with the method, including doing personal follow-ups on the condition of patients treated as early as 1965, supported by data collection by Zelman (1985, 1996), Hope (1999) and Kliman (2006), and making calculations of the dollar costs of Reflective Network Therapy implementation versus the dollar costs of several other forms of early childhood therapeutic intervention commonly used at taxpayer expense in public schools.

METHODS CONSIDERED FOR COMPARISON

1. Applied Behavioral Analysis (ABA), The Lovaas Method

ABA has been in use since 1977. The costs of this method when added to special education, in ways clearly shown to be effective in 40% of autistic preschoolers, are estimated conservatively as $40,000 per year per child. Two, three or four years of intervention are needed, about 40-60 hours per week. We estimate that each child's treatment, therefore, costs an average of $80,000 to $120,000 per child. To be conservative, some lower figures are used in accompanying charts.

The best study we have found of actual IQ testing as an outcome in ABA (rather than a comparison of developmental quotient baselines with later IQ testing, which weakens all the other ABA reports we have seen) is that of Eikeseth et al. (2007). Eikeseth reported on an ABA treatment group of 13 children in public kindergarten compared with an eclectically treated group of 11 children the same age treated in the same school system. The groups were assigned "independently based on the availability of qualified supervisors." Bayley Infant Scales of Intelligence (a flawed choice for an initial measure to compare with later IQ) or WPPSI-R IQ tests were given at baseline and three years later. Those children who had ABA 28 hours a week for at least two years had IQ rises averaging 25 points. The Eclectic Treatment group was treated 29 hours a week using combinations of ABA, TEACCH, and individualized educational approaches. The Eclectic Treatment also went on for at least two years and it resulted in only a 7 point IQ rise.

Though methodologically flawed, the 25 point IQ results of multi-year highly intensive ABA as reported by Eikeseth are remarkably similar to those of RNT treatment. They occur at much higher cost per child.

We estimate the costs as follows: Both the systematic ABA and Eikeseth's Eclectic Treatment groups used non-educator professional time of about 30 hours a week (including minimal administrative time) per child for 45 weeks a year for two years, totaling 2700 professional hours per child. Each child's therapist was paid, let us conservatively assume, $50 per hour. That expense for non-educator professional time was $135,000 per child. The ABA group of 13 children cost the school system 1,755,000 to produce the 25 point IQ rise. The Eclectic Treatment Group had about the same therapist time and cost and resulted in a 7 point IQ rise. In contrast, two classes of RNT treated children with 8 children per class totaling 16 children could have been treated with similar IQ results in one school year for less than $250,000. This would produce a saving of $1,505,000. Using Eikeseth's work, the scientifically best designed ABA study of IQ we could find, the cost-benefit ratio is very advantageous for RNT. We calculated it as ABA's $135,000 per child vs. RNT's range of $2,500 to $15,000 per child for similar IQ results. RNT shows over a ten-fold cost-benefit advantage over ABA. In addition, clinical (mental health) results would likely have been more marked because of the RNT focus on interpersonal relationships and reflective thinking.

2. TEACCH (Treatment and Education of Autistic and Communication related handicapped Children)

This method was originated by Schopler in the 1970's at the University of North Carolina. We are uncertain about its costs as a supplement to special education. IQ gain reports have been anecdotal. CGAS has not been systematically reported upon. However, the method has convincing clinical and cognitive outcomes on an anecdotal basis.

3. DIR (Developmental, Individual-Difference, Relationship Based) / Floortime

DIR/Floortime was created by Stanley Greenspan, MD around 1980. IQ gains resulting from the DIR method are not reported in a collected fashion, but claimed. Knowing the integrity of persons involved, we believe the claims are not only credible but genuine, though not yet available in systematic reports. Improvements take two to eight years and additionally require thousands of hours of parent-child sessions. Twenty percent of autistic children benefit markedly. Measures similar to CGAS were used and showed improvements though these results are not directly translatable into CGAS scores. There is no manual for replication. Costs are comparable to RNT costs at about 20,000 per child per two years. However the method often requires many years to achieve its results. DIR typically costs $80,000 per child for eight years of treatment.

4. Individual Psychodynamic Psychotherapy (Pull-Out Therapy)

This method has been in use since the work of Anna Freud and Melanie Klein began with children early in the 1900's. In schools, child therapy is usually called "pull-out psychotherapy", a method of delivery in which an emotionally disturbed, aggressive, child—usually with a diagnosed psychiatric disorder which is interfering with her education or that of others—is taken out of class and treated in an office in the school rather than transported to a clinic or private office. Parents may or may not be systematically involved. We estimate the costs of this method at $100/hour spent with the child or parent. Even when used four or five times a week, no systematic study gives evidence that pull-out therapy would be reliably effective in making IQ gains for a seriously emotionally disturbed child or be clinically helpful to a child with autism spectrum disorder. In fact we find there is no collection of evidence that this commonly used method reliably helps autistic children.

From the point of view of classroom behavioral improvements, pull-out psychotherapy has several disadvantages. It is, by definition, temporarily child-isolating. In contrast to in- classroom methods such as ABA or Reflective Network Therapy, pull-out therapy removes the child from the scene of social and behavioral problems so that emotional immediacy is lost and the child is hard pressed to remember the precipitants and contents of symptomatic outbreaks days after they happen. The child also loses the help of peers and teachers about whom the child may care a good deal. Pull-out psychotherapy is less expensive than ABA. If given intensively such as four or five times a week it is probably clinically effective, like child analysis, but that question has not been studied specifically regarding school-based treatments. Given intensively, it is more expensive than Reflective Network Therapy.

Among seriously disturbed anxious, non-autistic children who do not have conduct disorders, there is positive evidence regarding the good effect of individual psychotherapy on CGAS measurement of mental health gains. The best study we could find of "pull-out" therapy is Fonagy and Target's (1996). Fonagy scrutinizes the results of a particularly excellent clinic (The Hampstead Clinic) which provides private psychodynamic or psychoanalytic psychotherapy of children by psychoanalyzed, highly supervised or already trained students of child psychoanalysis. This extensive and remarkably lucid study comprises over seven hundred very well documented cases of individual psychodynamic child psychotherapy in private or clinic offices (Fonagy and Target, 1995).

The study does not address IQ or cognitive gains, but does carefully retrospectively address Children's Global Assessment Scores. The authors report that autism and pervasive developmental disorders *were not responsive* to such in-office psychodynamic treatment. Anxiety disorders definitely respond well, and an important finding is an orderly correlation of CGAS improvement with number of treatment sessions. This finding is similar to large scale studies of long term versus short term psychotherapy of adults, (Leichsenring & Rabung, October 1, 2008).

5. Reflective Network Therapy (RNT)

In use since 1965, created by Gilbert Kliman, MD with co-founder Elissa Burian, RNT was originally known as the Cornerstone Therapeutic Preschool Method. (Multiple applications have included the word "Cornerstone" in the naming of their preschool programs.) As a supplement to special education, RNT costs about $11,000 per child per year. Significant clinical and cognitive improvements occur in short time spans, from a few months to one or two years. RNT is manualized for consistent replication to achieve strong outcomes. Sustained IQ rises from 14 to 28 points are the norm for SED and PDD children who are IQ testable. Children on the autism spectrum and traumatized children benefit markedly. It is suitable for a full range of psychiatric disorders. Results include improved sociability, development of empathy, positive behavioral changes, increased vocabulary and communication skills, and increased receptivity to learning. One-on-one aides are unnecessary.

CONCLUSIONS

Of these methods, the one which seems to help mid to high functioning children on the autism scale to achieve academic functional levels and IQ gains similar to RNT results is the ABA (Lovaas) method. Lovaas does not think his method will produce IQ gains among severely retarded autistic children. In contrast, TEACCH and Reflective Network Therapy both have data showing they measurably helped some severely autistic children. Greenspan's data on 200 autistic young children suggests but does not clearly enumerate the same kinds of improvements. A continuing defect we have already complained about in most Lovaas method studies (including Eikeseth et al, 2007) is that using comparisons between Bayley Scores or Developmental Quotients on one hand and Wechsler Scales of Preschool Intelligence on the other hand is misleading. *There are excessive degrees of variance between the two measures.* Unfortunately, Lovaas and his followers have relied heavily on this low-validity follow up method. Therefore, their data may show inflation of follow-up IQ's among children who were initially unable to take a Wechsler test. A better method would be to do a first Wechsler, as soon as feasible, to provide a meaningful comparison of initial testing to follow-up test results. Similarly, DIR/Floortime data is weakened because it lacks a correlation of its clinical measures with CGAS.

In contrast, our presentation of RNT data deliberately slanted our IQ results *unfavorably* to ensure that our results are stated conservatively, and:

(a) We focus our outcome data collection reporting on comparisons of comparable tests.

(b) If a child cannot be tested by the Wechsler or Stanford-Binet method, we do not include that child in the IQ follow-up until the child is Wechsler testable.

(c) In cases where the Stanford Binet was used with a child, we accept research by others that ordinarily a follow-up test by the Wechsler method will show a reduction of IQ. (Moriarty, 1966)

Thus our findings are even more significant because almost all of the testable children showed IQ rises with RNT treatment even when declines were expectable.

Child analysis and presumably school based pull-out therapy's dose relationship or total sessions correlation with CGAS outcome results (Fonagy and Target, 1995) is very much what has been found with both CGAS gains and IQ gains with Reflective Network Therapy treatment in all diagnostic categories to date. These gains occur not only with neurotic, anxious or traumatized children but also with autistic and conduct-disordered children treated by Reflective Network Therapy. In the population studied by Fonagy, individual psychotherapy had its best results with childhood anxiety disorders, and its worst results with conduct-disordered and autistic categories of children. Of those children with childhood anxiety disorders treated by child analysis and presumably by pull-out therapy, the very best results are with treatment four times a week, over multiple years of therapy. The cost for effective individual psychotherapy for one seriously emotionally disturbed child with an anxiety disorder can be calculated by estimating the cost for four years of treatment (800 sessions) at $100 per session. That amounts to $80,000 or $20,000 per year. This is certainly a large multiple of the costs for RNT treatment for a single child. Further adding to cost benefits, there are no extra time, space or transportation costs for a child receiving RNT treatment in his existing school.

Reflective Network Therapy also has the advantage of very high likelihood (over 90%) of cognitive as well as clinical mental health gains among testable children. Further, RNT's strong clinical and cognitive results are not limited to anxious children. Reflective Network Therapy procedures are easily tailored for children with pervasive developmental disorders, including the entire autism spectrum as well as children with SED.

Reflective Network Therapy is the most clinically versatile of the five treatments reviewed because it is readily individualized for almost all preschool psychiatric disorders. It can be used with the whole gamut of preschoolers with autism spectrum disorders. It is easily tailored for seriously emotionally disturbed preschoolers, producing strong, measurable cognitive and clinical effects. It is inclusive, clinically versatile and feasible (see tables 9.4, 9.5 and 9.8) to carry out in: public school special education, community based mental health facilities and in privately operated therapeutic preschools. Over 90% of all IQ testable children in any diagnostic category including autism have an average Full Scale IQ rise of 12 to 28 points over 8 months of Reflective Network Therapy treatment (see table 9.6). The method is manualized for replication and the manual is augmented by instructional videos of actual treatment sessions which are keyed to the manual, (see table 9.7).

Because ABA is probably the most widely studied and widely used method for treating autism spectrum preschoolers throughout the world, we have focused on it in comparison with RNT. Reflective Network Therapy work contrasts with the non-inclusive (socially isolating) effect of ABA's pairing of a child with a one-on-one behavioral aide in the classroom. Such pairing of an adult with an autistic or severely disturbed child is frequent in the Lovaas method as commonly used in public schools today.

COMPARISON OF EARLY INTERVENTION METHODS:
FEATURES AND BENEFITS

INTERVENTION		*Criterion:* **INCLUSIVENESS** Deliberate inclusion of peers, teachers and parents. Real-life classroom interpersonal relations are a focus.
RNT Reflective Network Therapy	Yes	Inclusion of peers is a vital part of reflective network treatment, and the development of peer to peer empathy is often a powerful component. Parents and teachers are an integral part of the treatment technique, have frequent modeling by the psycho-therapist, and rapidly learn about important communications the child makes during treatment sessions. The psychotherapist has immediacy of observation, and can discuss interpersonal events with a patient and his teacher right as they happen. A treatment session in the classroom has the advantage of real life emotional charge –for example of jealousy, anger, curiosity, love– and allows a no-waiting intervention with the child's defenses and adaptation to the interpersonal processes.
PULL-OUT Psychotherapy in a school setting	No	Privacy from peers is a hallmark of treatment. Parents and teachers are usually isolated from the treatment, in the name of privacy, have little modeling by the psychotherapist, and learn about the child's important themes without immediacy. The psychotherapist in turn does not have simultaneous observation of the child in classroom and is often dealing with peer-relationship events which the child can no longer readily remember or feel are important.
ABA (Applied Behavioral Analysis)	No	A one on one aide tends to make an adult-child dyad, to the exclusion of full peer interaction. High frequency of formal inclusion of teachers, peers and parents in the behavioral modification process is difficult.
TEACCH	Yes	Normal classroom activities are enhanced. Empathy among peers and parent-child dyads is a goal, as is teacher empathy for the child.
DIR /Floortime	No	This therapy of parent and child usually but not necessarily excludes peers and teachers.

Table 9.4. Comparison of Interventions: Inclusiveness

Stanley Greenspan (1992) advocates a critical look at intensive (20-40 hours a week) behaviorally focused approaches to autistic children. A pioneer in the enhancement of mother-child relationships to evoke developmental progress, Greenspan expresses his keen disappointment with behavioral methods which produce development of "splinter skills" without recognizing that wholeness of interpersonal relationships is needed to overcome the learning problem:

> Autistic children often evidence severe biologically based thinking and language problems. They have deficits related to clear biological problems, such

INTERVENTION		Criterion: CLINICAL VERSATILITY Versatility Across Diagnostic Categories
RNT Reflective Network Therapy	Yes	Customizable and effective for SED and PDD. Helps autistic children in the entire spectrum from severe to mild. SED includes anxiety disorders, obsessive compulsive disorder, hyperactivity, attention deficit, posttraumatic stress disorders, conduct disturbances and depressive disorders. IQ and CGAS gain effects are regularly found among IQ testable RNT treated children in all diagnostic categories.
PULL-OUT Psychotherapy in a school setting	No	Not useful for most autistic children. Useful with seriously emotionally disturbed children having anxiety disorders. IQ changes amongst pull-out treated children are not currently reported.
ABA (Applied Behavioral Analysis)	Limited	Best with moderate to mildly retarded autistic children. No studies reported with seriously emotionally disturbed children. If used for three years, marked IQ gains are regular with autistic children but baseline measures are flawed.
TEACCH	No	Best with severely mentally retarded autistic children, where a few cases are reported of marked IQ gain.
DIR /Floortime	Not established but thought to be likely	A technique for putting a parent (mostly a mother) in tune with her autistic child, and bringing the child into richer affective contact with her. Very good clinical and cognitive effects on 20% of autistic preschool children. Diagnostic versatility is not established but Kliman thinks it is likely.

Table 9.5. Comparison of Interventions: Clinical Versatility

INTERVENTION	Criterion: IQ GAINS (Does the Method Regularly Produce Major IQ Gains?)
RNT Reflective Network Therapy	12-28 points over 8 months in over 90% of IQ testable children treated, whether autistic or any other diagnostic category.
PULL-OUT Psychotherapy in a school setting	Not well studied except by Heinicke for reading ability in children post preschool age.
ABA (Applied Behavioral Analysis)	Claims 12-28 points over 36 months, but developmental measures used at baseline and IQ tests at follow-up were not validly comparable.
TEACCH	28 points among several severely retarded autistic children, duration of treatment not stated.
DIR /Floortime	20% of IQ testable autistic preschoolers have IQ gains

Table 9.6. Comparison of Interventions: IQ

INTERVENTION	Criterion: MANUALIZED METHOD Replication Manual	Criterion: VIDEO ILLUSTRATIONS Keyed to the Manual
RNT Reflective Network Therapy	Yes	Yes
PULL-OUT Psychotherapy in a school setting	No	No
ABA (Applied Behavioral Analysis)	Yes	No
TEACCH	No	No
DIR /Floortime	No	No

Table 9.7. Reflective Network Therapy is Manualized with Video Illustrations Keyed to the Manual

as poor ability to process sounds, comprehend words, and plan sequential movements. Diagnosed between 18 months and 4 years of age, many of these youngsters display a variety of symptoms—wandering aimlessly, compulsively flapping their arms, continuously rubbing a spot on the carpet, repeatedly opening and closing a door, painstakingly marshaling small objects into rigidly straight lines—but almost no ability to respond to even the most basic attempts at com-

INTERVENTION	Criterion: FEASIBILITY Feasibility as indicated by use in a variety of settings
RNT Reflective Network Therapy	Public school special education classes, private therapeutic preschools, mental health centers, day care centers, shelter classrooms for homeless children, Head Starts, private regular preschools.
PULL-OUT Psychotherapy in a school setting	Public school special education classes, private therapeutic preschools, mental health centers, day care centers, private preschools.
ABA (Applied Behavioral Analysis)	Public school special education classes, private therapeutic preschools, mental health centers, day care centers, homes.
TEACCH	Public school special education classes, private therapeutic preschools.
DIR /Floortime	Similar venue versatility to ABA

Table 9.8. Comparison of Interventions: Feasibility

munication. Therapeutic programs for such severely challenged youngsters have traditionally concentrated on trying to teach them language or selected cognitive skills such as making particular sounds, acting out various social conventions, or imitating certain actions—the sort of isolated actions without context that we call "splinter skills." But even when these children learn to construct sentences, tie their shoes, or bang on drums, their actions usually do not show joyful spontaneity and zest, flexible problem solving, and emotional openness that should come naturally at their age. We have, for example, observed children with autistic symptoms in intensive behavioral programs (20 to 40 hours a week). Many, when they did speak, tended to exhibit rote and stereotyped quality in their thinking, though we felt they had the potential for more creative, abstract thought and greater creative imagination and closer peer relationships.

We have had different results with a program of emotional cuing, which begins at the point where the child finds himself turning away from his parents' smiles and overtures. This intervention program exploits the role of affect in mental development together with working with individual processing differences. It appears more effective in fostering healthy intellectual and emotional patterns than are strategies of direct cognitive stimulation (Greenspan, 1992). While children vary in their course of progress depending in part on the severity of biologically based processing deficits, this approach has enabled a number of children to work around specific disabilities by wooing them first into relationships and then into countless emotional exchanges with a caregiver, often beginning with simple facial expressions and gestures." (Greenspan, 1992)

Greenspan's commendable use of the interpersonal "wooing" approach with autistic children has not been reported on as a systematically used classroom-based approach. Although used in private practices and mental health clinics, DIR has not yet been subjected to controlled, comparison or random assignment studies. There is also not yet an uninterrupted series of preschool autistic children or seriously emotionally disturbed preschool children treated by Greenspan's methods with psychometric and CGAS outcome data.

Therefore, we do not yet have a means for a public school or other facility to adequately compare DIR/Floortime results and costs on a population basis to those of the school-based methods (including RNT) summarized in this chapter. Based on my own RNT work with autistic preschoolers and their parents as well as my own dyadic private practice with autistic children and their parents, I do have some predictions about what IQ, CGAS and CARS random assignment controlled studies will show. I forecast that Greenspan's dyadic (parent-child) method will be found more effective for autism spectrum disorders than ABA. But DIR /Floortime will be less effective than RNT because of the latter's more inclusive multiple-person reflective network which includes interpersonal wooing and the development and use of peer-empathy.

We considered the comparatively greater costs for the use of one-on-one aides on which the ABA (Lovaas) method depends in table 9.9. By having one RNT therapist performing individual therapy for multiple children within the classroom during short psychotherapy sessions each day of class, therapeutic personnel costs plummet while cognitive/clinical gains are achieved more quickly than with ABA. The budgetary difference turns out to be a savings of 600 to 1000 per cent or more over a conservatively estimated ABA behavioral aide approach. Put another way, the RNT classroom in a special education setting costs less than one sixth the expense incurred by using the one-on-one ABA model. Although the Lovaas method is helpful to many children and is deservedly well respected in many public school systems, it is definitely not the most cost effective method.

Special education is costly even without special education enhancements. We are not yet certain what percentage of autistic RNT treated children completely lose their initial need for special education services. Our conservative estimate (awaiting more rigorous follow up data) is that after eight months, at least 60% of RNT treated autism spectrum children who are IQ-testable when they start treatment go on to full time use of some regular classes within two years, and that a year later 80% of the same IQ testable children are even more fully integrated into regular public school classrooms.

It is important to underscore the fact that like ABA, Reflective Network Therapy also definitely modifies behavior. But it does so more richly. Positive and global behavioral improvements certainly result from this therapy. However, RNT is intentionally much broader in its goals and process, more peer-inclusive, more interpersonally complex, family engaging and emotionally fortifying than ABA is or is intended to be. Reflective Network Therapy is a psychological and social network therapy which blends individual psychotherapy, education (classroom curriculum), peer-interaction and cognitive as well as empathic exercising within the natural classroom setting. All of these beneficial components synergistically cause clinical and cognitive gains which are further supported by structured guidance and support for parents or primary caregivers. Positive changes in behavior and cognition result. RNT treatment induces intensive cognitive stimulation combined with movement toward clinical recovery from prior emotional deficits and disturbances. Clinical recovery is hastened by cognitive stimulation, including a very high volume of mentalizing, mirroring and reflective events during treatment sessions. Mental health gains, in turn, promote the rapidity of additional behavioral changes and cognitive growth. With RNT treatment, a small number of *severely* autistic children may fully recover and become richly empathic and cognitively well adapted to social and work life, with a marked IQ gain, clinically arriving at the point of becoming undiagnosable as autistic years later. (See chapter 4 for an example.)

The relative socializing and interpersonal benefits (mental health gains) of both ABA and RNT can be compared using standard tools such as CGAS to measure specific improvements. A meaningful cost-benefit comparison between the widely employed Lovaas method and Reflective Network Therapy must also include consideration of what is provided for the money spent.

Many school systems are burdened by high budgets not only for in-class special education aides but also for scientifically less proven "pull-out therapies" in which children are taken out of class for individual play therapy. In Reflective Network Therapy, pull-out sessions are eliminated; the child's individual therapy is fully integrated into the classroom experience; and, as stated elsewhere, in our experience, children who started RNT treatment with an ABA aide in tow do not need the aide after a month or less of RNT. Individual pull-out therapists and ABA aides are often assigned to children who could be much more intensively, effectively, economically and peer-inclusively helped within RNT groups. Pull-out therapists can be taught to perform RNT and thus improve the cost-effectiveness of their budgetary lines.

Table 9.9 (*Comparing Costs of Two Special Education Enhancements*) is a simple calculation regarding savings which can be realized by using RNT rather than ABA in a public school special education program. For this calculation, we used arbitrary and conservative salary figures, with a bias against our own method: $40,000 per year for a one-on-one ABA aid and $50,000 for a half time RNT therapist. Actual salary amounts will vary from community to community. There is no additional cost for a teacher's assistant or aide in most special education environments which can use RNT. That is because such environments usually have not only a teacher but also a teacher's assistant. There is also no additional cost if the special education system diverts a "pull-out" therapist to doing RNT. But to be conservative and biased against our own method, we introduce that therapist's salary as a cost in the calculations.

In her article, "Educators Deal with the Growing Problem of Autism," Fran Smith (2008) summarized special education costs which "skyrocket to 75,000 or more" per child with the addition of supplements such as one on one aides:

> Even merely adequate is expensive: A study by the Special Education Expenditure Project (conducted for the U.S. Department of Education) found that special classes, therapists, aides, transportation, and facilities for an autistic student cost an average of nearly $19,000 a year, or roughly triple the cost for a typical child. When districts go beyond adequate to establish intensive one-on-one programs or support a full array of speech, play, and occupational therapies, spending can skyrocket to $75,000 or more [per child]. (Smith, 2008)

In table 9.9 we used the conservative calculation of $40,000 per year for all costs associated with the use of a one-on-one ABA aide.

COMPARING COSTS OF TWO EARLY INTERVENTION METHODS: STAFF TIME AND SALARIES FOR SPECIAL EDUCATION ENHANCEMENTS

Enhancement for eight (8) difficult to educate children (ages two to seven) who have Serious Emotional Disturbances or Pervasive Developmental Disorders including Autism and Asperger's disorder.	
Method 1) ABA Applied Behavioral Analysis (Autistic and PDD children only)	Method 2) RNT Reflective Network Therapy (Autistic children, children with other forms of PDD, children with SED)
Requires a full time Aide for each child, added to existing special education classroom costs	Requires one in-classroom therapist added to existing special education classroom costs.
8 full time ABA Aides at the additional cost of 40,000 per Aide The children may be distributed among various special education classes or may all be in one larger class	50,000 for a half time RNT therapist The children may be distributed among various special education classes or may all be in one larger class
Total annual additional costs for 8 children's ABA aides = 320,000	Total annual additional costs for 8 children's RNT treatment = 50,000
TOTAL ANNUAL SAVINGS USING RNT RATHER THAN ABA Treating 8 children with RNT vs. using ABA: Savings = 270,000 Treating 80 children with RNT vs. using ABA: Savings = 2,700,000	

Table 9.9.   Comparing Costs of Two Special Education Enhancements

Lidia Wasowicz underscores additional line item costs associated with ABA and gives a grim picture of the financial burden to parents and taxpayers associated with this method.. For example, teaching an autistic child to wave goodbye can take up to 40 hours of repetition which would cost more than $1,000. Wascowicz further reported:

> If not carried out in a school-supported program, most of that cost for applied behavioral analysis intervention likely will be paid out of pocket since, with the exception of a few companies that offer reimbursement as part of their health benefits, the majority of insurers do not cover therapy for developmental disorders like autism.

That's despite a government endorsement of such treatments, which can set parents back in the neighborhood of $25,000 to $60,000 annually—and run up to as much as $80,000 to $100,000 a year for care in a residential school... A National Academy of Sciences panel convened by the U.S. government to evaluate existing research urged all autistic children, regardless of the severity of their impairment, be made eligible for special-education services. It also recommended a minimum of 25 hours per week of intensive, year-round training for [autistic] tots as young as 2. (Wasowicz, 2007)

In the Reflective Network Therapy model used in Table 9.10 *(Typical Staff Time and Related Costs)* we could look at the RNT marked cost advantage from another viewpoint. The same dollars used by public schools employing behavioral aides to supplementally educate and treat 8 children using ABA could instead be used to supplementally educate and treat 48 seriously

RNT: TYPICAL STAFF TIME PER WEEK AND RELATED COSTS FOR A 45 WEEK SCHOOL YEAR

HOUR PER WEEK FOR 8 CHILDREN, FIVE DAYS/WEEK	HOURS CLASS TIME	HOURS PARENT CONFERENCES	TEAM MEETINGS	HRS MISC	RECORD KEEPING	HOURS PER WEEK
Head Teacher Already in place at most special education services	31	6	1.5	0.5	1.0	**40**
Asst. Teacher Already in place at most special education services	38	0	1.5	0	0.5	**40**
Therapist	13	2	1.5	0	1.5	**18**
ANNUAL COST FOR RNT THERAPIST After the second year an RNT team with a licensed therapist can be self-supervising.						
If a therapist on staff is deployed for training and use in the RNT classroom	NO ADDITIONAL SALARY EXPENSE					
If a therapist is added to staff	ESTIMATED ANNUAL COST: $40,500					
Basic Costs for first year, second year and subsequent years: Training and Supervision						
START UP COSTS FIRST YEAR in a school or agency which already employs a suitable therapist who can be trained to perform RNT in the classroom	INITIAL INTENSIVE TRAINING, ONGOING TRAINING AND SUPERVISION IN RNT FOR THERAPIST AND TEACHERS				$20,000	
SECOND YEAR	WITH REDUCED SUPERVISION				$10,000	
SUBSEQUENT YEARS	SELF SUSTAINING: No Additional Costs				N/A	
START UP COST PER CHILD:						
1) COST PER CHILD FIRST YEAR: IF A THERAPIST MUST BE HIRED	$ 7,562					
2) COST PER CHILD FIRST YEAR: IF AN EXISTING THERAPIST IS TRAINED	$ 2,500					

Table 9.10. Typical RNT Staff Time and Related Costs Per 45 Week Full Day Full School Year

disturbed and/or autistic preschoolers children using Reflective Network Therapy.

With Cornerstone treatment, consistent and sustained results are achieved more quickly and with less time and money investment. Table 9.10 (included in the replication manual, chapter 3) considers information similar to that in Table 9.9, restated in terms of staff time dedicated to RNT child-pupils. Costs for the first year include orientation, initial intensive training, multiple half-day in-service, on site trainings and/or videoconferenced supervision and discussion throughout the first year. (No class days are lost as training revolves around applying the method hands-on with the children.)

The tables demonstrating financial feasibility and may provide school districts with budgetary motivation to use RNT. It is a major economy as well having qualitative and humanitarian advantages of marked improvement in the emotional and cognitive lives of pupils.

SUMMARY OF RNT ADVANTAGES WITH
FAVORABLE COST IMPACTS

1. Quantifiable Cognitive Development Gains: IQ improvements produced by the RNT method with autistic children are not systematically reported in pull-out therapies. RNT IQ gains are equivalent and often superior to IQ gains using the Lovaas method.

2. Rapidity of Results: Measurable mental health and cognitive gains are usually produced in a single school year by the Reflective Network Therapy method. This rapidity of efficacy reduces the treatment timeline and therefore all costs. The Lovaas method, TEACCH, and DIR require multiple years of 40 or more hours per week intervention to produce similar cognitive results. Pull-out therapy has no body of data on such results for autistic children.

3. Reduction of Existing Costs: (a) RNT usually eliminates the costly necessity for existing one-on-one behavioral aides within one month. Among more than 60 twice tested children in RNT archives and prospective study those several children who started treatment with an aide did not require a one-on-one behavioral aide after one month. The cost of a single one-on-one ABA aide to help a single child would just about cover the entire salary of an RNT therapist helping eight children. (b) Pull-Out Therapies: RNT eliminates all costs associated with pull-out therapy. The budget line for a pull-out therapist can be used for in-classroom RNT. Reflective Network Therapy achieves results using only 15-20 minutes per classroom day of professional psychodynamic therapist time with each child in the

RNT classroom. Therefore, a single RNT therapist can multiply the evident effectiveness of her or his time-use with the help of the in-classroom method, treating eight children four times a week in less time than it would take to take the same number of children out of the classroom for 50-minute psychotherapy sessions twice a week. Up to12 children can be well served in a single RNT classroom group, a limit we observe to keep track of the children's numerous communications in Reflective Network Therapy.

4. Feasibility: RNT has been successfully tested in highly varied educational and community based settings: public school special education classrooms, private therapeutic preschools, mental health clinics, shelters, day care centers, Head Starts and in another culture (Argentina).

5. Versatility: RNT is successful for children on the autism spectrum as well as for disturbed children having a full range of emotional (SED) and developmental disorders (PDD) while Lovaas' ABA method has no stated psychotherapeutic goals; ABA is primarily viewed as an educational response to ASD. Reflective Network Therapy works best for up to eight disturbed children per classroom, ages two to seven, who form the RNT classroom group. Twelve is the maximum number of children with serious SED or PDD (including Autism) who can be served in one classroom group. Each child can be treated efficiently every day the class meets, using less than three hours of a therapist's time in the classroom per day, giving each child in the group individual psychotherapy in that amount of time. Children can be served in a part time activity group, or a full-time special day class of their own. They can be part of a larger special education program or an even more inclusive class that meets for the rest of the day.

COMPARISON OF IQ OUTCOME DATABASES

The number of teams contributing to the IQ data base on which we draw is larger than we drew on for Lovaas method data base. At this writing, it appears that systematic Lovaas (ABA) IQ test follow up data is not only methodologically dubious but limited to about 50 well studied children in three generally well carried out projects. In contrast, Reflective Network Therapy draws on data from a larger number of children at multiple sites (see Tables 9.1, 9.2 and 9.3). In addition to RNT data flowing from a large number of reporting teams, the cumulative total number of control and comparison children correctly twice-tested for IQ change appears larger than we could find in the three best studies of ABA's IQ outcome data. We relied on combining Eikeseth's (2007) data, The Wisconsin Early Autism Project (Sallows and

Grauptner, 2005) and Lovaas' (1987) "IQ gain" reports. Smaller numbers of IQ outcomes were found in TEACCH and DIR reports.

The prospective study of a consecutive series of ten San Mateo, California RNT treated patients (Hope, 1999) has confirmed the IQ findings of the 11 prospectively studied and archival studies of 42 twice-tested RNT treated children in New York, (Zelman, Samuels and Abrams 1996, 1999). Other subjects in our cumulative total come from San Francisco and Piedmont, California and Buenos Aires. The California study added six control and three comparison children. An excellent comparison group is an independent study of IQ among 12 autistic preschoolers given an "eclectic" hodge-podge of applied behavioral analysis with occupational therapy, speech therapy, and other modalities to supplement special education and 13 given ABA (Eikeseth 2007). Eikeseth's 12 eclectic special education served children are useful as an unintended comparison treated series. They had a 7 point IQ rise. Kliman's non-RNT work with foster children and their IQ change data (Westchester County, New York) added 65 comparison treated twice-tested cases who received either 15 or 40 individual supportive-expressive psychotherapy sessions.

STATISTICAL SIGNIFICANCE

We are told by statisticians, such as Michael Acree, PhD, who did the meta-analysis of our data, that the phenomenon of IQ rise in Reflective Network Therapy is highly significant. It appears to be the only interpersonal psychotherapy method with such results. ABA is considered an educational method, not psychotherapy. ABA has IQ results similar to those of RNT, but ABA requires a much longer period of much more costly treatment to get those similar results.

Among the prospectively sampled RNT children were the ten autism spectrum (ASD) patients served in a California public school special education program. Similar findings of IQ rises have now been seen among IQ-testable autistic patients treated at three other sites: San Francisco, Piedmont, and Buenos Aires. So far only two of all IQ testable children in any of the sites and with any diagnosis have failed to show an IQ gain. This regularity indicates the IQ rise phenomenon in Cornerstone is robust among initially testable children. Zelman reports that about 40% of his archival Cornerstone RNT series of 42 subjects had pervasive developmental disorder (PDD). The others had a variety of serious emotional disorders (SED. The pervasive developmental disorder children did as well from an IQ rise point of view as the other 60% with serious emotional disorders. The number of twice-tested children treated with Reflective Network Therapy continues to grow as more IQ testable children are retested; we have over 20 previously tested children waiting for follow up testing (retesting) as we go to press.

The IQ rise benefits seen in children treated by Reflective Network Therapy are particularly significant in light of a large body of scientific literature regarding the stability of IQ. It is generally found in psychological studies of intelligence that children's IQs do not change much over time (Jonsdottir, et al., 2006). This contrasts markedly with treatment findings in RNT's outcome data. IQ gains from RNT treatment have been sustained up to 40 years. (See www.reflectivenetworktherapy.org for video of a follow-up interview.) The longest Lovaas follow-ups are 27 years, probably because the method was invented after RNT.

Table 9.11 shows the IQ changes among RNT treated twice-tested children. It indicates there is an orderly and direct correlation between the number of RNT treatments and rises in IQ.

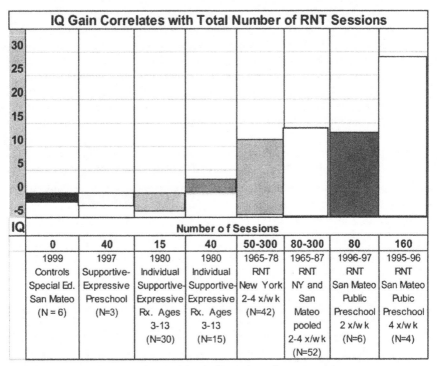

IQ Gain Correlates with Total Number of RNT Sessions							
Number o f Sessions							
0	**40**	**15**	**40**	**50-300**	**80-300**	**80**	**160**
1999 Controls Special Ed. San Mateo (N = 6)	1997 Supportive- Expressive Preschool (N=3)	1980 Individual Supportive- Expressive Rx. Ages 3-13 (N=30)	1980 Individual Supportive- Expressive Rx. Ages 3-13 (N=15)	1965-78 RNT New York 2-4 x/w k (N=42)	1965-87 RNT NY and San Mateo pooled 2-4 x/w k (N=52)	1996-97 RNT San Mateo Public Preschool 2 x/w k (N=6)	1995-96 RNT San Mateo Pubic Preschool 4 x/w k (N=4)

Table 9.11. IQ Gain Correlates with Total Number of RNT Sessions

CRITIQUES OF APPLIED BEHAVIOR ANALYSIS

Because ABA is probably the most widely studied and widely used method for raising IQ while treating autism spectrum preschoolers throughout the world, we focus particularly on ABA in comparison with RNT. A brief description of the common denominators in the many behavioral modification techniques currently in practice, including those employed by Lovaas occurs in an article by Dr. Kostas Francis:

> Thus, with the term 'behavioral treatments' we refer to those interventions where the Skinnerian-based techniques form the predominant feature of the approach. Although behavioral methodology has been evolving and new techniques have been introduced, applied behavior analysis and discrete trial learning still remain the core feature of behavioral intervention in autism, following the work carried out over the last 30 years by Dr. O. Ivar Lovaas, at the University of California, Los Angeles, USA.
>
> Skills in receptive/expressive language, attending to social stimuli, imitation, pre-academics (e.g. rote counting, knowledge of spatial relationships, etc.), and self-help that are deficient, are broken into discrete components. They are then taught on a one-to-one basis, in school and/or at home, using rewards for the successful completion of each step. Behavioral techniques of reinforcement (mainly positive), backward chaining (i.e. the process of teaching each component of a behavior starting with the last step needed to complete the sequence), shaping, and prompt and prompt fading are used. Physical aversives are no longer employed. Initially, food and favorite objects are used as reinforcers, and are later replaced by more social ones, such as praise. Learned responses are repeated until firmly embedded. (Francis, 2005)

In his review, Francis' evaluation of Lovaas is that "its original effectiveness claim is overstated." (Francis, 2005) The data and methodology used in Lovaas studies used as evidence of results have been criticized by many independent sources. Follow-up studies have been done which attempt to address some of these criticisms. Researchers and the senior medical consultant for the Office of Health Technology Assessment, Center for Health Services and Policy Research at the University of British Columbia provided a rigorous critical appraisal of two sources presenting the Lovaas method cost-benefits. In their executive summary, Bassett, Green and Kazanjian (2000) assert:

> It was found that both cost-benefit analyses are based on models biased in favor of Lovaas treatment. In neither instance do any children not receiving Lovaas children treatment appear in the functionally-normal category, despite research evidence showing that about 10-20% of a population of children with autism achieve employment, independent of specific treatment programs. At the same

time, only 10% of the group receiving Lovaas treatment remained in the group having the highest service requirements. (Bassett, 2000)

Investigators concluded that: data on competing alternatives were not well developed; effectiveness was "virtually unaddressed;" costs were not itemized and therefore it was not evident that important costs and consequences were adequately valued; no comprehensive description of the competing alternatives was provided; and that Jacobson et al. made assumptions based on an uncritical acceptance of the Lovaas research results. Further, they found that:

This model simply asserts a truism, namely, if an effective treatment for autism were available that achieved its effect at an early age, it would reduce public service costs over the lifetime of a person with autism. ...The alternative to Lovaas treatment is simply described as children who 'do not receive effective intervention or who otherwise continue to need intensive supports'...At best, these cost-benefit models demonstrate the obvious: if an effective treatment for autism were available that resulted in normally-functioning children starting at an early age, it would massively reduce public service costs (as well as human suffering) over the lifetime of a person with autism. (Bassett, 2000)

Similarly, the Jacobson and Mulick paper, which purported positive cost-benefit evidence in favor of the Lovaas method was critically reviewed with a different result in "Benefit-cost analysis and autism services: A response to Jacobson and Mulick" by Marcus, Rubin and Rubin who state:

In their article on system and costs issues in programs for children with autism, Jacobson and Mulick (2000) deal with the importance of examining the economic environment surrounding provision of effective services. However, their arguments are based on faulty assumptions, inadequate research findings, and misuse of benefit–cost analysis methods. Rather than providing an objective, systematic review of what is known and accepted about existing early intervention programs, the article comes across as a promotion for one approach, early intensive behavior intervention (EIBI).

If we agree that the intent of benefit–cost analysis is to help establish priorities for scarce resources, then the Jacobson and Mulick effort fails in this task. ...They fail to consider that resources may be limited... and that alternative services and treatments may be more efficient. (Marcus, Marcus, J.S. and Rubin, M.A., 2000)

I am generally satisfied that even though its data is muddled, the Lovaas method in fact does achieve and maintain statistically significant IQ gains, as does Cornerstone. However, I notice—in the article posted online at the NAS website (National Autistic Society), quoted below—how readily costs of the Lovaas method escalate. In order to realize the optimal gains cited by Lovaas, at least 40 hours per child per week of one on one work were required. I use the term, "at least", because apparently the cost of ongoing training and supervision of the behavioral aides was not counted as time nor factored as cost. It seems of limited practicability in many communities and living situations to have any behavioral aide become a veritable member of the family household at full-time working hours over any period of time. Lovaas described his findings from the experimental group as follows:

> A recoverable group of individuals who, following intervention, no longer demonstrated the characteristics of autism. *47% of children who worked 40 hours at home per week* [emphasis added] achieved normal functioning by the time they successfully entered full-time mainstream education at the age of seven. b) An intermediate group (40%) made substantial progress but still displayed autistic characteristics. Many of them retained language difficulties or an intellectual disability. (National Autistic Society, Lovaas-NAS, 2010)

RNT findings concur that more therapy produces more IQ gains in PDD and adds that the same is true of RNT treatment of children in SED categories. Researchers have established an orderly correlation between the frequency of RNT treatment and significant IQ rises (as discussed above). Most importantly, RNT requires far fewer than 40 treatment hours a week to achieve these results. Almost all of the children who received only a few hours a week of RNT treatment achieved measurable gains on mental health scores and experienced IQ gains. This comparison alone is a striking indicator of the cost-benefit advantages of using this method.

RNT's work contrasts with the non-inclusive or socially isolating effect of ABA pairing a child with a one on one behavioral aide in the classroom. Full-time pairing of an adult with an autistic or severely disturbed child is standard in the Lovaas method as commonly used in public schools today.

Stanley Greenspan (1992) also advocates a critical look at intensive (20-40 hours a week) behaviorally focused approaches to autistic children. A pioneer in the use of mother-child relationships to evoke developmental progress, Greenspan expresses his disappointment with behavioral methods which produce development of "splinter skills" without a wholeness of interpersonal relationships being part of the learning problem:

> Autistic children often evidence severe biologically based thinking and language problems. They have deficits related to clear biological problems, such as poor ability to process sounds, comprehend words, and plan sequential movements. Diagnosed between 18 months and 4 years of age, many of these youngsters display a variety of symptoms—wandering aimlessly, compulsively flapping their

arms, continuously rubbing a spot on the carpet, repeatedly opening and closing a door, painstakingly marshaling small objects into rigidly straight lines—but almost no ability to respond to even the most basic attempts at communication. (Greenspan 1992)

Therapeutic programs for such severely challenged youngsters have traditionally concentrated on trying to teach them language or selected cognitive skills such as making particular sounds, acting out various social conventions, or imitating certain actions—the sort of isolated actions without context that we call "splinter skills." But even when these children learn to construct sentences, tie their shoes, or bang on drums, their actions usually do not show joyful spontaneity and zest, flexible problem solving, and emotional openness that should come naturally at their age. We have, for example, observed children with autistic symptoms in intensive behavioral programs (20 to 40 hours a week). Many, when they did speak, tended to exhibit rote and stereotyped quality in their thinking, though we felt they had the potential for more creative, abstract thought and greater creative imagination and closer peer relationships.

Greenspan's commendable use of the interpersonal "wooing" approach with autistic children has not been reported on as a systematically used classroom-based approach. Used in private practices and mental health clinics, it has not yet been subjected to manualization or controlled, comparison or random assignment studies. We look forward ourselves to including Greenspan's DIR/Floortime method with individual families as a comparison group in a future study. Most importantly for administrators of public taxpayer supported services, there is not yet a series of autistic children or seriously emotionally disturbed preschool children treated by Greenspan's methods with data on psychometric and CGAS outcomes. Therefore we do not yet have a means for a public school or other facility to compare its results and costs on a population basis to those of the methods summarized here which do have such outcome data. DIR costs are probably comparable to pull-out therapy.

Based on my own four-plus decades of RNT work with autistic preschoolers and parents and my own dyadic (parent-child) work with autistic children and their parents, I do have some predictions about what IQ and CGAS studies will show. I forecast that Greenspan's dyadic (parent-child) DIR method is more effective for autism spectrum disorders than Fonagy and Target found with the dyadic method of child analysis. DIR will be found to be less effective than the more inclusive multiple person network, interpersonal wooing and peer-empathy building approach of Reflective Network Therapy.

We highlighted the costs for the use of one-on-one aides on which the ABA (or Lovaas) method relies (in Table 9.9). By having one RNT therapist performing individual therapy for multiple children within the classroom (therapeutically utilizing hundreds of moments of real life events) therapeutic personnel costs plummet compared to ABA. The budgetary advantage for RNT use is a savings of 300 to 600 per cent, depending on which ABA program is used for comparison. Put another way, the RNT classroom costs one third or one sixth of the expense incurred by using the one on one ABA model which the Lovaas method requires. Although the Lovaas is effective and deservedly well respected in many public school systems, it is definitely not the more cost effective method.

Great taxpayer savings occurred for each autistic or severely emotionally disturbed child treated by RNT whose case history is discussed in this book. Had the Lovaas method been used with the autistic children (which was an option for most of the California children) there would have been taxpayer expenses of over $40,000 a year per child for a special Applied Behavioral Analysis aide and if the Lovaas' template had been followed, this much higher cost would have continued for several years.

The Reflective Network Therapy method is quite cost-effective because it eliminates the need for allocation of considerable public school special education funds for multiple full or half-time behavioral aides to cover each child separately. The use of one on one aides for children in special education children requires taxpayers to support high costs, The additional weekly cost is about $6400 a week for eight children, using 8 part time aides (20 hours/week) at $40 an hour ($800 per week per child). The behavioral aides cost is in addition to the classroom teachers costing $1200/week, for a total of $7600/week in salary costs or 342,000 per year for a 45 week program. The RNT model of integrating eight children into one classroom with a teacher and a teacher's assistant, one therapist and no one-on-one aides has salary costs well under $100,000 for treating eight children for a full school year (45 weeks). It saves $220,000 versus the anti-inclusive and socially isolating requirement for multiple classroom aides in Lovaas (ABA).

It is also interesting to consider the independent assessment of behavior modification treatment done by British counterparts of the Canadians who evaluated Lovaas studies, perhaps more objectively because of their own even greater non-involvement in the politics of U.S. education (Dyson, 2004). An assessment was done at the University of Manchester which considered the component costs (additional staff, etc.) as well as the additional social costs associated with treating autistic children in terms of family and in-home supports. This excerpt from Dyson's analysis of cost-benefits of early interventions emphasized that the best results for Lovaas were documented by Lovaas supporters and practitioners, while an independent study (Boyd and Corley, 2001) was unable to replicate the results:

There have been a large number of studies focusing on the impact of various interventions for ASD. Jordan et al (1998) surveyed the existing literature on educational interventions and concluded that we knew less than we would like about the impact of particular interventions. Our survey of research since their survey confirmed this pessimistic conclusion (see Dyson, 2004). These conclusions about inconclusiveness of research were broadly accepted although supporters of the Lovaas method—for example, Sallows (2002, 2005) and Eikeseth (2001)—have claimed that the Lovaas studies are robust.

There have been a number of additional studies of Early Intensive Behavioral Interventions which are variations on ABA. Sallows and Graupner (1999), Eikeseth et al. (2000), Sheinkopf and Siegel (1998) and Bibby et al. (2001)—have all shown some success for the Lovaas method although only Sallows and Graupner were able to show results comparable to the original Lovaas results of over 40% of the children achieving "normal function" after three years. Other studies of EIBI, for example, Boyd and Corley (2001), failed to reproduce the results. (Dyson, 2004)

Dyson discusses concerns about the integrity of the Lovaas data when replicated in different environments (e.g., individual homes with student behavioral aides) where supervision is performed by reportage to and discussion with primary supervisors who are removed from the actual treatment or benefit of first hand observation:

A concern about treatment integrity—that is, the extent to which the treatment is replicated in different environments—is a criticism often leveled at the Lovaas EIBI (Early Intensive Behavioral Intervention or ABA) method, although it appears that EIBI is one of the best documented of all the programs and is usually—though not always—implemented with trained and accredited support and supervision. However, notwithstanding the extent of documentation and the care for treatment integrity in existing small-sample trials, there must remain some concern about the possibility of maintaining treatment integrity for large samples. The "supervision chains" will become longer so that the link between the experts developing the program and those implementing it is likely to become more tenuous. In addition, since many programs require large numbers of trained personnel, treatment of large samples is likely to require the use of less skilled personnel. (Dyson, 2004)

Dyson's report also mentions research suggesting that home-based behavioral programs have little effect on long-term outcomes. Whether or not this proves to be true, the potential negative impact of ABA on normal family life suggested by common sense may be impossible to isolate out and evaluate. Nevertheless, this potential as a socially negative effect (in addition to the obvious and implicit additional costs of home-based treatment) must be taken into consideration. In terms of Lovaas follow-up studies, the issue of limited sampling and lack of control group is also raised in Dyson's analysis. Long term follow-up is a weakness in all studies described by Dyson:

> Some studies have attempted to follow up children in particular studies in order to assess the long-term impact of the intervention. Again, EIBI proponents have been the most active in this respect. McEachin et al (1993) followed up at age 12 the nine "successes" of the original Lovaas group and found that eight of them could still be considered as functioning normally. These same children were followed up as young adults, when the gains were shown to be maintained, and they are currently being followed up once more. However, this follow-up is extremely limited. Not only is the sample very small but there is no follow-up of the control group (nor of the other members of the treatment group) and so it is difficult to be confident that the long-term effects are the result of treatment. (Dyson, 2004)

The study entitled "Early Intensive Behavioral Treatment: Replication of the UCLA Model [Lovaas] in a Community Setting" (Cohen, 2006) was a significant effort to replicate Lovaas findings independently using two comparison groups of 21 children each. (Subjects were not selected on a random assignment basis but by parental preference.) Despite 35 to 40 hours of Lovaas treatment for the first group, (the second was a special education class which did not employ one on one behavioral aides), there were no outcome differences in language comprehension or nonverbal skill. Only 6 of the 21 children receiving Lovaas treatment fully transitioned into regular education after 3 years, although 11 others were able to be included in regular education with the ongoing support of behavior modification.

> Although previous studies have shown favorable results with early intensive behavioral treatment (EIBT) for children with autism, it remains important to replicate these findings, particularly in community settings. The authors conducted a 3-year prospective outcome study that compared 2 groups: (1) 21 children who received 35 to 40 hours per week of EIBT from a community agency that replicated Lovaas' model of EIBT and (2) 21 age-and IQ-matched children in special education classes at local public schools. A quasi-experimental design was used, with assignment to groups based on parental preference. Assessments were conducted by independent examiners for IQ (unfortunately including Bayley Scales of Infant Development to compare with later Wechsler Preschool and Primary Scales of Intelligence), language (Reynell Developmental Language Scales), nonverbal skill (Merrill-Palmer Scale of Mental Tests), and adaptive behavior (Vineland Adaptive Behavior Scales). Analyses of covariance, with baseline scores as covariates and Year 1-3 assessments as repeated measures, revealed that, with treatment, the EIBT group obtained significantly higher IQ

(F = 5.21, p = .03) and adaptive behavior scores (F = 7.84, p = .01) than did the comparison group. No difference between groups was found in either language comprehension (F = 3.82, p = .06) or nonverbal skill. Six of the 21 EIBT children were fully included into regular education without assistance at Year 3, and 11 others were included with support; in contrast, only 1 comparison child was placed primarily in regular education. (Cohen, 2006)

Cohen summarizes this study by citing "a trend towards" language comprehension and stating that differences between the Lovaas-treated children and the comparison group were smaller than found in earlier Lovaas outcome studies. He does not comment on the scientifically flawed use of Bayley measures for IQ, a considerable methodologic difficulty as the correlation of Bayley scales with WPPSI IQ scores is poor:

> On the primary outcome measure of IQ, the EIBT group showed a gain of 25 points, which was statistically significant compared to the gain of 14 points in the comparison group. Similar effects were found on measures of adaptive behavior. The increases in test scores are similar to these reported in Lovaas' original EIBT study and in some recent investigations. However, the difference between the EIBT group and the comparison group on outcome measures was smaller than in other studies, as the comparison group also made gains. (Cohen, H., 2006)

We have already elaborated the evidence for the fact that Reflective Network Therapy achieves equal or better results when compared with Lovaas outcome studies. RNT's track record with ASD children, in addition to its more cost effective structure and testing in several community settings should encourage its wider application in public schools. In addition, autistic children often have other disturbances, such as traumatizing experiences for which RNT is also proven effective. In the public school setting, children with a full range of SED diagnoses require treatment for which Lovaas is not suited but for which RNT is eminently suited. Thus, Reflective Network Therapy is superior for peer-inclusive applications, not only because it results in large dollar savings in comparison to Lovaas, but also because it offers a methodological process which can be individualized to the needs of children in many conditions, allowing the RNT psychotherapist to tailor the content of individual treatment for children with a broad range of difficulties. It can also be done in the midst of a normal preschool class if desired.

A rich discussion of the unique clinical benefits of Reflective Network Therapy is interwoven throughout this book, in the case studies and scientific papers as well as in the narratives of actual classroom sessions incorporated into the manual chapter. The structured multiplication of social therapeutic events which seem to accelerate recoveries and produce cognitive gains in a short time frame is discussed in chapter one of this book under Concepts and Processes. An entire chapter on theory explaining the RNT clinical and cognitive effects follows this one.

The reduction of time investment for similar or better results must be taken into account when comparing the RNT with the Lovaas method to the extent that "time is money" especially in light of the likelihood of the long term benefits of earlier rather than later mental health and IQ gains for the children. In this aspect, Lovaas (ABA) and Reflective Network Therapy are not equivalent methods in value; RNT has the clear advantage. In most cases, children "graduate" from RNT's therapeutic environment after only eight months of treatment, having sustained marked IQ and clinical improvements.

Additional taxpayer cost savings are also apparent when using the Reflective Network Therapy with foster children. RNT significantly reduces the odds of "bouncing" in foster care. Bouncing, also called "unplanned transfer among foster homes" is associated with behavioral repetition compulsions which cause children to be rejected and result in multiple foster placements. Stabilizing foster care placements has important positive impact on the children's school continuity, their mental health, and cognitive abilities (Kliman 2006). It has numerous financially advantageous benefits, especially the immediate financial benefit of reducing social service administrative costs for managing unplanned transfers (Kliman 2006) and reducing the academic problems of transfers among schools when a foster child bounces from home to home and school districts are thus changes.

A foster care case worker's salary is about 900 a week (depending upon the community and locale). With overhead added, the true cost would be more. To select and orient a new foster family for a particular child with SED or even an adjustment reaction disorder requires additional administrative time. Training and supporting the foster parents to help the separation-distressed child typically requires 40 more hours. Case worker visits and supervision of the new home over ordinary levels takes another half week the first year. For these items we can represent direct costs as at least 2.5 weeks = $2,500. Associated record-keeping and administrative costs are about equal to these direct costs. Thus, the total savings from each saved transfer is conservatively $5,000. With a half million children placed in foster care annually in the U.S., their established need, humane considerations and long term benefits to society should prompt inclusion of more foster children in Reflective Network Therapy.

LONG TERM FINANCIAL BENEFITS

We also need to consider the lifelong contributions to society of children who have been helped to recover from severe emotional and cognitive disturbances and (conversely) the economic strain and drain on society precipitated by costly needs of ongoing support for those who are not helped to recover. Since Reflective Network Therapy tends to cause significant rises in IQ, the individual and society benefit from the positive correlation between higher IQ and higher earned income. We have shown that early interventions using RNT produce mental health and general intelligence improvements in a shorter period of time than other therapies. We have shown that the method produces substantial IQ gains equal to and sometimes better than those achieved by the socially isolating constant companion behavioral aide technique. We have detailed significant cost savings when RNT is used in a regular public special education context. Let us not lose sight of the economic value long term improvements in quality of life for the individual, including the recovered child's improved ability to benefit from higher education, earn higher income over his or her lifetime, and thus potentially become a contributor to the wider social good. The opposite is also true. For example, children who keep bouncing among foster homes wind up all too often in jails, and are among society's angriest criminals. It is reasonable to expect that stopping the cycle of foster care rejections and bouncing greatly reduces the likelihood of a foster child becoming a criminal. Similarly, children who remain in a state of anxiety or psychological traumatization are unlikely to fulfill their economic potentials.

For autistic children, time-use consideration is a high priority when choosing treatment. An entire family and many social resources may need to be involved in order for an autistic child to recover or reach good levels of empathy, playfulness, social flexibility, and an IQ in the normal range. Greenspan comments on the high demands on families of autistic children in his study of DIR/Floortime. Reporting on 200 children treated by that method, he notes a definite connection between quantity of intervention and the improvements, (Greenspan, and Weider, 2005).

The 20 percent of DIR treated children with the best outcomes had received large quantities of sessions and they required up to eight years of this treatment.

A short series of additional tables simplifies an overview of information that is critical for understanding the differences among treatments discussed in this chapter: RNT, ABA, DIR and Pull Out (individual psychotherapy). Table 9.12 summarizes outcome concerning the percentage of autistic children with IQ rise (by treatment modality), which methods have CGAS data, the time it takes for these methods to complete treatment, and what each method costs.

A further breakdown concerning the time each method requires to get results is presented in Table 9.12 (*Time and Costs to Achieve IQ and Global Mental Health Gains*). It summarizes outcome concerning the percentage of

	RNT	ABA	DIR	Intensive
TIME AND COSTS TO ACHIEVE IQ AND GLOBAL MENTAL HEALTH GAINS				
INTERVENTION	Reflective Network Therapy	Applied Behavioral Analysis(1)	/Floortime	**Psychoanalytic Pull-Out** Psychotherapy
Number of children systematically studied in best examples of research on the method	69	25	200	763
Number of twice-tested autistic children	33	25	200	Unknown
Number of children twice tested with fully comparable IQ tests used at first and second testing	69	Unknown	Unknown	Unknown
IQ rises significantly among IQ testable autistic children	Yes	Yes	Unknown	Not Tested
Percent of studied IQ testable children with IQ rises	90%	Unknown	20%	N/A
CGAS or equivalent rises regularly with SED or autistic children	Yes	Unknown	Yes for CGAS equivalent. (CGAS not used)	Yes for children with anxiety disorders
Years needed for significant IQ rise among IQ testable autistic children and other IQ testable SED children	1 school year	2 to 4 years with at least 2,520 hours alone in an office with ABA therapist	2 to 8 years	Unknown re IQ gains
Cost for IQ or CGAS effects per child in dollars as a supplement to public special education	6,000 to 12,000	Est. 40,000 to 100,000	Est. 80,000	Est. 80,000 to 160,000

(1) Eikeseth 2007 included unstated number of Bayley infant intelligence tests to compare with later WISC-R. (2) Target and Fonagy (1996) studied child analyses by retrospective CGAS scoring.

Table 9.12. Method Comparison: Time and Costs Involved for IQ and Global Mental Health Gains as Method Outcomes

autistic children with IQ rise (by treatment modality), shows which methods have CGAS data, the time it usually takes for these methods to complete treatment, and what each method costs.

Table 9.13 *(What Is Needed to Raise IQ)* describes gains for autistic children in correlation with the number of sessions, and the overall time required to induce positive results. The RNT advantage is particularly strong in this

INTERVENTION	CHARACTERISTIC: **WHAT IS NEEDED TO RAISE IQ** **Number of sessions, time and years needed for statistically significant IQ gains from treatment of autistic and non autistic children.**
RNT Reflective Network Therapy	90 fifteen minute sessions (twice a week for 45 weeks) produced IQ gains averaging 15 points among 69 IQ testable autistic and non-autistic children. 180 sessions/45 weeks nearly doubles the IQ gain. Most IQ testable children treated for 8 months achieve these results regardless of diagnosis. Of 33 autism spectrum children included over 90% showed IQ rises at second testing with fully comparable tests.
PULL-OUT **Psychoanalytic** Psychotherapy in a school setting	50 to 200 one hour sessions a year, usually for two or more years. No IQ effects known.
ABA (Applied Behavioral Analysis)	Eikeseth (2007) used 2,520 hours a year for two years. Percentage of treatable and percentage of IQ testable children is not clear. Comparability of first and second testing is flawed. Non-autistic children are not treated.
TEACCH	Not determined.
DIR /Floortime	Two to five hours a day, for two to eight years. Significant IQ gains reported among 20% of 200 autistic children. No data on non-autistic children.

Table 9.13. Comparison: Amount of Sessions, Time, and Years Needed for Measurable Gains

view because the low amount of time required per session and the high frequency of these short sessions (every day the class meets) lowers the cost of the in-classroom therapist's time, resulting in effective treatment of more autistic children for less money.

A summary of some advantageous factors—results, replication, research, inclusion of peers and teachers and clinical versatility—is used to compare methods discussed in this chapter in table 9.14.

Reflective Network Therapy has passed scientific study thresholds of feasibility, retrospective, prospective, consecutive, controlled and comparison treatments research. It has crossed the threshold for broader replication with the publication of the manual in this book. It is demonstrably cost efficient. Studies completed so far demonstrate superior, sustained results of RNT treatment for autistic and SED children, with both cognitive gains and mental health gains versus treatment by other methods in the same amount of treatment time. Further studies are in progress and future

ADVANTAGEOUS FACTOR	RNT	ABA	DIR	TEACCH	Pull Out
Manualized for independent replication	Y	Y	N	N	N
Instructional videos keyed to Manual	Y	N	N	N	N
Peers regularly included	Y	N	N	Y	N
Teachers regularly included	Y	N	N	Y	N
Some long term follow ups	Y	Y	Y	?	N
Clinical versatility demonstrated for non-autistic children with serious emotional disturbances (SED)	Y	N	?	Y	Y

Table 9.14. Summary Comparison of Advantageous Factors in RNT, ABA, DIR, TE-ACCH and Pull-Out Therapies

independent as well as collaborative studies are anticipated. We especially look forward to criterion based studies of videotaped sessions. Such work may begin to operationalize how to identify factors in Reflective Network Therapy which explain why children treated with this method get better more often, in more ways and more quickly than children treated by other methods.

In light of all the data and comparisons assembled to date, we encourage replication of Reflective Network Therapy for preschoolers in need of treatment for PDD or SED. We encourage application of RNT using the manual (Chapter 3), sticking to what is working. We are ready to train new teams in techniques of the method and offer technical and supervisory support for new service applications.

We expect the legal and political future will allow a contractual process between therapists and school districts wishing to serve their severely disturbed preschoolers in a minimally restrictive way, as RNT allows, right in their own classrooms rather than in pull-out therapy. Thus upcoming generations of child therapists may have a significant public health contribution to make in providing classroom-based treatment. We look forward to helping more impaired children to overcome mental health obstacles to their education, in this relatively inclusive way. There is more than sufficient scientific data to justify treatment of more children with PDD or SED in special education classrooms beginning at the preschool level, rather than depending mainly on behavioral aides, medications or pull-out therapies in public or private offices, clinics, day-hospitals and residential facilities.

OUR PERSPECTIVE ON RNT'S POTENTIAL TO HELP
LARGER NUMBERS OF SPECIAL EDUCATION CHILDREN

RNT teams should be set up with binding contractual collaboration agreements. The program and the children's clinical and cognitive improvements are too vulnerable to discontinuities if stability is highly dependent on the careers of individual administrators.

The best place for a Reflective Network Therapy service to help the most children is to make it available where the most children are: in public school systems. Ideally, our agency would form contractual relationships with public school public special education programs in several more states to train new RNT teams for those programs. Remote learning techniques are already working for such purposes with private agencies (using videoconferencing combined with on site supplemental guidance from our agency's senior certified RNT therapists). Additionally, an even larger body of outcome data would result, for further research and collaborative study. Further, some school districts (or municipalities on their behalf) might successfully apply for major foundation, state or federal grants to support implementation of this evidence based method. This is especially likely for schools where most children do not have family resources to support other forms of psychotherapy, in school districts where the tax base does not richly support special education enhancements.

We also look for improvements in types and scope of school-based outcome measures. A variety of practical "shoe-leather" means exist for judging child behavioral outcomes. Schools can follow not only IQ and CGAS but also track whether there is reduced need for special education classes and aides. With RNT, schools should also expect improved academic performance, reduction of behavioral infractions, increased regularity of attendance, reduction or elimination of symptoms of conduct disorders, improved empathic capacity and interpersonal communication, and long term improved academic achievement test scores. Comparisons with untreated cohorts from prior years should be possible, as well as comparisons with costs and results of pull-out therapies and in-classroom aides.

FINAL SUMMARY OF REFLECTIVE
NETWORK THERAPY BENEFITS

We conclude that Reflective Network Therapy, among the major methods reviewed, is probably the most cost-effective. It is a versatile educationally and clinically useful and scientifically proven method for simultaneously raising

IQ and improving the mental health of children with multiple diagnoses, including PDD and a host of psychiatric diagnoses. The method works well and cost-effectively for autistic as well as SED preschoolers. Significant mental health gains and IQ rises regularly occur in shorter time spans than expected with other methods which have been shown to produce such achievements. The RNT method is soundly grounded in psychoanalytic and psychiatric knowledge and theory, yet the powerful techniques, once practiced, feel almost intuitive. Start-up status is easily acquired by teachers and therapists alike with only three days of initial intensive training followed by low cost in-service training and support during the first two years.

Reflective Network Therapy is tailor-made for the individual child. Each child receives the direct, focused therapeutic attention of an interactive reflective network team related to his or her unique psychological life. The method uses what is going on with that child in the moment in his real school activities. It focuses on the here and now of what he is feeling, doing, thinking, his interactions with other people in the classroom, his behaviors and symbolic expressions in the immediacy of real life space. In the rich interpersonal and informational environment of a classroom, using Reflective Network Therapy techniques and procedures described in this book, children awaken to and respond with their full potential for loving and learning.

Chapter Ten

Theory of What Happens in Reflective Network Therapy

In this 45th year of Reflective Network Therapy use, it is still helpful for any theory of its therapeutic actions to stay near to quantitative data, while not excluding the qualitatively rich clinical complexity it has provided. Quantitatively, it is the only interpersonal psychotherapy we know which regularly produces data showing significant IQ gains while treating the whole child. Similarly, it is the only interpersonal psychotherapy we know which reduces transfers among foster homes. Qualitatively the realm of data to include is dauntingly large and will require much more investigation before theory of what happens can be more than very preliminary. It is a great advantage in forming a theory of therapeutic action that parents have so generously permitted video recording. Observationally, watching videos of the children's treatment sessions helps introduce qualitative elements into theory formation by providing visible and audible evidence that the children are not only becoming brighter but also calmer. From the start to the end of a quarter hour in-classroom psychotherapy session, the viewer of most RNT treatment videos will witness distinct motoric changes for the better. There is commonly a perceptible slowing of a child's previously over-rapid, agitated behavior. Often within minutes and regularly within a few weeks, anger and avoidant behaviors change into visible friendliness and social proximity-seeking. The calming and socializing effect of the method continues to grow and becomes stable over weeks or months of time in RNT classrooms. Such observations, literally plain to see, are combinations of qualitative and quantitative clues which we must explore in more detail, and for which we have only the beginnings of a theory of therapeutic action.

THEORIES OF CAUSAL FACTORS
IN CHILD PSYCHOPATHOLOGY

Before going further with a theory of "what we are doing in Reflective Network Therapy," let us look briefly at theories of what we are trying to reverse. That is, what can we reasonably (or even hopefully) theorize are the targets, the causes of childhood psychopathologies which we are trying to reverse with RNT and other treatments? Researchers are at early stages of developing a body of knowledge about causes of very diverse childhood psychiatric pathologies. There are presumably great differences in the genetic and experiential causes of most early arising psychiatric disorders. Our profession calls them by varied names: anxiety disorder, neurosis, attention deficit disorder, reactive attachment disorder, oppositional-defiant disorder, posttraumatic stress disorder, psychoses and bipolar disorders, to list just a few. The causes of those disturbances almost certainly differ greatly among them and even more from the causes of what are called pervasive developmental disorders, such as autism. Unfortunately, modern texts and curricula for training mental health clinicians are rich in descriptions of signs and symptoms of these psychopathologies but very sparing in stating even what little is definitely known about their causes, (Stubbe, et al. 2008). In the spirit of disclosing my own biases, which may influence the value and limitations of my thinking, the reader should know that in my own work, I have been operating with numerous theoretical bases, biases and views while formulating and practicing preventive and early treatment methods for children. Among the factors influencing my theory building are that:

- There are not enough well established tests to operationally study therapeutic action theories.
- There are few widely accepted ways to check clinically on the many, diverse etiological theories about childhood disturbances.
- There is little certainty as to why the incidence of some childhood disorders is on the rise throughout the world, and such understanding should be part of therapeutic theory building
- Biological approaches in genetics and neuroscience have a lot to offer in pointing out correlations of psychological disorders with chromosomal, gene, mitochondrial, psychophysiologic and neuroanatomic abnormalities. The genetic physiologic and anatomic abnormalities are various. They include many chromosomal and gene abnormalities, excesses of some stress hormones and neurotransmitters, deficits of others, as well as deficiencies or excesses of the total brain volume or certain parts of brain volume or function and sometimes abnormalities in the microscopic structure of syn-

apses and connective fibers in various parts of the brain associated with various disorders. We'll come to some correlations with RNT below.

- When a theory of clinical action is being tested, separating out the factors in a treatment technique itself can help lead to discovery of what factors are necessary for a particular outcome benefit obtained. For example, in RNT, if we hold other variables constant and study outcomes in association with low and high quantity of sessions, that could lead to understanding the relevance of session quantity to a certain outcome measure such as CGAS. Quantity of sessions then could be correlated with other theory about the practice effects of reflective exercise on IQ gain or reduction of children's transfers among foster homes. Such studies of clinical action are similar to physical medicine studies of antibiotics, where dose and duration of are commonly accepted parts of building tests of effective treatment.

- Similarly, if we reduced the parent contacts or educational classroom hours, we might discover thresholds for a factor beyond which a lower number of contacts produced no measurable outcome such as IQ gain, CGAS change or reduction of foster home transfers.

- Similarly, totally omitting psychoanalytic interpretation in an interpersonal therapy for comparison purposes should tell us something about whether interpretation and response to interpretation are essential ingredients for an optimal outcome. We have developed an elaborate set of criteria for studying these parts of therapeutic action.

- Although some major treatments (and theories relating to those treatments) of some disorders of childhood are beginning to be established, most of the data discussed in this book are not readily explained by current theories. There is unlikely to be a single theory of what causal processes RNT is reversing even in one disorder and how they are being reversed. That difficulty is consistent with the field's early state of explanations for why *any* child psychotherapy is effective, not just Reflective Network Therapy. Careful research by Fonagy et al. (2005), for example, showed that the specific high value of child analysis for children with anxiety disorders is clear, but it is not accompanied by a full explanation of the specificity of this exceptionally good therapeutic action. That is so partly because we don't even know with certainty what causes childhood anxiety disorders among some children and not among others.

There are, however, an increasing number of excellent, peer-reviewed studies of the brain, neuronal, connectivity and genetic bases for the important preschool age disorders lumped as autism spectrum disorders (among the severest of pervasive developmental disorders). Especially explanatory are Marcel Just's report (Just et al., 2004) on f-MRI evidence of white matter deficiencies in the connections between different brain centers in autistic persons and Hutsler and Zhang's (2010) post-mortem histologic work on excess connective obstruction among synaptic architecture in the cerebral cortex of children with autism. More detailed and compelling theories which take these findings into account are probably not far off.

We also strongly suspect that deficiencies in autistic people's ability to learn about others is related to reduced function in mechanisms used by the brain's mirror neuron systems (Oberman et al., 2005, 2007). Those systems help each of us perceive and connect to other people's motor manifestations of emotion. Other neurologic problems with likely social consequences are present in autism. Oberman et al. (2007) point out and Brang and Ramachandran (2010) also note that among the neurologic problems (associated with autism) may be deficiencies of the olfactory bulb, which is oxytocin and vasopressin rich, and among other mammals is highly involved in social recognition, (Hammock and Young, 2006; Tobin et. al. 2010). On the other hand, Ramachandran, Mitchell and Ropar (2010) found that "...individuals with autism spectrum disorders (ASD) could, surprisingly, infer traits from behavioural descriptions" and were subsequently able to associate traits, facts and names with the appropriate persons.

Autistic children certainly show a lack of connection to others, including lack of interest in others. This is a probable correlate of their lacking a theory of the mind of others. That is, they have great difficulty being socially curious, imagining or perhaps even thinking about other people's internal experience. As a result, to some degree, depending upon the severity of the pervasive developmental disorder or the autism, children do not know how others feel and may not comprehend expressions of feeling. They therefore fail to be empathic, to love, and to learn (Siegel, 2003).

It is widely agreed that the autism spectrum deficiencies of interpersonal connection almost certainly have some basis in the brain. The suspected brain basis may be caused by environmental effects on certain gene processes that control brain development, or "gene expressions" (Walker and Wilshire, 2006) which are at least partially distinct from genetic inheritance. "Fine-mapping" gene studies are locating some of the vulnerable genes related to autism, (Cantor et al., 2005; Nguyen, A. et al., 2010; Sarachana et al., 2010; Spence et al., 2006; Stone et al., 2004; Bucan et al., 2009; Hu et al. 2006; Alvarez-Retuerto, 2006; Duvall et al., 2007; Russo A.J. 2009; Nishiyama, T. et al., 2009; Munesue, T. et al., 2010). Whether genes and gene expressions of autistic individuals are damaged by toxins, allergic reactions, dietary problems, family risk factors, inoculations, or viral infections is still being hotly argued by researchers, (Lauristen, et al., 2005).

Unlike autism, the widespread form of anxiety disorder called childhood posttraumatic stress disorder (PTSD) definitely can be attributed in large part to the causal effects of clearly external precipitating events. Causal events include traumatic physical injury, suffering or witnessing ongoing abuse, witnessing or experiencing severe, disfiguring injuries, sexual abuse or rape and exposure to conditions of generalized threatening social conflict including family and community violence and war, (Eth and Pynoos, 1985). Yet we know that some children (and the social networks that support them) are more resilient than others. We know that environmental, social, family, and genetic factors are all implicated in why some children succumb to a trauma which would be causal for most children, and others do not (American Psychiatric Association, *DSM-IV-TR* , 2000).

My own best bet is that we will soon have consensus that most childhood psychiatric disorders have *multiple* genetic penetrance determinants and multiple relational and environmental determinants as well. By that hypothesis I mean that no one factor but rather a combination of biological processes, physical environmental influences, social environment, and interpersonal experience will all prove to be determinants. My theoretical biases (prejudices which influence my work) can be determined by noting that I suspect the most likely multiple determinants of quite a few childhood disorders have commonalities in the biological, interpersonal and physical realms, in the following categories:

- Both parents' combined contributions to the child's genetic susceptibilities.
- Immune system dysfunctions and allergic reactions that affect the developing brain beginning in utero.
- Viral infections during pregnancy and early infant development.
- Pathologic variations in chemical activity of neurotransmitters (substances which carry information and stimulate activity among brain neurons and other nervous system cells).
- Toxic ingestions of very various substances and types, ranging from insecticide use to cocaine abuse severe enough to cause brain developmental difficulties in utero and/or early childhood.

Beyond genetic and physiologic factors which produce vulnerabilities, the likely combinations of experiential and interpersonal levels of adversities involved in co-determining the emergence of a child's psychiatric disorder may include:

- Being born to uncaring primary caregiver(s), early or prolonged neglect, rejection or abandonment. This is unlikely to fully account for severe cases of pervasive developmental disorder, and has nothing to do with Rett's Syndrome or Fragile X Syndrome for example, but can greatly contribute to a large variety of childhood psychiatric disorders.

- Primary caregiver was not attuned or empathic during the first years of life.
- Primary caregiver was depressed for long periods during infancy.
- Attachment between infant/toddler and primary caregiver was insecure, irregular, erratic or hostile.
- Failure to thrive due to physical threats, disorders or disease.
- Repeated traumatic medical procedures.
- Physical injury.
- Physical abuse.
- Sexual overstimulation or assault.
- Witnessing domestic violence, especially over prolonged periods.
- Experiencing serial unreliability or loss of parents, through death, rejection, or abandonment to multiple foster placements.
- Pre-existing learning disabilities, particularly nonverbal ones, followed by psychological trauma.
- Having parents who unwittingly transmit their own trauma (Weingarten, 2003).
- Repeated, especially prolonged bullying or physical humiliation by sibling(s), foster siblings, primary caregiver(s), schoolmates or others.
- Experience of chronically terrorizing social environments, such as occur during violent social conflicts or conditions of war and siege.
- Social isolation; lack of opportunity to be brain-stimulated into states of social desire, curiosity and emotionally charged interaction.
- Conditions of social upheaval including experience of loss, danger or injury due to the immediate effects or aftermath of natural disaster.
- Psychological development proceeds in an orderly fashion which can be readily interrupted by many of the above factors, leading to processes of developmental arrest, fixations or weakness related to a specific phase at which the insults or interruptions occurred.

The impact these factors have on any one child at any one developmental epoch and in any one set of social circumstances exposed to any adversity varies greatly. For example, wide ranging manifestations of post-traumatic disorders are readily seen among refugee children in response to severe adversities, such as genocidal wars (Kliman,2003), or among child survivors of massive disasters like the 2004 Tsunami, Hurricane Katrina in 2005 or the 2010 Haitian earthquake. Even with catastrophic, clearly psychologically harmful events, some children and their social networks are markedly more, or less, resilient or vulnerable than others. There is ample evidence that the cumulative effects of multiple or chronic traumas are worse than the effects of single traumatic experiences (Dube et al. 2003). The effects of prior adversities of many kinds are sometimes multiplied by new adverse environmental factors. Studies of large populations receiving health care following such events show the likelihood of psychiatric disorder, of further victimization, and even of becoming a perpetrator committing intimate violence oneself is increased by a variety of traumas when they are multiple. Each adversity added builds the odds of a bad outcome, physically, psychosomatically, and psychologically (Chapman et al., 2004; Edwards et al., 2003; Fivush and Edwards, 2004; Dong et al., 2003; Dube et al., 2001, 2002, 2003). Physical health deteriorates measurably and medical costs rise for children (and continue to rise for adults) with a history of multiple childhood adversities (Biggs et al., 2003, 2004; Yehuda et al., 2003). Structural and physiological brain changes have been clearly demonstrated in chronic posttraumatic disorders (Bremner et al., 1995, 1997; Bremner, 1999; Krystal et al., 1995).

In light of the above facts and theories of cause, we can begin building a theory of therapeutic action about how what we do in Reflective Network Therapy that is helpful. We can make a start by considering what reflective function is. The following quote from Meehan and Levy (2009) gives a definition of reflective function, (a capacity intentionally exercised by Reflective Network Therapy), which is a good beginning point for theory building regarding therapeutic action of the method:

Reflective Function [RF] (is) the developmental achievement whereby children acquire the capacity to mentalize the thoughts, feelings, intentions and desires of self and others... Reflective Function has been found to mediate the relationship between parental attachment security and infant attachment security in the Strange Situation (Fonagy et al. 1995) and to mediate the relationship between atypical maternal behaviors and attachment security in infants (Grienenberger et al. 2005). RF has been found to change through psychotherapy (Levy et al. 2006). RF has also been related to external measures of neurocognitive functioning, including attentional capacities, executive functioning, and impulsivity (Levy et al. 2005)

A basic difficulty among children with autistic forms of PDD is a failure in the search for a reflected self, represented in another person's mind. The presence of a reflected self is a necessary part of becoming a self-recognized person. Fonagy et al. (2002) theorized that "a fundamental need of every infant is to find his own mind, or intentional state, in the mind of the object". The authors went on to argue that "this capacity to mentalize is a key determinant of self-organization and affect regulation". We agree with this formulation, and regard what we are doing with RNT as along those lines: treating children with techniques that tend to enable them to develop a way which makes them become able to efficiently organize and process cognitive and affective information about self and others. Reflective Network Therapy as used in a preschool classroom attempts to enhance children's reflective self-recognizing functions and related attentional, executive functions and impulse controls. Although we have scientific studies and videotaped treatments demonstrating surprising effects (such as cognitive development accompanied by statistically significant rises in IQ) we have not yet developed an easy way to test scientific theories to explain those results. Facts to consider in developing a theory of how Reflective Network Therapy works include the procedures employed.

As practiced in a preschool classroom Reflective Network Therapy is an integrated cycle of technical procedures. All the procedures are interpersonal. All are socially communicative. None take place in a pure dyad, and most occur in a multi-person setting. Each procedure feeds back to the child thoughts and processed emotions and each feedback cycle ultimately includes the child's peers and adults (teachers, the therapist and parents). Each procedure uses words, attitudes, emotions and behaviors. Each procedure provides a recursion or reflection of affectively charged information for repeated processing by the mind of a child and each procedure may ultimately influence the child's family and how that family thinks about and relates to the child.

RNT procedures are grounded in combinations of theory and practice of child psychoanalysis, early childhood education, child development, neuroscience, systems theory, and social network therapy. Psychoanalysis in general, and particularly as applied to children in a therapeutic classroom, addresses more than interpreting a child's unconscious processes (Kliman, 1970). It includes encouraging a child's learning to "mentalize" her own and other's actions and experiences, and to develop coherent thinking within a world of meaningful relationships, (Fonagy and Target, 1996); 2000, Target and Fonagy 1996; Fonagy et al. 2000) Mentalizing means the child is making sense of her own thoughts and powerful internal physiological experiences and ultimately developing a clear self-concept as well as a concept and theory of the mind of others. Further, psychoanalytic work in RNT, as in private practice outside the classroom is aimed at using interpretations for unhitching developmental arrests and fixations, allowed the natural developmental process to continue (Freud, A 1939,1962,1966/1946). Still further application of psychoanalytic understandings about development allows interpretations and activities which encourage the child to accept corrective relationships (Alpert

1941, 1943, 1954). Thus he can work through his resistance to having those relationships.

Systems and network theories we employ further embrace a great complexity of processes. These include individual psychological and neurophysiological events. Emerging findings from neuroscience afford exciting possibilities for explaining some of how the reflective network process embedded in Reflective Network Therapy works on an individual child within a particular developmental epoch. Systems and network theories can accommodate efforts to include neurobiology as well as reciprocally shaping relationships among child, schoolmates and siblings, analyst, teachers, family, and the family's network of kin, friends, and other service providers. All these "network relevant" events occur in the context of institutional and cultural systems that define internal and external obstacles and opportunities for facilitating a child's personal growth.

That rich complexity is why we sometimes use a symphony, opera or ballet metaphor to make sense of what we do in Reflective Network Therapy. Our choice of a musical metaphor enables us to think about simultaneous multiple themes from a variety of relevant voices and discourses, with flexibility and respect for the primacy of the clinical material of an individual child. Reflective Network Therapy involves a group of performers fluently articulating a set of unique psychological themes, generating a symphonic effect as the themes influence the harmonics and respond to each other, operating simultaneously and polyphonically. Each child is given a solo role every treatment day, and also directs the expressions of others who collaborate with her. The RNT classroom is an ever-changing creative "performance," like real life elsewhere. It has its own varying rhythms, momentum and flow. Certain technical rhythms permeate it reliably—the briefings, individual therapy sessions in the real life space, debriefings, and weekly parent guidance sessions—all a multi-pathway set of communications with regularity of timing and periodically returning to the individual child.

Each child has her own themes and dances, each family, teacher and therapist her own melodies and enacted stories. There is a conductor, a therapist who often interprets the score. The child is a singer, dancer, actor and at different times the composer/author or director/ collaborator in the complex unfolding of a developing (and sometimes opera-worthy) story of her own. The spirit of the music of Reflective Network Therapy (and the tone of the classroom) when it is at best is fluent, creative, and ultimately affectionate. It can lead to close harmony or group distress. It always includes all members of the orchestra, and all their glad and sad and angry songs and their jealous and altruistic stories.

THEORY ABOUT THE IN-CLASSROOM
THERAPIST'S STATE OF MIND

Despite the complexity of the phenomena and the theories we use to understand them, the classroom therapist as an RNT practitioner is trained to be and most often is operating in a state of mind known as "flow" (Csikszentmihalyi, 1990). He or she is absorbed in the moment, operating with intuitive facility, with ready access to internal creative resources and with little experience of deliberate effort.

In some ways the classroom setting, division of responsibilities, and deliberate teamwork of Reflective Network Therapy treatments, assists a psychotherapist to become better functioning than he could be otherwise. Reflective Network Therapy is richer and more complex for all its participants than is usual within individual child analysis. That is so because a whole network and social ecology (rather than an isolated dyad) is involved. However, RNT treatments can function very much like a child analysis for fifteen to twenty minutes at a time, multiple times a week, with the exception that it takes place in the public sphere of a shared classroom, with the intermittently overt and constantly real involvement of other children and adults.

FREE-FLOATING ATTENTION

I recently was starting to teach the method to a new RNT therapist, (perhaps the 25th person I personally trained), describing how she could best place herself in a frame of mind to carry out the method. She was not a psychoanalyst, and previously had only treated a few children more than twice a week. Seeing her at work in a busy homeless shelter classroom, where particularly needy and traumatized children struggle for attention, I saw that she was a bit tense and working too hard. I asked if she could to try to put herself in a relaxed receptive state of mind when starting a session with each child patient in Reflective Network Therapy. I suggested she could trust the teachers to do the teaching and intrusive impulse control of the other children, allowing her to just freely hover mindfully near a child, somewhat as if in a trance. Could she then also chat, giving thoughtful attention and dialogue with one child for 15 or 20 minutes?

She found this an intriguing idea and was able to relax and find herself not too busy with other stimuli in the room, outside of her own immediate patient's activities and expressions. The value of a therapist giving very relaxed and at the same hyperfocused attention only to one patient at a time (the index child) is very high in RNT. It resembles a psychoanalyst's free-floating attention to associations and resonance with one patient at a time.

Free-floating attention is also key to what psychoanalysts of adults describe as being in a state of "hovering". Hovering is a condition in which the analyst imagines himself or herself as a reflecting observer. He or she may be psychologically floating around weightlessly and uncritically, literally and figuratively above, beside or near the patient. The analyst tries to give hovering or free-floating reflection, with definite interest but without interfering with the patient's thoughts. He is listening, resonating and freely associating while endeavoring not to inhibit or criticize but rather to encourage the continuing expressiveness of the analysand. This state is a derivative of a state of mutual focus. Freud originally achieved this state by inducing hypnosis in his early patients and analysands (Freud, S. 1965/1891; Breuer and Freud, 1965/1893).

As the RNT therapist then may be in a somewhat meditative state, it is essential that teachers be available to do the impulse controlling and safety management work which a good analyst should not be doing hands-on. The analyst is thinking, responding, resonating, mentalizing, placing thoughts and emotions of the child into words for the child and also expressing the child's behavioral activities in a semantically encoded fashion. The last thing the psychotherapist wants to do in such an ideal reflective state of mind is to have a hands on, motion stopping, impulse controlling interaction. Such rightly belong to the teachers. In our experience, this proper role differentiation has never been much of a problem, probably because teachers are used to taking responsibility for order and discipline in the classroom.

EXPANSION OF THE PSYCHOTHERAPIST'S AND TEACHERS' OBSERVATIONAL FIELDS AND ABILITIES

Teachers expand the psychotherapist's observational range, and ideally can help create a family like atmosphere in which the psychotherapist participates in the classroom and in weekly team conferences. This is not only helpful in producing transference material. I have also noticed that a well functioning Reflective Network Therapy team influences itself so that the adults help each other increasingly attune with a particular child. This is professionally transformational for both educational and mental health disciplines.

Soon in the career of a Reflective Network Therapy teacher she or he becomes very alert to what the analyst finds interesting, important or puzzling about a particular child. In her debriefings and briefings she is practicing a function which is separate from interpretation but underlies interpretation supportively. That is, the teacher is practicing the function of empathic attunement, (Gallese, Keysers and Rizzolatti, 2004). Surrounded by a team of empathically attuned adults, all the children in the classroom tend to become empathically attuned over time as well. The children reflect upon each other during each child's sessions and in between. They are thinking all the time, as are their teachers and analyst. This is an amazing process which sometimes we have captured on video showing the children acting in a therapeutic fashion for each other, learning what are each other's needs and thoughts as well is emotions. This is another aspect of the in-classroom combination of education and therapy which promotes the development of empathy as well as altruism. Seldom have I seen altruism develop so well in a regular preschool with normal children. Again, this developmental result requires much practicing of the technique, and may be difficult to sustain as well in a non-intensive application of the method (one in which children are in the RNT classroom less than four or five times a week).

SETTING THE PACE

Many of our children are frantic and frenetic, hyperactive when they first enter a Reflective Network Therapy class. My technical advice to new RNT therapists is that, as part of their engagement, attunement and hovering state of mind, they should not move around a great deal physically. Children will ultimately model themselves after the relatively stationary or slow moving analyst. They will often show their resistance to the work by leaving the analyst's vicinity (and will show their receptivity to the work by physically seeking closer physical proximity). The analyst should express the fact that he or she is thinking about what the child is thinking and doing as the child is leaving the vicinity of a resisted work. In effect, this is an early interpretation of resistance by simply calling the child's attention to the need to understand his flight. When a child leaves the analyst's vicinity, the analyst should follow slowly, and comment on and interpret the child's avoidance and resistance slowly and calmly, not at the child's frantic pace. This reflective response helps the child to mirror and identify with binding up impulse and motion by example, and places a premium on abstract thought rather than concrete action or reactive behavior.

ONE-MINDEDNESS

One-mindedness is a state in which the analyst and child come to feel they are attuned, "of one mind", as described by Roy Aruffo, MD (researcher, child and adolescent psychoanalyst and member of the scientific board of advisors of the Children's Psychological Health Center) in a personal communication to me (2007). Cultivation of this state is an intentional aspect of Reflective Network Therapy in practice. In the state of one mindedness, the analyst has feelings and thoughts which hopefully are very close to those of the child, but the analyst has intermittently a highly adult perspective on those processes and can convey them in a tamed as well as an attuned fashion to the child. The analyst is sufficiently identified with a mental representation of the child in the analyst's mind that the analyst can make some predictions about what the child will do or say next.

This process of one-minded hovering, thoughtful, affectionate attunement to the child is at the heart and in the mind of the analytic therapist and child. As the child patient feels appreciated by the analyst, gradually increasingly understood, a child evolves a sense of having a unique experience. It may be the first time in this child's life in which an adult is paying frequent close attention to each and every gesture, even the direction of gaze manifested by the child. For most children this is an intense and empowering experience. It may be one of the first times the child has felt he has moved an adult person to intensely focus on his mental life in a highly valued, detailed, constructive, interested, absorbed fashion. He is aware that for all of a brief but coveted time he is the center of an adult's mental universe, and the adult is actually fully there, reflecting and revolving about the child in a way not ordinarily experienced. Further, the therapist is encouraging others in the classroom to do the same. All persons in the classroom are to some extent palpably struggling to understand, reflect upon and resonate with each and every little bit of the child's behavior and communications.

THEORY ABOUT THE CHILD PATIENT'S PROCESS AND NEEDS

Transference: In the artificial family of a Reflective Network Therapy classroom, where teachers and therapists are easily perceived as figures similar to parents and peers are perceived as similar to siblings, it is natural for old patterns of relational feelings and behavior to be transferred into the new family situation. The preschool forms of transference are numerous (Harley 1963). The process of transference is a rich bed in which the seeds of transference neurosis can grow. By transference neurosis I mean here: the evolution during a psychodynamic treatment of new or markedly exaggerated symptoms mainly in the treatment situation rather than elsewhere. These phenomena, occurring in the laboratory of the treatment situation where they can be detected are golden as material for interpretation by the psychotherapist.

Safety and nonjudgmental license for self expression: As in child analysis, the RNT method provides each child patient with a safe space, a social bubble of protection in which the child can freely express his inner life without criticism shame or guilt of being imposed by the outer world. An environment which encourages the child patient to freely express himself is especially necessary for children who are inhibited and is revelatory when treating children who are psychotic. The state of mind involved in child analysis and in Reflective Network Therapy is evocative and permits a creative enterprise which is rarely shared between adults and children. We suspect that this creativity coupled with the high value placed on thought and verbalization, is part of what leads to the IQ growth which RNT treated children experience.

Limits on narcissistic regression and gratification: In the midst of this seemingly oceanic, emotionally regressed, shared inner world of therapist and child there might seem to be a regressive pull. This pull does exist in the direction of attachment and affection seeking and against premature autonomy or defensive solitude. However the presence of impulse control help by teachers is an extraordinary advantage for the treatment. It allows the child to keep his sight on social decorum and boundaries. He increasingly appreciates what the limits are on his affectionate and aggressive strivings.

Reciprocity and Reward: Jealousy naturally develops and is gradually converted to altruism: Watching another child being treated and valued arouses envy. Jealousies and aggression are activated toward other children, but these are tamed in order that the other children will tolerate his own turn at exclusive treatment session time. There is reciprocity about the regularly occurring necessity for respecting other children's primacy when it is their turn with the therapist. Children quickly children learn that there is an immediate premium, a reward associated with sharing with others. Each child sees the others get their turn as the index child and know that their turn will come. That premium allows sharing ultimately to evolve into appreciation of what is on the other children's minds and further fosters the development of empathy and altruism.

PRACTICE IN MENTALIZING

As the analyst becomes increasingly attuned with his child patient, the child's affection, jealousies and aggression are more and more easily and rapidly appreciated and anticipated by the analyst. The child feels himself perceived and understood, and in turn becomes more thoughtful in regard to emotions and impulses of which he has been barely conscious in the past. This encourages him to feel it is possible to comprehend and master his own emotional and behavioral life with a new and comprehending ally. All of his emotional life is increasingly expressed in a mentalized fashion, (Fonagy and Target, 1996). The child models his own expressive repertoire on the mentalizing analyst and teachers and feels them working harmoniously on his behalf, having a highly novel experience of adults literally reflecting back and forth about him, respectfully and sincerely asking for his verbal contribution to the briefings and debriefings. This modeling happens hundreds of times a year for each child in his own treatment, and he sees it thousands of times a year in the treatment of others in his classroom. The process evokes powerful feelings of being loved, and with this affective charge, his thoughts are more likely than not to be permanently encoded in procedural and explicit memory. With practice, they also become less and less charged, far more conflict-free, emotionally neutral and manageable (Hartmann, H., 1958).

Neuroplasticity: In biological terms, it is likely that Reflective Network Therapy's IQ rise phenomenon among children with a variety of diagnoses, including those with pervasive developmental disorders depends upon the neuroplasticity of young children's brains. The areas most in need of development in autistic children are probably the white myelinated fibers which connect various brain centers. According to the work of Marcel Just et al. (2004), the centers themselves are intact but the connections between them are deficient. The process of exercising emotional investments in thoughts and interpersonal representations of those thoughts may well help exercise the neurologic connections amongst speech centers and emotion processing centers and information storage centers, particularly Broca's area and the limbic system as well as the frontal lobes. It is my hope that functional magnetic resonance imaging and magnetoencephalographic studies ultimately will show before and after changes in autistic and other children who experience IQ gains with Reflective Network Therapy treatment. Imaging studies show atrophic brain pathology occurs in children and young adults with PDD (Kosaka 2010). I expect these changes are being detectibly reversed by RNT, but have yet not succeeded in carrying out the necessary studies to test this hypothesis.

It is no coincidence, in my view, that certain atrophic changes and various deviations from the volumetric norm of various areas of the emotion and memory processing brain regions are present in the brains of patients with either autism or posttraumatic stress disorder. My hypothesis in this regard is that autistic children are the unfortunate victims of a kind of genetically or congenitally induced hypervigilance like the later arising hypervigilance of patients with PTSD. The reductions of interpersonal anxieties which occur during the practice of RNT communications may be an essential effect induced by the method which allows autistic children to thrive in the interpersonal world of the RNT classroom, evidenced by their increased receptivity to both learning and loving. A similar process is observed among children in Reflective Network Therapy who suffer from post traumatic stress disorders. These are two hypervigilant and defensively avoidant diagnostic groups of children who benefit cognitively and clinically from RNT treatments, and I think that it is no coincidence.

What we are producing may be the opposite of neuronal deaths which occur from flooding with stress hormones such as cortisol. We may be producing a protective, recuperative and growth-promoting effect on brain neurons. As the children grow less anxious they secrete less fear and stress hormones, particularly less molecules of catecholamines and cortisol and they secrete more of neuronal growth-promoting oxytocin. Inevitably, such reductions of neuron killing substances are beneficial to reducing the symptoms of hypervigilance and interpersonal avoidance.

QUANTITY OF THERAPY AS A FACTOR IN OUTCOMES

A number of strong and straightforward findings others have published about good child therapy treatment outcomes are relevant. Some of the best designed studies' outcome findings are about child psychoanalysis, a method long and closely studied and practiced intensively at The Hampstead Clinic in England. Target and Fonagy (1996) used the Hampstead archives to retrospectively create Children's Global Assessment Scores (CGAS). They showed correlations of many variables with those scores. They have shown with statistical power that intensive child analysis is markedly helpful in the outcome of several childhood disorders. Their large-scale study of over 700 children treated at the Hampstead Clinic finds child analysis to be particularly effective for those children whose disorders have primarily anxious features, rather than those with oppositional, autistic, or behavioral/conduct disorders. Target and Fonagy (1996) also found a relationship between quantity of treatment and good outcome on the CGAS measure. The total amount of treatment received correlates to quantity of CGAS improvement. Zelman (1996), Zelman, Abrams and Samuels (1985); Samuels (1985); Lopez and Kliman (1980), Hope (1999) and Kliman (1968. 1970, 2006, 2008) have reached similar conclusions about Reflective Network Therapy treatment. Particularly they conclude that the amount of treatment correlates with RNT's effect of raising children's Wechsler and Stanford Binet IQ scores. RNT treatment is structured such that the frequency of therapeutic sessions is not only much higher than that of most other interpersonal methods, but also, provides *additional multiple interventions in the form of daily therapeutic encounters* involving a complex multi-person network.

DIFFERENCES AND SIMILARITIES: REFLECTIVE
NETWORK THERAPY AND DYADIC PSYCHOANALYSIS

It appears theoretically important that Reflective Network Therapy is effective for the same disorders as is classical individual child analyses, disorders with primarily anxious components. However, the evidence to date suggests that RNT may be unique among psychodynamic therapies, in that it also regularly helps autistic children and those with several other conditions that usually *do not* respond significantly to child analysis: oppositional, defiant, and attention disordered children, children with conduct disorders, attention deficit disorders, and pervasive developmental disorders (Zelman, 1996, Hope, 1999).

IQ gain is only rarely studied or reported with classical child analyses or psychodynamic therapies of any interpersonal nature (Zelman and Samuels, 1996; Heinicke, 1966). In contrast, IQ rises are common and significant with Reflective Network Therapy. This correlates positively with the total amount of RNT treatment (Hope, 1999; Zelman, 1996). To put this essential point another way, Reflective Network Therapy and Lovaas methods are both distinguished by rises of IQ. Only a few other methods are (Greenspan, 2005). This distinction between Reflective Network Therapy and the Lovaas method on one hand and classical child analysis, regular special education, and therapeutic approaches of all other types on the other hand may have a simple but unlikely explanation. It may be that child analysts and other dyadic therapists (*other than* Heinicke, Zelman, Greenspan and Kliman) simply are not noticing that their patients are becoming brighter. They may therefore not have an interest in studying the IQ outcomes of their work. More likely there are other reasons, such as the aversion of many psychoanalysts to the "harder" sciences, including psychometric sciences.

In contrast to psychoanalysts, medical researchers and psychologists interested in social influences have been much more interested in IQ outcomes than psychotherapists generally. Since the mid 1940s, over a dozen longitudinal studies of stressful medical or social environmental factors among non-patients have included IQ as an outcome variable. All report findings show that IQ scores can drop greatly in apparent response to harmful environmental factors ranging from X-ray treatments of the brain for tumors to adverse interpersonal environment (Bayley, 1955; Bayley and Schaefer, 1964; Bradway, 1945; Bradway and Robinson, 1961; Honzik, Macfarlane and Allen, 1948; Honzik, 1957; Kagan and Freeman, 1963; Kagan, Sontag, Baker and Nelson, 1958; McCall, Appelbaum and Hogarty, 1973; Moriarty, 1966; Rees and Palmer, 1970; Sontag, Baker and Nelson, 1958; Wiener, Rider and Oppel, 1963; Pinneau, 1961).

TESTABLE THEORY ABOUT RNT'S
COGNITIVE AND CLINICAL GAINS

Traumatic experiences such as domestic violence are substantial reducers of IQ over time (Delaney-Black et al. 2002). IQ is influenced by the way a child is psychologically nurtured by family, school and community (Skeels and Dye, 1939; Money, 1983; Hope, 1999, Cornelius, 2010) and how he or she is educated (Barnett, 1995; Barnett and Hustedt, 2005; Kliman et al., 1982; Johnson, W. 2009; Zigler and Valentine, 1979; Zigler et al. 1982).

In the other direction, the positive IQ raising effects of middle class parents versus lower class parents during foster parenting were documented by Freeman et al. (1928) and Kliman et al. (1982). In a forerunner of our own interest in IQ as an outcome measure, psychoanalyst Christoph Heinicke (1983) found that word recognition ability was improved in elementary school boys treated psychoanalytically. Zelman reported (1996), Heinicke (1966) and Heinicke and Ramsey-Klee (1986) also found IQ was not changed by individual psychoanalytic psychotherapy, even at a four times a week frequency delivered by well-trained psychoanalytic therapists. Improvement in word recognition was associated with quantity of sessions, the more frequently seen children showed a striking gain. Other than Heinicke's report of word recognition tests and Zelman's IQ studies, only a few studies or reviews of psychotherapy outcomes in any disorder have focused on the possibility that psychological influences might be associated with favorable IQ, neuronal or brain changes (Schore and Schore, 2008).

I take an operationally testable position when building a theory of therapeutic action on this issue. Cognitive improvements with RNT therapy are conceptualized by us as involving brain functions changing in the opposite direction from the pathologies being combated. With RNT we are reversing the presumably brain-based affect declines of IQ seen in PTSD and the regulating deficits, attentional deficits and other cognitive dysfunctions seen in PDD. Thus my operationally testable position is that ultimately brain imaging studies will show that RNT treatment, more than control and comparison treatment, is associated with measurable recovery of the atrophic areas. This would require pre-treatment and post-treatment brain imaging studies using RNT as the therapy, and hopefully including a random assignment controlled methodology so that other treatments can be simultaneously studied.

I have elsewhere proposed a "Unifying Theory of Childhood Posttraumatic Stress Disorder" (Kliman 2008). In that proposal, as in this essay, I draw upon consilient thinking (Wilson, 1998) regarding evolutionary and neuropsychological data. I regard a number of childhood psychiatric disorders, particularly PTSD, as personality impoverishing and brain-impoverishing, mostly because of the neuron-damaging and neuron-killing effects of anxiety. PTSD is an anxiety disorder characterized by intrusive fearful thoughts about real, terrifying events. In PTSD a child is all too often awash not only in reverberating memories but also seems to be in a physiologic state of fear associated with fear hormones, expressed in sweating, rapid pulse, pale skin and feelings of dread. Some aspects of my theory may apply to chronic childhood anxiety states in general (Kliman, 2008), as PTSD is only one of a spectrum of anxiety disorders. PTSD involves an impoverishment of many psychological and neurological sorts. Brain neurons, pathways and areas of the brain shrink. Long and short term memory access become constricted, early childhood amnesia creeps forward and covers more of memory than in other patients (Scovis-Westin, 2006; Parkes and Stevenson-Hinde and Marris, 1982; Parkes, et al. 1991). The future is seen as ominous through traumatized lenses, (Terr, 1991), and social transactions regress to constricted and primitively viewed qualities.

All of those neuropsychological qualities, we believe, are to some extent reversed by Reflective Network Therapy. We also theorize that many SED children have impoverishments similar to those found with PTSD, though less obviously so, and this has not yet been verified by brain-based studies. RNT's inducement of mind-enriching and cognition enhancing therapeutic changes, spanning months of practice with mentalizing and attunement, may be exercises of just the parts of the brain needing strengthening. In other words, the CGAS gains and IQ rises resulting from the method may be due to processes in the opposite direction from the brain pathologic processes and IQ drops seen in PTSD (De Bellis et al. 2009; Yaffe et al., 2010).

Excessive cortisol and catecholamines (adrenaline and noradrenaline, also called epinephrine and norepinephrine) in anxiety disorders over time probably lead to impoverishment of the brain whether the hypercortisolemia and hypercatecholaminemia is due to adversities, loss of good relationship with caregivers, or to clear traumas, (Kliman 2008). Not only do some brain regions get smaller. IQ drops. The IQ drops associated with untreated PTSD appear quite long-term (Pluck et al., 2010; Yaffe 2010). PTSD produces affect regulating, attentional, short-term memory, working memory and other cognitive deficits and information processing disorders and there is MRI evidence of atrophic brain changes (Bremner et al. 1995, Bremner et al. 1997, Kliman 1996). Dementia is a surprisingly common correlate of PTSD, (Yaffe 2010). Thus we advise that seriously emotionally disturbed children (SED) who have had traumatic experiences must be studied with IQ as an outcome. Zelman (1996) has noted traumatized children as particularly benefitting from Reflective Network Therapy, and we have seen that connection regularly verified by outcome data. For example, Oscar, (the domestic violence victim child described in earlier in this book) had the highest IQ rise among the 10 children studied in his preschool cohort. The significant IQ improvements we see in traumatized children treated with Reflective Network Therapy may involve therapeutic reversals of, or compensations for, specific trauma-induced brain pathology. Reflective Network Therapy's effect of IQ rise may turn out to be similar to symptomatic improvements that may occur with administration of the drug escitalopram, which increases serum brain-derived neurotrophic factor during studies of its administration to PTSD patients (Berger et al., 2010). Similar thinking has led Olff (2010) to propose study of the effects of giving the hormone oxytocin to PTSD patients.

INCHING TOWARD THEORETICAL CONCLUSIONS

Reflective Network Therapy is probably a more reliably powerful treatment than other child therapies (especially more reliable and powerful for pervasive developmental disorders) because of enriching effects on emotionally influenced cognitive functions. Cognitive enrichment is best measured by comparing IQ at two points in time using the same test measure. We think the RNT advantage occurs because of a synergy between education and therapy in the classroom, permitting a coordinated effect within a network of neuronal and psychological influences. The combination of influences promotes children's tranquility, receptivity, and tender feelings toward psychotherapist and teachers. The effects are hypothesized as including reduction of stress hormones, increase of affinity and attachment hormones, improvement of dyadic relations, production of insight and reduced resistance to learning and relationship with teachers via interpretation. There is a positive cycle in the network. The teachers help the child feel safe in dealing with unconscious material. The therapists help the child be less resistant to natural curiosity and desire to learn. Both the teachers and therapists encourage learning, though at different levels. Peers are encouraging stimulators of curiosity and teamwork in learning.

Among foster children, an additional benefit is measurable: the reduction of discontinuities of care. We believe this is a result of theory-driven treatment which aims at the reversal of the child's own unconscious repetition compulsions and reduction of the complicity of adult networks in enabling this repetition (Kliman 2006).

THE MORE RNT TREATMENT
CHILDREN GET, THE MORE IQ RISES

Quantity of influence is important. The higher the number of Reflective Network Therapy sessions the greater the measurable IQ gains. Quantity of parent as well as child sessions per week is correlated with quantity of IQ gain. By involvement of the family, the RNT social network is activated to the great advantage of the child. Our findings indicate that the following should be considered established by future studies testing Reflective Network Therapy procedures:

• Choice of comparable baseline and outcome measures matters. Future studies of all methods should include the CGAS.
• When studying IQ change, apples should be compared with apples, not developmental quotients compared with intelligence quotients as has happened with ABA studies we reviewed. Our views about the value of the Wechsler Preschool Scale of Intelligence for studying outcome in autism, are supported by Mottron (2004), who found that there was the least likelihood of error when using the Wechsler Scales with patients with autism and PDD, as compared to a picture vocabulary scale like the Peabody Picture Vocabulary Test or the Raven Progressive Matrices. We find the Lovaas IQ outcome data deeply flawed because of persisting use of misfits between baseline measures of developmental quotients or Bayley scales and outcome measures of IQ.
• Insight matters. There is great technical commonality between the insight producing and transference-dependent effects of child analysis and the individual analytic aspects of Reflective Network Therapy. Our considerable studies of non-interpretive comparison psychotherapy methods yielded no IQ gains.
• Quantity matters. More sessions rather than fewer sessions are favorable in Reflective Network Therapy, Lovaas, DIR (Floortime) and child analysis treatments. The effect of quantity of sessions on IQ is highly orderly for IQ in the first three methods and for CGAS in child analysis.
• The regularity of response matters enough to warrant further study. IQ rise is regular among IQ testable children treated by Reflective Network Therapy.
• Diagnosis appears unrelated to IQ effect among our IQ testable children. IQ effect is independent of diagnosis but dependent on quantity of RNT sessions.
• CGAS improvement matters enough to require much further study and occurs in RNT regardless of diagnosis. With child analysis CGAS does not improve among PDD patients.

It seems likely to us that there is a set of reasons why the multidisciplinary network of RNT improves the mental health (measured by CGAS) of children with pervasive developmental disorder conditions, and that traditional, dyadic child analysis does not. The reasons include the more deliberately limited technology of child analysis. Child analysis by design thrives in isolation, promoting the private projective functions of a child's mind. It does not regularly deal with real life social spaces, or include a combination of social network components comparable to RNT's full integration of a handful of such components. Child analysis necessarily avoids the analyst's partnering intimately with use of classroom education, does not contain immediate focus on promotion of skills and sublimations, lacks on the spot verbalized reflections by multiple cooperating adults, has minimal teacher and parent modeling by the analyst, uses no peer group effects and in many cases may occur without weekly parent guidance.

I propose that exactly the usually absent combination of converging school, parent, teacher and analyst's reflective resources in child psychoanalysis is exactly what is needed in many cases. It usually raises IQ as well as CGAS in PDD children treated by RNT. The combination of resources produces a more effective and more developmentally and cognitively specific response to some PDD therapeutic needs than does unaided child analysis or the Lovaas method. Usually a major benefit and function of child analysis is to provide a child with insight. Insight as a child analytic technique generally does not easily change arrested development which has organic basis such as occurs with pervasive developmental disorders. Insight without containment of impulses also does not easily change cruel, unempathic, dysregulated, impulsive, defiant, oppositional and inattentive behavior. It is definitely insufficient (regardless of quantity) for optimal outcomes with children suffering from either PDD or serious conduct disorders (Fonagy 1999).

Improvement in conduct requires change in the context of school discipline, parenting style and peer interaction. RNT treatment produces and supports behavioral and conduct improvements more naturally than do classical child analytic therapies in addition to providing child patients with reflective insight during individual sessions and during additional structured interactions. Necessary for overcoming disruptive behavior, attentional disorder, and deficient impulse regulation is a well regulated home and school educational process. In RNT the schooling-specific educational process is carried out by the teachers and that process is enhanced by method-specific practices which utilize all of the interpersonal and intersubjective interactions occurring in that real life space, including the child's individual therapy in the classroom context.

Overcoming or mitigating pervasive developmental disorders, including autistic disorders, means correcting the associated mental impoverishments. Success in the treatment endeavor requires a child to develop of a theory of the mind and empathy for multiple others. That is a task for which classical child analytic therapy is not designed or well suited and for which it provides little immediate real exercise with peers. Reflective Network Therapy provides exactly those needed factors.

THE ROLE OF FEAR-RESPONSE AND AFFINITY-SEEKING HORMONES

One can see while observing videos of the RNT treatment of autistic and/or traumatized children how they become less anxious, less fearful of approaching, touching, being touched and staying physically near adults and peers. Surely this reduction of anxiety is not only a psychological epiphenomenon or solely the result of interpersonal practice. It looks as though reduced anxiety has underlying physiological accompaniments which are expressed in the child's body language, rhythms, postures, tone of voice, facial expressions and affects. And it is reasonable to postulate that such a changed state of mind and behavior must have associated body physiology changes—especially in endocrine, sympathetic, parasympathetic and brain neurologic processes. To feel loved and understood for hundreds of school days a year must be an experience with physical effects. Hormones such as oxytocin (prolactin), which encourages affinity and contact seeking, are probably increased at the same time as fear hormones are reduced in Reflective Network Therapy, (Carter, 2003). Certainly many talented and caring teachers and therapists using other methods with seriously disordered children care for them deeply and endeavor to express that love. The advantage RNT has in this regard is that opportunities for inducing positive physiological responses are not only multiplied by the multi-person network effect, but also every such opportunity is available for intentional use in helping the child's mentalizing.

THE PROCESS OF INSIGHT DEVELOPMENT

Trying to explain the power of Reflective Network Therapy, I often think of my best and perhaps most profound interpretive work with classical child psychoanalysis—which I have often used on a one on one basis. Whether working in my private office or in Reflective Network Therapy practice, I keep in mind a set of criteria by which I judge whether a psychoanalytic process is occurring within any psychodynamic psychotherapy. (A list of these criteria is posted at www.reflectivenetworktherapy.org). We ask our therapists and researchers to keep these criteria in mind when writing about a session or reviewing a videotape of a session.

From the first publication about this method, Psychological Emergencies of Childhood (Kliman, 1968), it has been my impression that the creation of a transference neurosis has been the most essential and valuable criterion for existence of a successful psychoanalytic process. It is a feature of those RNT cases in which children had profound successes and this has been my experience in private practice as well. Even among autistic children, transference can and does occur. I point to the example of Larry who developed a transference neurosis that was documented on treatment videos. He expressed to me his idea that I was nervous about him while we were separated during the Christmas vacation. He was projecting onto me that which he experienced in my absence while he wondered whether I was well and whether I would return to help him again. In a sense this was a new and artificial, as well as analyzable disturbance—anxiety about the analyst. He described, as part of that transference neurosis, his fantasy of my upset state, my "nervousness". In the context of talking about my "worrying" about him over Christmas vacation, Larry imagined in a post-Christmas play session how he himself had to be a superhero who rescued people from a burning train. He did marvelous work with a giant fire hose. He also expressed a variety of worried fantasies about germs harming me. The character of Larry's transference process on this occasion confirmed an obvious underlying experience of identification and bonding with me which enhanced his receptivity to my interpretations, as was borne out as he progressed through treatment to a successful conclusion.

Thus, Larry's post-vacation fantasies were part of a new and valuable, though distressed emotional process about him and his analyst and their relationship to each other. In addition, that struggle for a mutually affectionate relationship was transformative in his behavior with others. For example, he would say about himself, "It's my 'ponsibility to play with the other children and talk with them," clearly identifying with me as his and others' analyst, the person who in reality had that responsibility. That same day, Larry expressed concern about another child's difficulty in sharing his play things with children in the classroom. He soon became a close friend of that empathically appreciated peer. I also regard this sibling peer relationship as part of a transference to an artificial or therapeutic family, permitting the emergence of affection which otherwise was much resisted by this child, and previously transformed into dangerous and self-defeating aggressivity.

"WORKING THROUGH IN THE TRANSFERENCE"

In an early paper on Reflective Network Therapy (then known as the Cornerstone Therapeutic Preschool Method) I discussed the child "Jay" and his transference neurosis, regarding the teacher. He was fearful of going into the school basement, and imagined she had a bucket full of penises in the basement (Kliman, 1970). This was a transference of his dread and concern about his own mother who (in reality) often would bite his buttocks so hard and gnash her own teeth so strongly that on one occasion she broke one of her own teeth. The concept of "working through"—beyond the concept of the insight gained through interpretation—has a place in Reflective Network Therapy. Once a child has been understood and has a glimpse of his own inner life: that does not suffice. He must work on and through many examples, derivatives, and corollaries of the insight to make a lasting, positive change. Opportunities to do so and for the child to be guided in deepening his understanding are frequent and rich in Reflective Network Therapy. Even when the analyst is not in the classroom, teachers observe this effort to work through an insight, and can report back to the analyst how the child is endeavoring to come to grips with the psychological themes delineated in the psychotherapy sessions. Thus the classroom time, which is much longer than the treatment time, becomes a multiplier of the analytic process and allows carefully controlled working through. It measurably reduces repetition compulsions when circumstances permit measurement, as among series of foster children.

BEING CARED FOR AND REFLECTED ON RAISES SELF ESTEEM

There is a great self-esteem building value in a child psychoanalytic process. While not all interpretations made by the RNT therapist or observations made by teachers are accurate, they carry a deep meaning for the child's development as evidence that the adults place a high value on his mental life. Profound caring is part of the thoughtfulness and mentalizing on the part of the treating and educating adults. Not only are the adult reflections nurturing the child, but they are also fueling esteem for his own reflected upon self. The child's self-concept is further enriched by his perception that peers are thinking about him, even in their own childish ways. He is in a hall of complicated human mirrors, where many caring people are developing representations of him and reflecting back to him what they feel, think and showing him models of their mentalizing functions.

THE CHILD'S MIRROR NEURON SYSTEM IS
EXERCISED BY REFLECTIVE NETWORK THERAPY

Almost certainly we must consider the brain's mirror neuron systems. It is a conceptual leap to move from reflective behavior to reflective neurons. Gallese has written convincingly regarding "mirror neurons and the neural underpinnings of interpersonal relationships" and intentional attunement, (Gallese, 2001, 2003, 2005, 2007). His thinking is attuned to the preference of E. O. Wilson's landmark book about consilience (2008). He, his colleagues and other eminent scientists are looking for what Gallese has called "the quest for a common mechanism" (Gallese, 2003). I am encouraged to make the leap to a direct connection between RNT's techniques and mirror neuron exercises. If I am correct, there is large volume of mirror neuron exercising in RNT, and associated empathy as well as cognitive development. In doing this kind of theory building, I rely on the work of multidisciplinary scientists like E. O. Wilson. He defines consilience as the "jumping together" and application of principles of knowledge and theory from one branch of empirical science and events to another branch, for example, explaining behavioral data by means of neurological data, (Wilson, 1998). Learning certainly does appear to have marked neurologically based and social dimensions in many species that involve mirror neurons. Birds and fish appear to learn about dangers and preferred directions for travel by perceiving each others' slightest movements, thus better protecting themselves in flocks and schools. Mammals, especially primates, have a well-developed system of "mirror neurons" (Fadiga et al., 2000; Rizzolatti and Arbib, 1998; Rizzolatti, Fogassi and Gallese, 2001; Rizzolatti and Craighero, 2004).

Mirror neurons constitute about 10% of the human brain's many millions of motor neurons. They are activated when one individual observes the actions of others (Iacoboni et al., 2000; Gallese et al., 1996). The motor areas of the observing animals and humans behave in a remarkable way. The electrical activity of the observer's mirror neurons in the motor areas is the same as if the observer were conducting rather than simply watching the observed action. I hypothesize that such neuron systems are especially activated during learning in small peer and multi-age group situations such as Reflective Network Therapy provides. Our species probably developed under circumstances that favored children learning in small family and tribal groups. I further hypothesize that dyadic therapy—including one-on-one psychoanalysis and behavioral aide relationships, with fewer and less complex interactions—does not tend to activate as many brain centers involved in object representations and as many of the contained children's mirror neurons and therefore is less likely to provide the same enrichment of learning. This might explain why rises in IQ are not generally a feature of that intervention. However, if the treatment released a child for more parent, peer and teacher social involvement early enough, IQ rises could certainly occur.

Neuronally, mirroring is apparently an evolutionarily important part of learning. It is a widely used didactic procedure. Without knowing of mirror neurons, much teaching has occurred throughout human history by eliciting mirror responses to visual examples. Among autistic children (and we think among numbed children with PTSD) the use of the mirror neuron system is markedly reduced. Our theory of RNT's good effects on empathy and the development of children's ability to understand the minds of others include that Reflective Network Therapy makes up for these neurological deficiencies through constant interpersonal exercises, orchestrated during briefings and debriefings. RNT aims at developing the mirror neuron system through thousands of practicing episodes concerning behavior, emotion, and we think it also works ultimately through subtle modeling and teaching of empathy. Empathy's development depends on a child's observations and attention to other persons' muscular position and tension changes, facial expressions, postural, kinesthetic information, and odor and the hearing of increasingly meaningful vocalizations. The opportunity to hear, see, identify with and actively reflect back and forth of social observational and learning processes is immense in Reflective Network Therapy.

OTHER NEUROLOGIC CONSIDERATIONS

Recent neurological research already cited could, I think, be expanded to focus prospectively on an exploration of why RNT and child analysis are differentially effective with autistic children. It would be a scientific advance to use brain imaging to find evidence which might help explain treatment outcomes. .It might tell us how and why pervasive developmental disorders, including its most extreme form, autism, is ordinarily unresponsive to psychoanalytic methods (Target and Fonagy,1994) but is responsive to Reflective Network Therapy. We think it will be demonstrated that RNT induces growth of connective areas such as the corpus callosum, fibers between limbic systems and frontal lobes, and an increase of grey matter in limbic and frontal lobe areas as well as in the olfactory bulb. We suspect that cerebellar abnormalities (Wegiel et al., 2010) thought to be common in autism might also be reversible if autism can be successfully treated by RNT. Autism might then be viewed as similar to a cerebral palsy disorder, in which areas of neuron and muscle connection deficiency are often capable of rehabilitation through high degrees of frequent, persistent exercise over time.

Traumatic disorders as well as autistic disorders require some rehabilitation of deficient and pathologic brain functions, connectivity and distribution in the emotion-processing areas of the brain. We propose that some of the major neurobiological findings of others in the psychologically numbed patients with posttraumatic disorder and with autism suggest some common explanatory pathways for the two groups. The areas of brain atrophy or underdevelopment found on the f-MRI studies of patients in both groups are somewhat similar (Just, et al., 2004, 2007; Bremner, Krystal and Charney, 1995). Though many conceptual leaps of neuropsychological levels are involved, and any hypothesis is years away from definitive testing, it seems a reasonable possibility that RNT treatment outcome findings of benefits for both groups could be a result of the interpersonal exercises for the two clinical groups having similarities of neuronal effects.

Magnetic Resonance Imaging studies of patients with chronic Posttraumatic Stress Disorder show deficits in the form of atrophic changes in several areas of the brain, particularly in the limbic, thalamic, and prefrontal regions. These areas greatly influence learning, emotional processing and complex cognitive functions (Bremner et al., 1997; Bremner, 1999) in PTSD, not unlike some of the problems in the much earlier arising disorder of autism.

We know that Pervasive Developmental Disorder, particularly autism, is a very different clinical condition from Posttraumatic Stress Disorder in the early timing of one and the unpredictable precipitation of onset in the other, and in most features and symptomatology. But there are avoidant, anxious, numbed as well as hypervigilant features of both disorders. In autism spectrum disorders, as in PTSD, a strong tendency to hypervigilance includes keen avoidance of unfamiliar caregivers and saying no to many interpersonal processes, a pathologic defense which closes off much interpersonal learning. In chronic posttraumatic stress disorders, defensive "numbing" (van der Kolk 2006) also includes a "loss of interest in previously important relationships and activities" (DSM-IV-TR, 2000) which secondarily closes off interpersonal learning. In both conditions there is more than an interpersonal effect: there are neurologic atrophies in the patients' brains. The atrophies are sufficient to show significant changes in specific brain area volumes. MRI studies of autistic children show a deficient volume of limbic system, including thalamus and prefrontal areas (Ciaranello and Ciaranello, 1995), not identical to but similar to the smallness of the limbic system among traumatized children. Autistic patients also have deficient neuronal connection pathways such as between the prefrontal region and the limbic system in their brains. Autistic patients have an especially deficient amount of large pathway connections in the hardwiring of the white matter paths between a number of brain centers and in the corpus callosum itself which carries information between brain hemispheres (Just, 2004, 2007).

It seems to me that both autistic and traumatized children have difficulty with interpersonal learning because of the underlying pathology of limbic, thalamic, prefrontal, and several other interpersonally active, communication processing and memory-encoding areas. Further, probably vitally involved are the connections between these areas. All needed for success processing and integrating emotions aroused by interpersonal experiences.

There are also "distributive functions of the brain" about which there is new information and theory. Information received through hearing and vision is distributed far more widely than through the visual and auditory parts of the brain, (Kulesza and Mangunay, 2008). In fMRI studies, the distribution is more limited than normal in autism. RNT's multiple inputs, reflections of inputs and reflections of reflections probably powerfully exercise the distribution of information through the child's brain. These affectively charged inputs promote wide connectivity, a deficient process in autism and probably among severely traumatized children who are also excessively vigilant and avoidant of new experiences.

My own view is that Reflective Network Therapy's interpersonal exercises produce neuronal growth-stimulating effects not unlike those of some medications. Relevant to the effects of therapy on autistic as well as traumatized children is that an underlying physiologic effect on neurons is possible through social rather than simply through chemical experiences. Any such neuronal growth would be occurring with and because of associated chemical influences. That neuronal growth occurs throughout life and is possible with chemical influences is already fairly well established. Studies of psychotropic agents such as Prozac indicate the agents induce growth of brain neurons in mammals beyond that in control states (Castren and Ranamaki, 2010). My admittedly speculative ideas about a physical basis for positive IQ change in Reflective Network Therapy treatment also have a basis in the reverse. That is, there is a drop of IQ under certain conditions. There are many undisputed medical facts about conditions known to reduce IQ. Among well demonstrated detrimental physical influences on brain function are psychological trauma, physical malnutrition, brain radiation for leukemia, and lead poisoning. All are associated with a reduction of children's IQ. There is an orderly or dose-related negative correlation between the amounts of these adverse environmental experiences, and the reduction of IQ, (Cousens et al., 1998). Studies of chronic psychological adversity and trauma (Breslau et al., 2001; Carrey et al., 1995) and sensory and relational deprivation in infancy and early childhood (Spitz and Wolf, 1946) also reveal a drop in cognitive development, including of IQ. In anaclitic depression cases with hospitalism and marasmus, Rene Spitz observed chronically neglected hospitalized infants developed an aversion to interaction with caregivers, thus closing off much interpersonal learning (Spitz, 1946, 1964).

Along opposite and positive lines, concerning growth rather than reduction of intelligence, there are interpersonally oriented studies of IQ growth. Beneficial psychological experiences can lead to very significant rise in IQ. Skeels' social preventive work with the institutionalized infants of mentally retarded girls shows highly significant later IQ differences between those infants who had been neglected and those who were well attended to (Skeels and Dye 1939). Foster children placed in intellectually stimulating homes regularly have a small but significant rise of IQ (Freeman, Holzinger and Mitchell 1928; Kliman et al., 1982). Some Head Start programs have also shown marked IQ gains (Zigler, 1979), though they were usually not enduring gains.

Reflective Network Therapy, we hypothesize, reopens closed or atrophic pathways to interpersonal learning by providing an abundance of intensified, complex interactive encounters which exercise affectively charged brain functions required for relational experience. The chances for positive cognitive and brain growth outcomes are profoundly enhanced by the high frequency of Reflective Network Therapy. These are neuroplastic opportunities which the emotionally intensive therapy structure seems to guarantee so that almost all IQ testable children have IQ gains with Reflective Network Therapy.

NEUROHORMONAL CONSIDERATIONS

The natural and developmentally vital attachment of human beings to each other is promoted by hormonal actions very early in life. We think soothing interpersonal conditions allow a reduction of stress hormones such as adrenaline, noradrenaline (from the adrenal medulla), cortisol (from the adrenal cortex) and adrenal corticotrophic hormone (from the pituitary), to name a few. In order to receive information a child should not be numbed by trauma's effects on endorphins (Van der Kolk and Saporta, 1991). The hypothalamus and olfactory bulb, both rich in oxytocin, are both known to make that interpersonally affiliative influence available. We theorize that all these neurohormonal actions occur in a good psychotherapy experience, but especially when the social network's power is working on the developing preschool child.

LOVE IN REFLECTIVE NETWORK THERAPY

In another essay on theory we will further address the question of RNT and the physiology and psychology of love in depth, asking, "What theory can explain how the RNT treated children have grown both healthier emotionally and measurably more intelligent than with other methods we used?" When we think back on over four decades with over twenty teams of teachers and therapists who have used this treatment method successfully, the emotional recoveries and intellectual gains demand still further categories of scrutiny and explanation. We who originated the method have by introspection acquired a belief that its effectiveness has something to do with special circumstances for appropriately reciprocal love and recapturing of the ability to love. Love, in this method, is an interpersonal activity of reciprocal attunement, engagement, with caring, tender, nurturant interest and strong investment in another person's mind and emotions. It leads to one mindedness. It is a process that has been forgotten all too often in modern, more behaviorally oriented settings, including many day care centers, preschools, public and private kindergartens.

Children who love their teachers, peers and therapist become calm for longer periods than they previously or recently experienced. Their more prolonged attention during the loving state allows brain processing of more and more complicated mental matters, with the serenity necessary for concentration and multiple layers of mental work from concrete to abstract. New informational and procedural learning grows with the rewarding interactions that receptivity to teachers allows. Instead of using misguided defenses for shutting out their adult helpers and peers, children treated with Reflective Network Therapy—even though previously avoidant, unreceptive, oppositional, inflexible or numb—can now allow information to be received and processed in useful, flexible and creative ways. The new data coming into their perception and active tasks are processed in ever more refined and symbolic ways, sublimated and neutralized instead of in the raw primitive, defensive manner of autistic or traumatized minds.

Learning is promoted by loving, and children soon realize that they are loved even more because they are learning. Positive mutual reinforcements are abundant, interpersonally charged, rather than in behaviorally sterile manners. Thalamic and hippocampal centers of the brain which orchestrate the encoding of emotionally charged data and memory become increasingly active and flexible. The storehouses of memory widely scattered in the brain become enriched and well coordinated as the many practices of encoding emotionally pleasant and positively charged events make the access to data easier, more interconnected and even self-rewarding, rather than feared or trauma driven.

Extending the metaphor in which I likened Reflective Network Therapy to a symphony or a dance performance, the method similarly harnesses an interdependent set of players so that the harnessed energy of each supports the best outcome for all. It uses a social, thinking and loving network in contrast to other "solo" methods used by individuals helping children one-on-one in isolation, in a play-therapy room or tutoring office. The method releases tenderness in a whole classroom, in a society of hearts and minds which includes parents, children, teachers, and a therapist. Other forms of therapies sometimes have become one-size-fits all templates or behavioral recipes for inhibiting pathologic behavior, and some therapies are even exclusively pharmaceutical. While behavioral inhibitions and rewards, discipline, and chemical treatment methods are often very useful, children are not merely a set of chemicals, neurons, reflexes or symptoms to be retrained and restrained. Nor can children apparently reliably grow as much intellectually during dyadic therapies that isolate a child with a therapist. Not much intellectual growth reliably occurs in psychoanalytic work that solely relies on a therapist and child's feelings, insight and the power of psychoanalytic interpretation. In contrast, synergy (defined as a multiplication of energies and forces applied in the same direction) is at work in Reflective Network Therapy. RNT uses a synergistic combination of simultaneous affectionate educational and therapeutic attachments and influences which is limited in other therapies. This synergy could not be so fully and *reliably* present in other early childhood interventions.

In the Reflective Network Therapy method, combined interpersonal forces reliably cause a channeling of excitement, narcissistic pride, curiosity, jealousy, adventurousness, and mentally assertive, cognitively exploratory impulses. It happens, in other words, through the stimulation and activity of developmentally appropriate love in a family-like group which gives an affective, positively pleasurable charge to learning. The learning in RNT occurs in the service of seeking increasingly desired attachments, interpersonal relationships, exploring of those interpersonal intimacies, and the energetic, love-charged distribution of that intellectually adventurous process through the developing child's mind and brain.

Since we think the method ultimately depends on a sublimated, tender form of love among the participants—promoted and encoded into practical and psychoanalytically informed techniques—it is no accident that Reflective Network Therapy was originally invented and intended for orphaned children, who had lost their givers of love. The essential features of Reflective Network Therapy require the establishment of a kind of family in a school. Those features include the role of interpersonal interaction among the team as a whole, the importance of each child, his parents, his peers, and each team member. In an RNT classroom, children are encouraged to develop and use high levels of age appropriate skills, and equally helped to recognize and seek satisfaction for their less mature needs and quest for nurture. Every feature of psychotherapy appropriate to a particular child's capacities is used within the classroom. Every educational means for regulating and socializing the particular child's impulses and promoting cognitive growth is used by the teachers. Parents are integrally involved in helping, using and increasing the team's information and influence on their children. The children respond to love with love and in this therapeutic climate they learn. Society—especially parents, caregivers and teachers of young children—can gain further important psychological support, skills and wisdom by learning about Reflective Network Therapy's complex treatment combination of loving and caring education and what makes it work.

We think that love stimulates learning and is a necessary factor in children's cognitive development. Love is an evolutionarily driving force for the adventurous minds of children in our species. Reflective Network Therapy harnesses that force.

References and Suggested Readings

Achenbach, T. M. & Howell, C. T. (1993). Are American children's problems getting worse? A 13-year comparison. *Journal of the American Academy of Child & Adolescent Psychiatry, 32*(6), 1145–1154.

Ackerman, B. P. & Brown, E.D. (2006). Income poverty, poverty co-factors, and the adjustment of children in elementary school. *Advances in Child Development and Behavior, 34,* 91–129.

Adams, C. (2005). *A real boy: A true story of autism, early intervention and recovery* (1st ed.). Berkeley, CA: University of California Press.

Adler, G. (1980). Transference, real relationship and alliance. *International Journal of Psycho-Analysis, 61,* 547–558.

Aichhorn, A. (1935/1925). *Wayward Youth.* (Elizabeth Bryant, Julia Deming, Mary O'Neil Hawkins, George J. Mohr, Esther J. Mohr, Helen Ross & Hildegarde Thun, Trans.) New York: Viking Press. Translation of *Verwahrloste jungend* (2nd ed.) Leipzig Vienna and Zurich: Internationaler Psychoanalytischer Verlag. (Original work published 1925.)

Allen, D. A. (1988). Autism spectrum disorders: Clinical presentation in preschool children. *Journal of Child Neurology, 3*(1), Suppl. S48–S56.

Allen, D. A. (1989). Developmental language disorders in preschool children: Clinical subtypes and syndromes. *School Psychology Review, 18*(4), 442–451.

Allen, D. A., Mendelson, L. & Rapin, I. (1989). Syndrome-specific remediation in preschool developmental dysphasia. In J. H., Harel, S., Caesar, P., Gottlieb, M. I., Rapin, I. & De Vivo, D. C., (Eds.), *Child Neurology and Developmental Disabilities.* Baltimore, MD: Paul Brooks, 233–243.

Allen, D. A. & Mendelson, L. (December 2000). Parent, child, and professional: Meeting the needs of young autistic children and their families in a multidisciplinary therapeutic nursery model. *Psychoanalytic Inquiry, (20)*5, 704–731.

Alpert, A. (1941). Education as therapy. *Psychoanalytic Quarterly, 10*(3), 468–474.

Alpert, A. & Rapin, I. (1953). Treatment of a child with severe ego restriction in a therapeutic nursery. *The Psychoanalytic Studies of the Child, 8,* 333–354.

Alpert, A. (1954). Observations on the treatment of emotionally disturbed children in a therapeutic center. *The Psychoanalytic Study of the Child, 9,* 334–343.

Altschul, S. (1988). *Childhood Bereavement and Its Aftermath.* Madison, CT: International Universities Press.

Alvarez-Retuerto, A., Cantor, R. M., Gleeson, J. G., Ustaszewska, A., Schackwitz, W. S., Pennacchio, L. A. & Geschwind, D. H. (Dec. 15, 2006). Association of common variants in the Joubert syndrome gene (AHI1) with autism. *Human Molecular Genetics, 17*(24), 3887–3396.

American Psychiatric Association. (2000). *Diagnostic and Statistical Manual of Mental Disorders (4th ed. Text Revision)* (DSM-IV-TR). Washington, DC.

Andra, R. F., Brown, D. W., Felitti, V. J., Bremner, J. D., Dube, S. R. & Giles, W. H. (May 2007). Adverse childhood experiences and prescribed psychotropic medications in adults. *American Journal of Preventive Medicine, 32*(5), 389–394.

Andra, R.F., Dong, M., Bown, D.W., Felitti, V. J., Giles, W. H., Perry, G. S., Valerie, E. J. & Dube, S. R. (April 2009). The relationship of adverse childhood experiences to a history of premature death of family members. *BMC Public Health, 16.* 9–16.

Angelsen, N. K., Vik, T., Jacobsen, G. & Bakketeig, L. S. (2001). Breast feeding and cognitive development at age 1 and 5 years. *Archives of Disease in Childhood, 5*(3), 183–188.doi:10.1136/adc.85.3.183.

Ater, J. L., Moore, B. D. 3rd, Francis, D. J., Castillo, R., Slopis, J. & Copeland, D. R. (1996). Correlation of medical and neurosurgical events with neuropsychological status in children at diagnosis of astrocytoma: Utilization of a neurological severity score. *Journal of Child Neurology, 11*(6), 462–469.

Aust, P. (1981). Using the life story book in treatment of children in placement. *Child Welfare, (6)*8, 535–560.

Auvrignon, A., Leverger, G. & Lasfargues, G. (February 2008), How to discuss death with a dying child: Can a story help? (Article in French) *Bulletin of the National Academy of Medicine, 192*(2), 393–400. Retrieved from PMID: 18819691.

Axline, V. (1949). Mental deficiency: Symptoms or disease. *Journal of Counseling Psychology, 13,* 313–327.

Ayres, J. A. (1979). *Sensory integration and the child.* Los Angeles: Western Psychological Services.

Balter N. & Lopez T. (1990). Psychological Help for a Disadvantaged Preschool Boy. *Journal of Preventive Psychiatry and Allied Disciplines, 4*(4), 329–344.

Barbas, H. (1995). Anatomic basis of cognitive-emotional interactions in the primate prefrontal cortex. *Neuroscience and Biobehavioral Reviews, 19,* 499–510.

Barbell, K. (1997). Foster care today: A briefing paper. Washington, DC: Child Welfare League of America.

Barlow, H.B. (1980). Natures joke: A conjecture on the biological origins of consciousness. In B. D. Josephson. & V.S. Ramachandran, V. S., (Eds.), *Consciousness and the physical world* (pp. 81–94). Oxford, UK: Pergamon Press.

Barnett, W.S. (1995). Long term effects of early childhood programs on cognitive and school outcomes. *The Future of Children, 5(*3), 25–50. Princeton, NJ: Brookings.

Barnett, W.S. & Hustedt, J.T. (2005). Head Start's lasting benefits. *Infants & Young Children,* 18(1), 16–24.

Barry, H. & Lindemann, E. (1960). Critical ages for maternal bereavement in psycho-neuroses. *Psychosomatic Medicine, 22,* 166–181.

Bassett. K., Green, C. J. & Kazanjian, A. (July 2000) Autism and Lovaas treatment: A systematic review of effectiveness evidence. *Centre for Health Services and Policy Research, British Columbia Office of Health Technology Assessment, University of British Columbia.*

Bastiaansen, J. A. C. J., Thioux, M. & Keysers, C. (2009). Evidence for mirror systems in emotions. *Philosophical Transactions, Royal Society Biological Sciences, 364,* 2391–2404. doi:10.1098/rstb.2009.0058.

Bauman, M. L. & Kemper, T. L. (Eds.). (1994). *The neurobiology of autism.* (2nd ed.) Baltimore, MD: Johns Hopkins University Press.

Bayley, N. (1955). On the growth of intelligence. *American Psychologist, 10,* 805–818.

Bayley, N. & Schaefer, E. S. (1964). Correlations of maternal and child behaviors with the development of mental abilities: data from the Berkeley growth study. Monographs of the Society for Research in Child Development, 29, 1–80.

Beauchamp, J. P., Cesarini, D., Johannesson, M., Lindqvist, E. & Apicella, C. (July 6, 2010). On the sources of the height-intelligence correlation: New insights from a bivariate ACE model with assortative mating. *Behavior Genetics, Epublished ahead of print.* PMID: 20603722.

Beck, A. T., Sethi, B. B. & Tuthill, R. W. (1963). Childhood bereavement and adult depression. *Archives of General Psychiatry, 9,* 295–302.

Bedwell, J. S., Keller, B., Smith A. K., Hamburger, S., Kumar, S. & Rapaport, J. L. (1999). Why does postpsychotic IQ decline in childhood-onset schizophrenia? *American Journal of Psychiatry, 12,* 1996–1997.

Begley, S. (2007, January 19). How thinking can change the brain: Dalai Lama helps scientists show the power of the mind to sculpt our gray matter. *The Wall Street Journal,* p. B1. Retrieved from http://online.wsj.com.

Bellis, D. E., Hooper, S. R. Spratt, E. G. & Woolley, D. P. (2010). Neuropsychological findings in childhood neglect and their relationships to pediatric PTSD. *Journal of the International Neuropsychological Society, 15*(6), 868–878.

Bender, L. (1954). *A dynamic psychopathology of childhood.* Springfield, Illinois: Charles C. Thomas.

Berger, M. & Kennedy, H. (1975). Pseudobackwardness in children: Maternal attitudes as an etiological factor. *The Psychoanalytic Study of the Child, 30,* 279–306.

Berger W., Mehra, A., Lenoci, M., Metzler, T.J., Otte, C., Tarasovsky, G. …Neylan, T.C. (2010) Serum brain-derived neurotrophic factor predicts responses to escitalopram in chronic posttraumatic stress disorder. *Progress in Neuro-pharmacology & Biological Psychiatry.* (Epublished ahead of print) doi:10.1016/j.pnpbp.2010.07.008.

Bergman, T. & Freud, A. (1965). *Children in the hospital,* International University Press, New York.

Bernstein, N.R. & Menolascino, F.J. Apparent and relative mental retardation: Their challenge to psychiatric treatment. In F. J. Menolascino (Ed.), *Psychiatric approaches to mental retardation.* New York: Basic Books.

Berrueta-Clement, J.R., Schweinhart, L.J., Barnett, W.S., Epstein, A.S., & Weikart, D.P. (1984*). Changed lives: The effects of the Perry Preschool Program on youths through age 19.* [Monograph].Ypsilanti, MI: The High/Scope Press.

Bertolini, M. & Neri, F. (1998). Treatment outcomes: Psychotherapy. In J. G. Young (Ed.), *Designing mental health services and systems for children and adolescents: A shrewd investment.* Philadelphia, PA: Brunner/Mazel Publishers.

Bertrand, J., Mars, A., Boyle, C., Bove, F., Yeargin-Allsopp, M. & Decoufle, P. (2001). Prevalence of autism in a United States population: The brick township, New Jersey, investigation. *Pediatrics, 108*(5), 1155–61.

Bibby, P., Eikeseth, S., Martin, N. T., Mudford, O. C. & Reeves, D. (2001) Progress and outcomes for children with autism receiving parent-managed intensive interventions. *Research in Developmental Disabilities*, 22(6), 425–47.

Biggs, A.M., Ariz, Q., Tomenson, B. & Creed, F. (2003). Do childhood adversity and recent social stress predict health care use in patients presenting with upper abdominal or chest pain? *Psychosomatic Medicine 65*, 1020–1028.

Biggs, AM, Aziz, Q, Tomenson, B. & Creed, F. (February 2004) Effect of childhood adversity on health related quality of life in patients with upper abdominal or chest pain. *Gut, 53*(2), 180–186.

Blos, P. (1972). The Epigenesis of the adult neurosis. *The Psychoanalytic Study of the Child, 27,* 106–135.

Bonaparte, M. (1950/1939). *Five copy books* (Nancy Proctor-Gregg, Trans.). London: Imago. (Original work published 1939.)

Bondy, D., Davis, D. & Hagen, S. (1990). Brief, focused preventive group psychotherapy: Use of the personal life history book method with groups of foster children, *Journal of Preventive Psychiatry* 4(1), 25–38.

Boocock, S. S. (1995). Early childhood programs in other nations: Goals and outcomes. *The Future of Children:* 5(3), 94–114.

Bornstein, B. (1930). Zur psychogenese de pseudodebilitat. *International Journal of Psycho-Analysis, 16,* 378–399.

Bowlby, J. (1960). Separation anxiety. *International Journal of Psychoanalysis, 41,* 89–113.

Bowlby, J. (1969). *Attachment and Loss: Vol. 1, Attachment.* New York: Basic Books.

Bowlby, J. (1973). *Attachment and Loss: Vol. 2, Separation: Anxiety & Anger.* London: Hogarth Press.

Bowlby, J. (1980). *Attachment and Loss: Vol. 3, Loss, Sadness & Depression.* London: Hogarth Press.

Bowlby, J. (1988). *A secure base: Parent-child attachment and healthy human development.* New York: Basic Books.

Boyd, R. D. & Corley, M. J. (2001) Outcome survey of early intensive behavioral intervention for children with autism in a community setting. *Autism,* 5(4), 430–441.

Bradway, K. P. (1945). An experimental study of factors associated with Stanford-Binet IQ changes from the preschool to the junior high school. *Journal of Genetic Psychology, 66,* 107–128.

Bradway, K. P. & Robinson, N. M. (1961). Significant IQ changes in twenty-five years: A follow-up. *Journal of Educational Psychology, 52,* 74–79.

Bram, A. D. and Gabbard, G. O. (2001). Potential space and reflective functioning. *International Journal of Psycho-Analysis, 82*:685–699.

Brang, D. & Ramachandran, V. S. (May 2010) Olfactory bulb dysgenesis, mirror neuron system dysfunction, and autonomic dysregulation as the neural basis for autism. Medical Hypothesis, 4(5), 919–921.

Bremner J.D., Krystal J.H., Southwick. S. M. & Charney, D.S. (1995). Functional neuroanatomical correlates of the effects of stress on memory. *Journal of Traumatic Stress 8*, 527–554.

Bremner, J.D., Licinio J., Darnell, A., Krystal, J. H., Owens, J., Southwick, S. M., Nemeroff, C. B., & Charney, D. S. (1997): Elevated CSF corticotropin-releasing factor concentrations in posttraumatic stress disorder. *American Journal of Psychiatry 154*, 624–629.

Bremner, J.D. (1999). Does Stress Damage the Brain? *Biological Psychiatry 45*, 797–805.

Breslau, N., Chilcoat, H. D., Susser, E. S., Matte, T., Liang, K. Y. & Peterson, E. L. (2001). Stability and change in children's intelligence quotient scores: A comparison of two socioeconomically disparate communities. *American Journal of Epidemiology, 154*(8), 711–717.

Bretherton, I., Ridgeway, D. & Cassidy, J. (1990). Assessing internal working models of the attachment relationship; An attachment story completion task for 3-year-olds. In M. T. Greenberg, Cicchetti, & E.M. Cummings, (Eds.), *Attachment in the preschool years; theory, research and intervention,* Chicago: University of Chicago Press.

Breuer, J. & Freud, S. (1965/1893). On the psychical mechanism of hysterical phenomena: preliminary communication from studies on hysteria. In J. Strachey (Trans.), *The Standard Edition of the Complete Psychological Works of Sigmund Freud, Volume II (1893–1895): Studies on Hysteria,* 1–17. London: Hogarth Press and the Institute of Psycho-Analysis. (Original work published 1893) Retrieved from http://www.pep-web.org.

Brown, E. J., Amaya-Jackson, L., Cohen, J., Handel, S., de Bocanegra, H. T., Zatta, E., Goodman, R. F. & Mannarino, A. (2008). Understanding childhood traumatic grief: A multi-site empirical examination of the construct and its correlates. *Death Studies, 32* (10), 899–923. doi: 10.1080/07481180802440209.

Bucan, M., Abrahams, B. S., Wang, K., Glessner, J. T., Herman, E. I., Sonnenblick, L. I., Alvarez-Retuerto, A. I. ...Hakonarson, H. (June 2009), Genome-wide analyses of exonic copy number variants in a family-based study point to novel autism susceptibility genes. *PLoS Genetics 5*(6):e1000536. Epublished 2009 June 26. Retrieved from PMID: 19557195.

Buitelaar, J. K., Van der Weest M, Swaab-Barneveld, H. & Van der Gaag, R. J. (1999).Verbal memory and performance IQ predict theory of mind and emotion recognition ability in children with autism spectrum disorders and in psychiatric control children. *Journal of Child Psychology and Psychiatry and Allied Disciplines, 40*(6), 869–881.

Buxbaum, E, (1954). Technique of child therapy. *The Psychoanalytic Study of the Child, 9,* 297–333.

Buxbaum, E. (1964). The parents' role in the etiology of learning disabilities. *The Psychoanalytic Study of the Child, Vol. 19,* 421–447.

California DDS. (1999). Changes in the population of persons with autism and pervasive developmental disorders in California's developmental services system: 1987 through 1998: A report to the legislature March 1, 1999. Retrieved from http://www.dds.ca.gov.

Cantor, R. M., Kono, N., Duvall, J. A., Alvarez-Retuerto, A., Stone, J. L., Alarcon, M., Nelson, S. F. & Geschwind, D. H. (2005) Replication of autism linkage: fine-mapping peak at 17q21. *American Journal of Human Genetics, 76,* 1050–1056.

Carrey, N. J., Butter, H. J., Persinger, M.A. & Bialik, R.J. (1995). Physiological and cognitive correlates of child abuse. *Journal of the American Academy of Child and Adolescent Psychiatry, 34*(8), 1067–75.

Carrion, V. G., Weems, C. F., & Reiss, A. L. (2007). Stress predicts brain changes in children: A pilot longitudinal study on youth, stress, posttraumatic stress disorder, and the hippocampus. *Pediatrics, 119*(3) 509–516. doi:10.1542/peds.2006-2028.

Carter, C.S. (2003). Developmental consequences of oxytocin. *Physiological Behavior, 79,* 383–397.

Carter, C.S. (1998). Neuroendocrine perspectives on social attachment and love. *Psychoneuroendocrinology, 23,* 779–818.

Castren, E. & Ranamaki, T. (April 2010). The role of BDNF and its receptors in depression and antidepressant drug action: Reactivation of developmental plasticity. *Developmental Neurobiology, (70),* 289–97.

Chakrabarti, S. & Fombonne, E. (2001). Pervasive developmental disorders in preschool children. *Journal of the American Medical Association, 285*(24), 3141–3142.

Chakrabarti, S. & Fombonne, E. (June 2005). Pervasive developmental disorders in preschool children: Confirmation of high prevalence. *The American Journal of Psychiatry, 62*(6):1133–41.

Chang, K. S. F., Lee, M. M. C., Low, W. D. & Kvan, E. (1989). Height and weight of southern Chinese children. *American Journal of Human Biology, 1,* 397–408.

Chapman DP, Whitfield CL, Felitti VJ, Dube SR, Edwards VJ, Anda RF. (2004). Adverse childhood experiences and the risk of depressive disorders in adulthood. *Journal of Affective Disorders, 82*(2):217–25.

Children's Psychological Health Center (Producer). (1999). Autism Recovery: 33 Year Follow-Up. [Video]. Retrieved from http://www.cphc-sf.org/content/view/58/42/

Children's Psychological Health Center (Producer). (2009). Kliman G., Hirshfeld L., Kliman J. & Trimble D. Successful treatment of a mildly autistic boy. [Video].

Choi, J., Jeong, B., Rohan, M. L., Polcari, A. M. & Teicher, M. H. (February 1, 2009). Preliminary evidence for white matter tract abnormalities in young adults exposed to parental verbal abuse. *Biological Psychiatry, 65*(3), 224–34.

Ciaranello, A. L. & Ciaranello, R. D. (1995). The neurobiology of infantile autism. *Annual Review of Neuroscience, 18,* 101–128.

Clay, R. (1998, April). Today's foster-care system is facing new challenges: The number of children in the system has jumped 65 percent over the last decade. *American Psychological Association Monitor, (29)*4.

Cohen, D. J. & Volkmar, F. R. (1997). Conceptualizations of autism and intervention practices: International perspectives. In D. J. Cohen, & F. R. Volkmar (Eds.), *Handbook of Autism and Pervasive Developmental Disorders* (2nd ed.). New York: Wiley.

Cohen, H., Amerine-Dickens, M. & Smith, T. (2006). Early intensive behavioral treatment: Replication of the UCLA model in a community setting. *Journal of Developmental Behavioral Pediatrics, 27*(2 Suppl):S145–155.

Cohen, S. (1998). *Targeting autism.* Berkeley, CA: University of California Press.

Cornelius M. D., Goldschmidt L., De Genna, N.M., Richardson, G.A., Leech, S.L. & Day. R. (June 2010). Improvement in intelligence test scores from 6 to 10 years in children of teenage mothers. *Journal of Developmental and Behavioral Pediatrics, 31*(5), 405–13.

Courchesne, E.,Yeung-Courchesne, R., Press, G. A., Hesselink, J. R. & Jernigan, T.L. (1988). Hypoplasia of cerebellar vermal lobules VI and VII in autism. *New England Journal of Medicine, 318,* 1349–1354.

Cousens, P., Waters, B., Said, J. & Stevens, M. (1988). Cognitive effects of cranial irradiation in leukemia: A survey and meta-analysis. *Journal of Child Psychology and Psychiatry, 29*(6), 839–852.

Cunningham, J. B. (August 13, 2006). Remarks by U.S. Consul General James B. Cunningham–Asian Autism Conference 2006, The Hong Kong Academy of Medicine. Retrieved from http://hongkong.usconsulate.gov/cg_jc2006081301.html.

Csikszentmihalyi, M. (1990). *Flow: The psychology of optimal experience.* New York: Harper and Row.

Dapretto, M. D., Pfeifer, M.S., Scott, J. H., Sigman, A. A., Bookheimer, S. Y. & Iacoboni, M. (January 2006). Understanding emotions in others: mirror neuron dysfunction in children with autism spectrum disorders. *Nature Neuroscience, 9*(1), 28–30.

Dawson, G., Rogers, S., Munson, J. Smith, M. Winter, J., Greenson, J...Varley, J. (January 2010). Randomized, controlled trial of an intervention for toddlers with autism: the Early Start Denver Model. *Pediatrics, 125*(1), 17–23. doi:10.1542/peds.2009–0958.

DeCarli, C., Fugate, L., Falloon, J., Eddy, J., Katz, D. A., Friedland, R. P., Rapoport, S.I., Brouwers, P & Pizzo, P. A. (1991). Brain growth and cognitive improvement in children with human immunodeficiency virus-induced encephalopathy after 6 months of continuous infusion zidovudine therapy. *Journal of Acquired Immune Deficiency Syndromes, (6),* 585–599.

De Bellis, M. D., Hooper, S. R., Spratt, E. G. & Woolley, D. P. (2009). Neuropsychological findings in childhood neglect and their relationships to pediatric PTSD. *Journal of the International Neuropsychological Society, 15*(6), 868–878.

Delaney, R. C., McCarthy, G., Charney, D. S., & Innis, R. B. (1995). MRI-based measurement of hippocampal volume in patients with combat-related posttraumatic stress disorder. *American Journal of Psychiatry, 152,* 973–981.

Delaney-Black V., Covington, C., Ondersma, S.J., Nordstrom-Klee, B., Templin, T., Ager, J., Janisse J. & Sokol, R. J. (2002). Violence exposure, trauma, and IQ and/or reading deficits among urban children. *Archives of Pediatric Adolescent Medicine, 56*(3):280–5.

Deutsch, H. (1937). Absence of grief. *Psychoanalytic Quarterly, 6, 12–22.*

De Waal, F. (1996). *Good natured: The origins of right and wrong in humans and other animals.* Cambridge, MA: Harvard University Press.

Di Pellegrino, G., Fadiga, L., Fogassi, L., Gallese, V. & Rizzolatti, G. (1992). Understanding motor events: A neurophysiological study. *Experimental Brain Research, 91,* 176–180.

Doidge, N. (2001). Introduction to Jeffery: Why psychoanalysts have low mortality rates. *Journal of the American Psychoanlaytic Association, 49*(1), 97–102.

Dong, M., Anda, R.F., Dube, S. R., Giles, W. H. & Felitti, V. J. (2003). The relationship of exposure to childhood sexual abuse to other forms of abuse, neglect, and household dysfunction during childhood. *Child Abuse & Neglect, 27*(6):625–39.

Downey, T. (2001). Early object relation into new objects. *The Psychoanalytic Study of the Child, 56,* 39–67.

Dube, S. R., Andra, R. F., Felitti, V. J., Chapman, D. P. Williamson, D. F. & Giles, W. H. (December 2001). Childhood abuse, household dysfunction, and the risk of attempted suicide throughout the life span: findings from the Adverse Childhood Experiences Study. *Journal of the American Medical Association, 286*(24), 3089–3096.

Dube, S. R., Andra, R. F., Felitti, V. J., Edwards, V. J. & Williamson, D. F. (February 2002). Exposure to abuse, neglect, and household dysfunction among adults who witnessed intimate partner violence as children: implications for health and social services. *Violence and Victims, 1,* 3–17.

Dube, S. R., Felitti, V. J., Dong, M., Chapman, D. P., Giles, W. H. & Anda, R. F. (2003). Childhood abuse, neglect, and household dysfunction and the risk of illicit drug use: The adverse childhood experiences study. *Pediatrics, 111*(3) 564–572.

Duhrssen, A. (1972). Katamnestische ergebrnisse bei 1004 patienten nach analystischer psychotherapie. *Zeitshrift fur psychosomatische medizin, 7*(2), 94–113.

Duvall, J. A., Lu, Ake, Cantor, R. M., Todd, R. D., Constantino, J. N. & Geschwind, D. H. (April 2007). A quantitative trait locus analysis of social responsiveness in multiplex autism families. *The American Journal of Psychiatry,16.* Retrieved from doi: 10.1176/appi.ajp.164.4.656.

Duyme, M., Dumaret, A. & Tomkiewicz, S. (1999). How can we boost IQs of "dull children"?: A late adoption study. *Proceedings of the National Academy of Sciences, USA, 96*(15), 8790–8794.

Dyson, A. (2004). The Costs and Benefits of Earlier Identification and Effective Intervention, Final Report, *University of Manchester Research Report 505.*

Edwards, M. (1967). Libidinal phases in the analytic treatment of a preschool child. *The Psychoanalytic Study of the Child, 22, 199–215.*

Edwards, V. J., Holden, G. W., Felitti, V. J. & Anda, R. F. (2003). Relationship between multiple forms of childhood maltreatment and adult mental health in community respondents: results from the adverse childhood experiences study. *The American Journal of Psychiatry, 160*(8), 1453–1460.

Edgcumbe, R. (1975). The border between therapy and education. In *Studies in child Psychoanalysis: Pure and applied.* New Haven, CT, and London: Yale University Press.

Eikeseth, S. (2001). Recent critiques of the UCLA Young Autism Project. *Behavioral Interventions, 16,* 249–64.

Eikeseth, S., Smith, T., & Eldevik, E. & Jahr S. (2002). Intensive behavioral treatment at school for 4 to 7 year-old children with autism. *Behavior Modification, 26,* 49–68.

Eikeseth, S., Smith, T., Jahr, E. & Eldevik, S. (May 7, 2007). Outcome for children with autism who began intensive behavioral treatment between ages 4 and 7: A comparison controlled study. *Behavior Modification, 31*(3), 264–278.

Eisch, A, (2002). Adult neurogenesis: implications for psychiatry. *Progress in Brain Research, 138,* 315–42.

Eissler, K. R. (1955) *The psychiatrist and the dying patient.* New York: International Universities Press.

Emde, R. N. (1990). Mobilizing fundamental modes of development—an essay on empathic availability and therapeutic action. *Journal of the American Psychoanalytic. Association., 38,* 881–913.

Engert F. & Bonhoeffer, T. (6 May1999) Dendritic spine changes associated with hippocampal long-term synaptic plasticity. *Nature 399,* 66–70. doi:10.1038/19978.

Epstein, S. F. (2000) Prologue. *Psychoanalytic Inquiry, 20*(5) 631–636.

Erikson, E. H. (1950). *Childhood and society.* New York: Norton.

Eth, S. & Pynoos, R. S. (Eds.). (1985). *Post-traumatic stress in children.* Washington, DC: American Psychiatric Press.

Eth, S. & Pynoos, R.S. (1985). Developmental perspective on psychic trauma in childhood. In C.R. Figley (Ed.), *Trauma and its wake: The study and treatment of post-traumatic stress disorders.* New York: Brunner/Mazel.

Eth, S. & Pynoos, R. (1985). Interaction of trauma and grief in childhood. In S. Eth & R. Pynoos (Eds.), *Post Trauma and Stress Disorder in Childhood.* Washington, DC: American Psychiatric Press.

Fadiga, L., Fogassi, L., Gallese, V. & Rizzolatti, G. (March 2000). Visuomotor neurons: ambiguity of the discharge or 'motor' perception? *International Journal of Psychophysiology 35*(2–3) 165–177.

Fanshel, D. & Shinn, E. (1978). *Children in foster care: A longitudinal investigation.* New York, NY: Columbia University Press.

Faulkes, S. H. (1964). *Therapeutic group analysis.* New York: International University Press.

Feinberg, D. (1970). Preventive therapy with siblings of a dying child. *Journal of the American Academy of Child Psychiatry, 9*(4):644–668.

Fenichel, O. (1941). The ego and the affects. *Psychoanalytic Review, 28,* 47–60.

Ferrari, P. F., Gallese, V., Rizzolatti, G. & Fogassi, L. (2003). Mirror neurons responding to the observation of ingestive and communicative mouth actions in the monkey ventral premotor cortex. *European Journal of Neuroscience, 17,* 1703–1714.

Festinger, T. (1983). *No one ever asked us: A postscript to foster care.* New York, NY: Columbia University Press.

Fisch, G. S., Simensen, R., Tarleton, J., Chalifoux, M., Holden, J. J, Carpenter, N, & Fleming, J. (1963). Activation of mourning and growth by psychoanalysis. *International Journal of Psychoanalysis, 44,* 419–431.

Fivush, R. & Edwards, V. J. (2004) Remembering and forgetting childhood sexual abuse. Journal of Child Sexual Abuse, *13*(2),1–19.

Fleming, J. & Altschul, S. (1963). Activation of mourning and growth by psychoanalysis. *International Journal of Psychoanalysis, (44)*, 419–431.

Floud, R., Wachter, K. W. & Gregory, A., (1990). *Height, health and history: nutritional status in the United Kingdom, 1750–1980.* Cambridge, UK: Cambridge University Press.

Flynn, J. R. (2000). IQ gains, WISC subtests and fluid g: g theory and the relevance of Spearman's hypothesis to race. *Novartis Foundation Symposium, 233,* 202–216.

Fogassi, L. & Gallese, V. (2002). The neural correlates of action understanding in non-human primates. In M. I. Stamenov & V. Gallese (Eds.), *Mirror Neurons and the Evolution of Brain and Language* (pp. 13–35). Amsterdam: John Benjamins.

Fonagy, P. & Higgitt, A. (1985). Personality theory and clinical practice. London: Methuen.

Fonagy, P. & Moran, G. S. (1994). Psychoanalytic formulation and treatment of chronic metabolic disturbance in insulin dependent diabetes mellitus. In A. Erskine & D. Judd (Eds.), *The imaginative body: psychodynamic psychotherapy in health care* (pp. 6–86). London: Whurr Publications.

Fonagy, P., Steele, M., Steele, H., Leigh, T., Kennedy, R., Mattoon, G. & Target, M. (1995a). Attachment, the reflective self, and borderline states: The predictive specificity of the Adult Attachment Interview and pathological emotional development. In S. Goldberg, R. Muir, & J. Kerr (Eds.), *Attachment theory: Social, developmental and clinical perspectives* (pp. 233–278). New York: Analytic Press.

Fonagy, P., Steele, M., Steele, H., Leigh, T., Kennedy, R., Mattoon, G. & Target, M. (1995b). The predictive validity of Mary Main's Adult Attachment Interview: A psychoanalytic and developmental perspective on the transgenerational transmission of attachment and borderline states. In S. Goldberg, R. Muir, & J. Kerr (Eds.), *Attachment theory: Social, developmental and clinical perspectives* (pp. 233–278). Hillsdale, NJ: The Analytic Press.

Fonagy, P. (1995). Psychoanalytic and empirical approaches to developmental psychopathology: an object-relations perspective. In T. Shapiro & R. N. Emde (Eds.), *Research in psychoanalysis: Process, development, outcome* (pp. 245–260). Madison, CT: International Universities Press.

Fonagy, P. & Target, M. (1996). Playing with reality: I: Theory of mind and the normal development of psychic reality. *International Journal of Psycho-Analysis, 77,* 217–233.

Fonagy, P. & Target, M. (1996). Predictors of outcome in child psychoanalysis: A retrospective study of 763 cases at the Anna Freud Centre. *Journal of the American Psychoanalytic Association, 44,* 27–77.

Fonagy, P., Steele, M., Steele, H. & Target, M. (1998). *Reflective-functioning manual: Version 5.0 for application to the adult attachment interview.* London: University College London.

Fonagy P. (Ed.). (1999) *An open door review of outcome studies in psychoanalysis.* London: International Psychoanalytical Association Research Committee.

Fonagy, P. & Target, M. (2000). Playing with reality III: The persistence of dual psychic reality in borderline patients. *IJPA*, 81, 853–873.

Fonagy, P., Gergely, G., Jurist, E. L. & Target, M. (2002). *Affect regulation, mentalization and the development of the self.* New York; Other Press.

Fonagy, P. & Target, M. (2003). *Psychoanalytic theories of personality and its development.* London: Whurr Publications.

Fonagy, P., Target, M., Cottrell, D., Phillips, J. & Arabella Kurtz. (2005) *What works for whom?: A critical review of treatments for children and adolescents.* New York: Guilford Press.

Foulkes, S.H. (1964) *Therapeutic Group Analysis.* New York: International Universities Press.

Fraiberg, S. (1962). A therapeutic approach to reactive ego disturbances in children in placement. *American Journal of Orthopsychiatry, 32*(1), 18–31.

Francis, K. (2005). Autism interventions: A critical update. *Developmental Medicine and Child Neurology, 47*(7), 493–497.

Freeman, F. N., Holzinger, K. J. & Mitchell, B. C. (1928). The influence of environment on the intelligence, school achievement, and conduct of foster children. In *27th Yearbook of the National Society for the Study of Education Parts I-II,* pp. 103–217.

Freud, A. (1939) *The Ego and the Mechanisms of Defense: The Writings of Anna Freud, Vol. 2.* New York: International Universities Press.

Freud, A. & Dann, S. (1951). An experiment in group upbringing. *The Psychoanalytic Study of the Child, 6,* 7–168.

Freud, A. (1960). Discussion of Dr. John Bowlby's paper. *The Psychoanalytic Study of the Child, 15,* 53–62.

Freud, A. (1962). Assessment of childhood disturbances. *The Psychoanalytic Study of the Child, 17,* 149–158.

Freud, A. (1966/1946), *The psychoanalytical treatment of children.* New York: International Universities Press. (Original work published 1946)

Freud, A. (1966) A short history of child analysis. *The Psychoanalytical Study of the Child, 21,* 7–14.

Freud, A. (1967). Comments on psychic trauma. *The writings of Anna Freud: Vol. 5* (pp. 221–224). New York: International Universities Press.

Freud, A. (1968). Indications and contraindications for child analysis. *The Psychoanalytic Study of the Child, 23,* 37–46.

Freud, A. (1971/1936). The ego and the mechanisms of defense. In *The writings of Anna Freud: Vol. 2.* New York: International Universities Press. (Original work published 1936)

Freud, A. & Burlingham, D. (1973/1943). Infants without families. In *The writings of Anna Freud: Vol. 3,* 543 681. New York: International Universities Press (Original work published 1943).

Freud, A. (1979). The nursery school from the psychoanalytic point of view. In *The writings of Anna Freud: Vol. 8,* 315–330. New York: International Universities Press.

Freud, S. (1957/1917). Mourning and Melancholia. In J. Strachey (Ed. & Trans.), *The standard edition of the complete psychological works of Sigmund Freud: Vol. 14*. London: Hogarth Press (Original work published 1917).

Freud, S. (1960/1905). Jokes and their relation to the unconscious. In J. Strachey (Ed. & Trans.), *The standard edition of the complete psychological works of Sigmund Freud: Vol. 8*. London: Hogarth Press. (Original work published 1905)

Freud, S. (1964/1937). Analysis terminable and interminable. In J. Strachey (Ed. & Trans.), *The standard edition of the complete psychological works of Sigmund Freud: Volume 23*. London: Hogarth Press. (Original work published 1937)

Freud, S. (1965/1891). Hypnosis. In James Strachey (Trans). In James Strachey (Trans.), *The standard edition of the complete psychological works of Sigmund Freud, Volume 1. (1886–1899): Pre-psycho-analytic publications and unpublished drafts*, 3rd ed., 103–114. Vienna: Urban & Schwarzenberg. (Original work published 1891) Retrieved from http://www.pep-web.org

Friedman , S. B., Chodoff, P., Mason, J. W. & Hamburg, D. A. (1963). Behavioral observations on parents anticipating the death of a child. *Pediatrics 32*, 610–625.

Friedman, M. (1988). The Hampstead clinic nursery: the first twenty years. *Bulletin of the Anna Freud Centre, 11*, 227–288.

Furman, E. (1971). Some thoughts on reconstruction in child analysis. *The Psychoanalytic Study of the Child, 26*, 372–385.

Furman, E. (1981). *A child's parent dies: Studies in childhood bereavement*. New Haven: Yale University.

Furman, R. A. (1964). Death of a six-year-old's mother during his analysis. *The Psychoanalytic Study of the Child, 19*, 377–397.

Furman, R. A. & Katan, A. (Eds.). (1969). *The therapeutic nursery school: A contribution to the study and treatment of emotional disturbances in young children*. New York: International Universities Press.

Fuss, M., Poljanc, K. & Hug, E. B. (2000). Full Scale IQ (FSIQ). Changes in children treated with whole brain and partial brain irradiation. A review and analysis. *Strahlentherapie und Onkologie,176*(12), 573–581.

Gabbard, G.O., Gunderson, J. G. & Fonagy, P. (2002). The place of psychoanalytic treatments within psychiatry. *Archives of General Psychiatry, 59*(6), 505–510.

Galenson, E. (1971). The therapeutic nursery school: A contribution to the study and treatment of emotional disturbances in young children. *Psychoanalytic Quarterly, 40*, 682–685.

Gallese, V., Fadiga, L., Fogassi, L. & Rizzolatti, G. (1996). Action recognition in the premotor cortex. *Brain, 119*, 593–609.

Gallese, V. & Goldman, A. (1998). Mirror neurons and the simulation theory of mind reading. *Trends in Cognitive Sciences, 12*, 493–501.

Gallese, V. (2001): "The 'shared manifold' hypothesis: From mirror neurons to empathy, *Journal of Consciousness Studies , 8*, 5–87. Boston/London: Imprint Publishers.

Gallese, V. (2003). The manifold nature of interpersonal relations: the quest for a common mechanism. *Philosophical Transactions of the Royal Society, 358*, 517–528. London: Oxford University Press.

Gallese, V., Fogassi, L., Fadiga, L. & Rizzolatti, G. (2002). Action representation and the inferior parietal lobule. In W. Prinz & B. Hommel (Eds.), *Common mechanisms in perception and action: attention and performance, Vol. 19*, (pp. 334–355). New York, NY: Oxford University Press.

Gallese, V., Keysers, C. & Rizzolatti, G. (2004). A unifying view of the basis of social cognition. *Trends in Cognitive Sciences, 8*, 396–403.

Gallese, V. (2005) The intentional attunement hypothesis: The mirror neuron system and its role in interpersonal relations. In *Lecture Notes in Computer Science, 2005*(3725), 19–30. Berlin/Heidelberg: Springer.

Gallese, V. (March, 2007) Intentional attunement: Mirror neurons and the neural underpinnings of interpersonal relations, *Journal of the American Psychoanalytic Association, 55*(1), 131–175. doi:10.1177/00030651070550010601.

Geleerd, E. (1963, May). Transference in the preschool years. Paper presented at the annual meeting of the American Psychoanalytic Association, St. Louis, MO.

Giedd, J. N., Vaituzis, A.C., Hamburger, S. D., Lange, N., Rajapakse, J. C, Kaysen. D. Rapoport, J. L. (1996) Quantitative MRI of the temporal lobe, amygdala, and hippocampus in normal human development: ages 4–18 years. *The Journal of Comparative Neurology, 366*(2), 223–230.

Gold, S., Arndt, S., Nopoulos, P., O'Leary, D. S. & Andreasen, N. C. (1999). Longitudinal study of cognitive function in first-episode and recent-onset schizophrenia. *American Journal of Psychiatry, 156*(9), 1342–1348.

Goldberg, E. L., Kliman, G. & Reiser, M. F. (1966). Improved visual recognition during hypnosis. *Archives of General Psychiatry.* 14(1), 100–107.

Goldman, A. I. & Sripada, C. S. (2005). Simulationist models of face-based emotion recognition. *Cognition*, 94(3), 193–213. doi:10.1016/j.cognition.2004.01.005.

Goldstein, K. (1939). *The organism.* New York: American Book Company.

Goodman, J.F. & Cameron, J. (March 1978). The meaning of IQ constancy in young retarded children. *Journal of Genetic Psychology, 132*, 109–119.

Goodman, J. F., Cecil, H. S. & Barker, W.F. (1984). Early intervention with retarded children: some encouraging results. *Developmental Medicine and Child Neurology, 26*(1), 47–55.

Grandin, T. (1996). Thinking in pictures: And other reports from my life with autism. Vancouver, WA: Vintage Books.

Gratton, L., LaFrontaine, C. & Guibeault, J. (1966). Group psychoanalytic work with children. *Canada Psychiatric Association Journal, 11*, 432–442.

Green G. 1996 Early behavioural intervention for autism what does research tell us? In Maurice C., Green G., and Luce S. (Eds) *Behavioural Intervention for Young Children with Autism.* Austin, TX: Pro-Ed.

Greenacre, P. (1971). *On the development and function of tears. Emotional growth: Vol. 1*, (pp.249–259). New York: International University Press.

Greenson, R. R. (1965). The working alliance and the transference neurosis. *Psychoanalytic Quarterly, 34*, 155–181.

Greenspan, S. I. (1992). *Infancy and early childhood: The practice of clinical assessment and intervention with emotional and developmental challenges.* Madison, CT: International Universities Press.

Greenspan, S. I. (1992). Reconsidering the diagnosis and treatment of very young children with autism spectrum or pervasive developmental disorder. *Zero to Three Journal, 13,* 1–9.

Greenspan. S.I. (1998). Commentary: Guidance for constructing clinical practice guidelines for developmental and learning disorders: Knowledge vs. evidence-based approaches. *The Journal of Developmental and Learning Disorders, 2*(2), 171–192.

Greenspan, S.I. (2000). Children with autism spectrum disorders: Individual differences, affect, interaction, and outcomes. *Psychoanalytic Inquiry, 20*(5), 675–703.

Greenspan, S.I. & Wieder, S. (1997). Developmental patterns and outcomes in infants and children with disorders in relating and communicating: A chart review of 200 cases of children with autism spectrum diagnoses. *The Journal of Developmental and Learning Disorders. 1,* 87–141.

Greenspan, S.I. & Weider, S. (1997). An integrated developmental approach to interventions for young children with severe difficulties in relating and communicating. *Zero to Three Journal, 17*(5): 5–18.

Greenspan, S. I. & Wieder, S. (1998). *The child with special needs.* Reading, MA: Addison-Wesley.

Greenspan, S.I. & Weider, S. (1999). A functional developmental approach to autism spectrum disorders. *Journal of the Association for Persons with Severe Handicaps, 24*(3), 147–161.

Greenspan, S. & Weider, S. (2001). Asperger's Syndrome: The developmental, individual difference, relationship-based (DIR) approach to diagnosis and the intervention. *The Journal of Developmental and Learning Disorders, 4*(1), 45–68.

Greenspan, S. I. & Weider, S. (2005). Difference relationship-based (DIR) approach. *The Journal of Developmental and Learning Disorders, 9.*

Gregory, I. (1965). Anterospective data following childhood loss of a parent. *Archives of General Psychiatry, 13,* 99–109.

Grienenberger J., Kelly K. & Slade, A. (2005). Maternal reflective functioning, mother-infant affective communication and infant attachment: Exploring the link between mental states and observed caregiving behavior in the intergenerational transmission of attachment. *Attachment and Human Development 7*(3), 299–311.

Grill, J., Renaux, V.K., Bulteau, C., Viguier, D., Levy-Piebois, D., Sainte-Rose, C., Dellatolas, G., Raquin, M. A. ... Kalifa, C. (1999). Long-term intellectual outcome in children with posterior fossa tumors according to radiation doses and volumes. *International Journal of Radiation Oncology-Biology- Physics, 45(*1), 137–145.

Hagerman, R. J. (1996). A controlled study of longitudinal IQ changes in females and males with fragile X syndrome. *American Journal of Medical Genetics, 2,* 350–355.

Halfon, N., Berkowitz, G. & Klee, L. (1992). Mental health service utilization by children in foster care in California. *Pediatrics, 89,* (6 Pt. 2), 1238–1244.

Hammock, E. A. & Young, L. J. (2006). Oxytocin, vasopressin and pair bonding: implications for autism. Philosophical Transactions of the Royal Society of London, Series B, Biological Sciences, 361(1476), 2187–2198.

Harley, M. (May 1963). Transference in the preschool years. Presented at the Annual Meeting of the American Psychoanalytic Association, Chairperson: Elisabeth R. Geleerd. St. Louis, MO.

Harris, B., (1994). The height of schoolchildren in Britain, 1900–1950, In J. Komlos, (Ed.), *Stature, living standards and economic development*. Chicago, IL: University of Chicago Press.

Harris, S. L., Randleman, J. S., Gordon, R., Kristoff, B. & Fuentes F. (1991). Changes in cognitive and language functioning of preschool children with autism. *Journal of Autism & Developmental Disorders, 21*(3), 281–90.

Hartmann, H. (1958/1939). *Ego psychology and the problem of adaptation* (D. Rappoport, Trans.) New York: International Universities Press. (Original work published 1939.)

Harvey, John. H. & Uematsu, Mika A. (1995). Why we must develop and tell our accounts of loss. Paper presented at Society for Applied Research in Memory and Cognition, First Biennial Conference, Vancouver, Canada.

Heinicke, C. M. (1993). Integrating experientially based concepts and behavioral observations in developmental and intervention research. *Journal of the American Psychoanalytic Association, Empirical studies in psychoanalysis, 41(Suppl.)*, 353–368.

Heinicke, C. M. & Ramsey-Klee, D. M. (1986) Outcome of child psychotherapy as a function of frequency of session. *Journal of the American Academy of Child Psychiatry 25*(2), 247–253.

Heinicke, C. M. (1966). Frequency of psychotherapeutic session as a factor affecting the child's developmental status. *The Psychoanalytic Study of the Child, 20*, 42–98.

Hellman, I. (1954). Some observations on mothers of children with intellectual inhibitions. *Psychoanalytic Study of the Child, 9*, 259–273.

Herba, C. & Phillips, M. (October 2004). Annotation: Development of facial expression recognition from childhood to adolescence: behavioural and neurological perspectives. *Journal of Child Psychology and Psychiatry and Allied Disciplines, 45*(7), 1185–1198.

Hoeft, F. Carter, J. C., Lightbody, A., Hazlett, H. C., Piven, J. & Reiss, A. L. (May 18, 2010). Region-specific alterations in brain development in one- to three-year-old boys with fragile X syndrome. Proceedings of the National Academy of Sciences, 107(20), 9335–9339. Retrieved from: PMID: 20439717.

Honzik, M. P., MacFarlane, J. W. & Allen, L. (1948). The stability of mental test performance between two and eighteen years. *Journal of Experimental Education, 17*, 309–324.

Honzik, M. P. (1967). Environmental correlates of mental growth: Prediction from the family setting at 21 months. *Child Development, 38(2)*, 337–364.

Hope, M. D. (1999). *IQ scores and social behavioral ratings of preschoolers in special education and Cornerstone: Differential treatment efficacy*. Doctoral dissertation, Wright Institute, Berkeley, CA. Retrieved from http://www.cphc-sf.org/content/category/7/16/42/.

Horowitz, S., Simms, M. & Farrington, R. (1994). The impact of developmental and behavioral problems on the exit of children from foster care. *Journal of Developmental and Behavioral Pediatrics, 15*, 105–110.

Hosford, D. A., Simonato, M., Cao, Z., Garcia-Cairasco, N., Silver, J. M., Butlier, L., Shin, C. & McNamara, J. O. (March 1995). Differences in the anatomic distribution of immediate-early gene expression in amygdala and angular bundle kindling development. *The Journal of Neuroscience, 15*(3, Part 2), 2513–2523.

Howard-Peebles, P. N. & Maddalena, A. (1996). Longitudinal study of cognitive abilities and adaptive behavior levels in fragile X males: A prospective multicenter analysis. *American Journal of Medical Genetics, 4*(2), 356–361.

Howlin, P., Mawhood, L. & Rutter, M. (2000). Autism and developmental receptive language disorder: A follow-up comparison in early adult life. *Journal of Child Psychology and Psychiatry and Allied Disciplines, 41*(5), 561–578.

Hu, V. W., Frank, B. C., Heine, S., Lee, N. H. & Quackenbush, J. (May 2006). Gene expression profiling of lymphoblastoid cell lines from monozygotic twins discordant in severity of autism reveals differential regulation of neurologically relevant genes. *BMC Geonomics,18*(7). Retrieved from doi: 10.1186/1471–2164–7–118.

Hutsler, J. J. & Zhang, H. (January 14, 2010). Increased dendritic spine densities on cortical projection neurons in autism spectrum disorders. *Brain Research, 1309*, 83–94.

Iacoboni, M., Woods, R. P., Brass, M., Bekkering, H., Mazziotta, J. C. & Rizzolatti, G. (1999). Cortical mechanisms of human imitation. *Science, 286*, 2526–2528.

Iacoboni, M., Ptito, A. Weeks, N.Y. & Zaidel, E. (April 2000). Parallel visuomotor processing in the split brain: cortico-subcortical interactions. *Brain 123*(Pt. 4) 759–769.

Iacoboni, M. (2005). Understanding others: Imitation, language, empathy. In S. Hurley & N. Chater (Eds.), *Perspectives on imitation: From neuroscience to social science: Vol. 1*, (pp. 77–99). Cambridge, MA: MIT Press.

Iacoboni, M. & Lenzi G.L. (2005). Mirror neurons, the insula, and empathy. *Behavioral and Brain Sciences, 5*, 39–40.

Imanaka, A., Morinobu, S., Toki, S. & Yamawaki, S. (October 2006) Importance of early environment in the development of post-traumatic stress disorder-like behaviors. *Behavioral Brain Research, 173*(1) 129–137.

Itzchak, E. B., Lahat, E., Burgin, R. & Zachor, A. D. (2008). Cognitive, behavior and intervention outcome in young children with autism. *Research in Developmental Disabilities, 29*(5), 447–458.

Jacobson, J. W., Mulick, J. A. & Green, G. (1998). Cost-benefit estimate for early intensive behavioral intervention for young children with autism: General model and single state case. *Behavioral Interventions, 14*, 433–465.

Jacobson, J. W. & Mulick, J. A. (2000). System and cost research issues in treatments for people with autistic disorders. Journal of Autism and Developmental Disorders, *30*(6), 585–593.

Jellema, T., Baker, C. I., Wicker, B. & Perrett, D. I. (2000). Neural representation for the perception of the intentionality of actions. *Brain and Cognition, 44*, 280–302.

Joffe, W. G. & Sandler, J (1965). Notes on pain, depression, and individuation. *The Psychoanalytic Study of the Child, 20*, 394–424.

Johnson, D.E., Guthrie, D., Smyke, A.T., Koga, S. F., Fox, N. A., Zenah, C. H. & Nelson, C. (April 5, 2010). Growth and associations between auxology, caregiving environment, and cognition in socially deprived Romanian children randomized to foster vs. ongoing institutional care. *Archives of Pediatrics & Adolescent Medicine, 164*(6), 507–516.

Johnson, W., Deary, I. J. & Iacono, W. G. (September 1, 2009). Genetic and environmental transactions underlying educational attainment. *Intelligence, 37*(5), 466–478.

Jonsdottir, S. L., Saemundsen, E., Asmundsdottir, G., Hjartardottir, S., Asgeirsdottir, B. B., Smaradottir, H. H. ...Smari, J. (2006). Follow-up of children diagnosed with pervasive developmental disorders: Stability and change during the preschool years. *Journal of Autism and Developmental Disorders, 37*(7), 1361–1374.

Jordan, R., Jones, G. & Murray, D. (1998). Educational interventions for children with autism: A literature review of recent and current research. DfES Research Report No. RR77. London: Department for Education and Employment.

Just, M. A., Cherkassky, V. L., Keller, T. A. & Minshew, N. J. (2004) Cortical activation and synchronization during sentence comprehension in high-functioning autism: Evidence of underconnectivity. *Brain, 127*(8),1811–1821. doi:10.1093/brain/awh199.

Just, M. A., Cherkassky V. L., Keller, T. A. & Minshew, N. J. (2007) Functional and anatomical cortical underconnectivity in autism: Evidence from an fMRI study of an executive function task and corpus callosum morphometry. *Cerebral Cortex, 17*(4), 951–961. doi:10.1093/cercor/bhl006.

Kagan, J., Sontag, L. W., Baker, C. T. & Nelson, V. L. (1958). Personality and IQ change. *Journal of Abnormal and Social Psychology, 46,* 261–266.

Kagan, J. & Freeman, M. (1963). Relation of childhood intelligence, maternal behaviors, and social class to behavior during adolescence. *Child Development, 34,* 899–911.

Kandel, E. (1999). Biology and the future of Psychoanalysis: A new intellectual framework for psychiatry revisited. *American Journal of Psychiatry, 156,* 505–524.

Katan, A. (1961). Some thought about the role of verbalization in early childhood. *The Psychoanalytic Study of the Child, 16,* 184–188.

Kavushansky, A., Ben-Shachar, D., Richter-Levin, G. & Klein, E. (2009). Physical stress differs from psychosocial stress in the pattern and time-course of behavioral responses, serum corticosterone and expression of plasticity-related genes in the rat. *Stress, 12*(5), 412–425.

Keilp, J. G. & Prohovnik, I. (1995). Intellectual decline predicts the parietal perfusion deficit in Alzheimer's disease. *Journal of Nuclear Medicine, 36*(8), 1347–1354.

Kennedy, H. (1971). Problems in reconstruction in child analysis. *The Psychoanalytic Study of the Child, 26,* 386–402.

Kennedy, H. (1988). The pre-history of the nursery school. *Bulletin of the Anna Freud Centre, 11,* 271–276.

Keysers, C. & Perrett, D.I.(2004). Demystifying social cognition: A Hebbian perspective. *Trends in Cognitive Sciences, 8,* 501–507.

Klagsburn, S. C., Kliman, G. & Clark, E. J. (Eds.). (1989) *Preventive psychiatry: Early intervention and situational crisis management.* Philadelphia, PA: The Charles Press.

Klein, E. (1949). Psychoanalytic aspects of school problems. In *The Psychoanalytic Study of the Child, Vol. 4*, 369–390.

Kliman, G. (1955) Adrenal medullary function. In Gordon, G. S. (Ed.), *Yearbook of Endocrinology,* Chicago, IL: Yearbook Publishers

Kliman, G. (1967). The Cornerstone method of applied psychoanalysis in a therapeutic preschool. Presentation at Westchester Psychoanalytic Society, Rye, NY.

Kliman, G. (1967) Scientific program: Application of psychoanalytic technique in nursery and kindergarten classes. Correspondent: Milton Gray. Presented at Westchester Psychoanalytic Society, Chairmanship of Norbert Bromberg. Rye, New York.

Kliman, G. (1968). *Psychological emergencies of childhood.* New York: Grune & Stratton.

Kliman, G. (1968). Cornerstone treatment of a dying child. In Kliman, G. psychological emergencies of childhood, Bellak, L. (Ed.). New York, NY: Grune and Stratton.

Kliman, G. (1969). The Cornerstone Method. Unpublished manuscript, presented at the New York Academy of Child and Adolescent Psychiatry.

Kliman, G. (1970). Analyst in the nursery: application of child analytic techniques in a therapeutic nursery. In *The Psychoanalytic Study of the Child, 30,* 477–510.

Kliman, G. (1970). Treatment of a ghetto preschooler with drug-addicted parents. Paper presented at the Vulnerable Child Workshop, American Psychoanalytic Association, New York.

Kliman G. & Ronald, D. (1970). The unique function of the teacher in an experimental therapeutic nursery school. The Center for Preventive Psychiatry: White Plains, New York.

Kliman G. (1974). Death of a parent occurring during a child's analysis, In *Trauma: Monograph V* of the Monograph Series of the Ernst Kris Study Group, New York Psychoanalytic Institute. New York: International Universities Press.

Kliman G. (1974). A case of a dying child, In *Trauma: Monograph V* of the Monograph Series of the Ernst Kris Study Group, New York Psychoanalytic Institute. New York: International Universities Press.

Kliman, G. (1975) Experimental application of child analytic techniques in a therapeutic nursery. *The Psychoanalytic Study of the Child, 30,* 477–510.

Kliman, A. S. (1976). The Corning flood project: Psychological first aid following a natural disaster. In H. J. Parad, H. L. P. Resnick, L. G. Parad, (Eds.), *Emergency and disaster management: A mental health sourcebook.* Bowie, MD: Charles Press.

Kliman, G. (1977). Psychoanalysis and preventive psychiatry. Paper presented at a meeting of the Westchester Psychoanalytic Society, White Plains, NY.

Kliman, G. (1977). Preventive measures in childhood bereavement. In Linzer, N. (Ed.), *Understanding bereavement and grief.* New York: Yeshiva University Press.

Kliman, G. (1978). Treatment of vulnerable preschoolers. Paper presented at a meeting of the Vulnerable Child Workshop, American Psychoanalytic Association, New York.

Kliman G. (1978). Follow-ups of Cornerstone preschool patients. *Community Education Report* White Plains, NY: The Center for Preventive Psychiatry; Paper presented to American Psychoanalytic Association Workshop, Washington, DC.

Kliman, G., Feinberg, D., Stein, M., Lester, M. (1978) Clinical Status and IQ follow-ups on eleven Cornerstone treated children. Presentation at American Psychoanalytic Association, Spring Meeting, New York.

Kliman, G. (1979). Facilitation of mourning during childhood. In I. Gerber, A. Wiener, A. H. Kutscher, D. Battin, A. Arkin, & I. Goldberg (Eds.), *Perspectives on bereavement.* New York: Arno Press.

Kliman, G. (1979). Childhood mourning: A taboo within a taboo. In I. Gerber, A. Wiener, A. H. Kutscher, D. Battin, A. Arkin, & I. Goldberg (Eds.), *Perspectives on bereavement.* New York: Arno Press

Kliman, G. & Rosenfeld, A. (1980). *Responsible parenthood: The child's psyche through the six-year pregnancy.* New York: Holt, Rinehart and Winston.

Kliman, G., Schaeffer, M., Friedman, M. & Pasquariella, B. (1981). Children in foster family care: A preventive and research program for a high-risk population. *Journal of Preventive Psychiatry, 1,* 47–56.

Kliman, G., Schaeffer, M. H., Friedman, M. J. & Pasqueariella, B. (1982). Preventive mental health services for children entering foster care. Monograph of the Center for Preventive Psychiatry: White Plains, NY.

Kliman, G. & Shaeffer, M. (1983). Summary of two psychoanalytically based service and research projects: Preventive treatments for foster children. *Journal of Preventive Psychiatry,* 2(1).

Kliman, G. & Schaeffer, M. H. (1990). A breakthrough in prediction and prevention: diagnoses as social predictors for foster children. *Journal of Preventive Psychiatry and Allied Disciplines 4* (1), New York: Human Sciences Press.

Kliman G. & Schaeffer, M. H. (1990). Summary of two psychoanalytically based service and research projects: Preventive treatments for foster children. *Journal of Preventive Psychiatry and Allied Disciplines* (2)1. New York: Human Sciences Press.

Kliman G. (1990). Toward preventive intervention in early childhood object loss. In Noshpitz, J. D. & Coddington, R. D. (Eds.), *Stressors and clinical techniques in child psychiatry.* New York: John Wiley.

Kliman, G. (1992). Interpersonal schemas and a new theory of PTSD. Paper presented at the Center for the Study of Consciousness, University of California, San Francisco, CA.

Kliman, G. (1994). Toward a unifying theory of PTSD. Unpublished manuscript. Presented at a meeting of The International Association of Child and Adolescent Psychiatry & Allied Disciplines, San Francisco, CA.

Kliman, G. (1996) Use of a personal life history book in the treatment of foster children—An attempt to enhance stability of foster care placements. In Zelman A (Ed.), *Early Intervention with High-Risk Children: Freeing Prisoners of Circumstance.* Jason Aronson, Northvale, NJ. 105–124.

Kliman G. (1996) Field notes: foster care: the personal life history book: A psychoanalytically based intervention for foster children, *Journal for the Psychoanalysis of Culture & Society,* 1(2), 159–162.

Kliman, G. (1996). *My personal life history book: A guided activity workbook for children, their families, case workers and teachers,* (5th ed.) San Francisco, CA: The Children's Psychological Health Center. (Original work published 1985.)

Kliman, G. (1996). *The personal life history book method: A manual for preventive sychotherapy with foster children*, (5th ed.). San Francisco: The Children's Psychological Health Center. (Original work published 1985.)

Kliman, G. (1996) Toward a unifying theory of PTSD: Psychoanalytic, neurophysiologic, behavioral, memory and anatomic data. Paper presented at a meeting of the International Society for Traumatic Stress Studies, Maastricht, Netherlands.

Kliman, G. & Zelman, A. (1996). Use of a personal history book in the treatment of foster children—an attempt to enhance stability of foster care placements. In A. Zelman (Ed.). *Early intervention with high-risk children: Freeing prisoners of circumstance*. Northvale, NJ: Jason Aronson, 105–124.

Kliman, G. (1997). Child psychoanalysis applied in public special education classes: The Cornerstone project. *The American Psychoanalyst,* April 1997. The American Psychoanalytic Association, New York.

Kliman, G. (1997). Field notes on foster care. *Journal of Psychoanalysis of Culture & Society, 1,* 59–162.

Kliman, G. (1998). Videotaped consultations with traumatized children: Contribution of observable behavior to a unifying theory of PTSD. Paper presented at a meeting of the International Association of Child & Adolescent Psychiatry and Allied Disciplines. Stockholm, Sweden.

Kliman G, Hummer K, Dornic S, Schwartz M. (1998) *The Cornerstone Method: Three instructional DVDs for professional use.* San Francisco, CA: Children's Psychological Health Center.

Kliman, G. (Feburary 1999). A unifying new theory of posttraumatic stress disorder. *Scientific Bulletin of Children's Psychological Trauma Center.* San Francisco, CA: CPTC.

Kliman, G. (1999). Intensive in-classroom psychotherapy of preschoolers. Paper presented at the meeting of the Western Regional Association of Child Psychoanalysts, Vail, CO.

Kliman G. & Wolfe, H. (2003). *My book about war and terrorism: A guided activity workbook for children, families and teachers to encourage healthy expression, learning and coping.* San Francisco: The Children's Psychological Health Center.

Kliman, G. (2005) Video evidence of a psychoanalytic process and associated clinical and IQ gains in a therapeutic classroom; presentation at American Psychoanalytic Association, New York.

Kliman, G. (2006). Methods for maximizing good effects of foster care: Evidence-based strategies to prevent discontinuities of foster care and raise IQ. *International Journal of Applied Psychoanalytic Studies, 3*(3), 4–16. doi:10.1002/aps.46.

Kliman G., (December 2006). Responding to hurricanes Katrina and Rita, *The American Psychoanalyst 31*(2).

Kliman, G, Oklan, E., Oklan, A., Wolfe, H. & Kliman, J. (2006) *My Personal Story about Hurricanes Rita and Katrina: A guided activity workbook.* San Francisco: The Children's Psychological Health Center.

Kliman, G. (2007) Treatment of autistic preschoolers by an application of child analysis in a therapeutic preschool classroom. Presentation to a scientific meeting of San Francisco Center for Psychoanalysis, Jan 8, 2007.

Kliman, G. (2008). Toward a unifying theory of post-traumatic stress disorder: integrating data from studies of post-traumatic behavior, memory, symptom formation, physiology, cerebral imaging, psychoanalytic findings and evolutionary theory. Unpublished manuscript. Presented to the first joint scientific meeting of the American College of Psychoanalysts and the American Academy of Psychoanalysis and Psychodynamic Psychiatry, May 3, 2008, Washington DC.

Knapp M., Romeo R. & Beecham, J. (2009) Economic cost of autism in the UK. *Autism,13*(3):317–36. Retrieved from: doi:10.1177/1362361309104246.

Knights, R. M., Ivan, L. P, Ventureyra, E. C., Bentivoglio, C., Stoddart, C., Winogron, W. & Bawden, H. N. (1991). The effects of head injury in children on neuropsychological and behavioural functioning. *Brain Injury, 5*(4), 337–338.

Kogan M.D., Blumberg, S. J., Schieve, L.A., Boyle, C.A., Perrin, J.M., Ghandour, R.M. ...Van Dyck, P.C. (November 2009). Prevalence of parent-reported diagnosis of autism spectrum disorder among children in the US, 2007. *Pediatrics, 124*, 1395–1403. doi:10.1542/peds.2009–1522

Kohut, H. (1971). *The analysis of the self.* New York: International University Press.

Kohut, H. (1977). *The restoration of the self.* New York: International Universities Press.

Kohut, H. & Wolf, E. S. (1978). The disorders of the self and their treatment: An outline.*International Journal of Psychoanalysis, 59*, 413–425.

Kornhuber, H. H., Bechinger, D., Jung, H. & Sauer, E. (1985). A quantitative relationship between the extent of localized cerebral lesions and the intellectual and behavioural deficiency in children. *European Archives of Psychiatry and Neurological Sciences,235*(3), 129–133.

Kosaka H., Omori M., Munesue T., Ishitobi M., Matsumura Y., Takahashi. T. ... Wada Y. (2010). Smaller insula and inferior frontal volumes in young adults with pervasive developmental disorders. *NeuroImage 50*(4), 1357–1363.

Kreitler, S., Weyl, Arush, M., Eds. (2004) *Psychosocial Aspects of Pediatric Oncology*, The New England Journal of Medicine, *351*(2136–2137).Hoboken, NJ: Wiley. doi: 10.1002/0470020776.

Kranzler E. M., Shaffer D., Wasserman G. & Davies, M.A. (1990). Early childhood bereavement. *Journal of the American Academy of Child and Adolescent Psychiatry* 29:5139.

Kremen, W. S., Buka, S. L., Seidman, L. J., Goldstein, J. M., Koren, D. & Tsuang, M. T. (1998). IQ decline during childhood and adult psychotic symptoms in a community sample: A 19–year longitudinal study. *American Journal of Psychiatry, 5*, 672–677.

Kris, E. (1956). The recovery of childhood memories in psychoanalysis. *Psychoanalytic Study of the Child, 11*, 54–88.

Krystal, J. H., A. L. Bennett, J. D. Bremner, S. M. Southwick. & D. S. Charney. (1995) Toward a cognitive neuroscience of dissociation and altered memory. Retrieved from onlinelibrary.wiley.com doi/10.1111/j.1749–6632.1997.tb48270.x/pdf.

Kuhl, P.K. (2004). Early language acquisition: cracking the speech code. *Nature Reviews Neuroscience, 5*, 831–843.

Kulesza, R. J. & Mangunay, K. (March 2008) Morphological features of the medial superior live in autism. Brain Research, (1200) 132–137. doi:10.1016/j.brainres.2008.01.009.

Lagace, D., Noonan, M. & Eisch, A. (2007). Hippocampal neurogenesis: A matter of survival. *American Journal of Psychiatry, 164*(2), 205.

Lauritsen, M.B., Pedersen, C.B. & Mortensen, P.B. (2005) Effects of familial risk factors and place of birth on the risk of autism: A nationwide register-based study. *Journal of Child Psychology and Psychiatry, 46*(9), 963–971.

Lavigne, J. V., Arend, R., Rosenbaum, D., Binns, H. J., Christoffel, K. K. & Gibbons, R. D. (1998). Psychiatric disorders with onset in the preschool years: I. Stability of diagnoses *Journal of the American Academy of Child and Adolescent Psychiatry 37*(12), 1246–54.

Lavigne. J.V., Cicchetti C., Gibbons, R.D., Binns, H.J., Larsen, L. & DeVito, C. (2001). Oppositional defiant disorder with onset in preschool years: longitudinal stability and pathways to other disorders. *Journal of the American Academy of Child and Adolescent Psychiatry, 40*(12), 1393–400.

Lavigne, J.V., Lebailly, S. A., Hopkins, J., Gouze, K.R. & Binns, H. J. (2009) The prevalence of ADHD, ODD, depression, and anxiety in a community sample of 4–year-olds. *Journal of Clinical Adolescent Psychology, 38*(3), 315–328.

Lawrence, L. E., Viron, M., Johnson, J. E., Hudkins, A., Samples, G. & Kliman, G. (October 2006). A school-based mental health recovery effort, poster session presentation at the 58th annual meeting of the Institute on Psychiatric Services, New York.

Lawrence, L. E., Viron, M., Johnson, J. E., Hudkins, A., Samples, G. & Kliman, G. & O'Neill P. (June 2007). A school-based mental health recovery effort. Poster session presentation at the 33rd annual meeting of the Association of Directors of Medical Student Education in Psychiatry, Park City, UT.

LeDoux, J. E. (1994). Brain mechanisms of emotion and emotional learning. *Current Opinion in Neurobiology, 2*(2), 191–197.

LeDoux, J. E. (1994). Emotion, memory and the brain: The neural routes underlying the formation of memories about primitive emotional experiences, such as fear, have been traced. *Scientific American, 270*(6), 50–57.

Leichsenring, F. & Rabung, S. (October 1, 2008) Effectiveness of long-term psychodynamic psychotherapy: A meta-analysis. *Journal of the American Medical Association, 300*, (13), 1551–1565.

Leland, H., Walker, J. & Taboada, A. (1959). Group play therapy with a group of post-nursery male retardates. *American Journal of Mental Deficiency, 63,* 848–851.

Levy, K.N., Meehan, K.B., Reynoso, J.S., Lenzenweger, M.F., Clarkin, J.F. & Kernberg, O.F. (2005). The relation of reflective function to neurocognitive functioning in patients with borderline personality disorder. *Journal of the American Psychoanalytic Association, 53,* 1305–1309.

Levy, K. N., Meehan, K. B., Kelly, K. M., Reynoso, J. S., Weber, M., Clarkin, J. F. & Kernberg, O. F. (2006). Change in attachment patterns and reflective function in a randomized control trial of transference focused psychotherapy for borderline personality disorder. *Journal of Consulting and Clinical Psychology, 74*(6), 1027–1040.

Liotti, G. (1999). Understanding the dissociative processes. *Psychoanalytic Inquiry, 19*, 757–783.

Lofgren, L. B. (1966). On weeping. *International Journal of Psychoanalysis, 47*, 375–381.

Lopez, T. (1974). Psychotherapeutic assistance to a blind boy with limited intelligence. *The Psychoanalytic Study of the Child, 29*, 277–300.

Lopez, T. & Kliman, G. (1979). Memory, reconstruction, and mourning in the analysis of a 4–year-old child: maternal bereavement in the second year of life. *The Psychoanalytic Study of the Child, 34*, 235–271.

Lopez, T. & Kliman, G. (1980). The Cornerstone treatment of a preschool boy from an extremely impoverished environment. *The Psychoanalytic Study of the Child, 35*, 341–375.

Lopez, T., Balter, N., Howard, S., Stewart, R. & Zelman, A.B. (1996). Cornerstone: A therapeutic nursery for severely disadvantaged children. In A. Zelman (Ed.), *Early intervention with high-risk children: Freeing prisoners of circumstance* (pp. 23–64). Northvale, NJ: Jason Aronson.

Lovaas, O. I. (1981). *Teaching developmentally disabled children: The me book.* Austin, TX: Pro-Ed.

Lovaas, O. I. (1987). Behavioral treatment and normal educational and intellectual functioning in young autistic children. *Journal of Consulting and Clinical Psychology, 55*(1), 162–164.

Lovaas, O. I. (1993). The development of a treatment-research project for developmentally disabled and autistic children. *Journal of Applied Behavior Analysis, 26*(4), 617–630.

Lustman, S. L. (1970). Cultural deprivation. *The Psychoanalytic Study of the Child, 25*, 483–502.

Lynn, R., Hampson, S. L. & Mullineux, J. C. (1987). A long-term increase in the fluid intelligence of English children. *Nature, 328*(6133), 797.

Macri, S., Spinelli, S., Adriani, W., Dee Higley, J. & Laviola, G. (2007). Early adversity and alcohol availability persistently modify serotonin and hypothalamic-pituitary-adrenal-axis metabolism and related behavior: what experimental research on rodents and primates can tell us. *Neuroscience & Biobehavioral Reviews, 31*(2), 172–180.

Mahler, M. S. (1942). Pseudoimbecility: A magic cap of invisibility. *Psychoanalytic Quarterly, 11*, 149–164.

Mahler, M. S. & Furer, M. (1960). Observations on research regarding the 'symbiotic syndrome' of infantile psychosis. *Psychoanalytic Quarterly, 29*, 317–327.

Mahler, M. S. (1968). *On human symbiosis and the vicissitudes of individuation.* New York: International Universities Press.

Main, M., Kaplan, K. & Cassidy, J. (1985). Security in infancy, childhood and adulthood: A move to the level of representation. In I. Bretherton & E. Waters (Eds.), *Growing points in attachment theory and research.* Monographs of the Society for Research in Child Development, *50*(1–2, Serial No. 209), 66–104.

Maletic-Savatic, M., Malinow, R. & Svoboda, K. (1999). Rapid dendritic morphogenesis in CA1 hippocampal dendrites induced by synaptic activity. *Science, 283,* 1923–1927.

Mannoni, M (1972). *The backward child and his mother.* New York: Pantheon Books.

Marcus, L. M., Rubin, J. S. & Rubin, M.A. (2000). Benefit-cost analysis and autism services: A response to Jacobson and Mulick. *Journal of Autism and Developmental Disorders, 30,* 595–598.

Maughan, B. & McCarthy, G. (January 1997). Childhood adversities and psychosocial disorders. *British Medical Bulletin, 53*(1), 156–169.

Maurice, C. (1993). *Let me hear your voice: A family's triumph over autism.* New York: Knopf.

McCall, R. B., Appelbaum, M. I. & Hogarty, P. S. (1973). Developmental changes in mental performance. *Monographs of the Society for Research in Child Development, 38*(3, Serial 150).

McDonald, M. E. & Paul, J.F. (March 15 2010). Timing of increased autistic disorder cumulative incidence. *Environmental Science & Technology, 44*(6) 2112–2118.

McEachlin, J. J., Smith, T. & Lovaas, O. I. (1993). Long-term outcome for children with autism who received early intensive behavioral treatment. *American Journal on Mental Retardation, 97,* 359–372.

McKracken, J. (February 5, 2010). [Quoted in] L.A. confidential: seeking reasons for autism's rise, by Melinda Beck, *Wall Street Journal*: Retrieved from www.online.wsj.com.

Meehan, K. B., Levy, K. N., Reynoso, J., Hill, L. & Clarkin, J. (2007, January). Measuring reflective function with a multi-dimensional questionnaire: Comparison to scoring reflective function on the AAI. Paper presentation at a meeting of the American Psychoanalytic Association, New York.

Meehan, K. B. & Levy, K. N. (2009). Psychodynamic theories of relationships. In H. Reis & S. Sprecher (Eds.), *Encyclopedia of Human Relationships.* (pp. 1299–1302). Thousand Oaks, CA: Sage Publications.

Meers, D. R. (1970). Contributions of a ghetto culture to symptom formation. *The Psychoanalytic Study of the Child, 25,* 209–230.

Meers, D.R. (1973). Psychoanalytic research and intellectual functioning of ghetto-reared black children. *The Psychoanalytic Study of the Child, 28,* 395–418.

Meers, D. R. (1975). Precocious heterosexuality and masturbation. In I. M. Marcus & J. J. Francis (Eds.), *Masturbation from infancy to senescence* (pp. 411–438). New York: International University Press.

Melhem, N. M., Moritz, G., Walker, M., Shear, M. K. & Brent, D. (2007) Phenomenology and correlates of complicated grief in children and adolescents. *Journal of the American Academy of Child & Adolescent Psychiatry, 46*(4), 493–499.

Miles, J., McCathren, R. B., Stichter, J. & Shinawi, M. *(April 13, 2010).* Autism Spectrum Disorders, In Pagon, R.A., Bird, T.C., Dolan, C.R. & Stephens, K., (Eds.), *GeneReviews, NCBI Online Bookshelf.* (Original posting August 27, 2003) Retrieved from http://www.ncbi.nlm.nih.gov/bookshelf/br.fcgi?book=gene&part=autism-overview.

Miller, J. (1988). A child losing and finding her objects: An unusual therapeutic in the nursery school. *Bulletin of the Anna Freud Centre, 11,* 75–89.

Mishkin, A. D., Viron, M., Lawrence, L. E., Johnson, J. E,, Samples, G. & Kliman G. (October 2007). Reducing post-traumatic stress after Hurricane Katrina: a school-based intervention. Poster presentation at the 59th annual meeting of the Institute on Psychiatric Services, New Orleans, LA.

Moffitt, T. E., Caspi, A., Harkness, A.R. & Silva, P. A. (1993). The natural history of change in intellectual performance: who changes? How much? Is it meaningful? *Journal of Child Psychology and Psychiatry and Allied Disciplines, 4*(4), 455–506.

Molfese, V. J. & Holcomb, L. C. (1989). Predicting learning and other developmental disabilities: assessment of reproductive and caretaking variables. *Birth Defects Original Article Serices, 25*(6), 1–23.

Money, J., Annecillo, C. &, Kelley, J. F. (1983). Growth of intelligence: Failure and catch-up associated respectively with abuse and rescue in the syndrome of abuse dwarfism. *Psychoneuroendocrinology, 8*(3), 309–319.

Moriarty, A. E. (1966). *Constancy and IQ change: A clinical view of relationships between tested intelligence and personality.* Springfield, IL: Charles C. Thomas.

Morrissey, J. R. (October 1964), Death anxiety in children with fatal illness. *American Journal of Psychotherapy, 18,* 606–615.

Mottron, L. (2004). Matching strategies in cognitive research with individuals with high functioning autism: Current practices, instrument biases, and recommendations. *Journal of Autism and Developmental Disorders, 34*(1), 19–27.

Mundy, L. (1957). Therapy with physically and mentally handicapped children in a mental deficiency hospital. *Journal of Clinical Psychology, 13(1),* 3–9.

Nacewicz, B. M., Dalton, K. M, Johnstone, T., Long, M. T., McAuliff, E. M., Oakes, T. R.,Alexander, A. L. & Davidson, R. J. (2006). Amygdalya volume and non-verbal social impairment in adolescent and adult males with autism. *Archives of General Psychiatry, 63*(12), 1417–28.

Nagera, H. (1963). The developmental profile—Notes on some practical considerations regarding its use. *The Psychoanalytic Study of the Child, 18,* 511–540.

Nagera, H. (1966). Early childhood disturbances, the infantile neurosis, and the adulthood disturbances. New York: International Universities Press.

Nagy, M. (1948). The child's theories concerning death. *The journal of genetic psychology, 73* (First Half) *3–27.* Retrieved from PMID: 18893204.

National Autistic Society, Lovaas-NAS. (2010). Lovaas. Retrieved from: www. autism.org.uk.

National Institute of Mental Health. (2010) Autism spectrum disorders (pervasive developmental disorders); Autism Intervention for toddlers improves developmental outcomes.Retrieved from: www.nimh.nih.

Neubauer, P. B., Beller, E. K. (1958) Differential Contributions of the. Educator and Clinician *in* Diagnosis. In Krugman, M. (Ed.), *Orthopsychiatry and the School.* Greenville, SC: American Orthopsychiatric Association.

New York State Department of Health Early Intervention Program. (1999) *Clinical practice guideline: Report of the guideline recommendations. Autism/pervasive developmental disorders, assessment and Intervention for young children (age 0–3 years)*, Publication 4215. New York: New York State Department of Health.

Nguyen, A., Rauch, T. A., Pfeifer, G. P. & Hu, V. W. (August 2010). Global methylation profiling of lymphoblastoid cell lines reveals epigenetic contributions to autism spectrum disorders and a novel autism candidate gene, RORA, whose protein product is reduced in autistic brain. *The FASEB Journal, official publication of the Federation of American Societies for Experimental Biology,* 24(8)m 3036–3051. Retrieved from PMID: 20375269.

Nishiyama, T., Notohara, M., Sumi, S., Takami, S. & Kishino, H. (December 2009) Major contribution of dominant inheritance to autism spectrum disorders (ASDs) in population-based families. *Journal of Human Genetics, 54*(12):721–726.

Norden, V. & Gillberg, C. (1998). The long-term course of autistic disorders: Update on follow-up studies. *Acta Psychiatrica Scandinavica, 97*(2), 99–108.

Novick, J. (1970). The vicissitudes of the working alliance in the analysis of a latency girl. *The Psychoanalytic Study of the Child, 25,* 231–256.

Novick, J. (1980). Negative therapeutic motivation and negative therapeutic alliance. *The Psychoanalytic Study of the Child, 35,* 299–320.

Novick, J. (1992). The therapeutic alliance: A concept revisited. *Child Analysis, 3,* 90–100.

Novick, J. & Novick, K. K. (2000). Parent work in analysis: Children, adolescents, and Adults. Part one: The evaluation phase. Journal of Infant, Child, and Adolescent Psychotherapy, *1*(4), 55–77.

Novick, K. (August 1991). The therapeutic alliance in work with parents. Paper presentation at a meeting of the American Psychological Association, San Francisco, CA.

Nyden, A., Billstedt, E., Hjelmquist, E. & Gillberg, C. (2001). Neurocognitive stability in Asperger syndrome, ADHS, and reading and writing disorder: A pilot study. *Developmental Medicine and Child Neurology, 43*(3), 165–171.

Oberman, L.M., Hubbard, E.M., McCleery, J.P., Altschuler, E.L., Ramachandran, V.S. & Pineda, J.A. (2005). EEG evidence for mirror neuron dysfunction in autism spectrum disorders. *Cognitive Brain Research, 24,* 190–198.

Oberman, L. M., McCleery, J. P. & Ramachadran, J. A. (2007) EEG evidence for mirror neuron activity during the observation of human and robot actions: Toward an analysi of the human qualities of interactive moods. *Neurocomputing 70*(13–15, 2194–2203. doi:10.10.1016/j.neurocom.2006,02.024.

Oberndorf, C. P. (1939). The feeling of stupidity. *International Journal of Psycho-Analysis, 20,* 443–451.

Olch, G. B. (1971). Technical problems in the analysis of the preoedipal and preschool child. *Journal of the American Psychoanalytic Association, 19,* 543–551.

Olff, M., Langeland, W. Witteveen, A. & Denys, D. (August 2010). A psychobiological rationale for oxytocin in the treatment of posttraumatic stress disorder. *CNS Spectrums, 15*(8), 522–530.

Osofsky, J. D. (1988). Attachment theory and research and the psychoanalytic process. *Psychoanalytic Psychology, 5,* 159–177.

Pardeck, J. (1983). An empirical analysis of behavioral and emotional problems of fosterchildren as related to replacement in care. *Child Abuse & Neglect, (7)* 75–83. doi:10.1016/0145–2134(83)90033–9.

Pardeck, J. (1984). Multiple placement of children in foster care: An empirical analysis. *Social Work, 29,* 506–509.

Parkes, C. M. & Stevenson-Hinde, (Eds.). (1982). *The place of attachment in human behavior.* New York: Basic Books.

Parkes, C.M., Stevenson-Hinde, J. & Marris, P. (Eds.). (1991). *Attachment across the life cycle.* London/New York: Routledge.

Parnes J. S. (2001) Testimonial of a public school administrator. Retrieved from http://www.cphc-sf.org/content/category/5/14/37/.

Pearson, D, McGrath, N. M., Nozyce, M., Nichols, S. L., Raskino, C., Brouwers, P., Lifschitz, M. C. & Englund, J. A. (December 2000). Predicting HIV disease progression in children using measures of neuropsychological and neurological functioning. *Pediatrics, 106*(6), e76.

Piaget, J. (1928). *The child's conception of the world.* London: Routledge and Kegan Paul.

Perry, B.D. (1996). Incubated in terror: Neurodevelopmental factors in the "cycle of violence." In J.D. Osovsky (Ed.), *Children, Youth and Violence: Searching for Solutions.* New York: Guilford Press.

Pinneau, Samuel R. (1961). *Changes in intelligence quotient infancy to maturity: New insights from the Berkeley Growth Study with implications for the Stanford-Binet Scales and applications to professional practice.* Boston, MA: Houghton Mifflin.

Piven, J., Harper, J., Palmer, P. & Arndt, S. (1996). Course of behavioral change in autism: A retrospective study of high-IQ adolescents and adults. *Journal of the American Academy of Child and Adolescent Psychiatry, 35*(4), 523–529.

Planck, E. (1964). Pavanne for a dead infant, *Medical Times Newsletter, 92*(7), 639.

Pluck, G., Lee, K. H., David, R., Macleod, D. C., Spence, S. A. & Parks, R. W. (March 2010). Neurobehavioural and cognitive function is linked to childhood trauma in homeless adults. *The British Journal of Clinical Psychology.* (Epublished ahead of print) retrieved from PMID: 20230661.

Ramachandran, V.S. (May 29 2000) Mirror neurons and imitation learning as the driving force behind "the great leap forward" in human evolution. *Edge, 69.* Retrieved from http://www.edge.org/3rd_culture/ramachandran/ramachandran_p1.html.

Ramachandran, V. & Oberman, S. (2006). Broken mirrors: A theory of autism. *Scientific American, 295*(5), 62–69.

Ramachandran, R., Mitchell, P. & Ropar D. (October 2010). Recognizing faces based on inferred traits in autism spectrum disorders. *The International Journal of Research and Practice,* [Epublished ahead of print] Retrieved from PMID: 20923892.

Rank, B. (1949). Adaptation of the psychoanalytic technique for the treatment of young children with atypical development. *American Journal of Orthopsychiatry, 19*(1), 130–139.

Rank, B. (1955). Intensive study and treatment of preschool children who show marked personality deviations, or "atypical development," and their parents. In

G. Caplan (Ed.), *Emotional problems of early childhood*, 51–84. New York: Basic Books.

Rapaport, D. (1953). On the psychoanalytic theory of affects. *International Journal of Psychoanalysis, 34,* 177–198.

Rapaport, D. (1960). On the psychoanalytic theory of motivation. In M. Jones (Ed.), *Nebraska Symposium on Motivation,* 173–247. Lincoln, NE: University of Nebraska Press.

Redl, F. (1959). Strategy and techniques of life-space interview. *American Journal of Orthopsychiatry, 29*(1), 1–18.

Reddy, L. & Pfeiffer, S. (1997). Effectiveness of treatment foster care with children and adolescents: A review of outcome studies. *Journal of the American Academy of Child and Adolescent Psychiatry, 36*(5), 581–588.

Rees, A. H. & Palmer, F. H. (1970). Factors related to change in mental test performance. *Developmental Psychology, 3*(2, Pt.2), 1–57.

Remus-Araico, J. (1965). Some aspects of early-orphaned adults' analyses. *Psychanalyatic Quarterly, 34,* 316.

Renick, O. (1995). The role of an analyst's expectations in clinical technique: Reflection on the concept of resistance. *Journal of the American Psychoanalytic Association, 43,* 83–94.

Rimland, B. (1964). *Infantile autism.* New York: Appleton-Century Crofts.

Rippon, G., Brock, J., Brown, C. & Boucher, J. (2007). Disordered connectivity in the autistic brain: challenges for the 'new psychophysiology'. *International Journal of Psychophysiology, 63*(2), 164–172. doi:10.1016/j.ijpsycho.2006.03.012.

Rizzolatti, G., Fadiga, L., Fogassi, L. & Gallese, V. (1996). Premotor cortex and the recognition of motor actions. *Cognitive Brain Research, 3,* 131–141.

Rizzolatti, G. & Arbib, M. A. (1998). Language within our grasp. *Trends in Neurosciences, 21,* 188–194.

Rizzolatti, G., Fogassi, L., & Gallese, V. (2001). Neurophysiological mechanisms underlying the understanding and imitation of action. *Nature Review Neuroscience, 2,* 661–670.

Rizzolatti, G. & Craighero, L. (2004). The mirror-neuron system. *Annual Review of Neuroscience, 27,* 169–192.

Rome, R., Byford, S. & Knapp, M. (September 2005). Economic evaluations of child and adolescent mental health interventions: a systematic review. *Journal of Child Psychology and Psychiatry, 46*(9), 919.

Rogers, S. J. & Lewis, H. (1989). An effective day treatment model for young children with pervasive developmental disorders. *Journal of the American Academy of Child and Adolescent Psychiatry, 28,* 207–214.

Rosenblitt, D. L. (1996). States of overstimulation in early childhood. *The Psychoanalytic Study of the Child, 51,* 542–561.

Rosenblitt, D. L. (2005). Translating child analysis from the playroom to the classroom *Journal of the American Psychoanalytic Association, 53,* 189–211.

Roth, A. & Fonagy, P. (1996). *What works for whom? A critical review of psychotherapy research.* New York: Guilford Press.

Rutter, M. (1968). Concepts of autism: A review of research. *Journal of Child Psychology and Psychiatry and Related Disciplines, 9*(1), 1–25.

Russo A. J., Krigsman, A., Jepson, B. & Wakefield, A. (November 2009). Decreased serum hepatocyte growth factor (HGF) in autistic children with severe gastrointestinal disease *Biomark Insights, 4*, 181–190. Retrieved from PMID: 20029653.

Salo, F. & Friedman, M. (1988). The runaway bunny mother: The long term influence of the nursery school. *Bulletin of the Anna Freud Centre, 11*, 53–74.

Sallows, G. O. (2002). Educational interventions for children with autism in the UK. *Early Child Development and Care, 163*, 25–47.

Sallows, G. O. & Graupner, T. D. (2005), Intensive behavioral treatment for children with autism: Four-year outcome and predictors. *American Journal on Retardation, 110*(6), 417–438.

Samuels, S. C. (1996) Treatment of foster children: working through life to facilitate attachment. In Zelman, A. (Ed.), *Early intervention with high-risk children: Freeing prisoners of circumstance*, 125–149. Northvale, NJ: Jason Aronson.

Sanchez, M. M., Ladd, C. O. & Plotsky, P. M. (2001). Early adverse experience as a developmental risk factor for later psychopathology: Evidence from rodent and primate models. *Development and Psychopathology, 13*(3, 419–449.

Sandler, J., Kennedy H. & Tyson, R. L. (1980). *The technique of child analysis*. Cambridge, MA: Harvard University Press.

Sarachana, T., Zhou, R., Chen, G., Manji, H. K., Hu, V. W. (April 2010). Investigation of post-transcriptional gene regulatory networks associated with autism spectrum disorders by microRNA expression profiling of lymphoblastoid cell lines. *Genome Medicine, 2*(4):23.Retrieved from PMID: 20374639.

Sheinkopf, S. J. & Siegel, B. (1998). Home—based behavioral treatment of young children with autism. *Journal of Autism and Developmental Disabilities, 28*(1), 15–23.

Schneider, C. & Midgley, N. (2009). Validation and application of the child psychotherapy Q-sort and adolescent psychotherapy. Presentation to Windholz Foundation, San Francisco, CA.

Schopler, E. & Olley, J. G. (1982). Comprehensive educational services for autistic children: The TEACCH model. In C. R. Reynolds & T. R. Gutkin (Eds.), *The handbook of school psychology*, 629–643. New York: John Wiley.

Schopler, E., Reichler, R. J. & Renner, B. R. (1988). *The childhood autism rating scale (CARS)*. Los Angeles, CA: Western Psychological Services.

Schore, A. N. (1994). *Affect regulation and the origins of the self*. Hillsdale, NJ: Lawrence Erlbaum.

Schore, J. R. & Schore, A. N. (2008) Modern attachment theory: The central role of affect regulation in development and treatment. *Clinical Social Work Journal, 36*(1), 9–20.

Scovis-Westin T (2001) Templating of memory in twelve raped boys. doctoral dissertation.California School of Professional Psychology, Berkeley, CA.

Schreier, A., Wolke, D., Thomas, K., Horwood, J., Hollis, C., Gunnel, D., Harrison, G. (May 2009). Prospective study of peer victimization in childhood and psychotic symptoms in a nonclinical population at age 12 years. *Archives of General Psychiatry, 66*(5), 527–536.

Schweinhart, L. J., Barnes, H. V. & Weikart, D. P. (1993). *Significant benefits: The High Scope Perry Preschool study through age 27.* Monographs of the HighScope Educational Research Foundation, 10. Ypsilanti: HighScope Press.

Sehlmeyer, C., Schöning, S., Zwitserlood, P., Pfleiderer, B., Kircher, T., Arolt, V. & Konrad, C. (June 10, 2009). Human fear conditioning and extinction in neuroimaging: A systematic review. *PLoS One, 4*(6), e5865.

Seligman, M. E. P. (July 1996). Long-term psychotherapy is highly effective: The Consumer Reports study. *Harvard Mental Health Letter.*

Settlage, C. F. & Spielman, P. M. (1975). On the psychogenesis and psychoanalytic treatment of primary faulty structural development. *Association for Child Psychoanalysis: Summaries of Scientific Papers and Workshops, 2,* 32–63.

Shaffer, D., Gould, Brasic, J., Ambrosini, P., Fisher, P. Bird, H. & Aluwahlia, S. (1983). A children's global assessment scale (CGAS). *Archives of General Psychiatry, 40*(11), 1228–1231.

Shaffer, D., & Caton, C. (1984). *Runaway and homeless youth in New York City: A report to the Ittleson Foundation.* New York: The Ittleson Foundation.

Shapiro, T. (1994). Response to Francis Tustin's letter. *Journal of the American Psychoanalytic Association, 42,* 1309–1310.

Siegel, B. (1996). *The world of the autistic child.* New York: Oxford University Press.

Siegel, B. (2003). *Helping autistic children to learn.* London, UK: Oxford University Press.

Siegel, M. (1987). *Psychological testing for early childhood through adolescence: A developmental and psychodynamic approach.* Madison, CT: International Universities Press.

Siegel, S. (1956). *Nonparametric statistics for the behavioral sciences.* New York: McGraw Hill.

Skeels, H. M. & Dye, H. A. (1939). A study of the effects of differential stimulation in mentally retarded children. *Proceedings of the American Association of Mental Deficiency, 44,* 114–136.

Smith, F. (March 19, 2008). Educators deal with the growing problem of autism: As the number of special-needs students soars, schools grapple with ways to offer high-quality education without going broke. *Edutopia,* Retrieved from www.edutopia.org/autism-school-special-needs.

Smith, I., Beasley, M. G. & Ades, A. E. (1991). Effect on intelligence of relaxing the low phenylalanine diet in phenylketonuria. *Archives of Disease in Childhood, 66*(3), 311–316.

Smith, J. R. & Brooks-Gunn, J. (1997). Correlates and consequences of harsh discipline for young children. *Archives of Pediatrics & Adolescent Medicine, 51*(8), 777–786.

Sokoloff, M. (1959). A comparison of gains in communicative skills, resulting from group play therapy and individual speech therapy, among a group of non-severely dysarthric, speech handicapped cerebal palsied children. (Doctoral dissertation, New York University) *Dissertation Abstracts International, 20,* 803.

Solnit, A., & Provence, S. (1963). *Modern perspectives in child development.* New York: International Universities Press.

Sontag, L. W., Baker, C. T. & Nelson, V. L. (1958). Mental growth and personality development: A longitudinal study. *Monographs of the Society for Research in Child Development, 23*(2, Serial No. 68).

Speers, R. (1965). Group therapy in childhood psychosis. Durham, NC: University of North Carolina Press.

Speigel, D., Kraemer, H. & Gottheil, E. (1989). Effective psychosocial treatment on survival of patients with metastatic breast cancer. *Lancet, 2,* 888–891.

Spence, S. J., Cantor, R. M., Chung, L., Kim, S., Geschwind, D. H. & Alarcon, M. (2006). Stratification based on language-related endophenotypes in autism: Attempt to replicate reported linkage. *American Journal of Medical Genetics Part B (Neuropsychiatric Genetics) 141B,* 591–598.

Sperber, D. (November 19, 2004). "Mirror neurons" or "Concept neurons"? Dan Sperber, Nov 19, 2004 11:39 UT, Reply to Gallese, V., (2004) Intentional attunement. The mirror neuron system and its role in interpersonal relations. Retrieved from http://www.interdisciplines.org/mirror/papers/1.

Spitz, R. (1946). Hospitalism. *The Psychoanalytic Study of the Child, 2,* 113–117.

Spitz, R. & Wolf, K. (1946). Anaclitic depression: An inquiry into the genesis of psychiatric conditions in early childhood. *The Psychoanalytic Study of the Child 2,* 313–342.

Spitz, R. (1964). The derailment of dialogue. *Journal of the American Psychoanalytic Association, 12,* 752–775.

Spreckley, M. & Boyd, R. (March 2009). Efficacy of applied behavioral intervention in preschool children with autism for improving cognitive, language, and adaptive behavior: A systematic review and meta-analysis. *Journal of Pediatrics, 154*(3), 338–344.

Sprince, M. P. (1967). The psychoanalytic handling of pseudostupidity and grossly abnormal behavior in a highly intelligent boy. In E.R. Geleerd (Ed.), *The child analyst at work,* 85–114. New York: International Universities Press.

Staver, H. (1953). The child's learning difficulty as related to the emotional problems of the mother. *American Journal of Orthopsychiatry, 23,* 131–141.

Stein, M. & Ronald, D. (1974). Educational psychotherapy of preschoolers. *Journal of the American Academy of Child Psychiatry, 13*(4), 618–634.

Stein, M. B., Kerry, L. J., Taylor, S., Vernon, A. & Livesley, W. J. (October 2002) Genetic and environmental influences on trauma exposure and posttraumatic stress disorder symptoms: A twin study. *American Journal of Psychiatry, 159,* 1796–1797.

Stewart, R. & Mendik, L. (1996). Cornerstone, steppingstone, superstone: A three-phase, long-term intensive intervention for extremely stressed, emotionally disturbed children. In Zelman, A. (Ed.), *Early intervention with high-risk children: Freeing prisoners of circumstance,* (pp. 65–84).

Stone, J. L., Merriman, B., Cantor, R. M., Yonan, A. L., Gilliam, T. C., Geschwind, D. H. & Nelson, S. F. (2004). Evidence for sex-specific risk alleles in autism spectrum disorder. *American Journal of Human Genetics, 75*(6) 1117–1123. Epublished 2004 October 5. Retrieved from PMID: 15467983.

Stone, L. (1954). The widening scope of indications for psychoanalysis. *Journal of the American Psychoanalytic Association, 2,* 567–594.

Stone, L. (1961). *The psychoanalytic situation: An examination of its development and essential nature.* New York: International Universities Press.

Stubbe, D., Martin, A., Bloch, M., Belitsky, R., Carter, D., Ebert, M. …Leckman, J. F. (2008). Model curriculum for academic child and adolescent psychiatry training. *Academic Psychiatry, 32*(5), 366–376.

Sullivan, H. A. (1953). *The interpersonal theory of psychiatry.* New York: Norton.

Sullivan, R., Wilson, D. A., Feldon, J., Yee, B. K., Meyer, U., Richter-Levin, G. …Braun, K. (November 2006). The International Society for Developmental Psychobiology annual meeting symposium: Impact of early life experiences on brain and behavioral development. *Developmental Psychobiology, 48*(7), 583–602.

Susser, E. R. & Wallace, R. B. (1982). The effects of environmental complexity on the hippocampal formation of the adult rat. *Acta Neurobiologiae Experimentalis, 42*(2), 203–207.

Szatmari, P. & Streiner, D. L. (1996). The effect of selection criteria on outcome studies of children with pervasive developmental disorders (PDD). *European Child & Adolescent Psychiatry, 5*(4) 179–84.

Szatmari, P., Paterson, A. D., Zwaigenbaum, L., Roberts, W., Brian, J., Liu, X. Q., Vincent, J.B., Skaug, J. L. …Meyer, K.J. (2007). Mapping autism risk loci using genetic linkage and chromosomal rearrangements. *Nature Genetics 34*(3), 319–328. doi:10.1038/ng1985.

Szurek, S. A. & Berlin, I. N. (Eds.). (1973). *Clinical studies in childhood psychosis.* New York: Brunner/Mazel.

Tanner, J. M., (1962). *Growth at adolescence: With a general consideration of the effects of hereditary and environmental factors upon growth and maturation from birth to maturity.* (2nd ed.). Oxford, UK: Blackwell Scientific Publications.

Tanner, J. M. (1982). The potential of auxological data for measuring economic and social well-being, *Social Science History, 6,* 571–581.

Target, M. & Fonagy, P. (April 1994). The efficacy of psychoanalysis for children with emotional disorders. *Journal of the American Academy of Child and Adolescent Psychiatry, 3(3),* 772–784.

Target, M. & Fonagy, P. (October 1994). The efficacy of psychoanalysis for children: prediction of outcome in a developmental context. *Journal of the American Academy of Child and Adolescent Psychiatry, 33(8),* 1134–1144.

Target, M. & Fonagy, P. (1996). Playing with reality II: The development of psychic reality from a theoretical perspective. *International Journal of Psychoanalysis, 77,* 459–479.

Tarnower, W. (1966). Extra-analytic contacts between the psychoanalyst and the patient. *Psychoanalytic Quarterly, 35,* 399–413.

Terr, L. C. (1991). Childhood traumas: An outline and overview. *American Journal of Psychiatry 148*(1), 10–19.

Tobin, V.A., Hashimoto, H., Wacker, D.W., Langnaese, K. Caquineau, C. …Ludwig, M. (2010). An intrinsic vasopressin system in the olfactory bulb is involved in social recognition. *Nature, 464*(7287), 2187–2198.

Tottenham N. & Sheridan. MA. (2010) A review of adversity, the amygdala and the hippocampus: a consideration of developmental timing. *Frontiers in Human Neuroscience,* (Epublished September 21 2009) doi:10.3389/neuro.09.068.2009.

Tustin, F. (1992). *Autistic states in children* (Rev. ed.). London: Routledge & Kegan Paul.

Umilta, M. A., Kohler, E., Gallese, V., Fogassi, L., Fadiga, L., Keysers, C. & Rizzolatti, G. (2001). I know what you are doing: A neurophysiological study. *Neuron, 32*, 91–101.

U.S. Department of Health and Human Services, Administration for Children and Families, Children's Bureau Express. (February 2010). Adoption and foster care statistics: Trends in foster care and adoption. *Adoption and Foster Care Analysis and Reporting System.* Retrieved from: www.acf.hhs.gov/programs/cb/stats_research/index.htm#afcars.

Valenstein, A. (1975). Comments in scientific meeting: The analysis of (nonpsychotic) children with structural deviations. *Association for Child Psychoanalysis: Summaries of Scientific Papers and Workshops, 2*, 32–63.

Van der Kolk, B. & Saporta, J. (23 December 1991).The biological response to psychic trauma: mechanisms and treatment of intrusion and numbing. *Anxiety Research, 4*, 199–212.

Van der Kolk, B. (July 2006). Clinical implications of neuroscience in PTSD. *Annals of the New York Academy of Sciences, (1071)*, 277–293.

Vernick, J., & Karon, M. (1965). Who's afraid of death on a leukemia ward? *American Journal of Diseases of Children, 109*, 393–397.

Vygotsky, L. S. (1978). *Mind in society: The development of higher psychological processes.* Cambridge, MA: Harvard University Press.

Waelder, R. (1932). The psychoanalytic theory of play. *Psychoanalytic Quarterly, 2*, 208–224.

Wald, M. S., Carlsmith, J. M. & Leiderman, P. H. (1988). *Protecting abused and neglected children.* Stanford, CA: Stanford University Press.

Walker, J. R. & Wiltshire, T. (December 2006). Databases of free expression. *Mammalian Genome 17*(12), 1141–1146. doi:10.1007/s00335–006–0043–5.

Wallerstein, R. S. (1995). The effectiveness of psychotherapy and psychoanalysis: Conceptual issues and empirical work. In Shapiro T, & Emde, R. N. (Eds.), *Research in psychoanalysis: Process, development, outcome*, 299–311. Madison, CT: International Universities Press.

Wasowicz, L. (2007). Autism therapies vary: Timing is the key to treating autism. UPI Consumer Health. Retrieved from www.pedmed.com.

Wasserman, G. A., Liu, X., Lolacono, N. J, Factor, Litvak, P., Kline, J. K., Popovac, D., Morina, N. ... Graziano, J. H. (1997). Lead exposure and intelligence in 7–year-old children: The Yugoslavia prospective study. *Environmental Health Perspectives, 105*(9), 956–962.

Waters, E., Wippman, J. & Sroufe, L. A. (1979). Attachment, positive affect, and competence in the peer group: Two studies in construct validation. *Child Development, 50*(3), 821–829.

Watt, D. (2007). Toward a Neuroscience of Empathy: Integrating Affective and Cognitive Perspectives. *Neuropsychoanalysis, 9*(1), 119–140.

Wegiel, J., Kuchna, I., Nowicki, K., Imaki, H., Wegiel, E. M., Ma, S.Y., Chauhan, A., Chauhan, Wisniewski, T. (June 2010) The neuropathology of autism: defects of neurogenesis and neuronal migration, and dysplastic changes. *Acta Neuropathologica, 119*(6): 755–770. doi: 10.1007/s00401–010–0655–4.

Weider, S. I. & Greenspan, S, (2001). The DIR (developmental, individual-difference, relationship-based) approach to assessment and intervention planning. *Bulletin of Zero to Three, 21*(4), 11–19.

Weil, A. P. (1973). Ego strengthening prior to analysis. *The Psychoanalytic Study of the Child, 28,* 287–304.

Weiner, G., Rowland, V. & Oppel. W. (1963). Some correlates of IQ changes in children. *Child Development, 34*(1), 61–67.

Weingarten, K. (2003), *Common shock: Witnessing violence every day.* New York: Penguin Book Group USA.

Werner, H. (1940/1926). *Comparative psychology of mental development* (3rd Ed.). New York: International Universities Press. (Original work published 1926.)

Werner, H. (1957). The concept of development from a comparative and organismic point of view. In D. Harris (Ed.), *The concept of development,* 125–148. Minneapolis, MN: University of Minnesota Press.

Whalley, L. J. & Deary, I. J. (2001). Longitudinal cohort study of childhood IQ and survival up to age 76. *British Medical Journal, 322*(7290), 819.

White, T., Cullen, K., Rohrer, L. M., Karatekin, C., Luciana, M., Schmidt, M. Lim, K. O. (January 2008). Limbic structures and networks in children and adolescents with schizophrenia. *Schizophrenia Bulletin, 34*(1), 18–29.

Wilson, E. O. (1998). *Consilience: The unity of knowledge.* New York: Knopf.

Wilson, P. (1988). Therapeutic intervention through the nursery school. *Bulletin of the Anna Freud Centre, 11,* 307–316.

Winnicott, D.W. (1965). The theory of the parent-infant relationship. In *The maturational processes and the facilitating environment* (pp.37–55). New York: International Universities Press.

Wolfberg, P.J. (2003). *Peer play and the autism spectrum: The art of guiding children's socialization and imagination.* Shawnee Mission, KS: Autism Asperger Publishing Company.

Wolfenstein, M. & Kliman, G. (Eds.) (1965). *Children and the death of a president.* New York: Doubleday.

Wolfenstein, M. (1966). How is Mourning Possible? *The Psychoanalytic Study of the Child, 21,* 93–123.

Wolpert, D. M., Doya, K. & Kawato, M. (2003). A unifying computational framework for motor control and social interaction. *Philosophical Transactions of the Royal Society,Biological Sciences 358*(1413) 593–602. doi: 10.1098/rstb.2002.1238.

Woods, M. Z. (1988). Developmental help: Interventions in the nursery school. *Bulletin of the Anna Freud Centre, 11,* 295–306.

Yaffe, K., Vittinghoff, E., Lindquist, K., Barnes, D. Covinsky, K. E., Neyla, ...M. Marar, C. (June 2010). Posttraumatic stress disorder and risk of dementia among US veterans. *Journal of the American Medical Association, 303*(22), 2287–2288.

Yamanouchi, N. Okada, S. Kodama, K. Sakamoto, T., Sekine, H., Hirai, S., Murakami, A., Komatsu, N. & Sato, T. (2009) Effects of MRI abnormalities on WAIS-R performance in solvent abusers. *Acta Psychiatrica Scandinavica, 96*(1), 34–39. Epublished 29 January 2009. doi: 10.1111/j.1600–0404.1997.tb00235.x.

Yang, T. F., Wong, T. T., Cheng, L. Y., Chang, T. K., Hsu, T. C., Chen, S. J. & Chuang, T. Y. (February 1997). Neuropsychological sequelae after treatment for medulloblastoma in childhood—the Taiwan experience. *Child's nervous system, Journal of the International Society for Pediatric Neurosurgery, 13*(2), 77–80, discussion 81.

Yehuda, R., Yang, R.K., Guo, S.L. & Makotkine, Y. (2003). Relationship between dexamethasone-inhibited lysozyme activity in lymphocytes and the cortisol and glucocorticoid receptor response to dexamethasone. *Journal of Psychiatric Research, 37, 471–477.*

Zelman, A., Samuels, S. & Abrams, D. (1985). IQ changes of young children following intensive long-term psychotherapy. *American Journal of Psychotherapy, 39*(2), 215–217.

Zelman, A. & Samuels, S. (1996). Children's IQ changes and long-term psychotherapy: A follow up study. In Zelman, A. (Ed.), *Early intervention with high-risk children: Freeing prisoners of circumstance.* Northvale, NJ: Jason Aronson.

Zigler, E. (1979). Project Head Start: Success or failure? In E. Zigler & J. Valentine (Eds.), *Project Head Start: A legacy of the war on poverty.* New York: Free Press.

Zigler E., Abelson W.D., Trickett P.K. & Seitz V. (1982). Is an intervention program necessary in order to improve economically disadvantaged children's IQ scores? *Child Development, 53*(2), 340–348.

Zigler, E. & Bennett-Gates, D. (Eds) (1999). *Personality development in individuals with mental retardation.* Cambridge: Cambridge University Press.

Zimmerman, R. (1982). Foster care in retrospect. *Tulane Studies in Social Welfare: Vol. 14.* New Orleans, LA: Tulane University School of Social Work.

Appendix A

Resources for Therapists, Teachers, Researchers, Parents, Schools, and Mental Health Agencies

The Children's Psychological Health Center, Inc.—a nonprofit agency
2105 Divisadero Street, San Francisco, CA 94115
Phone (415) 292-7119 Fax (415) 749-2802
Visit our website for more information:
www.childrenspsychological.org / www.reflectivenetworktherapy.org

SUMMARY: TRAINING, SUPPORT AND CERTIFICATION IN REFLECTIVE NETWORK THERAPY

The Children's Psychological Health Center can provide experienced Cornerstone trainers, supervisors, and help launch a new site launch to carry out Reflective Network Therapy in classrooms. Training mental health professionals and educators is a major service, aiding many hundreds of children and families by enhancing the knowledge of their helpers. Qualified therapists and researchers may sign Confidentiality Agreements to obtain materials from an extensive archive of treatment videos. (See Appendix B for a comprehensive overview of the training program.) In addition, our website provides more detail regarding training, seminars, workshops, and presentations, research opportunities and internships. Gilbert Kliman, MD may be contacted directly with training requests or inquiries regarding research opportunities: gilbert.kliman2008@gmail.com

CONFIDENTIALITY AGREEMENT

Access to training videos (DVD format) illustrating a spectrum of Reflective Network Therapy techniques require completion and acceptance of a CPHC Confidentiality Agreement for Professional Research or Educational Study of Videotape Archives. The requisite confidentiality agreement may be downloaded from our website or requested from the CPHC office by phone or by fax. There is no charge for these DVDs; they are not for sale. They must not be copied or shown to other persons; they are not for public viewing. They are a valuable archive of briefings, debriefings, and full therapy sessions with individual children in the classroom which illustrate uses of RNT techniques, children's immediate responses, therapeutic turning points, and long term changes. Organized by case study, by service site and by subject, hundreds of cross-sectional and longitudinal studies (studies that follow the same child, over time) of emotionally and cognitively improving children treated by this method are an archive for which parental permission has been generously given for training and scientific study.

GUIDED ACTIVITY WORKBOOKS

For Therapists, Teachers, Researchers, Parents Schools, Mental Health Services, Foster Child Services and Agencies and Agencies Responding to Mass Disasters

A series of Guided Activity Workbooks developed by CPHC helps parents, teachers, therapists and disaster relief responders working with foster children or families traumatized by natural or man-made disasters. These resources are derivatives of Reflective Network Therapy designed to provide psychological first aid. They help prevent, minimize or treat posttraumatic stress disorders (PTSD). Guided Activity Workbooks have been specialized to help highly stressed children and families cope with specific disasters: terror attack, hurricane, earthquake, flood, tornado, fire, tsunami and the trauma of long term regional conflict. Additionally, we created a guided activity workbook specialized to help homeless and recently homeless children and families in transitional housing.

Individuals and Families can download free copies from our website or purchase printed copies.

Free downloads (PDF format) are available in the Disaster Help section of our website under "How To Order." In that section, books available for purchase from Amazon are also identified and linked directly to that source.

LICENSES FOR MASS REPRODUCTION BY SOCIAL SERVICE SYSTEMS, PRIVATE AGENCIES, SCHOOLS AND GOVERNMENT AGENCIES

Disaster responders may contact CPHC directly to obtain a license for mass reproduction at the nominal cost of 25 cents per book to print and distribute 100 or more copies. Please telephone or send an email directly to Gilbert Kliman, MD: gilbertkliman2008@gmail.com

ASSISTANCE AND COLLABORATION

CPHC has assisted with training on-the-ground responders via SKYPE. Please contact Gilbert Kliman, MD directly with requests for collaboration or assistance with training regarding a helping agency's use of a Guided Activity Workbook for a specific mass disaster response effort. Examples of our agency's collaboration with agencies responding to mass disasters include Mercy Corps (2008 Sichuan earthquake, and Hurricanes Katrina and Rita); and a collaboration with the Massachusetts School of Professional Psychology and Ekòl Akasya (École Acacia; The Acacia School) in Pétion-Ville, Haiti (Haiti earthquakes and aftermath).

PREVENTION OF DISCONTINUITY TRAUMA IN FOSTER CARE: THE PERSONAL LIFE HISTORY BOOK METHOD

The Personal Life History Book Method is a preventive narrative therapy in the form of a Guided Activity Workbook. A Manual for use with this tool is also available. DVDs are available as training instruments for use of the Personal Life History book for foster care parents, case workers, and private or public foster care agency supervisors and administrators.

GUIDED ACTIVITY WORKBOOKS FOR USE AFTER NATURAL DISASTERS

My Story about The Hurricane (generic updated workbook for all U.S. applications)
My Story about Hurricanes Katrina and Rita
Istwa Pa M Sou Tranblemannte Ayiti a Mon Histoire
Sur Le Tremblement De Terre En Haiti

My Own Story about the Earthquake in Haiti—English
My North American Story about the Earthquake in Haiti—English
My Sichuan Earthquake Story—Mandarin
My Sichuan Earthquake Story—English
My Tornado Story
My Flood Story
My Fire Story
My Earthquake Story (1989 Loma Prieta earthquake, San Francisco edition)
Mi Historia de la Tormenta Stan—Spanish
My Story about Tropical Storm Stan—English

WORKBOOK FOR HOMELESS CHILDREN AND RECENTLY HOMELESS CHILDREN IN TRANSITIONAL HOUSING

My Personal Story about Being Homeless

GUIDED ACTIVITY WORKBOOK FOR FOSTER CHILDREN AND MANUAL FOR PREVENTIVE PSYCHOTHERAPY

My Personal Life History Book: A Guided Activity Workbook for Foster Children
The Personal Life History Book Method: A Manual for Preventive Psychotherapy with Foster Children

GUIDED ACTIVITY WORKBOOKS FOR TRAUMA FROM WAR AND ATTACK OR THREAT OF ATTACK AND DURING REGIONAL CONFLICT

My Personal Story about Living in Gaza—Arabic
My Personal Story about Living in Gaza—English
My Story about Living in Israel with Terror Attacks—Hebrew
My Story about Living in Israel with Terror Attacks—English
My Book about the Attack on America
My Book about War and Terrorism
My Story about the Gulf War

Appendix B

Reflective Network Therapy Training and Certification

GETTING STARTED: TRAINING AND SUPPORT PLAN

Often our Medical Director or another senior RNT therapist is asked to give a presentation about the method for a prospective site's decision making body as well as for a prospective reflective network team. Other times, a new service site is born after our agency provides free educational materials about the method, including videotapes of Reflective Network Therapy being used with real children who have autism or PDD, or SED. *(See Appendix A for information regarding Confidentiality Agreements for viewing treatment videos.)* Once the commitment is made, start-up training in Reflective Network Therapy typically follows this path:

1. Start Up. The First Year of a new service with a qualified RNT team begins with initial on site intensive training: three full days of educational and therapeutic staff training prior to implementing the method.
   (a) A senior certified Reflective Network Therapist who is also certified as a supervisor will conduct the initial training, assisted by an experienced RNT Teacher.
   (b) Nine half-days of additional on-site training during the start-up year will support increased skills and confidence while providing the RNT trainer first hand review of the treatment work being done. This will be followed by full discussion. This support program can be supplemented by arranging for additional telephone consultations and/or videoconferencing as needed.
2. Deepening use of the Method—The Second Year: During the second year of operating a new RNT site, supervision is provided by ten once a month 90-minute consultation sessions using video conferencing. The second

year is critical to ensure the highest outcomes for the staff and children. The second year's ten videoconferences are the minimum expectation for provision of appropriate review, supervision and guidance in carrying out the method. One or more on-site refresher trainings or "working seminars" may be arranged if the site desires. During refresher training, a senior Reflective Network Therapy Trainer and Supervisor will be in the classroom or watching a recent video with the practitioners, witnessing the work done by the team with their child pupil-patients done by the team. This visit will be followed by on-site time dedicated to feedback and discussion. Additional arrangements can also be made for telephone conferences, if these are needed.

INTRODUCTION TO TEACHER AND THERAPIST CERTIFICATION IN REFLECTIVE NETWORK THERAPY

CPHC provides onsite training, guidance and supervision for mental health professionals, including: psychiatrists, psychotherapists, psychologists, social workers MFTs and teachers leading to RNT Certification upon completion of course of study. In general, we strive to train the personnel to attune and focus on a child's interpersonal relationships and communication of here and now play, behavioral and emotional process, and to help the therapist, teacher and child mentalize that process. In addition to selected readings, the study of videotapes illustrating a spectrum of Reflective Network Therapy techniques is a unique and essential part of the training. These tapes are a valuable archive of briefings, debriefings, and full therapy sessions with individual children in the classroom which illustrate uses of a spectrum of dynamic techniques, children's immediate responses, therapeutic turning points, and long term changes.

THE REFLECTIVE NETWORK THERAPY MANUAL

The replication manual provides a strong working knowledge of basic concepts, processes and procedures. Study of the manual will facilitate the training process and further clarify requirements and expectations for certification. During training, the therapist will be guided regarding his or her responsibility to provide clinical leadership of the classroom team. If the trainee is a psychoanalyst, he or she is further guided in their work by the "Criteria for Judging the Existence of a Psychoanalytic Process".

Additional information is available on our website. (See Appendix A: Resources.)

TEACHER CERTIFICATION IN
REFLECTIVE NETWORK THERAPY

Head teachers must be licensed in their state or supervised by a state licensed teacher, and have training appropriate to the age levels of their pupils. Ideally but not necessarily, Special Education Certification is desirable for the head teacher. Teacher Training will be conducted by CPHC certified senior staff. Teacher's roles and responsibilities are detailed in the Reflective Network Therapy Manual. Teachers will study actual treatments by viewing selected RNT training DVDs. Explanation and discussion of the content these materials will be facilitated by the CPHC certified trainer or supervisor. These video-documentaries demonstrate many aspects of technique essential for carrying out the method. Teachers aiming at RNT certification will provide videotapes of their work to their CPHC trainer for review, discussion and guidance. In-classroom video documentation of the teacher-in-training's work in RNT should be should be made on at least ten occasions. Ongoing in-staff training includes the RNT trainer making periodic reviews of current videotaped or personally viewed treatments.

The therapist supports and guides teachers to attune to children's mental lives, develop or deepen their teacher-child engagement skills, achieve briefing and parent guidance performance expectations and learn method techniques both in action and through modeling. Briefings and debriefings and working in tandem in the classroom provide opportunities for teacher training as do the weekly staff meetings.

In order to be eligible for Certification, a Teacher must complete at least one semester of supervised practice in a Reflective Network Therapy classroom with at least five children, with two reaching a planned termination, at least one of the children being female, and at least one being autistic or on the Pervasive Developmental Disorder spectrum. He or she must have conducted at least 16 parent guidance sessions of 45 minutes duration.

Certified Therapists will regularly provide their RNT Supervisors with standardized reports which capture data on child patients. This includes WPPSI-R documentation of IQ changes, Mental Health Ratings in the form of CGAS score, and (if the child has pervasive developmental disorder) changes on the Child Autism Rating Scale (CARS). Tracking the number and frequency of children's individual treatment sessions and parent guidance sessions is essential.

Training Level One: Initial Training for Therapists and Teachers

A start-up weekend of training: This training is given by Gilbert Kliman, MD, Linda Hirshfeld, PhD, Alicia Mallo, MD, Catherine Henderson (or a combi-

nation of senior RNT therapists certified by The Children's Psychological
Health Center) together with a senior RNT teacher training is videotape-
based until the third day, when demonstrations are given with the site's actual
children in their real life classroom setting. The site's head teacher(s) is/are
chosen to help do briefings and debriefings, and one of the training therapists
does a demonstration with several children for a morning. Discussion is then
held in the afternoon, based on videotapes of the morning's work.

After the three days of initial training, a child therapist, child analyst or
child psychiatrist at the site begins its own work with continuing supervision.
A therapist who has previously treated at least two preschoolers in any other
intensive form of child psychotherapy for more than a year can usually begin
using the Reflective Network Therapy method immediately after the three
days of initial intensive training.

Most preschool teachers, even without therapeutic work experience, have
little difficulty getting started carrying out RNT, and they will rapidly become competent and confident using these new techniques as they continue to
grow under supervision. The most difficult part for teachers is often learning
to do the RNT form of parent guidance.

TRAINING STEP TWO: REVIEWING ACTUAL WORK
OF THE CLINICIAN CANDIDATE FOR CERTIFICATION

Ten videotaped sessions of the senior clinician's own Reflective Network
Therapy work should be reviewed during and as part of the first year's RNT
supervision. The review should be done by a therapist already trained in
Reflective Network Therapy. That supervisor can certify whether the work is
inclusive of and demonstrates reliable use of the basic techniques of Reflective Network Therapy, including successful use of interpretations and collaborative inclusion of material from teacher briefings. Some of the supervisory
sessions can be done using videoconferencing if the site's equipment permits
viewing at both ends of the conference, or if videotapes are available in advance for the supervisor's study.

Training Level Two: Mid-Level or Junior Psychotherapists
Using Reflective Network Therapy

Psychotherapists who lack other clinical certification (such as mental health
practitioner in their state or certification in psychoanalysis) can often be
very effective under supervision. A good but not essential criterion for prior
experience is to have had two preschool cases in long term intensive psycho-

therapy on an individual basis (several times a week for a couple of years per child). Some therapists and some interns with even less experience have been effective and have grown quickly from supervised experience with RNT practices. Depending on prior levels of training, junior and mid-level therapists will require more initial supervision than senior therapists such as licensed mental health providers, experienced child therapists, child analysts and Board Certified Child psychiatrists. Ideally they will receive at least 20 rather than ten supervised hours.

After the initial three days of start-up training the mid-level or junior therapist is likely to need some help understanding how powerful the intensive process is, how closely one must work with families, and how much teachers have to contribute to understanding of the children. Countertransference processes must be brought into awareness. That is particularly so if certification candidates have not been in an interpersonal treatment themselves, where their own defensive tendencies to avoid or disrupt intimacy has been modified.

Training Level Three: General Minimums for a Certified Psychoanalyst Using Reflective Network Therapy

Quantity of Sessions: To become RNT certified a certified psychoanalyst or Board Certified Child Psychiatrist therapist should conduct one hundred individual treatment sessions of 15 or more minutes per child. Four cases are needed, one of them on the autism spectrum. Others should conduct two hundred individual treatment sessions. At that point a preliminary certification will be issued. A satisfactory planned termination of a case will allow full therapist certification in Reflective Network Therapy when the other minimums are met.

Numbers of children treated: At least four children including one child whose treatment is deemed satisfactorily completed and whose treatment termination has been discussed with a supervisor. Treatment terminations include "graduation" or transitioning when a child becomes able to be mainstreamed.

Quantity of Videotaped Treatment Sessions for Review: Ten satisfactory videotaped sessions should be approved by a supervisor, documenting work with at least four children. One of the four children should be on the autism spectrum. At least one child's case should later be brought to successful planned termination, and the certificate finalized at that point.

Therapist Supervision of Teachers: At least ten hours of teacher-therapist conferences should have occurred and their contents discussed cogently with the RNT therapy trainee's supervisor as part of the overall supervision of cases.

Parent Guidance Sessions: A therapist must have conducted 10 sessions and supervised teachers in at least 20 sessions. (Teachers are expected to conduct parent guidance sessions with each child's parents 3 out of 4 weeks on an ongoing basis to make the network effect sufficiently powerful).

Substitution for Videotapes: In the absence of permission to videotape treatment sessions, two detailed case reports and an essay should be submitted for review by a supervisor, who should certify that the products show a grasp of basic features of the method including an understanding of transference and countertransference issues. Scientific and clinical reports and publications are encouraged and, at the discretion of a supervisor, may indicate readiness for certification before other standards are met.

Fast Track Certification as a Certified Senior RNT Therapist, Trainer/Supervisor

When a child psychoanalyst or Board Certified Child Psychiatrist becomes a local supervisor of in-classroom Reflective Network Therapy, the certification process can be simplified. If fast track certification is needed, training can be compressed in some locations—especially those with existing patient populations waiting to be served. Experience with four or more patients who receive a total of one hundred fifteen minute sessions of Reflective Network Therapy can lead an already well trained analyst or psychiatrist to certification as a Reflective Network Therapy supervisor. These quantities are equivalent to a half-time, five week long initial clinical immersion period which can result in immediate provisional certification as a Reflective Network Therapy Clinician/Supervisor. The supervisor can then take prospective junior and mid-level RNT clinicians into training, multiplying the number of staff and greatly increasing the number of children served.

The rationale for this fast track training is that Reflective Network Therapy is derived from and builds upon both therapeutic education and child psychotherapy. The most experienced and highly trained psychoanalytic therapists are encouraged to attempt the method and will usually require minimal training to get started doing independent work. After ten sessions of actual work being supervised by a trainer, the work will often be self-instructing, with optional but desirable refresher supervision, once or twice a year.

Thus, in a short time a Certified Senior Reflective Network Therapy clinician can learn the method and then become a supervisor of this form of very intensive psychotherapy. Certified child psychoanalysts and most experienced child psychiatrists have already learned to reliably conduct very intensive insight-oriented psychotherapies with preschoolers. They have already much experience working with schools, and even more experience working with parents and collaterals. They understand the technical problems of transference and countertransference, the value of supervision, and how to follow the effects of an interpretation. Therefore they can be expected to acquire skill in reflective psychotherapy methods much more quickly than less fully trained and experienced child therapists, and they can be certified quickly as trainers.

Senior Reflective Network Therapy practitioners often are previously very experienced supervisors themselves of intensive psychodynamic interpersonal therapy. They can be expected to transmit their understanding of the RNT experience to their own therapist-trainees after a hundred Reflective Network Therapy sessions have been conducted.

THE IDEAL SETTING

Those hundred sessions and ten supervisory sessions concerning the work can occur most easily when Reflective Network Therapy occurs in an already existing setting, with preschool patients already enrolled in a school or agency. In some circumstances one could start training by treating four children a day, work up to six or eight children a day, averaging five sessions a day four days a week—or at least 20 brief sessions a week. By treating children at that pace, perhaps in mornings only, a seasoned child analyst can perform a total of one hundred Reflective Network Therapy treatment sessions (of 15 or more minutes each) in five weeks. During that five-week timeframe there will also be weekly conferences with teachers and each child's family should be met with at least once for an hour.

Contact The Children's Psychological Health Center, Inc. for more information. *(See Appendix A)*

Appendix C

Professional Participants

TEACHERS, THERAPISTS AND OTHER PARTICIPANTS

Among the first Reflective Network Therapy (originally called "Cornerstone") teachers involved in pioneering the method were: Elissa Burian, Doris Gorin (later known as Doris Ronald), Florence Herzog, Susan Mandel, Renate Rossmere, and Marianne Schnall (later known as Marianne Rubin). We are grateful to over 20 RNT therapist-teacher teams, in addition to associated mental health professionals, education specialists, scientific advisors, forward thinking administrators of public school education, private therapeutic schools and other venues for Reflective Network Therapy who have contributed much to the development and success of the method, including:

David Abrams, PhD, Psychological Tester, White Plains, NY

Laura Ahn, Information Technologist, Wellspring Family Services, Seattle, WA

Jan Baeuerlen, MD, Supervisor, Piedmont, CA

Norma Balter, CSW, Therapist and Psychoanalyst, White Plains, NY

Betty Buchsbaum, PhD, Psychological Tester, White Plains, NY

Elissa Burian, MA, Educational Consultant, Teacher, White Plains, NY

Judy Burr-Chellin, LCSW, Therapist, Wellspring Family Services, Seattle, WA

Lynda Byrd, Head teacher, Cornerstone Therapeutic Preschool, San Francisco, CA

Harold Charney, PhD, Psychological Tester, White Plains, NY

Daniel Feinberg, MD, Therapist, White Plains, NY

Molly Franklin, MFTI, Therapist, San Francisco, CA

Audrey Harbur, LCSW, Therapist, White Plains, NY

Myron Harris, PhD, Psychological Tester, White Plains, NY

Alexandra Harrison, MD, Therapist, Psychoanalyst, Cambridge, MA

Catherine Henderson, PhD, Therapist, Psychoanalyst and Supervisor, Seattle, WA

Gayle Hernandez, Assistant teacher, San Mateo, CA

Florence Herzog, Teacher, White Plains, NY

Peggy Herzog, PhD, Therapist, White Plains, NY

Linda Hirshfeld, PhD, Therapist, Piedmont, CA

Miquela Diaz Hope, PhD, Therapist, Psych. Research Tester, SF & San Mateo, CA

Susan Howard, Therapist, White Plains, NY

Karita Hummer, LCSW, Therapist, San Jose, CA

Bevette Irvis, Director, Morningsong Early Learning Center, Wellspring, Seattle, WA

Kim Johnson, Teacher, Morningsong Early Learning Center, Wellspring, Seattle, WA

Gilbert Kliman, MD, Founder, Therapist, Supervisor, White Plains, NY, Seattle, WA, San Francisco, San Mateo and Piedmont, CA, Buenos Aires, Argentina

Marianne Kris, MD, Supervisor, White Plains, NY

Tina Lapides, PhD, Supervisor, Piedmont, CA

Marianne Lester, MA, Therapist, White Plains, NY

Ty Lewis, Teacher, Morningsong Early Learning Center, Wellspring, Seattle, WA

Thomas Lopez, PhD, Therapist, White Plains, NY

Harriet Lubin, MSW, Therapist, White Plains, NY

Alicia Asman Mallo, MD, Therapist and Director, Buenos Aires, Argentina

Susan Mandel, MA, Teacher, White Plains, NY

Mali Mann, MD, Supervisor, San Mateo, CA

Michael McDonald, M.Ed, Educational Director, San Francisco, CA

Melissa McRitchie, LCSW Therapist, Seattle, WA

Laurie Mendik, CSW, Therapist, White Plains, NY

Fran Morris, LCSW, Therapist, Norman, Oklahoma, OK

Keith Myers, LICSW, VP, Clinical & Training Services, WSF, Seattle, WA

Mary Jane Otte, MD, Therapist, San Mateo, CA

Jay S. Parnes, EdD, Senior Administrator, Special Education, San Mateo, CA

Deanna Reardon, MA, Therapist, San Francisco, CA

Doris Gorin Ronald, Teacher, Educational Director, White Plains, NY

Albert Rosenfeld, Author, White Plains, NY

Ruth Rosenfield, MA, Therapist, Psychoanalyst, White Plains, NY

Renate Rossmere, Teacher, White Plains, NY

Marianne Schnall Rubin, MA, Teacher, White Plains, Yonkers, NY

Leanne Runyon, MA, Head Teacher, San Mateo, CA

Shirley Samuels, EdD, Researcher, Psychoanalyst, White Plains, NY

M. H. Schaeffer, PhD, Exec. Dir. Center for Preventive Psychiatry, White Plain, NY

Karen Sheridan, LCSW, Therapist, Morningsong Early Learning Center, Seattle, WA

Miriam Siegel, PhD, Psychological Tester, White Plains, NY

Ann Spiegel, DMH, Therapist, Psychoanalyst, Mount Vernon, NY

Myron Stein, MD, Therapist, Supervisor, Assoc. Medical Director, White Plains, NY

Rita Stewart, MS, Teacher, White Plains, NY

Tish Teaford, MFTI, Therapist, San Mateo, CA

Dorian Tenore-Bartilluci, BA, Patient and Author, White Plains, NY

David S. Theis, DMH, Exec. Dir., Ann Martin Center, Piedmont, CA

Steve Tuber, PhD, Psychological Tester, White Plains, NY

Vanessa Vigilante, MA, Therapist, San Francisco, NY

Arthur Zelman, MD, Therapist, Supervisor, Medical Director, White Plains, NY

Appendix D

The Children's Psychological Health Center, Inc.

A California Public Benefit Corporation with Federal 501(c)3 Nonprofit Status
www.reflectivenetworktherapy.org or www.childrenspsychological.org

OUR MISSION

The Children's Psychological Health Center is dedicated to healing the hearts and minds of children suffering from autism spectrum disorders, developmental disorders and serious emotional disturbances. We do this through a leading edge treatment called Reflective Network Therapy (RNT), a social network therapy that enlists those closest to the children, including family members, teachers, and therapists as allies in the treatment process. Children are treated in classroom environments and in communities stricken by natural disasters. Children treated by Reflective Network Therapy achieve improved mental health, greater empathic capacity, improved social skills and cognitive gains and are helped to fulfill their human potential.

OUR BOARD OF DIRECTORS

Geoffrey Fletcher, Chairperson
Jason Erdell
Phyllis Fullmer
Roberta Hoffman
Gilbert Kliman, MD
Melissa King-Nuttall
Carolyn Lund

Amy Kux
Harriet Wolfe, MD

OUR SCIENTIFIC ADVISORY BOARD

Roy N. Aruffo, MD
Janis Baeuerlen, MD
David Brodzinsky, PhD
Elissa Burian, MA
Harry Coren, MD
Paul Jay Fink, MD
Alexandra Harrison, MD
Catherine Henderson, PhD
Joe Herzberg, MD
Linda Hirshfeld, PhD
Jodie Kliman, PhD
Christina Lapides, LCSW
Thomas Lopez, PhD
Henry Massie, MD
Fran Morris, MA
Jay Parnes, EdD
Shirley Samuels, EdD
Marjorie Schlenoff, LCSW
William Singletary, MD
Al Solnit, MD (deceased)
Ann Spiegel, MA
David Theis, DMH
David W. Trimble, PhD

We carry out our mission by seeking funding and resources to support training and certifying therapists and teachers in the replication of the Reflective Network Therapy method. We encourage independent and collaborative service and research, and public education regarding the individual and social benefits of using this in-classroom therapeutic method. We additionally support the continued evolution, distribution and use of a derivative of this method: Guided Activity Workbooks. These harness small social networks to reduce unplanned transfers in foster children (using the manualized Personal Life History Book method). We have produced a range of psychoanalytically informed guided activity workbooks for children stressed or traumatized by natural disasters or violent regional conflicts.

Index

About the Author

GILBERT KLIMAN, MD, *Medical Director The Children's Psychological Health Center, Inc., Distinguished Life Fellow of the American Psychiatric Association and Board of Psychiatry and Neurology, Life Fellow and Diplomate of the American Academy of Child and Adolescent Psychiatry, Certified Psychoanalyst for Children, Adolescents and Adults, American Psychoanalytic Association*

Dr. Kliman received his medical degree from Harvard Medical School and his child psychiatric training at the Albert Einstein College of Medicine, He has received many awards, including the 2008 Dean Brockman Award of the American College of Psychoanalysts for lifelong service and contributions to psychoanalysis and an international literary prize. After child psychiatric training, including an interdisciplinary Fellowship in Science and Psychiatry at The Albert Einstein College of Medicine, he founded three nonprofit organizations dedicated to childhood mental health services. All three were derived from the Cornerstone Reflective Network Therapy experience. He originated the Cornerstone Therapeutic Preschool Method of Reflective Network Therapy with the help of colleagues (including Elissa Burian) at The Center for Preventive Psychiatry which he founded in 1965. He next founded the Foster Care Study Unit at Columbia's University College of Medicine and Surgery, Department of Child Psychiatry, where he successfully worked on a systematic test of a derivative of the Cornerstone Method. He continued to refine the method at The Children's Psychological Health Center, Inc., (www.childrenspsychological.org) the third nonprofit he founded, where he has been the Medical Director since 1993. He is responsible for that agency's research and training. Using data and video archives from over 40 years of Reflective Network Therapy treatments, he is developing a controlled, multi-site project to further replicate and study RNT's clinical and IQ outcomes.

Currently working with a Bay Area sister site delivering Reflective Network Therapy services, the Ann Martin Center in Piedmont, California, he also supervises and consults at the first South American service site, Cornerstone Argentina in Buenos Aires. Collaborating with Alexandra Harrison, MD, Associate Professor of Harvard Medical School's Department of Psychiatry, he mentored her start of a new Reflective Network Therapy preschool project in Cambridge, Massachusetts. Collaborating with Wellspring Family Services of Seattle in 2007, he began training and supervising RNT service for traumatized homeless children at their Morningsong Preschool, and helped expand Wellspring's ability to accept other stressed preschoolers. His private practice of forensic child psychiatry (www.expertchildpsychiatry.com) has included testifying in over 275 federal and state cases on socially significant issues concerning children's well-being.

Applications of Dr. Kliman's guided activity workbooks also use RNT. He first developed the workbooks as a replicable and low cost social network harnessing method, at the Foster Care Study Unit, Columbia's University College of Medicine and Surgery, in the Department of Child Psychiatry. He ultimately developed a range of such network harnessing therapeutic workbooks—all using Reflective Network Therapy—to help children cope with earthquakes, wars, and hurricanes. They have been distributed by charitable agencies such as Mercy Corps and CPHC to over sixty thousand disaster-stricken families throughout the world. They are downloadable at www. childrenspsychological.org. A Mandarin workbook for survivors of the 2008 Sichuan earthquake has been used to help more than 35,000 Chinese children. Arabic versions have been used with 12,000 Gaza children. A Creole and French version is in use for Haitian children dealing with the 2010 earthquake. Dr. Kliman has appeared on national television features concerning psychological trauma and related children's issues (Barbara Walters, Straight Talk, 20/20, Health and Science News, The Today Show). He has authored over 70 scientific papers and several books, including *Psychological Emergencies of Childhood* and *Responsible Parenthood*. The latter, co-authored with Albert Rosenfeld, won the Janusz Korczak Prize for "world's best book concerning the well-being and nurture of children". He founded *The Journal of Preventive Psychiatry and Allied Disciplines*, and served as Editor-in-Chief.

Dr. Kliman has certifications from the American Psychiatric and American Psychoanalytic Associations, the New York Psychoanalytic Institute, and the American Academy of Child and Adolescent Psychiatry and has made scientific presentations at more than 100 scientific seminars, conferences and symposiums. He has been principal investigator for over 50 grant supported research and service projects regarding psychological illness and traumatic experiences concerning young children and families. His professional positions have included: Interdisciplinary Fellow in Science and Psychiatry at The Albert Einstein College of Medicine, Assistant Clinical Professor, Mount Sinai Medical School, Department of Psychiatry, New York; Director, Preventive Psychiatry Service, Elmhurst General Hospital, Queens, New York, Chief Psychiatric Consultant, Children's Garden, San Rafael, California, (a residential foster care facility) Director, Preventive Psychiatry Services and Unit for Study of Mass Violence and Genocide, St. Mary's Hospital, San Francisco; private practice of Psychiatry and Psychoanalysis (Adult, Child, and Adolescent) in San Francisco, New York and California; Director and Principal Investigator, Foster Care Study Unit, Columbia University, College of Physicians and Surgeons, New York; where he was also Associate Clinical Professor in the Department of Child Psychiatry. Currently Medical Director of The Children's Psychological Health Center in San Francisco, he is a supervisor at Wellspring Family Services of Seattle, Washington and The Ann Martin Center in Piedmont, California and is on the faculty of the St. Louis Psychoanalytic Institute, as well as The San Francisco Center for Psychoanalysis.

CONTRIBUTING EDITOR, **ELISSA BURIAN**, MA obtained her degree in educational psychology from Teachers College, Columbia University. She helped found the Center for Preventive Psychiatry and the method of Reflective Network Therapy Method (then called The Cornerstone Therapeutic Preschool Method), authored two chapters in Zelman's (1996) Early Intervention with High Risk Children, taught at Windward School, White Plains, New York, supervised students at Sarah Lawrence College Laboratory School, was a founder and Director of The Ethical Society Nursery School, White Plains, New York, Educational Psychotherapist and Clinical Coordinator for The Center for Preventive Psychiatry (Yonkers, New York) and a head teacher and supervisor. She consults regarding ongoing Reflective Network Therapy preschool service projects and video archives.

Made in the USA
Monee, IL
24 February 2022

91733576R00236